高橋和希

THIS HAPPENED TO ME A WHILE AGO. WHEN I WAS TAKING A WALK THE OTHER DAY, I SAW AN UNUSUAL STREET STALL. AN OLD MAN WHO LOOKED LIKE THE STOREKEEPER WAS SMILING AT ME.

THE SIGN SAID "CHECKMATE SHOGI." (SHOGI IS LKE JAPANESE CHESS.) IF YOU COULD SOLVE THE SHOGI PROBLEM, IT SAID, YOU'D WIN 30,000 YEN! SO, OF COURSE I ROSE TO THE CHALLENGE! ONE MOVE, TWO MOVES...BUT I FAILED ON THE EIGHTH MOVE!

THEN THE OLD MAN HELD OUT HIS HAND AND SAID SOME-THING...*HUH?!* 1,000 YEN FOR EACH MOVE?! THE SIGN DIDN'T SAY ANYTHING ABOUT *THAT!* AND THAT'S HOW I LOST 8,000 YEN.
—*KAZUKI TAKAHASHI, 1997*

Artist/author Kazuki Takahashi first tried to break into the manga business in 1982, but success eluded him until **Yu-Gi-Oh!** debuted in the Japanese **Weekly Shonen Jump** magazine in 1996. **Yu-Gi-Oh!**'s themes of friendship and fighting, together with Takahashi's weird and wonderful art, soon became enormously successful, spawning a real-world card game, video games, and two anime series. A lifelong gamer, Takahashi enjoys Shogi (Japanese chess), Mahjong, card games, and tabletop RPGs, among other games.

YU-GI-OH! VOL. 4
The SHONEN JUMP Graphic Novel Edition

This graphic novel contains material that was originally published in English from **SHONEN JUMP** #10 to #13.

STORY AND ART BY
KAZUKI TAKAHASHI

Translation & English Adaptation/Anita Sengupta
Touch-Up Art & Lettering/Kelle Han
Cover Design/Izumi Evers
Graphics & Layout/Sean Lee
Senior Editor/Jason Thompson

Managing Editor/Elizabeth Kawasaki
Director of Production/Noboru Watanabe
Executive V.P./Editor-in-Chief/Hyoe Narita
Sr. Director of Licensing & Acquisitions/Rika Inouye
V.P. of Sales & Marketing/Liza Coppola
V.P. of Strategic Development/Yumi Hoashi
Publisher/Seiji Horibuchi

PARENTAL ADVISORY
Yu-Gi-Oh! is rated "T" for teens. It may contain violence, language, alcohol or tobacco usage, or suggestive situations. It is recommended for ages 13 and up.

Printed in Canada.

Published by VIZ, LLC
P.O. Box 77010 • San Francisco, CA 94107

SHONEN JUMP Graphic Novel Edition
10 9 8 7 6 5 4 3 2
First printing, February 2004
Second printing, October 2004

www.viz.com

THE WORLD'S MOST POPULAR MANGA
SHONEN JUMP GRAPHIC NOVEL
www.shonenjump.com

SHONEN JUMP GRAPHIC NOVEL

Vol. 4

KAIBA'S REVENGE

STORY AND ART BY
KAZUKI TAKAHASHI

THE STORY SO FAR...

Shy and easily picked on, 10th-grader Yugi spent most of his time alone playing games...until he solved the Millennium Puzzle, a mysterious Egyptian artifact passed down from his grandfather. Possessed by the puzzle, Yugi became Yu-Gi-Oh, the King of Games, and challenged bullies and criminals to weird games where the loser loses their mind! But now, one of Yugi's past opponents has recovered from Yugi's "Penalty Game," and is preparing a special project of his own...

DARK YUGI

武藤遊戯
YUGI MUTOU

The main character. When he solved the ancient Egyptian Millennium Puzzle, he developed an alter ego, "Dark Yugi," which emerges in times of stress. Afterwards, the regular Yugi doesn't remember what happened.

真崎杏子

KATSUYA JONOUCHI

城之内克也

Yugi's classmate, a tough guy who gets into lots of fights. He used to think Yugi was a wimp, but now they are good friends. In the English anime he's known as "Joey Wheeler."

ANZU MAZAKI

Yugi's classmate and childhood friend. She fell in love with the charismatic voice of Yugi's alter ego, but doesn't know that they're the same person. Her first name means "Apricot." In the English anime she's known as "Téa Gardner."

海馬モクバ

海馬瀬人

MOKUBA KAIBA

Seto's little brother. He challenged Yugi to the collectible miniatures game "Capsule Monster Chess."

SETO KAIBA

An expert at the collectible card game "Duel Monsters." When he tried to steal a super-rare card from Yugi's grandfather, Yugi beat him at his own game, then trapped him in an illusionary world where he was eaten by the game's monsters.

武藤双六

本田ヒロト

HIROTO HONDA

Yugi's classmate, a friend of Jonouchi. In the English anime he's known as "Tristan Taylor."

SUGOROKU MUTOU

Yugi's grandfather, the owner of the Kame ("Turtle") game store.

Yu-Gi-Oh!

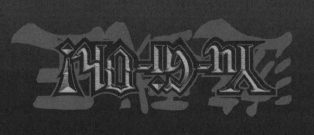

Vol. 4

CONTENTS

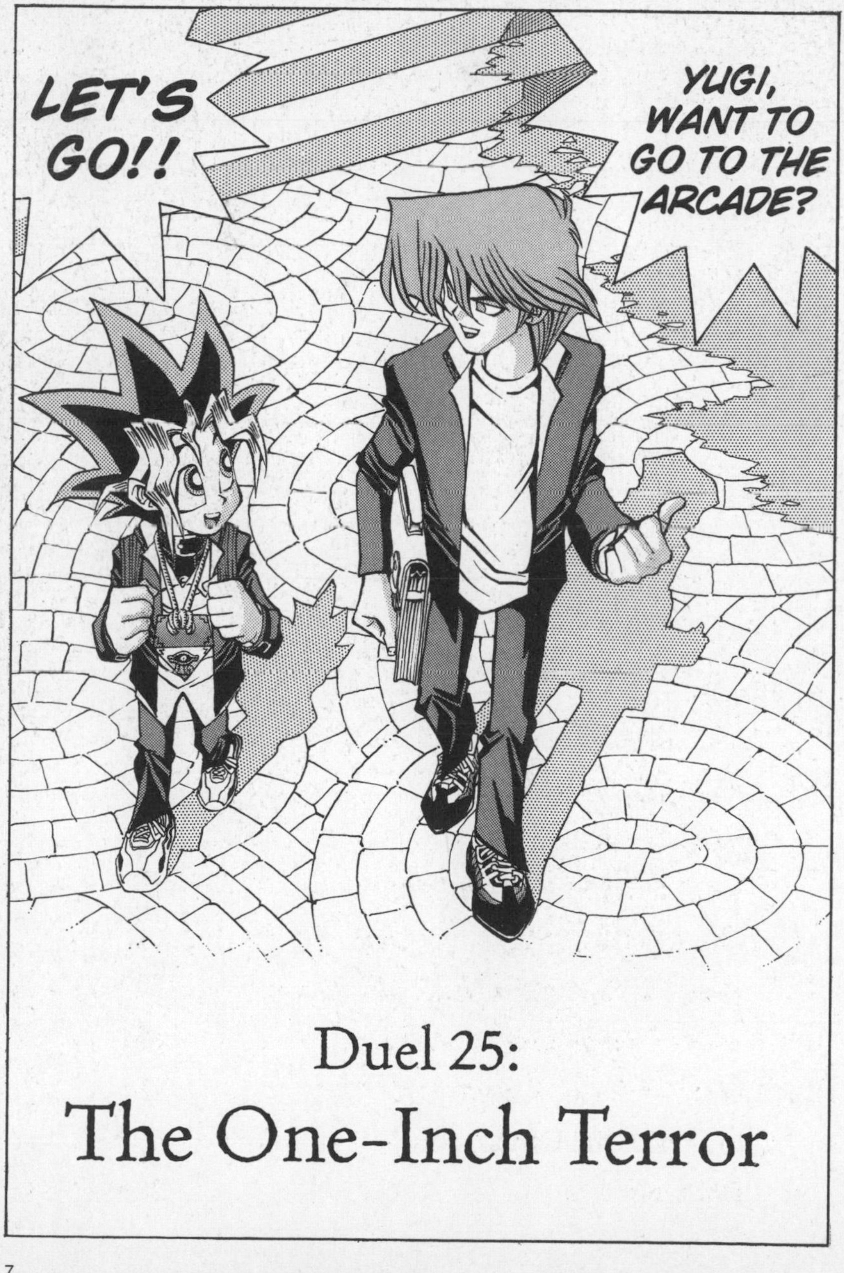
YUGI, WANT TO GO TO THE ARCADE?
LET'S GO!!

Duel 25:
The One-Inch Terror

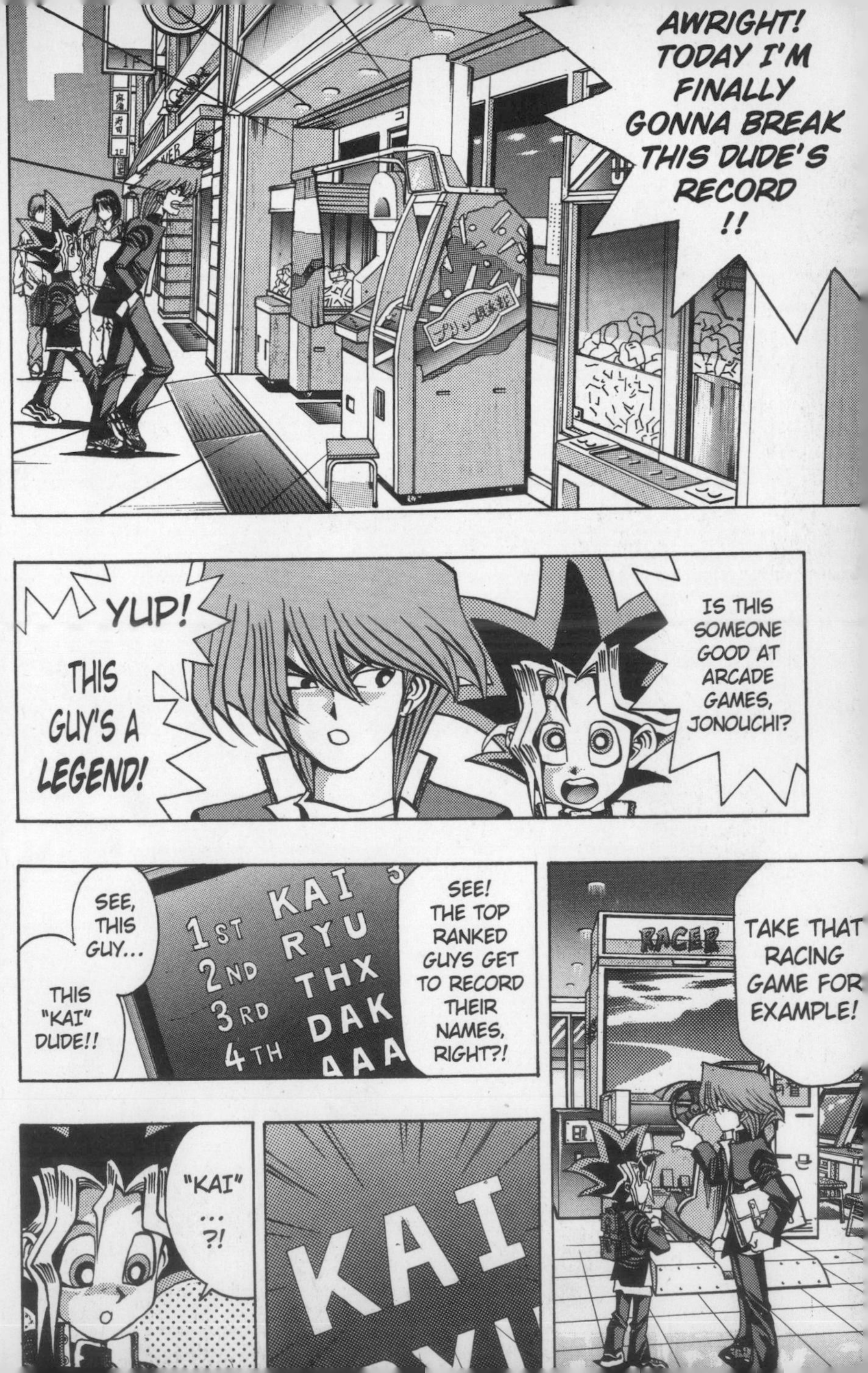
AWRIGHT! TODAY I'M FINALLY GONNA BREAK THIS DUDE'S RECORD !!
IS THIS SOMEONE GOOD AT ARCADE GAMES, JONOUCHI?
YUP!
THIS GUY'S A LEGEND!
TAKE THAT RACING GAME FOR EXAMPLE!
RACER
SEE! THE TOP RANKED GUYS GET TO RECORD THEIR NAMES, RIGHT?!
1ST KAI
2ND RYU
3RD THX
4TH DAK
AAA
SEE, THIS GUY...
THIS "KAI" DUDE!!
KAI
"KAI" ... ?!

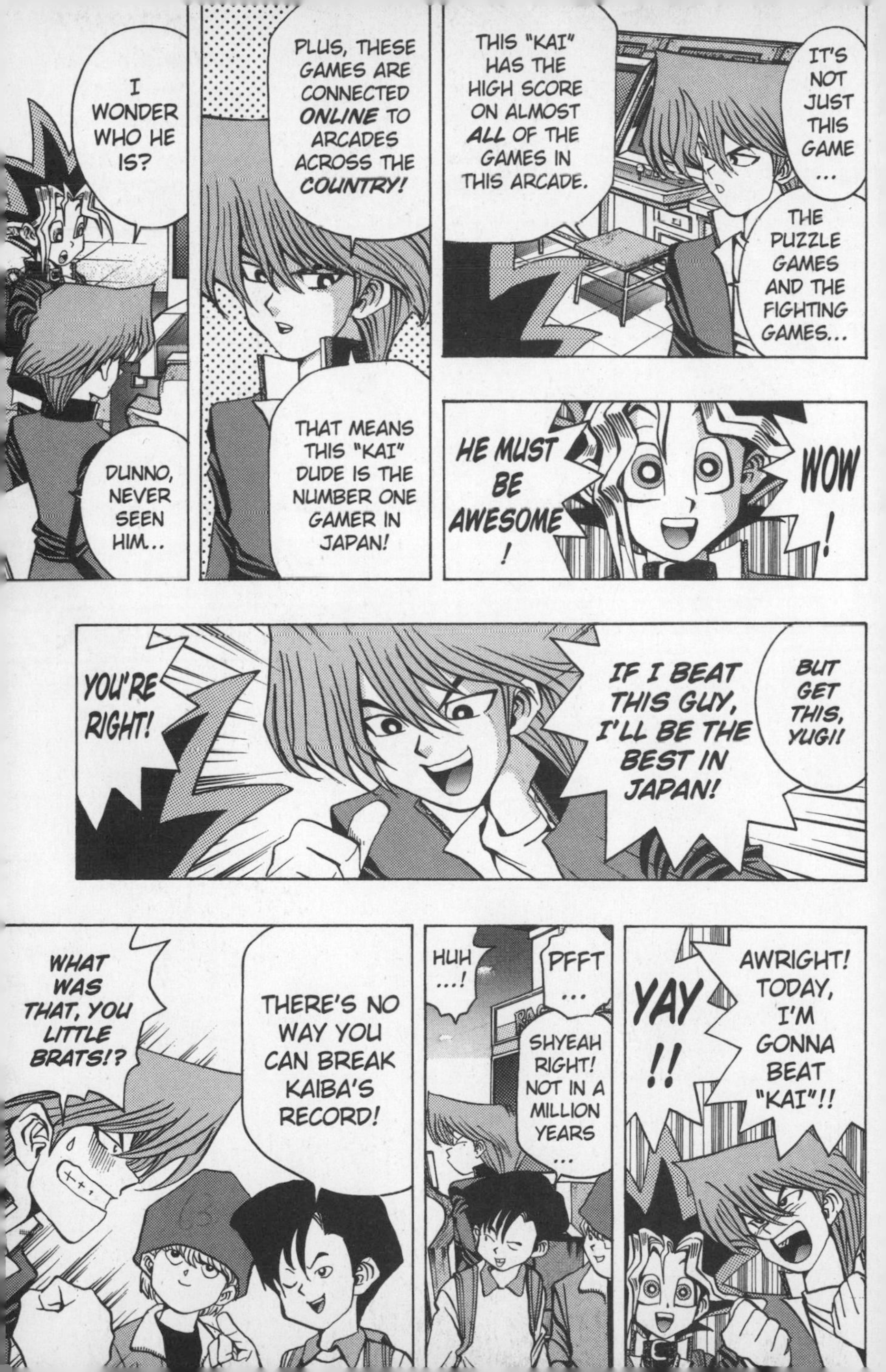
IT'S NOT JUST THIS GAME ...
THE PUZZLE GAMES AND THE FIGHTING GAMES...
THIS "KAI" HAS THE HIGH SCORE ON ALMOST ALL OF THE GAMES IN THIS ARCADE.
WOW !
HE MUST BE AWESOME !
PLUS, THESE GAMES ARE CONNECTED ONLINE TO ARCADES ACROSS THE COUNTRY!
THAT MEANS THIS "KAI" DUDE IS THE NUMBER ONE GAMER IN JAPAN!
I WONDER WHO HE IS?
DUNNO, NEVER SEEN HIM...
BUT GET THIS, YUGI!
IF I BEAT THIS GUY, I'LL BE THE BEST IN JAPAN!
YOU'RE RIGHT!
AWRIGHT! TODAY, I'M GONNA BEAT "KAI"!!
YAY !!
PFFT ...
HUH ...!
SHYEAH RIGHT! NOT IN A MILLION YEARS ...
THERE'S NO WAY YOU CAN BREAK KAIBA'S RECORD!
WHAT WAS THAT, YOU LITTLE BRATS!?

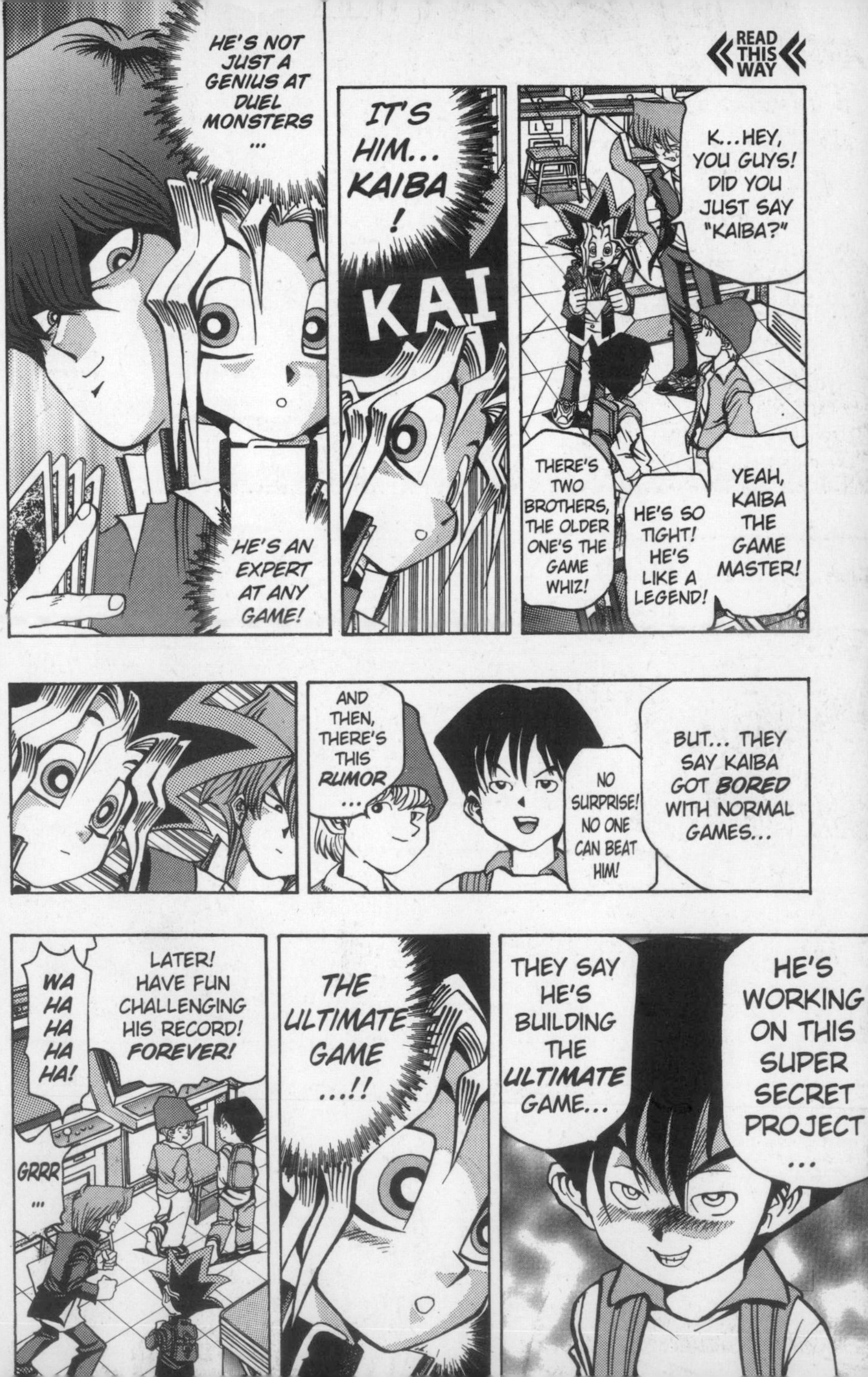
READ THIS WAY
K...HEY, YOU GUYS! DID YOU JUST SAY "KAIBA?"
YEAH, KAIBA THE GAME MASTER!
HE'S SO TIGHT! HE'S LIKE A LEGEND!
THERE'S TWO BROTHERS, THE OLDER ONE'S THE GAME WHIZ!
IT'S HIM... KAIBA!
KAI
HE'S NOT JUST A GENIUS AT DUEL MONSTERS ...
HE'S AN EXPERT AT ANY GAME!
BUT... THEY SAY KAIBA GOT BORED WITH NORMAL GAMES...
NO SURPRISE! NO ONE CAN BEAT HIM!
AND THEN, THERE'S THIS RUMOR ...
HE'S WORKING ON THIS SUPER SECRET PROJECT ...
THEY SAY HE'S BUILDING THE ULTIMATE GAME...
THE ULTIMATE GAME ...!!
LATER! HAVE FUN CHALLENGING HIS RECORD! FOREVER!
WA HA HA HA HA!
GRRR ...

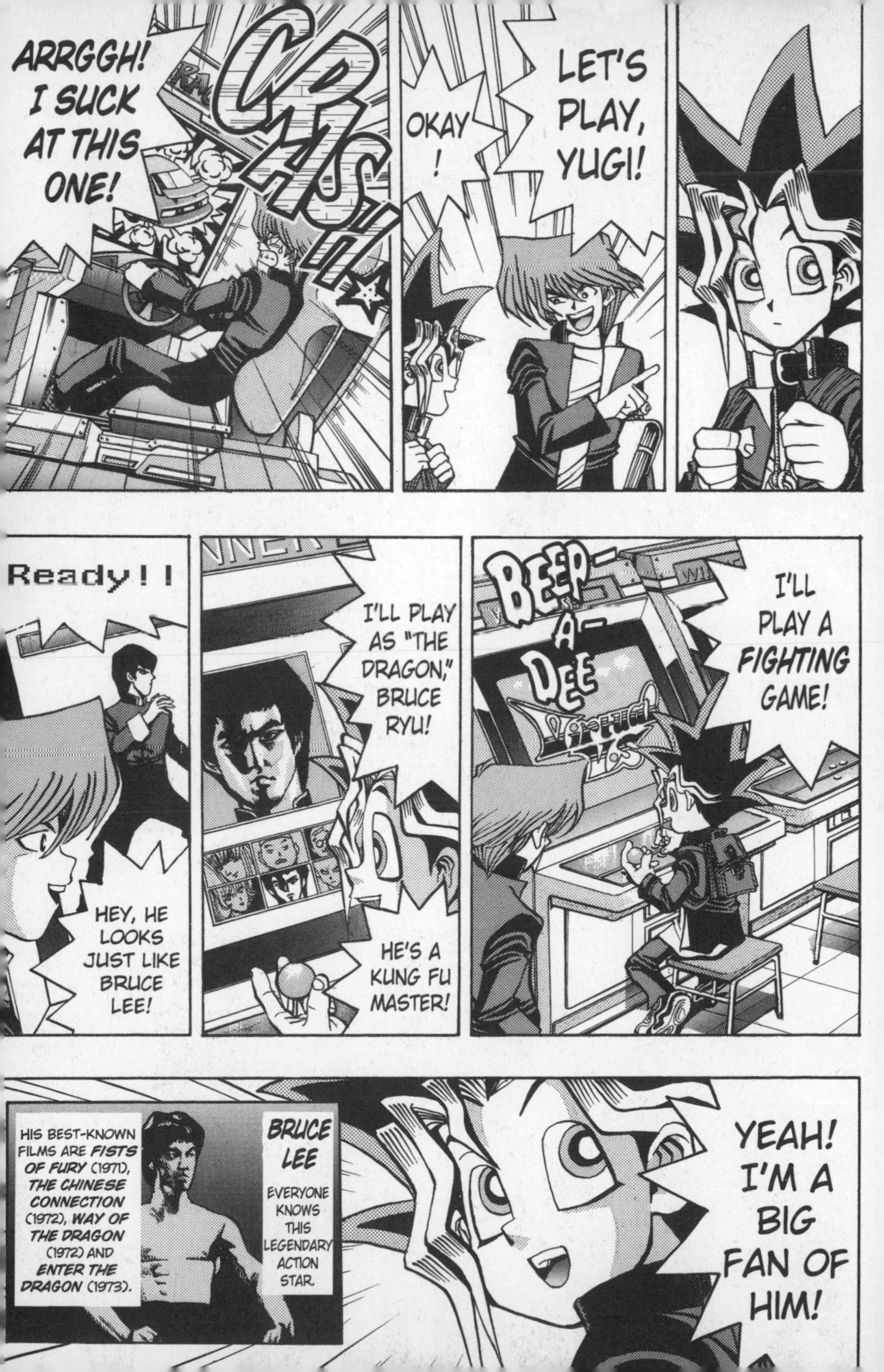
LET'S PLAY, YUGI!
OKAY!
ARRGGH! I SUCK AT THIS ONE!
CRASH!!
I'LL PLAY A FIGHTING GAME!
BEEP-A-DEE
I'LL PLAY AS "THE DRAGON," BRUCE RYU!
HE'S A KUNG FU MASTER!
Ready!!
HEY, HE LOOKS JUST LIKE BRUCE LEE!
YEAH! I'M A BIG FAN OF HIM!
BRUCE LEE
EVERYONE KNOWS THIS LEGENDARY ACTION STAR.
HIS BEST-KNOWN FILMS ARE FISTS OF FURY (1971), THE CHINESE CONNECTION (1972), WAY OF THE DRAGON (1972) AND ENTER THE DRAGON (1973).

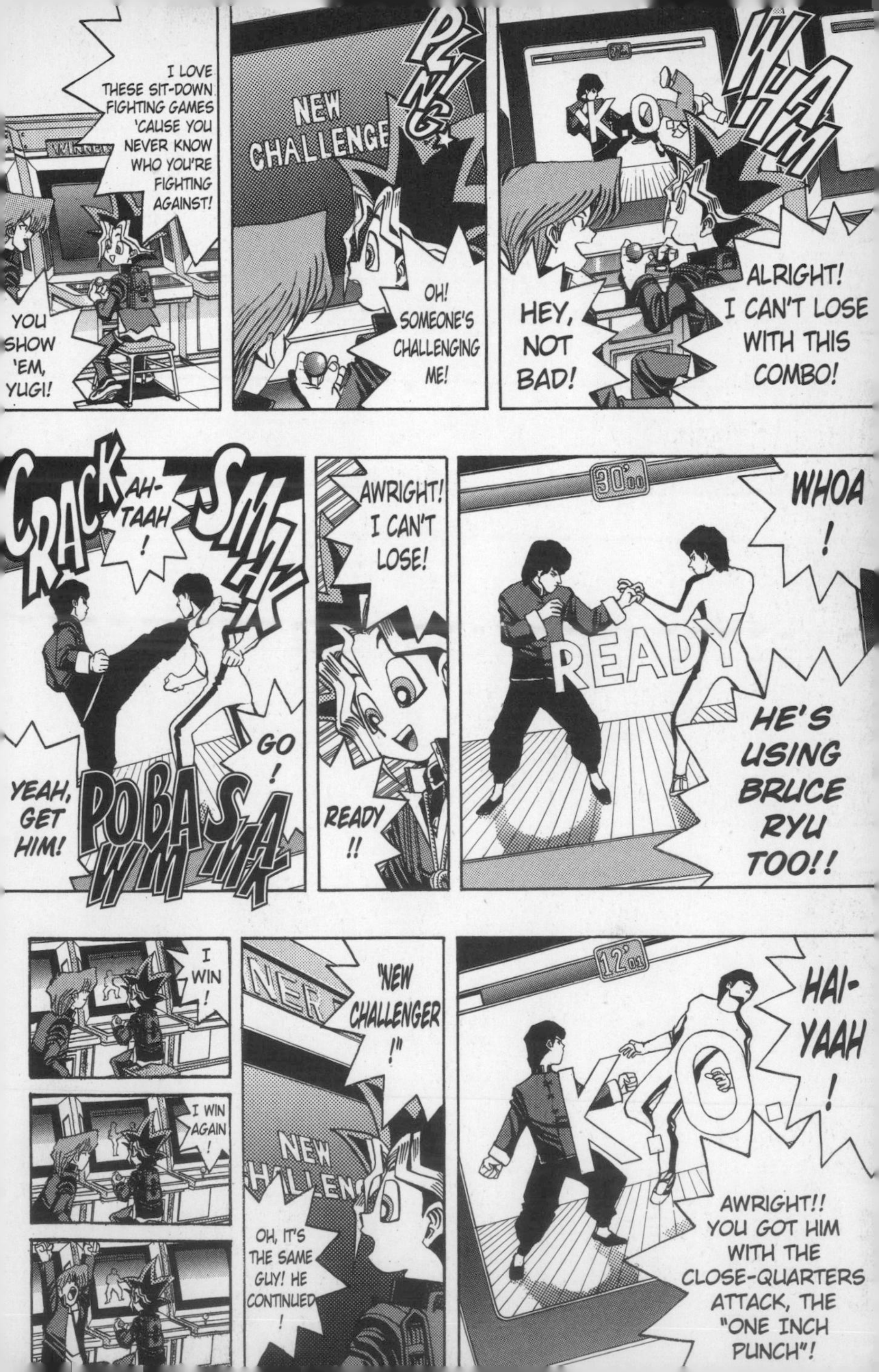
WHAM
K.O.
ALRIGHT! I CAN'T LOSE WITH THIS COMBO!
HEY, NOT BAD!
PLING
NEW CHALLENGE
OH! SOMEONE'S CHALLENGING ME!
I LOVE THESE SIT-DOWN FIGHTING GAMES 'CAUSE YOU NEVER KNOW WHO YOU'RE FIGHTING AGAINST!
YOU SHOW 'EM, YUGI!
WHOA!
READY
HE'S USING BRUCE RYU TOO!!
AWRIGHT! I CAN'T LOSE!
READY!!
CRACK
AH-TAAH!
SMACK
GO!
POWBAMSMACK
YEAH, GET HIM!
HAI-YAAH!
K.O.
AWRIGHT!! YOU GOT HIM WITH THE CLOSE-QUARTERS ATTACK, THE "ONE INCH PUNCH"!
"NEW CHALLENGER!"
NEW CHALLENGE
OH, IT'S THE SAME GUY! HE CONTINUED!
I WIN!
I WIN AGAIN!

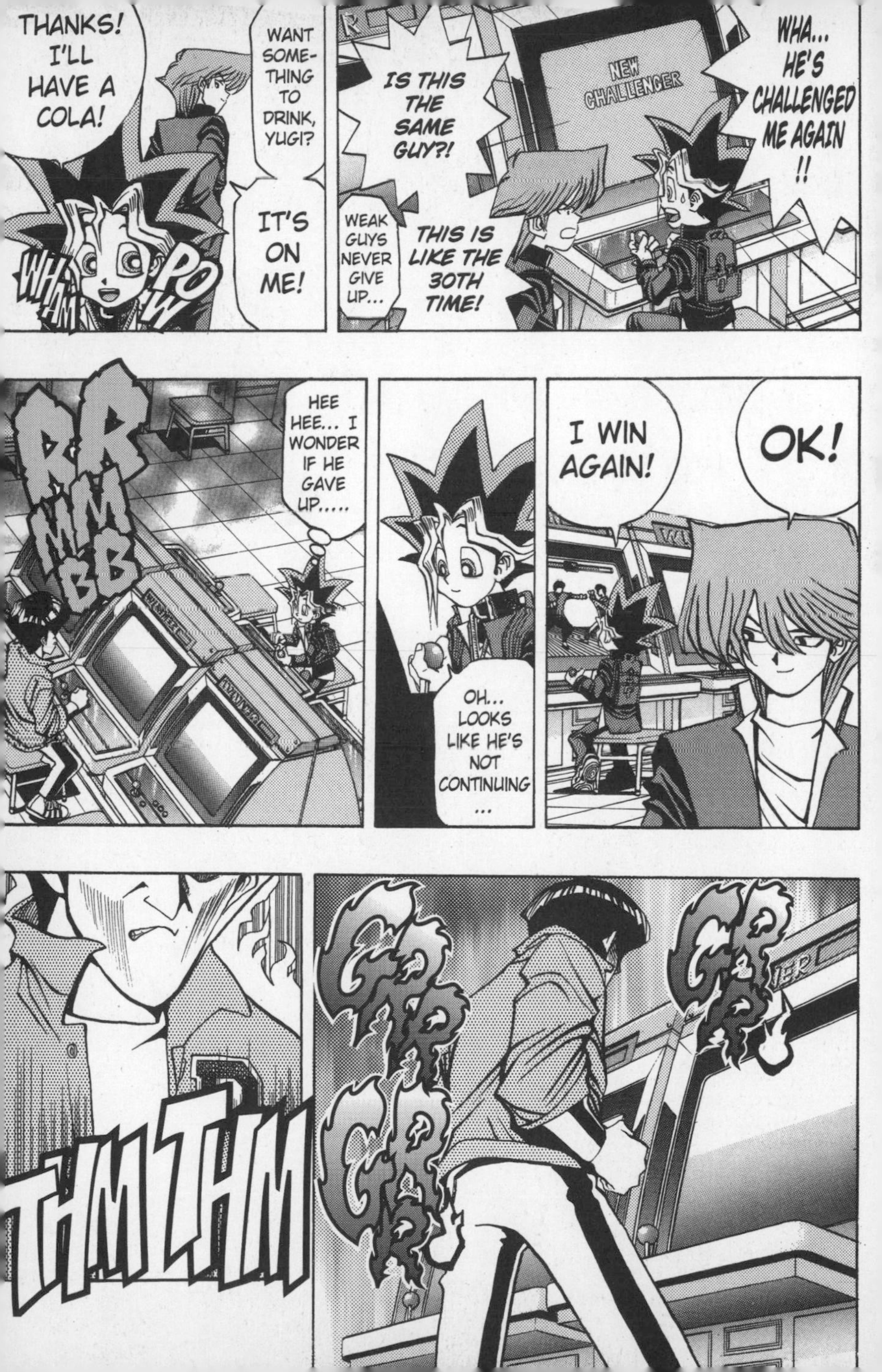
NEW CHALLENGER
WHA... HE'S CHALLENGED ME AGAIN !!
IS THIS THE SAME GUY?!
THIS IS LIKE THE 30TH TIME!
WEAK GUYS NEVER GIVE UP...
WANT SOME-THING TO DRINK, YUGI?
IT'S ON ME!
THANKS! I'LL HAVE A COLA!
WHAM
POW
OK!
I WIN AGAIN!
OH... LOOKS LIKE HE'S NOT CONTINUING ...
HEE HEE... I WONDER IF HE GAVE UP.....
RRMMBB
THM THM

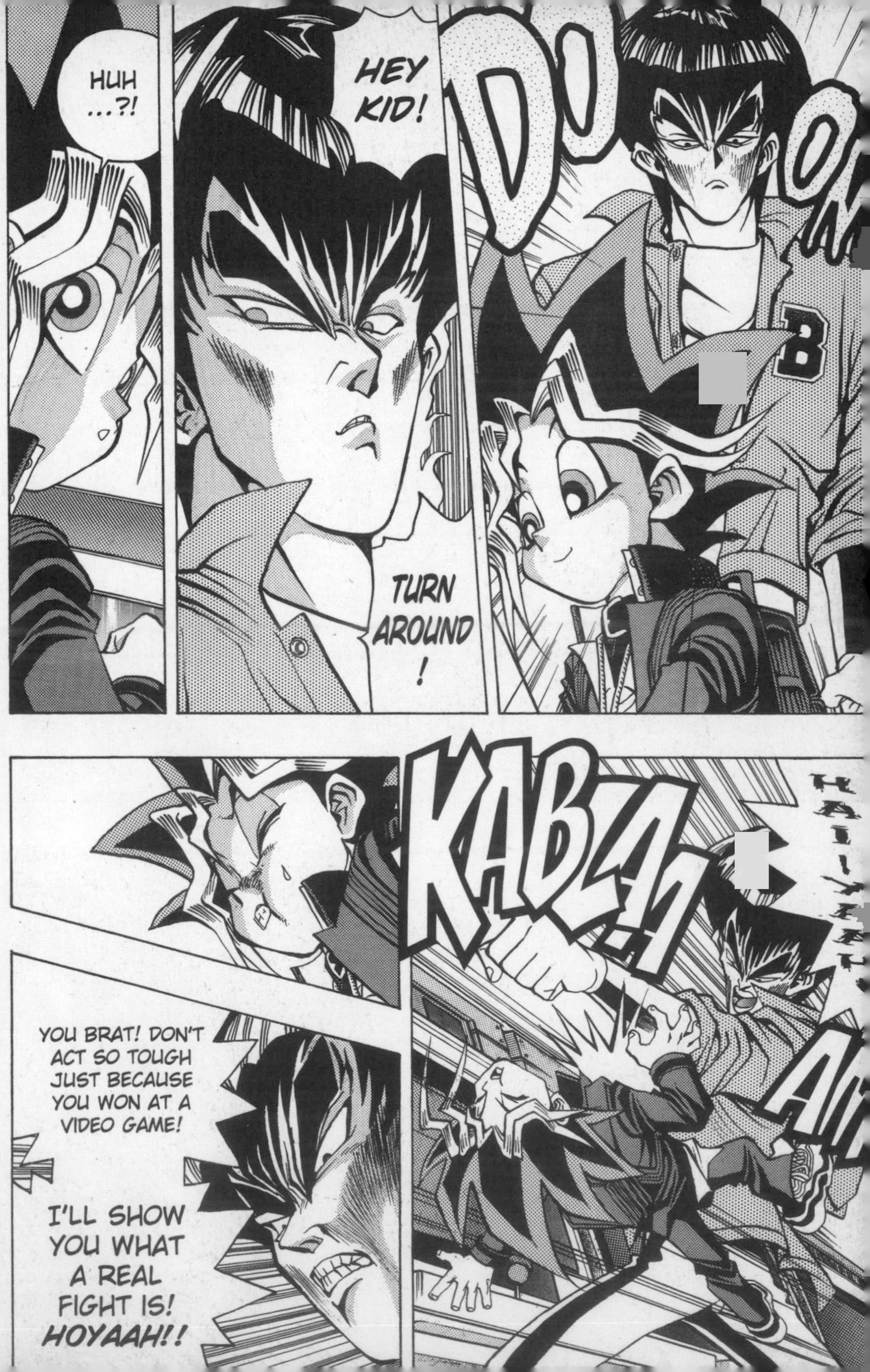
HEY KID!
TURN AROUND!
HUH ...?!
KABLAM
YOU BRAT! DON'T ACT SO TOUGH JUST BECAUSE YOU WON AT A VIDEO GAME!
I'LL SHOW YOU WHAT A REAL FIGHT IS! HOYAAH!!

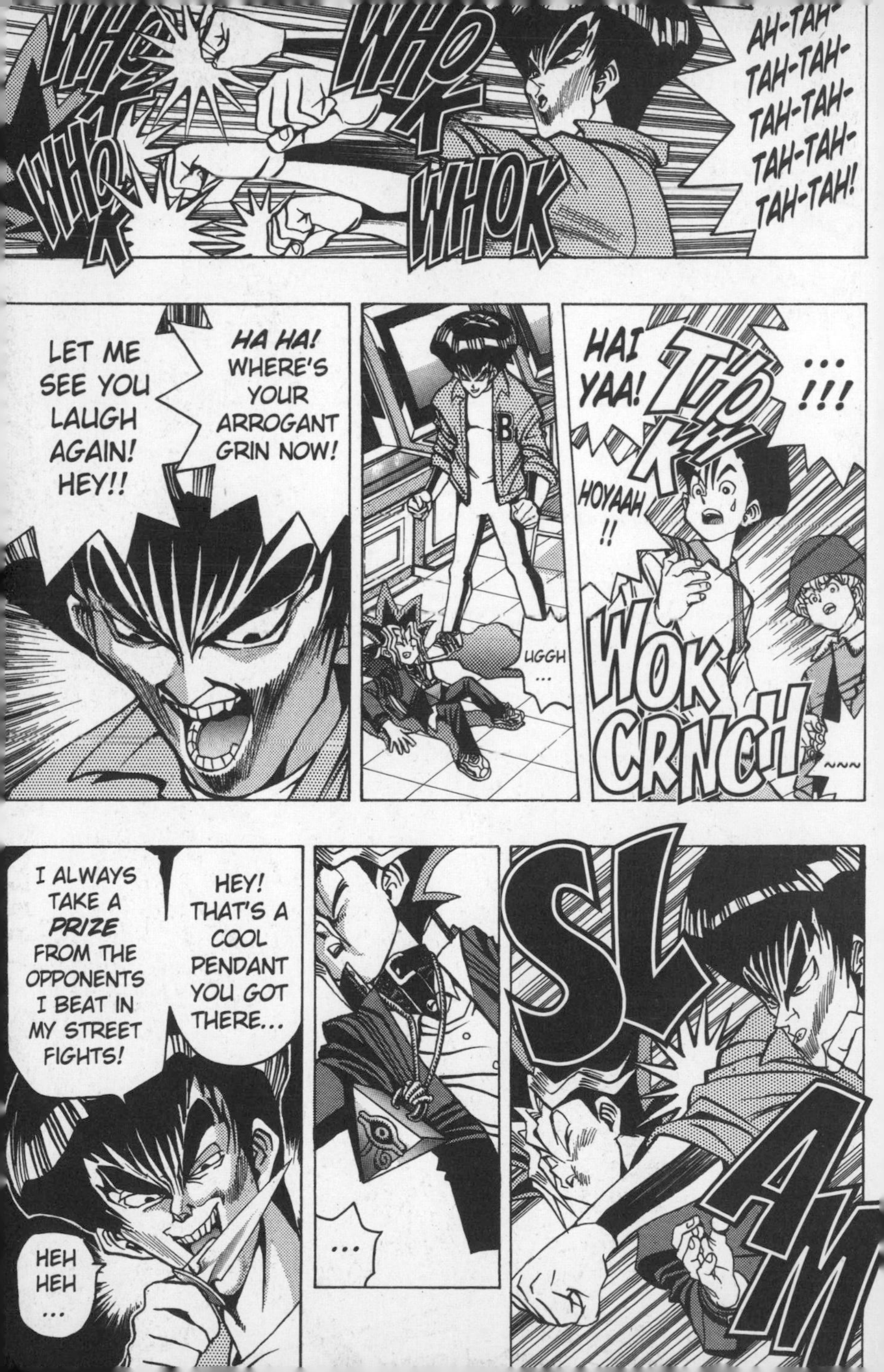
AH-TAH-TAH-TAH-TAH-TAH-TAH-TAH-TAH-TAH!
WHOK
WHOK
WHOK
WHOK
HAI YAA!
THWOK
...!!!
HOYAAH!!
WOK
CRNCH
UGGH...
HA HA! WHERE'S YOUR ARROGANT GRIN NOW!
LET ME SEE YOU LAUGH AGAIN! HEY!!
SLAM
...
HEY! THAT'S A COOL PENDANT YOU GOT THERE...
I ALWAYS TAKE A *PRIZE* FROM THE OPPONENTS I BEAT IN MY STREET FIGHTS!
HEH HEH ...

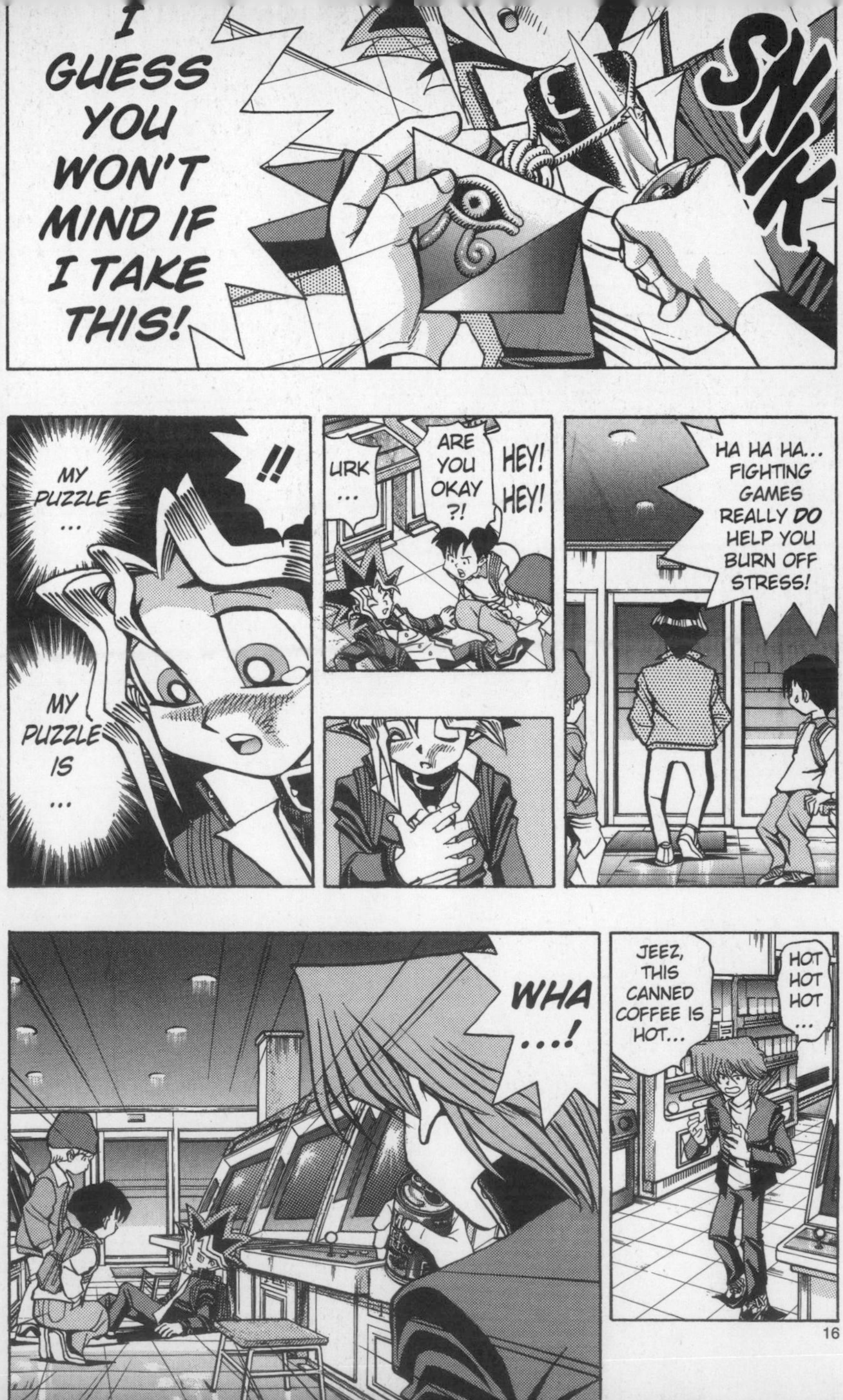
I GUESS YOU WON'T MIND IF I TAKE THIS!
SNIK
HA HA HA... FIGHTING GAMES REALLY DO HELP YOU BURN OFF STRESS!
HEY! HEY!
ARE YOU OKAY ?!
URK ...
!!
MY PUZZLE ...
MY PUZZLE IS ...
JEEZ, THIS CANNED COFFEE IS HOT...
HOT HOT HOT ...
WHA ...!

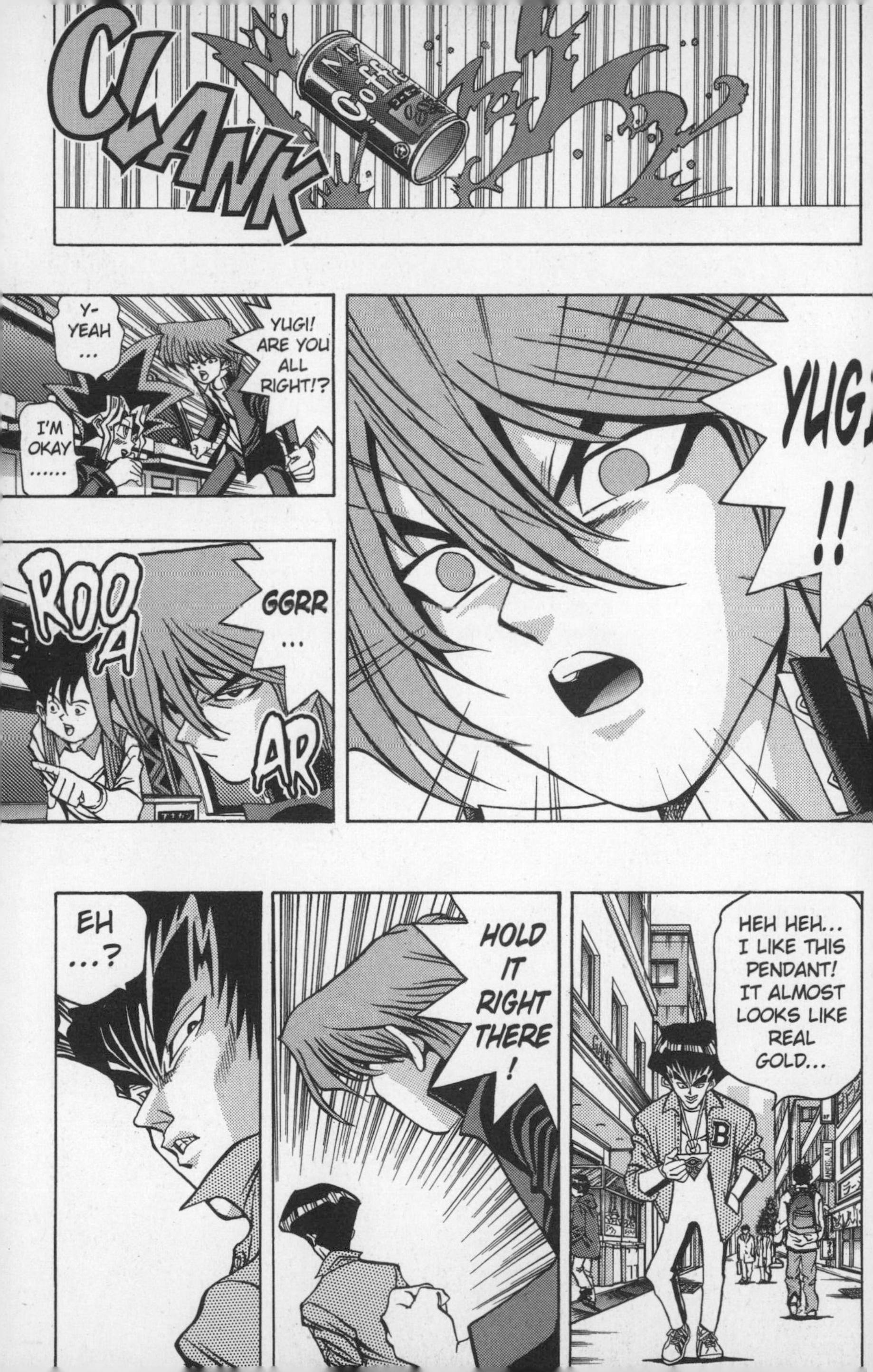
CLANK
YUG
!!
YUGI! ARE YOU ALL RIGHT!?
Y-YEAH ...
I'M OKAY ....
ROOAAR
GGRR ...
HEH HEH... I LIKE THIS PENDANT! IT ALMOST LOOKS LIKE REAL GOLD...
HOLD IT RIGHT THERE !
EH ...?

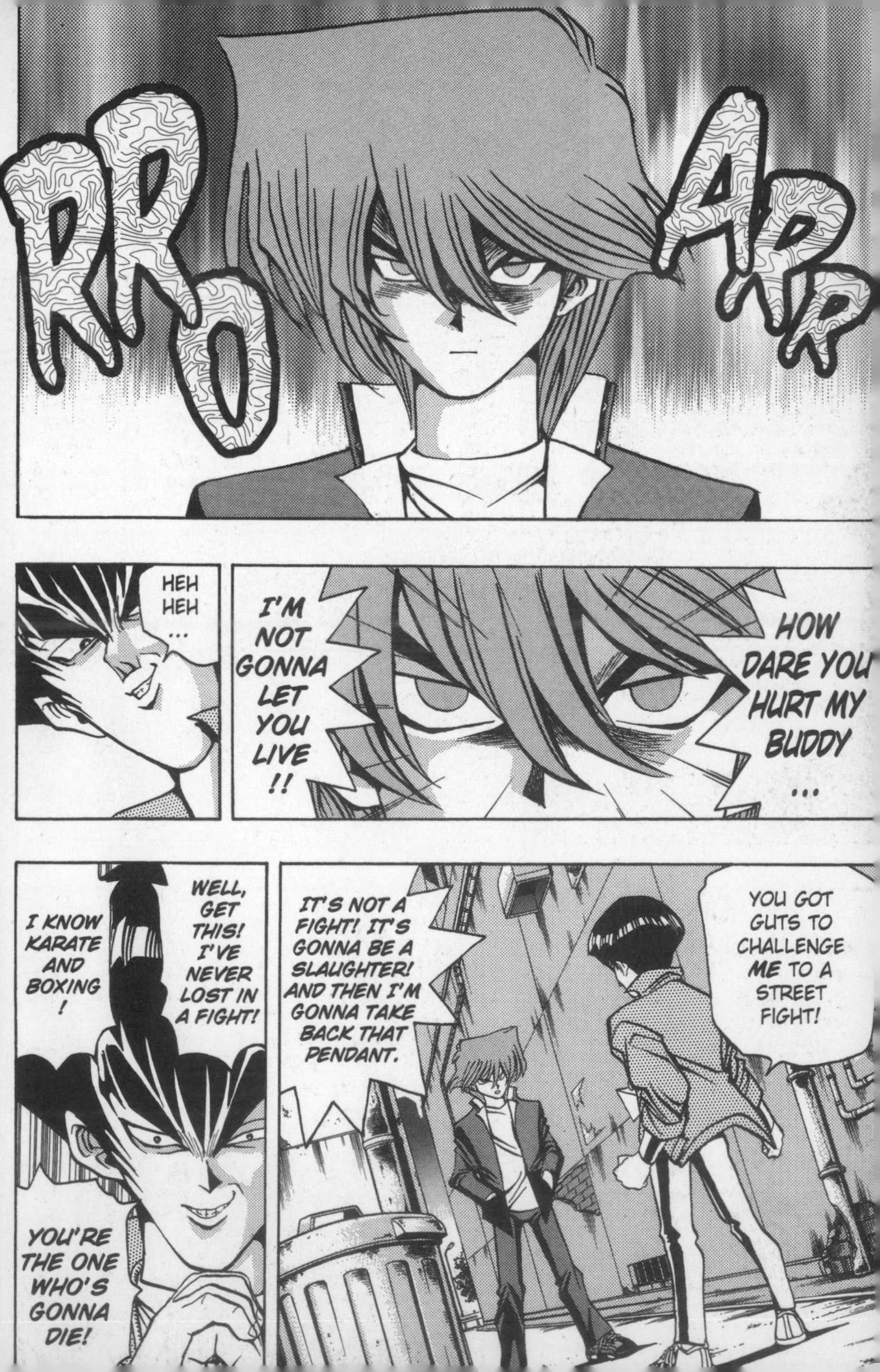
RROAR
HOW DARE YOU HURT MY BUDDY ...
I'M NOT GONNA LET YOU LIVE !!
HEH HEH ...
YOU GOT GUTS TO CHALLENGE ME TO A STREET FIGHT!
IT'S NOT A FIGHT! IT'S GONNA BE A SLAUGHTER! AND THEN I'M GONNA TAKE BACK THAT PENDANT.
WELL, GET THIS! I'VE NEVER LOST IN A FIGHT!
I KNOW KARATE AND BOXING !
YOU'RE THE ONE WHO'S GONNA DIE!

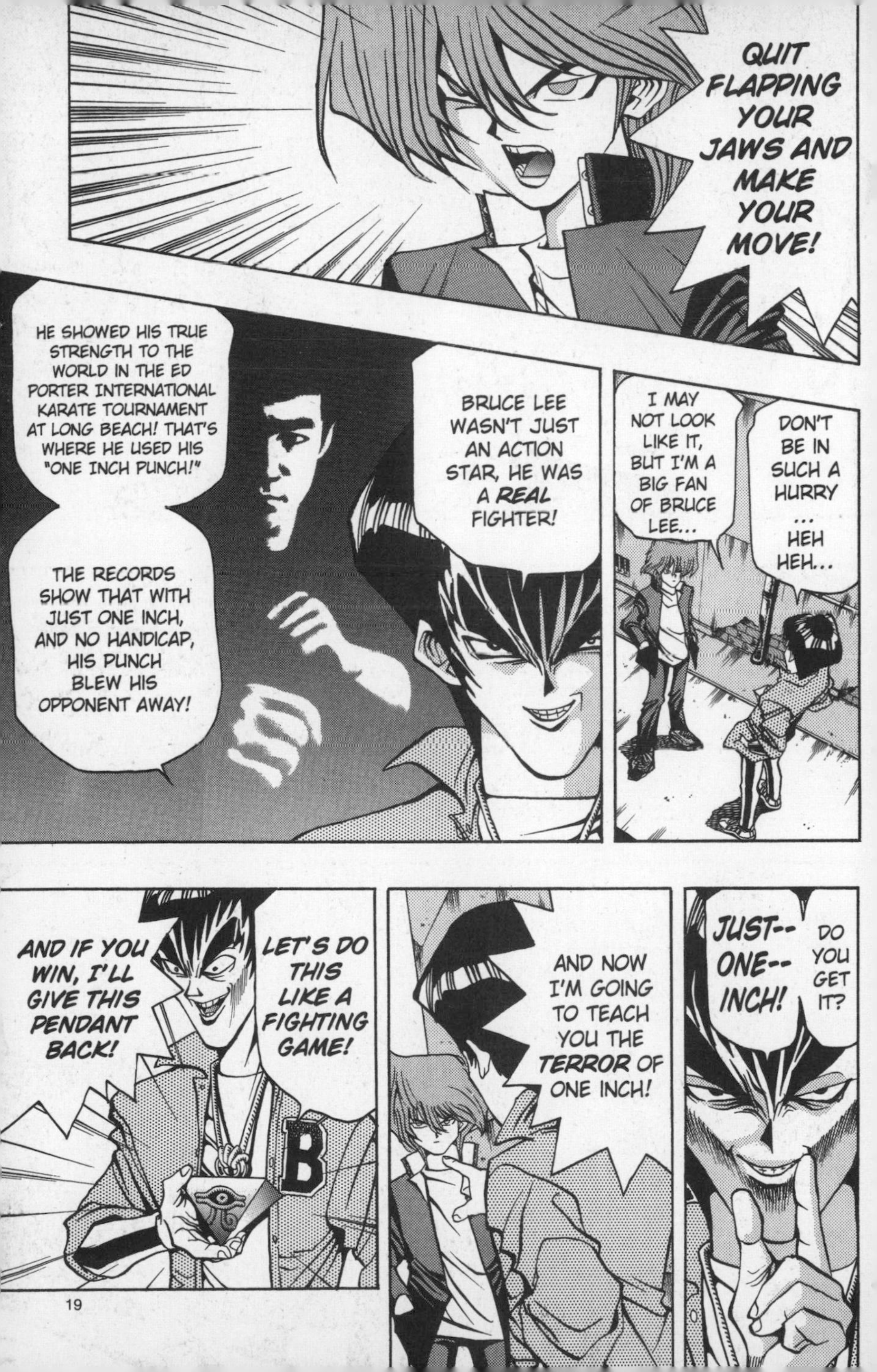
QUIT FLAPPING YOUR JAWS AND MAKE YOUR MOVE!
DON'T BE IN SUCH A HURRY ... HEH HEH...
I MAY NOT LOOK LIKE IT, BUT I'M A BIG FAN OF BRUCE LEE...
BRUCE LEE WASN'T JUST AN ACTION STAR, HE WAS A *REAL* FIGHTER!
HE SHOWED HIS TRUE STRENGTH TO THE WORLD IN THE ED PORTER INTERNATIONAL KARATE TOURNAMENT AT LONG BEACH! THAT'S WHERE HE USED HIS "ONE INCH PUNCH!"
THE RECORDS SHOW THAT WITH JUST ONE INCH, AND NO HANDICAP, HIS PUNCH BLEW HIS OPPONENT AWAY!
DO YOU GET IT?
JUST-- ONE-- INCH!
AND NOW I'M GOING TO TEACH YOU THE *TERROR* OF ONE INCH!
LET'S DO THIS LIKE A FIGHTING GAME!
AND IF YOU WIN, I'LL GIVE THIS PENDANT BACK!

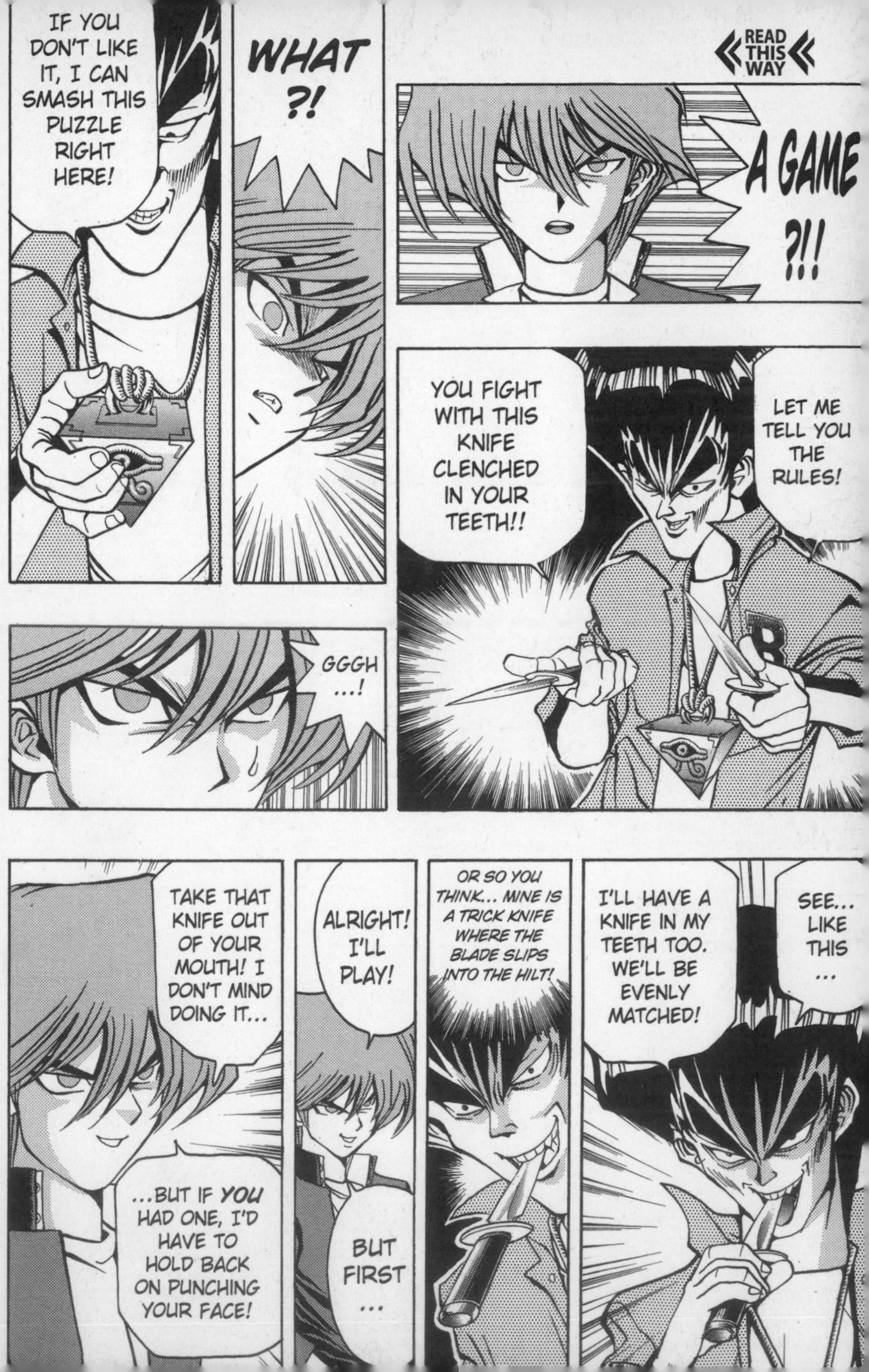
READ THIS WAY
A GAME ?!!
WHAT ?!
IF YOU DON'T LIKE IT, I CAN SMASH THIS PUZZLE RIGHT HERE!
LET ME TELL YOU THE RULES!
YOU FIGHT WITH THIS KNIFE CLENCHED IN YOUR TEETH!!
GGGH ...!
SEE... LIKE THIS ...
I'LL HAVE A KNIFE IN MY TEETH TOO. WE'LL BE EVENLY MATCHED!
OR SO YOU THINK... MINE IS A TRICK KNIFE WHERE THE BLADE SLIPS INTO THE HILT!
ALRIGHT! I'LL PLAY!
BUT FIRST ...
TAKE THAT KNIFE OUT OF YOUR MOUTH! I DON'T MIND DOING IT...
...BUT IF *YOU* HAD ONE, I'D HAVE TO HOLD BACK ON PUNCHING YOUR FACE!

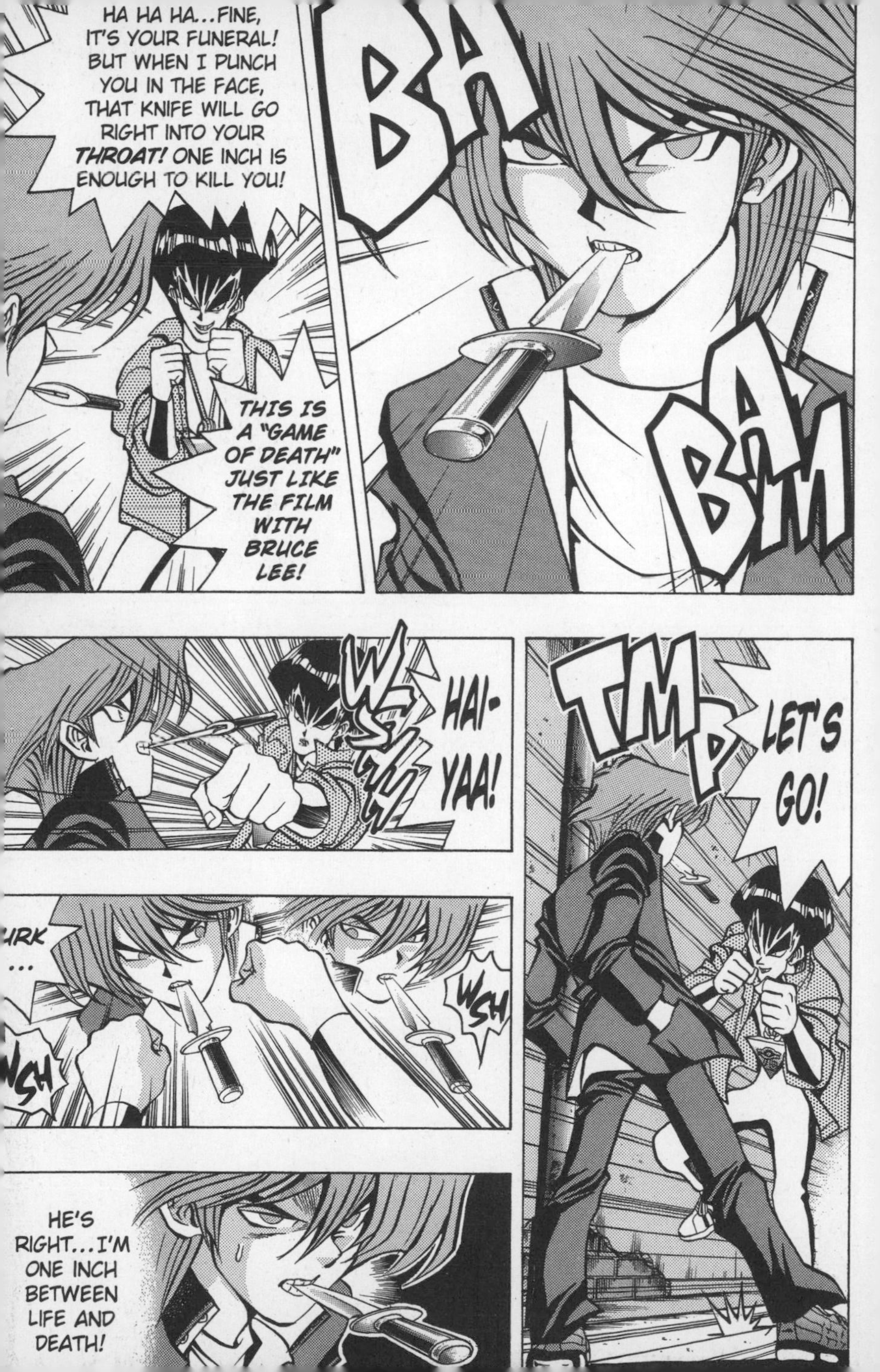
BA
BAM
HA HA HA...FINE, IT'S YOUR FUNERAL! BUT WHEN I PUNCH YOU IN THE FACE, THAT KNIFE WILL GO RIGHT INTO YOUR *THROAT!* ONE INCH IS ENOUGH TO KILL YOU!
THIS IS A "GAME OF DEATH" JUST LIKE THE FILM WITH BRUCE LEE!
TMP
LET'S GO!
WSH
HAI-YAA!
WSH
URK ...
WSH
HE'S RIGHT...I'M ONE INCH BETWEEN LIFE AND DEATH!

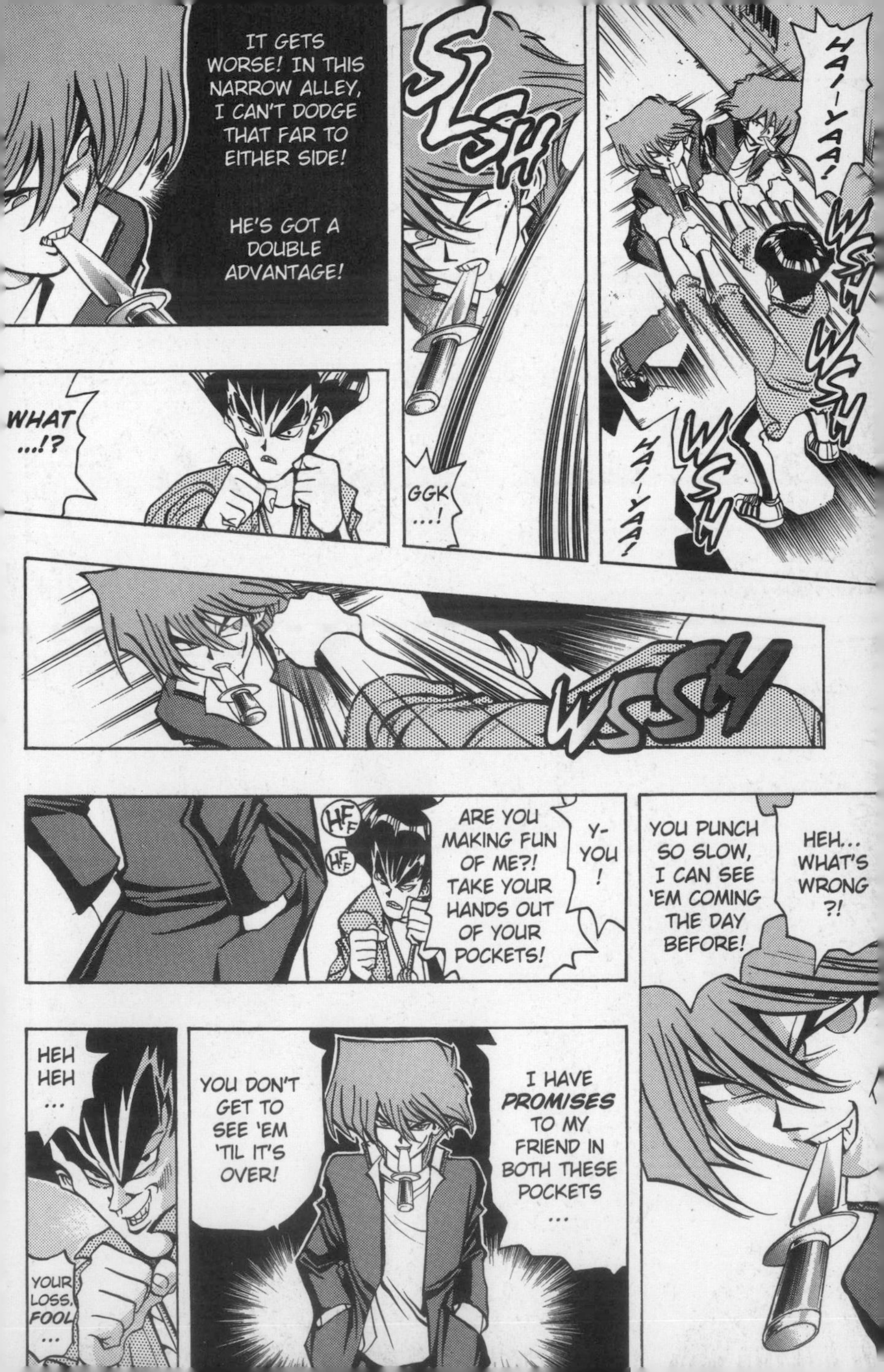
HA-YAA!
WSH
WSH
WSH
WSH
HA-YAA!
SLSH
GGK ...!
IT GETS WORSE! IN THIS NARROW ALLEY, I CAN'T DODGE THAT FAR TO EITHER SIDE!
HE'S GOT A DOUBLE ADVANTAGE!
WHAT ...!?
WSSH
HEH... WHAT'S WRONG ?!
YOU PUNCH SO SLOW, I CAN SEE 'EM COMING THE DAY BEFORE!
Y-YOU !
ARE YOU MAKING FUN OF ME?! TAKE YOUR HANDS OUT OF YOUR POCKETS!
HF
HF
I HAVE *PROMISES* TO MY FRIEND IN BOTH THESE POCKETS ...
YOU DON'T GET TO SEE 'EM 'TIL IT'S OVER!
HEH HEH ...
YOUR LOSS, *FOOL* ...

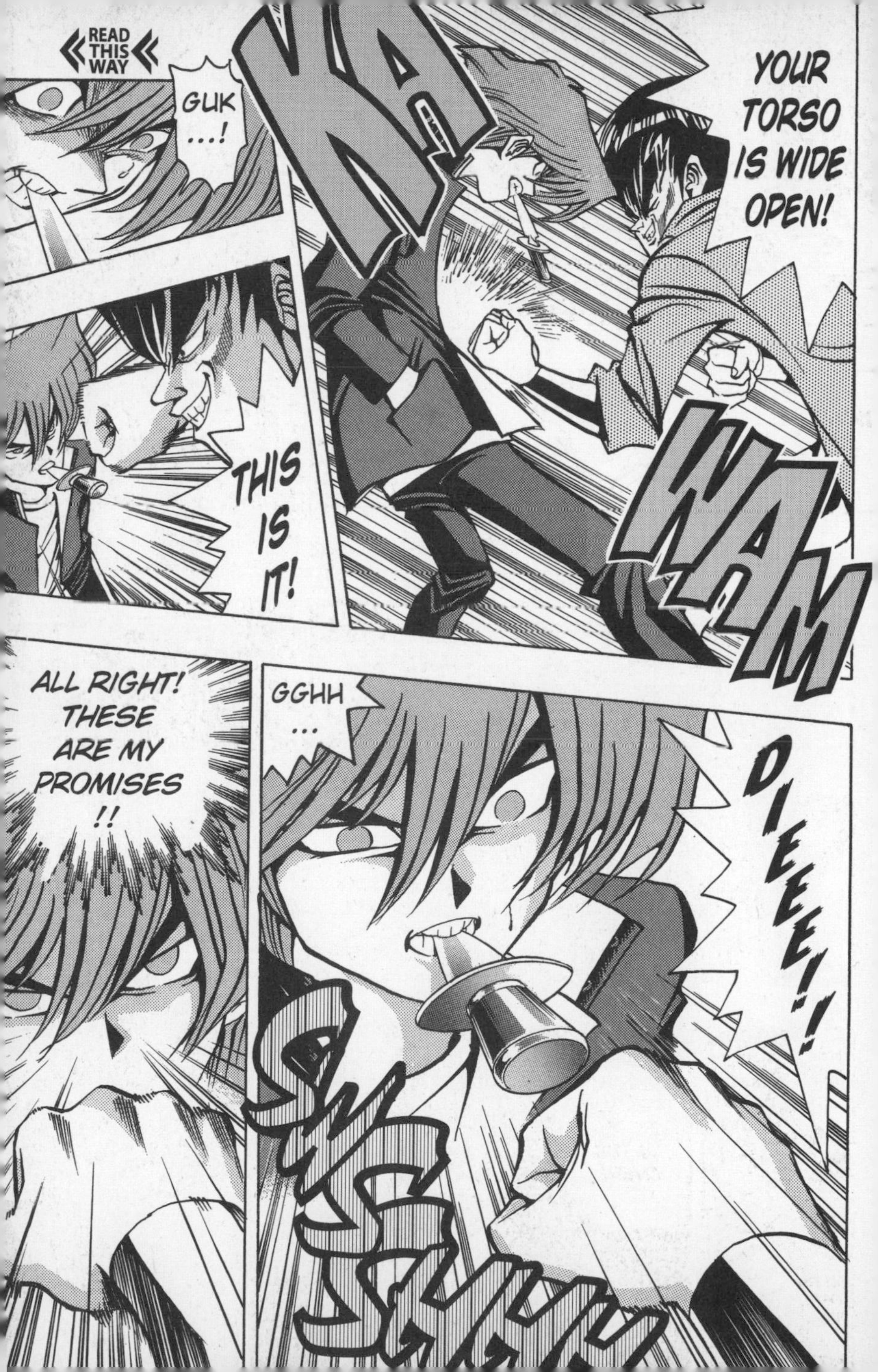
YOUR TORSO IS WIDE OPEN!
WHAM
READ THIS WAY
GUK ...!
THIS IS IT!
GGHH ...
DIEEE!!!
ALL RIGHT! THESE ARE MY PROMISES !!

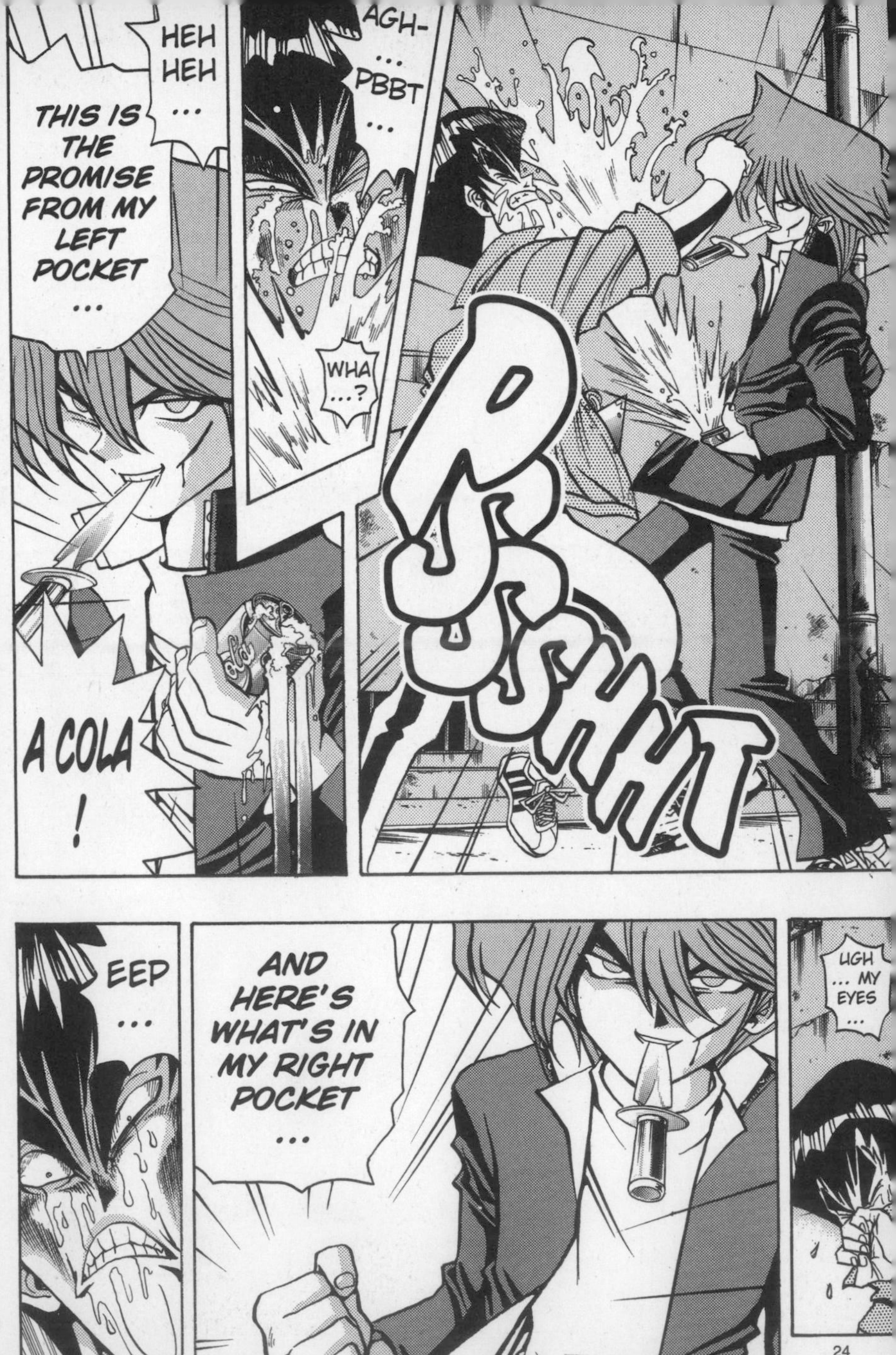
PSSHT
AGH- ... PBBT ...
WHA ...?
HEH HEH ...
THIS IS THE PROMISE FROM MY LEFT POCKET ...
A COLA !
UGH ... MY EYES ...
AND HERE'S WHAT'S IN MY RIGHT POCKET ...
EEP ...

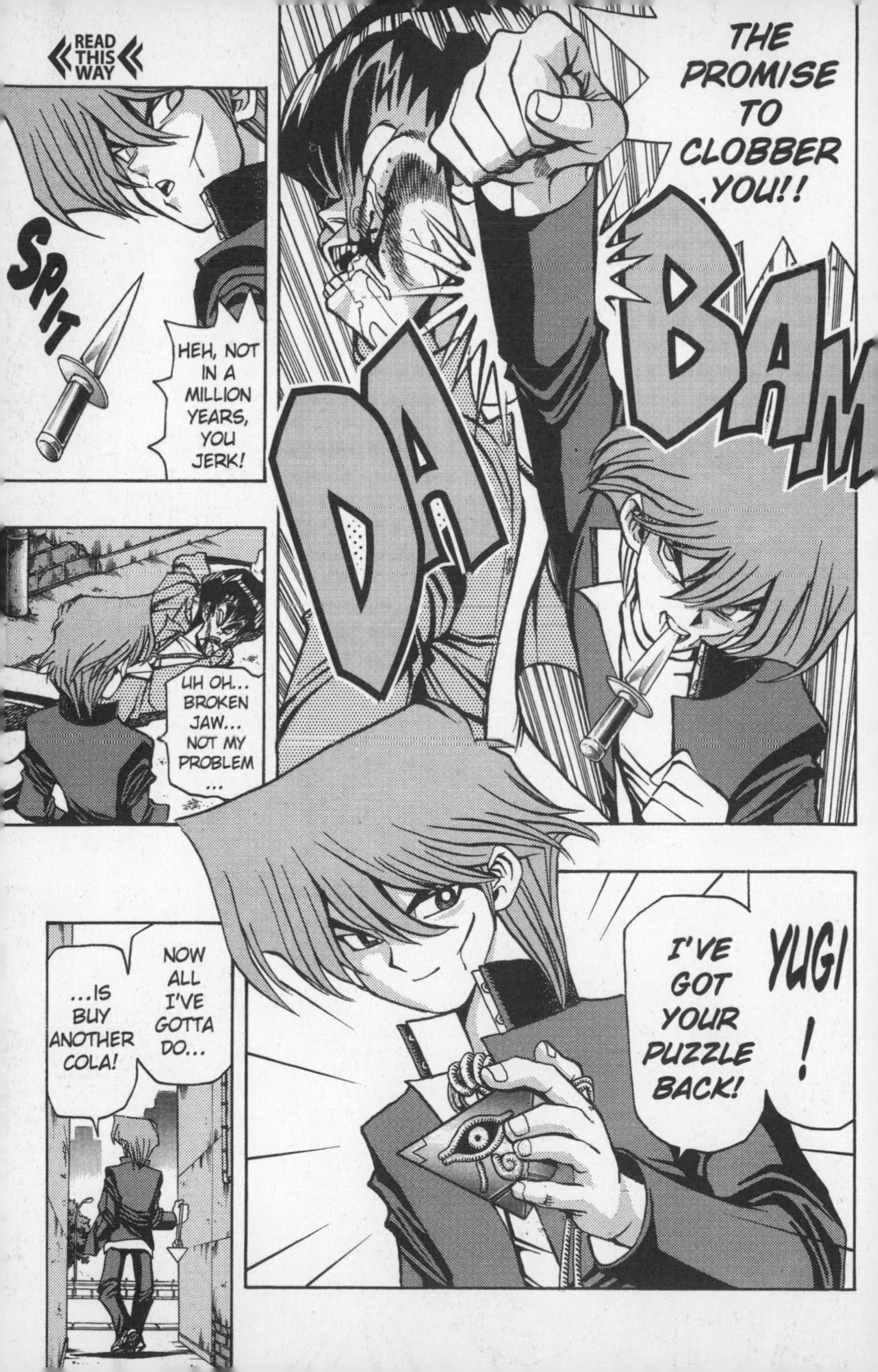
READ THIS WAY
THE PROMISE TO CLOBBER YOU!!
BAM
DA
SPIT
HEH, NOT IN A MILLION YEARS, YOU JERK!
UH OH... BROKEN JAW... NOT MY PROBLEM ...
I'VE GOT YOUR PUZZLE BACK!
YUGI !
NOW ALL I'VE GOTTA DO...
...IS BUY ANOTHER COLA!

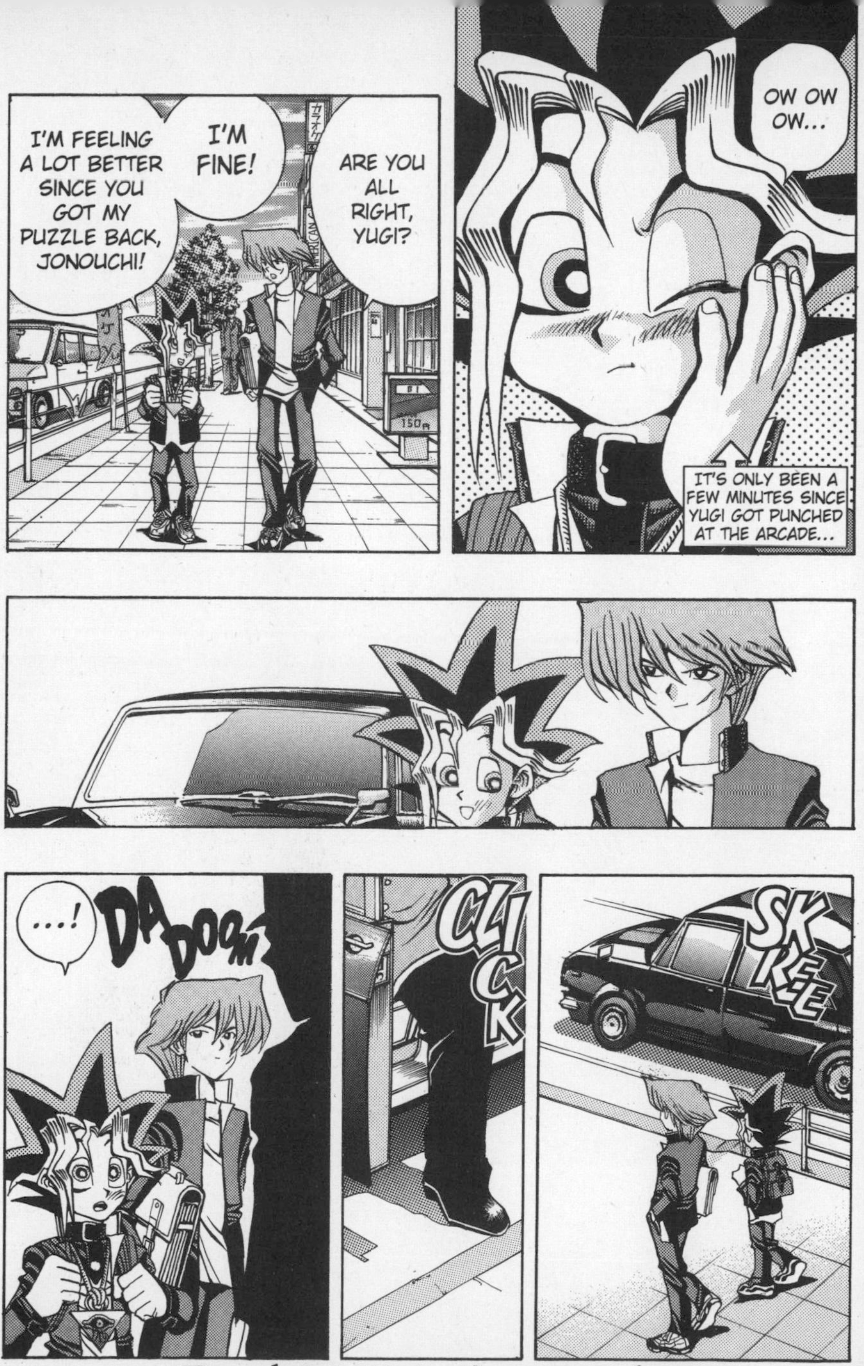
OW OW OW...
IT'S ONLY BEEN A FEW MINUTES SINCE YUGI GOT PUNCHED AT THE ARCADE...
ARE YOU ALL RIGHT, YUGI?
I'M FINE!
I'M FEELING A LOT BETTER SINCE YOU GOT MY PUZZLE BACK, JONOUCHI!
SKREEE
CLICK
DADOOM
...!

Duel 26: Russian Roulette

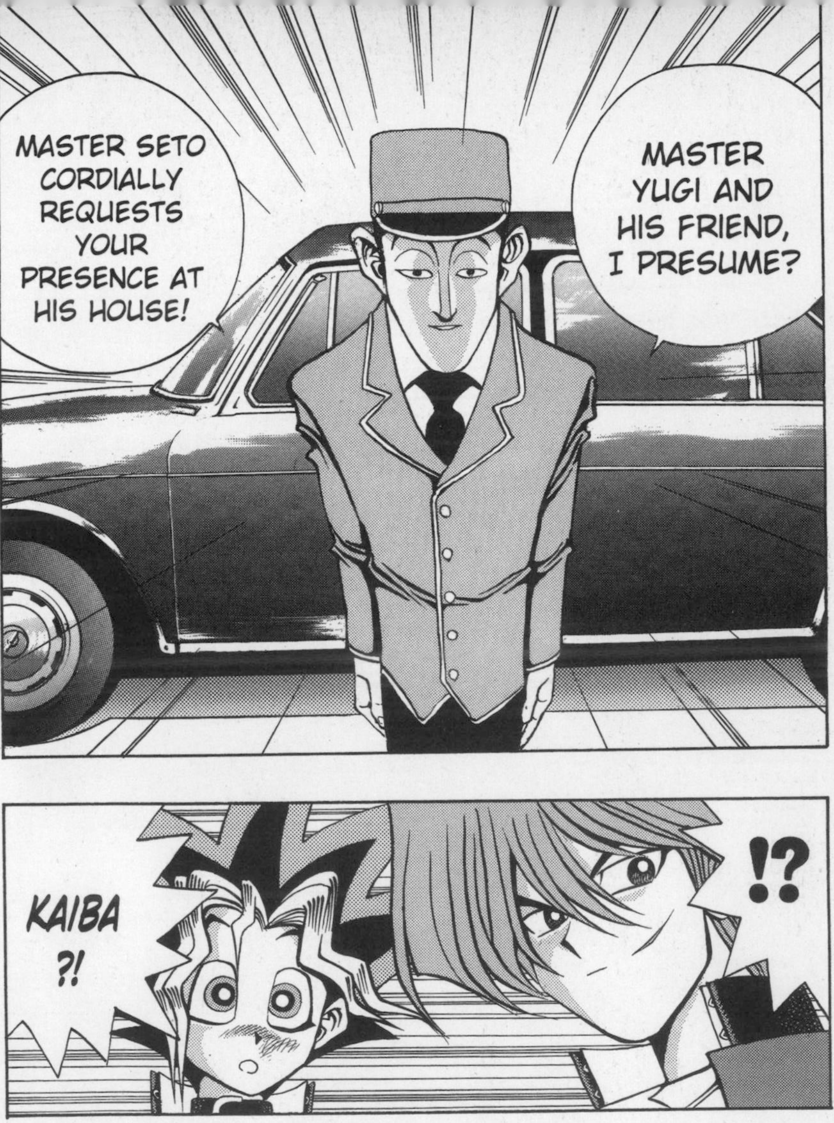
MASTER YUGI AND HIS FRIEND, I PRESUME?
MASTER SETO CORDIALLY REQUESTS YOUR PRESENCE AT HIS HOUSE!
!?
KAIBA ?!

Duel 26: Russian Roulette

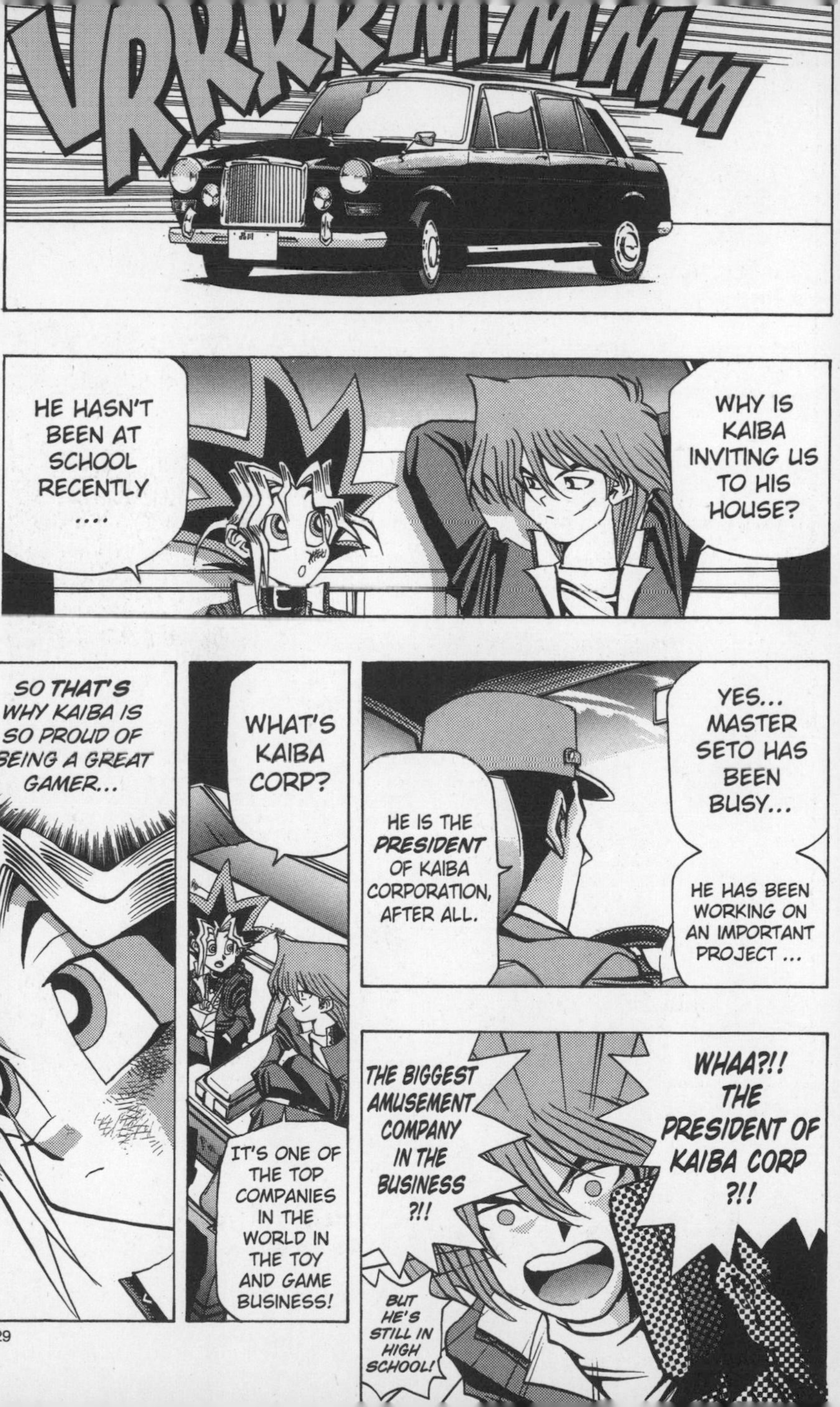
VRRRRMMMMM
WHY IS KAIBA INVITING US TO HIS HOUSE?
HE HASN'T BEEN AT SCHOOL RECENTLY ....
YES... MASTER SETO HAS BEEN BUSY...
HE HAS BEEN WORKING ON AN IMPORTANT PROJECT ...
HE IS THE PRESIDENT OF KAIBA CORPORATION, AFTER ALL.
WHAA?!! THE PRESIDENT OF KAIBA CORP ?!!
THE BIGGEST AMUSEMENT COMPANY IN THE BUSINESS ?!!
BUT HE'S STILL IN HIGH SCHOOL!
WHAT'S KAIBA CORP?
IT'S ONE OF THE TOP COMPANIES IN THE WORLD IN THE TOY AND GAME BUSINESS!
SO THAT'S WHY KAIBA IS SO PROUD OF BEING A GREAT GAMER...

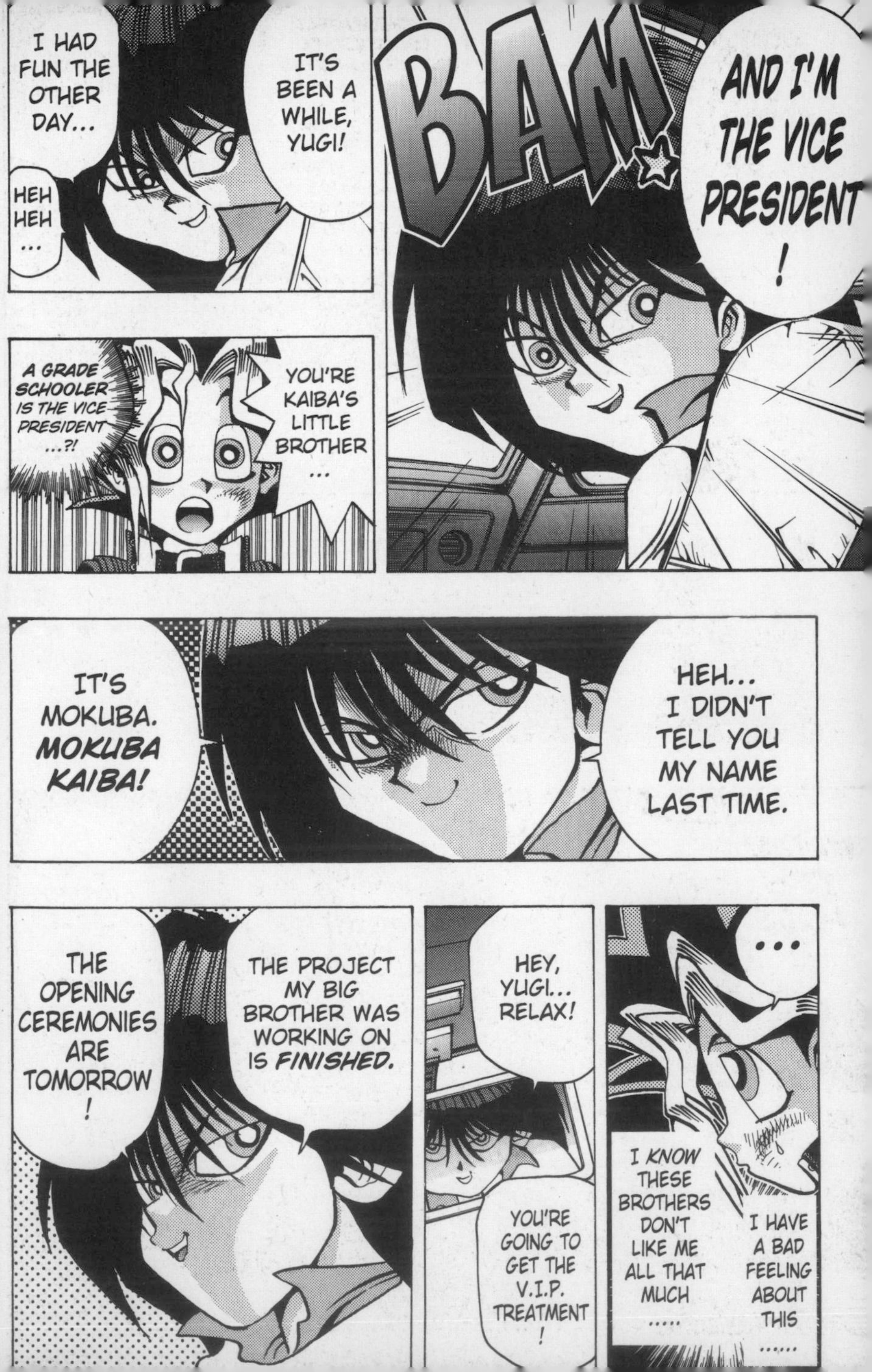
AND I'M THE VICE PRESIDENT !
BAM!
IT'S BEEN A WHILE, YUGI!
I HAD FUN THE OTHER DAY...
HEH HEH ...
YOU'RE KAIBA'S LITTLE BROTHER ...
A GRADE SCHOOLER IS THE VICE PRESIDENT ...?!
HEH... I DIDN'T TELL YOU MY NAME LAST TIME.
IT'S MOKUBA. ***MOKUBA KAIBA!***
...
HEY, YUGI... RELAX!
YOU'RE GOING TO GET THE V.I.P. TREATMENT !
I *KNOW* THESE BROTHERS DON'T LIKE ME ALL THAT MUCH .....
I HAVE A BAD FEELING ABOUT THIS ......
THE PROJECT MY BIG BROTHER WAS WORKING ON IS ***FINISHED.***
THE OPENING CEREMONIES ARE TOMORROW !

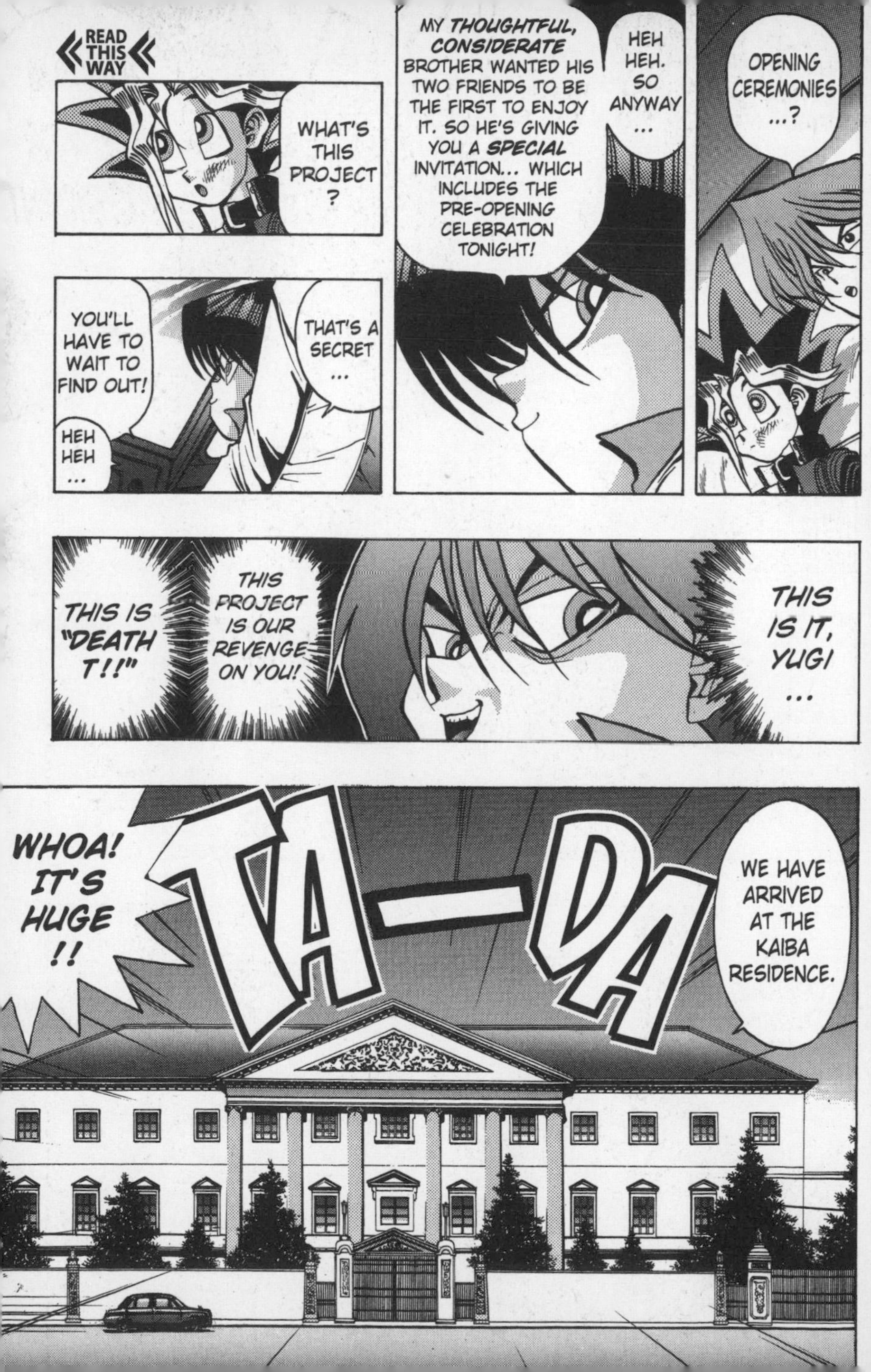
READ THIS WAY
OPENING CEREMONIES ...?
HEH HEH. SO ANYWAY ...
MY *THOUGHTFUL, CONSIDERATE* BROTHER WANTED HIS TWO FRIENDS TO BE THE FIRST TO ENJOY IT. SO HE'S GIVING YOU A *SPECIAL* INVITATION... WHICH INCLUDES THE PRE-OPENING CELEBRATION TONIGHT!
WHAT'S THIS PROJECT ?
THAT'S A SECRET ...
YOU'LL HAVE TO WAIT TO FIND OUT!
HEH HEH ...
THIS IS IT, YUGI ...
THIS PROJECT IS OUR REVENGE ON YOU!
THIS IS "DEATH T!!"
WE HAVE ARRIVED AT THE KAIBA RESIDENCE.
TA-DA
WHOA! IT'S HUGE !!

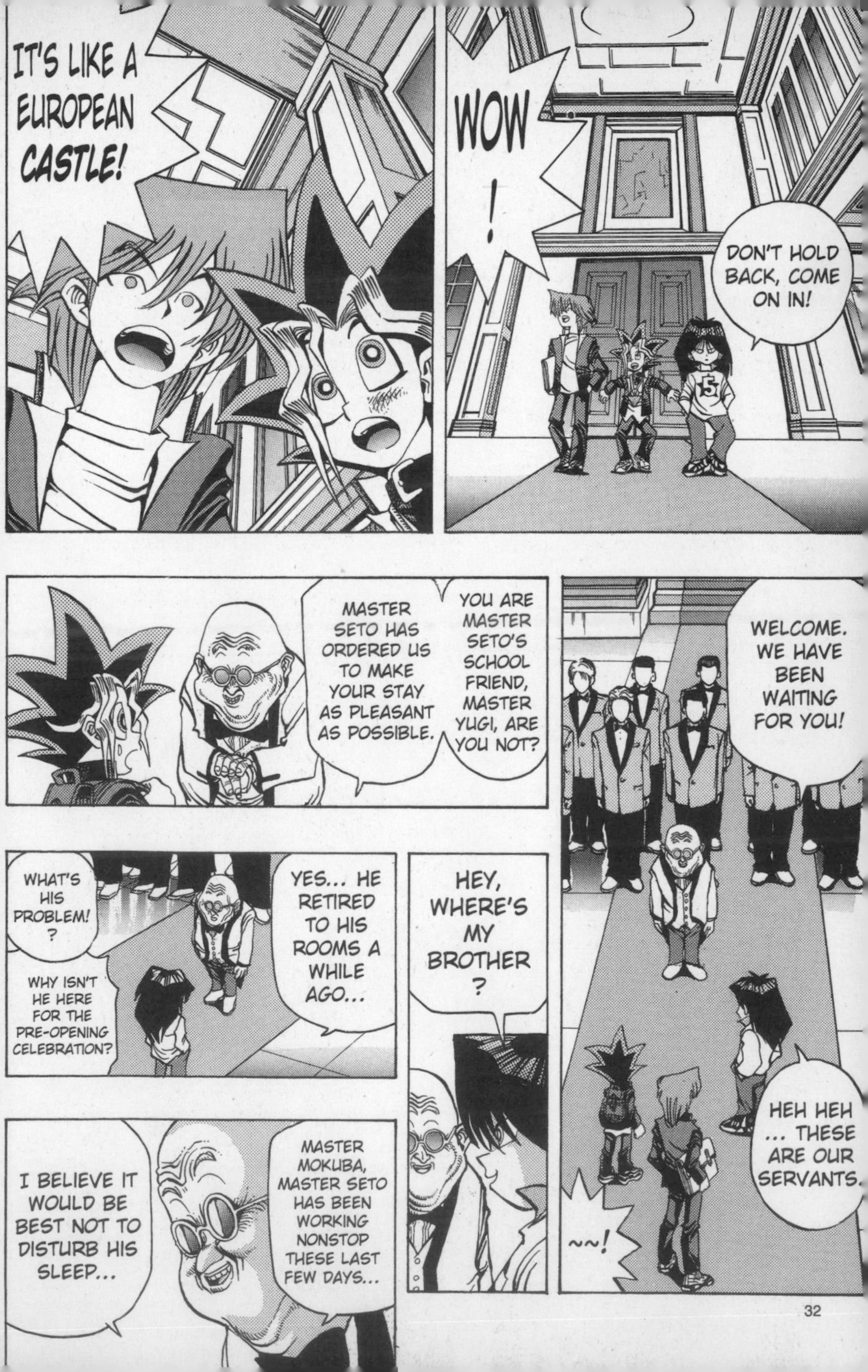
DON'T HOLD BACK, COME ON IN!
WOW!
IT'S LIKE A EUROPEAN CASTLE!
WELCOME. WE HAVE BEEN WAITING FOR YOU!
HEH HEH ... THESE ARE OUR SERVANTS.
~~!
YOU ARE MASTER SETO'S SCHOOL FRIEND, MASTER YUGI, ARE YOU NOT?
MASTER SETO HAS ORDERED US TO MAKE YOUR STAY AS PLEASANT AS POSSIBLE.
HEY, WHERE'S MY BROTHER?
YES... HE RETIRED TO HIS ROOMS A WHILE AGO...
WHAT'S HIS PROBLEM!?
WHY ISN'T HE HERE FOR THE PRE-OPENING CELEBRATION?
MASTER MOKUBA, MASTER SETO HAS BEEN WORKING NONSTOP THESE LAST FEW DAYS...
I BELIEVE IT WOULD BE BEST NOT TO DISTURB HIS SLEEP...

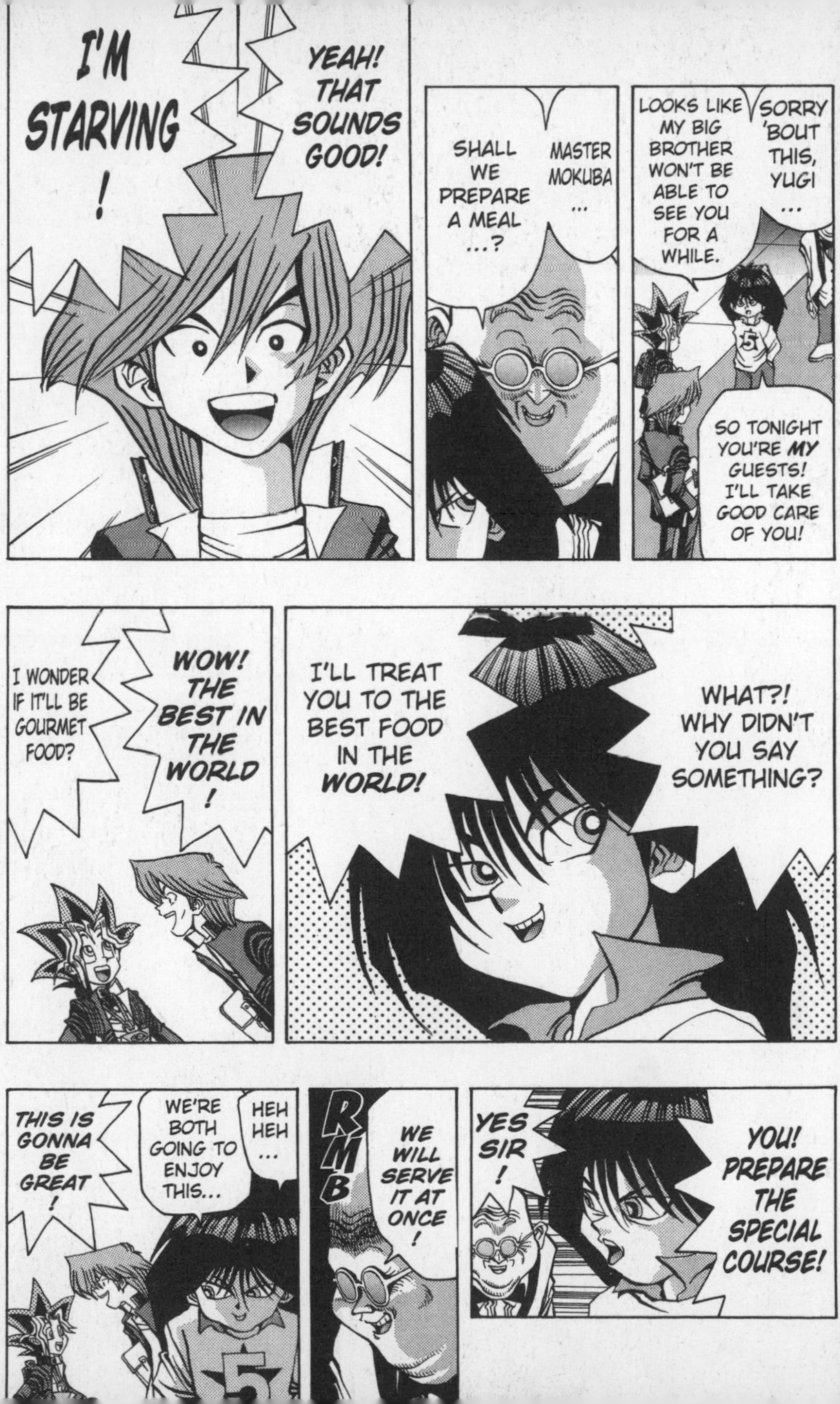
SORRY 'BOUT THIS, YUGI ...
LOOKS LIKE MY BIG BROTHER WON'T BE ABLE TO SEE YOU FOR A WHILE.
SO TONIGHT YOU'RE MY GUESTS! I'LL TAKE GOOD CARE OF YOU!
MASTER MOKUBA ...
SHALL WE PREPARE A MEAL ...?
YEAH! THAT SOUNDS GOOD!
I'M STARVING!
WHAT?! WHY DIDN'T YOU SAY SOMETHING?
I'LL TREAT YOU TO THE BEST FOOD IN THE WORLD!
WOW! THE BEST IN THE WORLD!
I WONDER IF IT'LL BE GOURMET FOOD?
YOU! PREPARE THE SPECIAL COURSE!
YES SIR!
WE WILL SERVE IT AT ONCE!
RMB
HEH HEH ...
WE'RE BOTH GOING TO ENJOY THIS...
THIS IS GONNA BE GREAT!

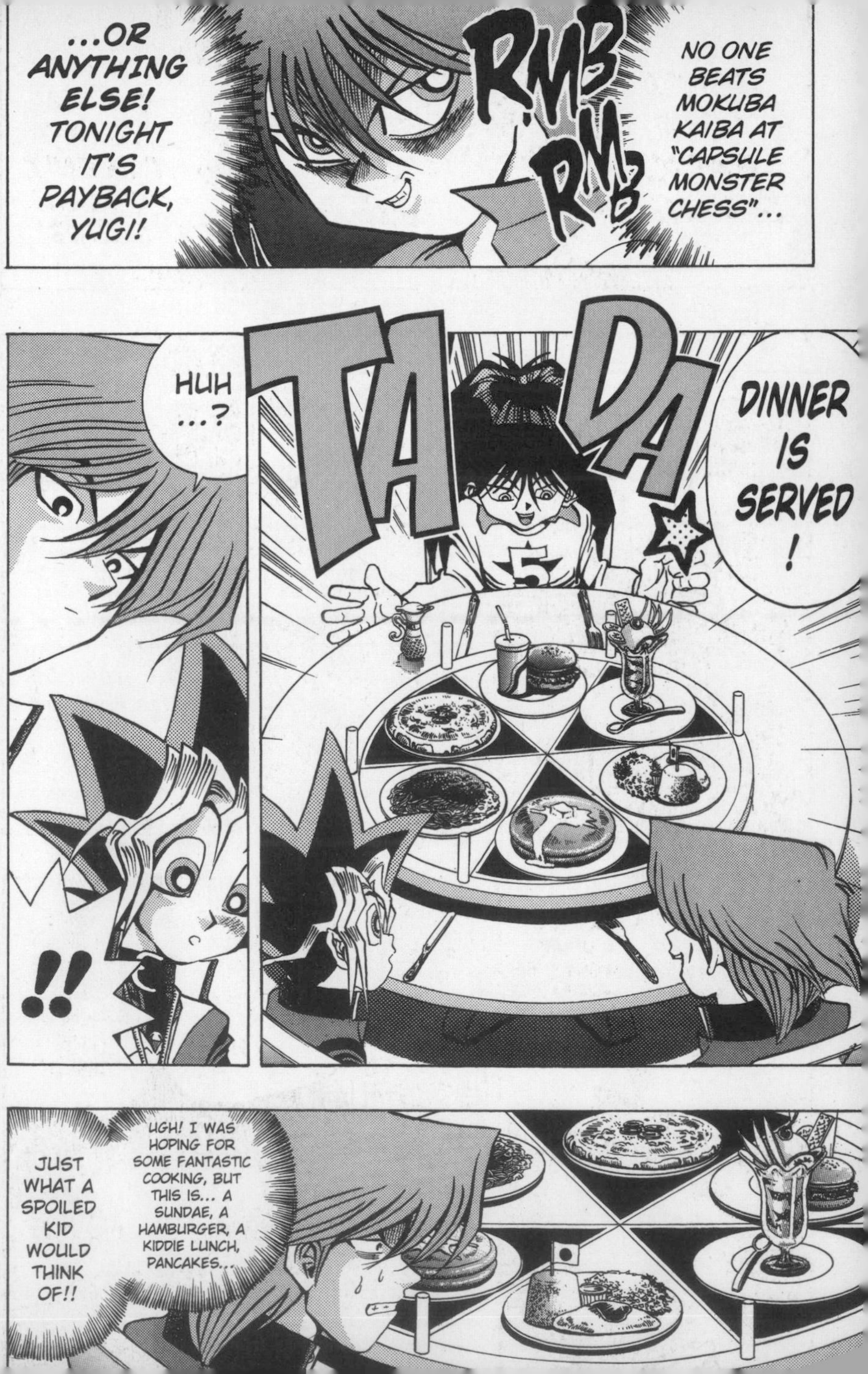
NO ONE BEATS MOKUBA KAIBA AT "CAPSULE MONSTER CHESS"...
RMB RMB
...OR ANYTHING ELSE! TONIGHT IT'S PAYBACK, YUGI!
DINNER IS SERVED!
TA DA
HUH ...?
!!
UGH! I WAS HOPING FOR SOME FANTASTIC COOKING, BUT THIS IS... A SUNDAE, A HAMBURGER, A KIDDIE LUNCH, PANCAKES...
JUST WHAT A SPOILED KID WOULD THINK OF!!

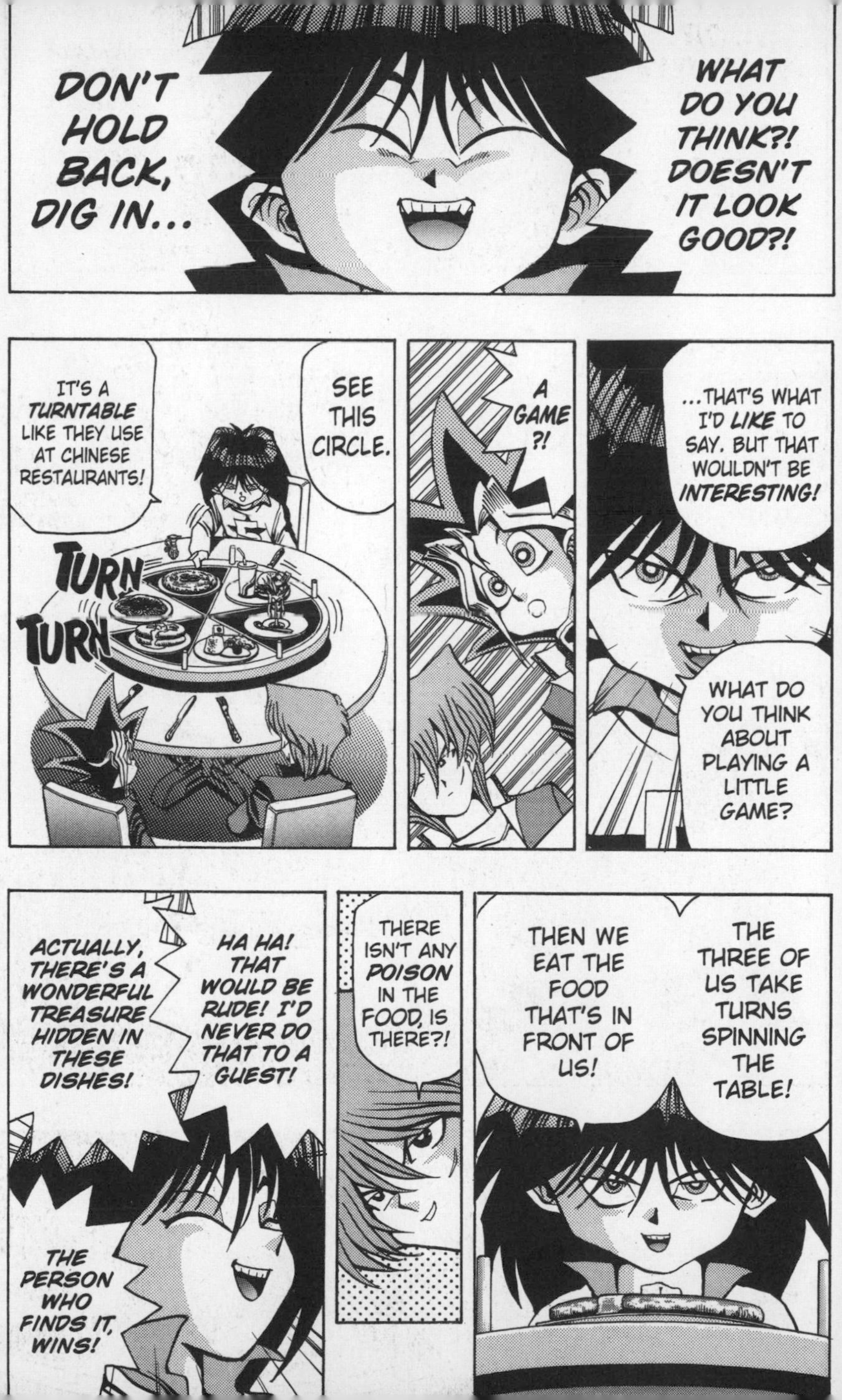
WHAT DO YOU THINK?! DOESN'T IT LOOK GOOD?!
DON'T HOLD BACK, DIG IN...
...THAT'S WHAT I'D LIKE TO SAY. BUT THAT WOULDN'T BE INTERESTING!
WHAT DO YOU THINK ABOUT PLAYING A LITTLE GAME?
A GAME ?!
SEE THIS CIRCLE.
IT'S A TURNTABLE LIKE THEY USE AT CHINESE RESTAURANTS!
TURN
TURN
THE THREE OF US TAKE TURNS SPINNING THE TABLE!
THEN WE EAT THE FOOD THAT'S IN FRONT OF US!
THERE ISN'T ANY POISON IN THE FOOD, IS THERE?!
HA HA! THAT WOULD BE RUDE! I'D NEVER DO THAT TO A GUEST!
ACTUALLY, THERE'S A WONDERFUL TREASURE HIDDEN IN THESE DISHES!
THE PERSON WHO FINDS IT, WINS!

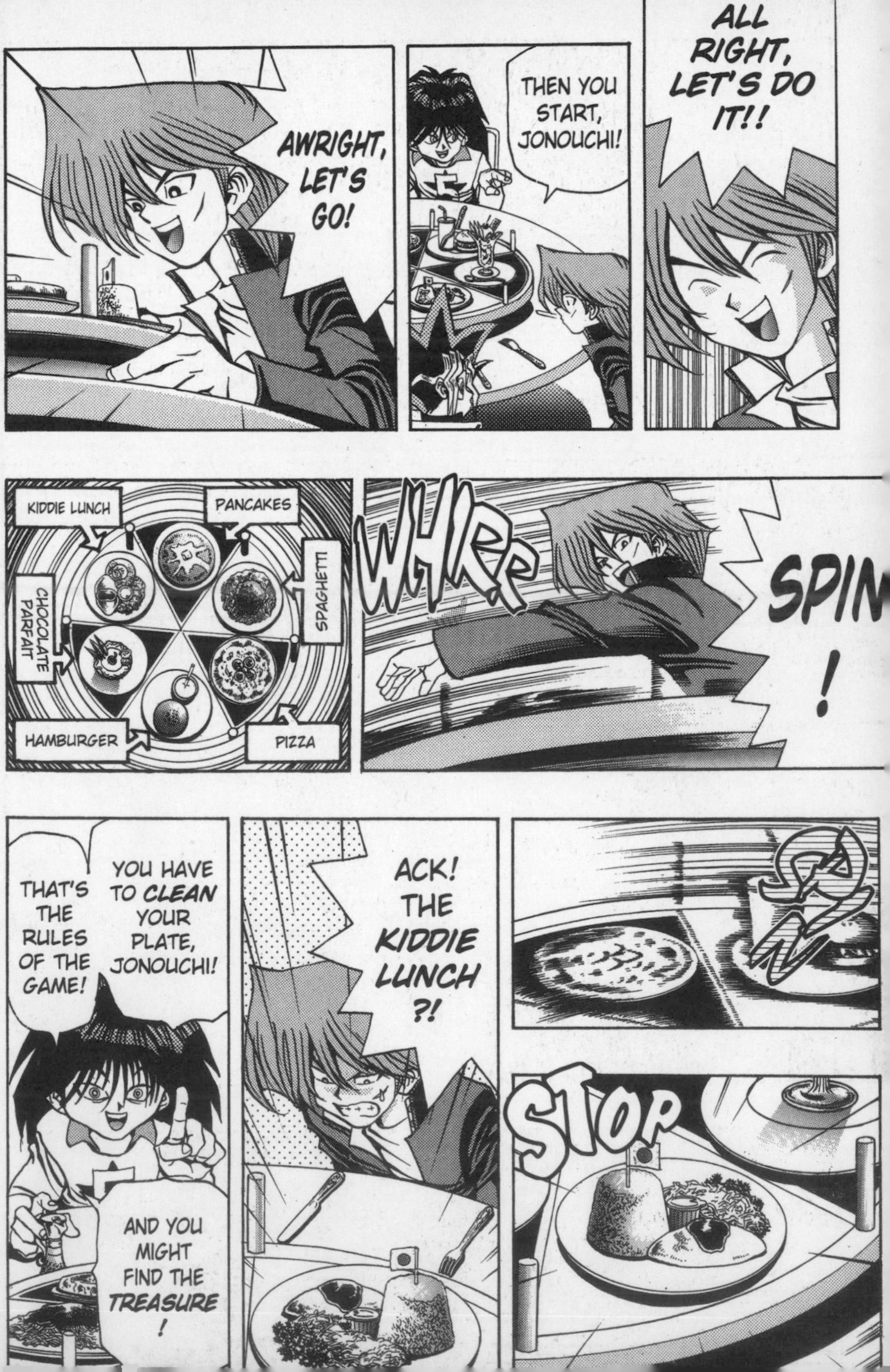
ALL RIGHT, LET'S DO IT!!
THEN YOU START, JONOUCHI!
AWRIGHT, LET'S GO!
WHIRR
SPIN!
KIDDIE LUNCH
PANCAKES
SPAGHETTI
CHOCOLATE PARFAIT
HAMBURGER
PIZZA
STOP
ACK! THE KIDDIE LUNCH ?!
YOU HAVE TO CLEAN YOUR PLATE, JONOUCHI!
THAT'S THE RULES OF THE GAME!
AND YOU MIGHT FIND THE TREASURE!

READ THIS WAY

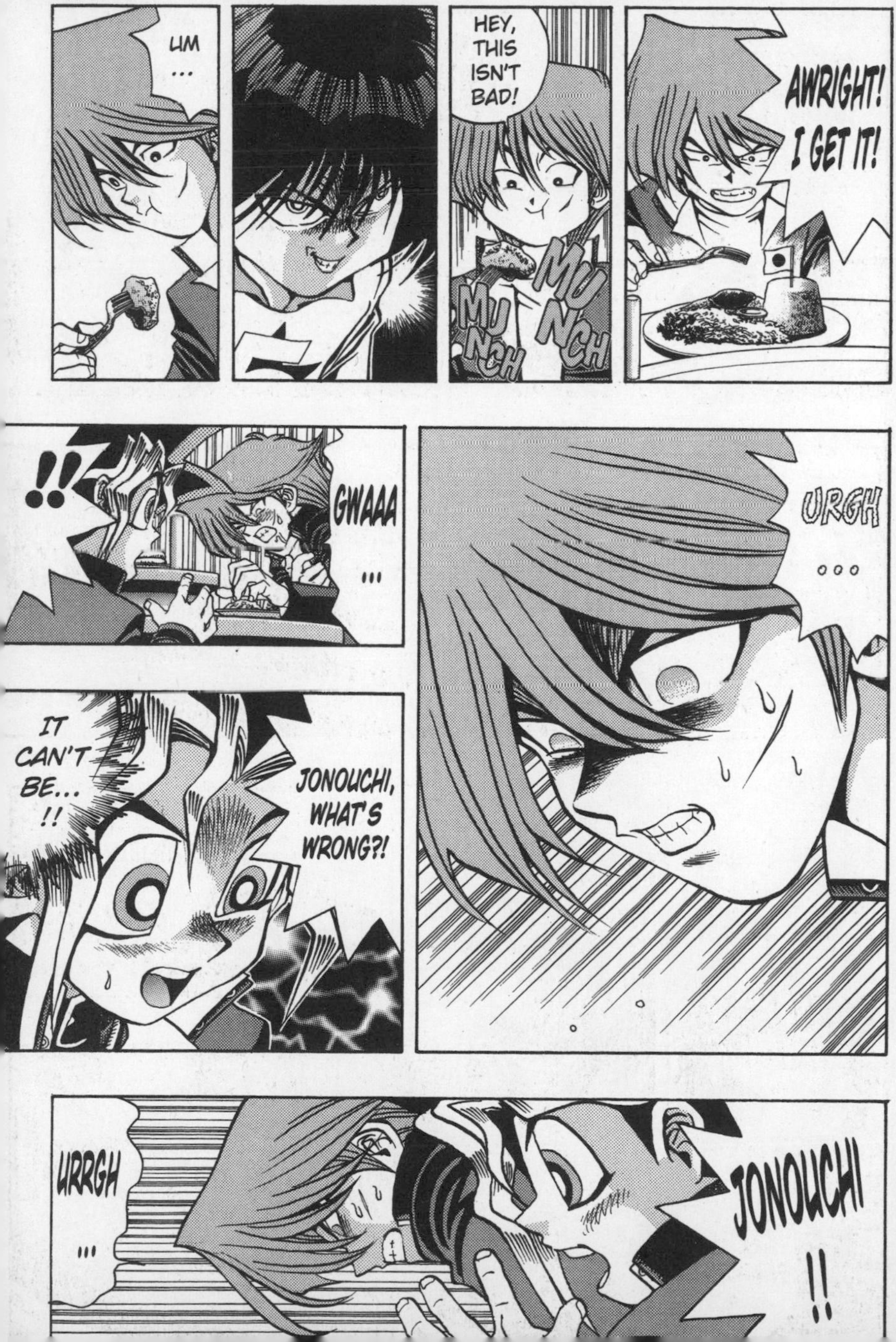
AWRIGHT! I GET IT!
MUNCH MUNCH
HEY, THIS ISN'T BAD!
UM ...
URGH ...
!!
GWAAA ...
JONOUCHI, WHAT'S WRONG?!
IT CAN'T BE... !!
JONOUCHI !!
URRGH ...

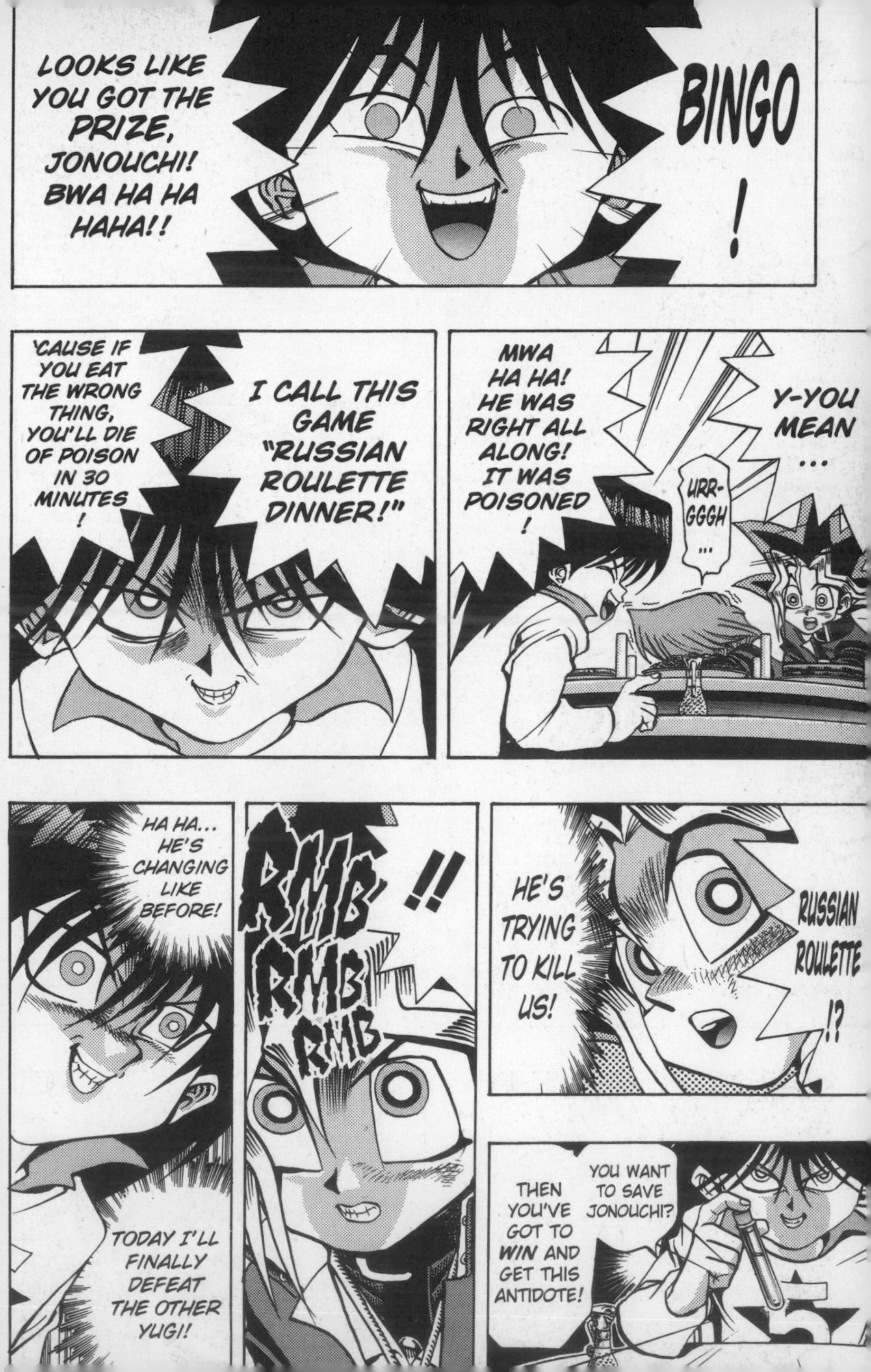
BINGO!
LOOKS LIKE YOU GOT THE PRIZE, JONOUCHI! BWA HA HA HAHA!!
Y-YOU MEAN...
URR-GGGH...
MWA HA HA! HE WAS RIGHT ALL ALONG! IT WAS POISONED!
I CALL THIS GAME "RUSSIAN ROULETTE DINNER!"
'CAUSE IF YOU EAT THE WRONG THING, YOU'LL DIE OF POISON IN 30 MINUTES!
RUSSIAN ROULETTE!?
HE'S TRYING TO KILL US!
YOU WANT TO SAVE JONOUCHI?
THEN YOU'VE GOT TO WIN AND GET THIS ANTIDOTE!
RMB RMB RMB !!
HA HA... HE'S CHANGING LIKE BEFORE!
TODAY I'LL FINALLY DEFEAT THE OTHER YUGI!

READ THIS WAY

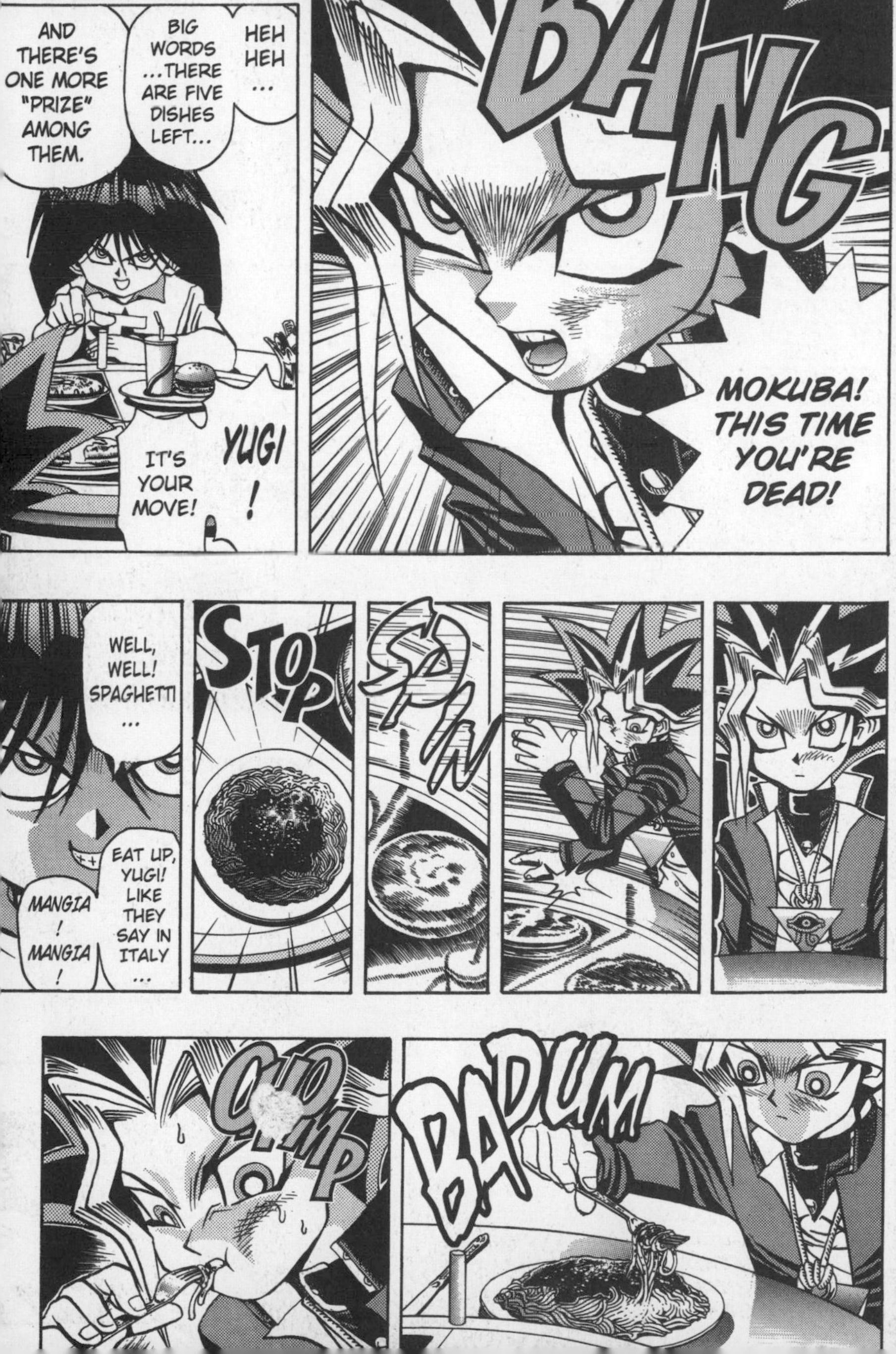
BANG
MOKUBA! THIS TIME YOU'RE DEAD!
HEH HEH ...
BIG WORDS ...THERE ARE FIVE DISHES LEFT...
AND THERE'S ONE MORE "PRIZE" AMONG THEM.
YUGI !
IT'S YOUR MOVE!
SPIN
STOP
WELL, WELL! SPAGHETTI ...
EAT UP, YUGI! LIKE THEY SAY IN ITALY ...
MANGIA ! MANGIA !
BADUM
CHOMP

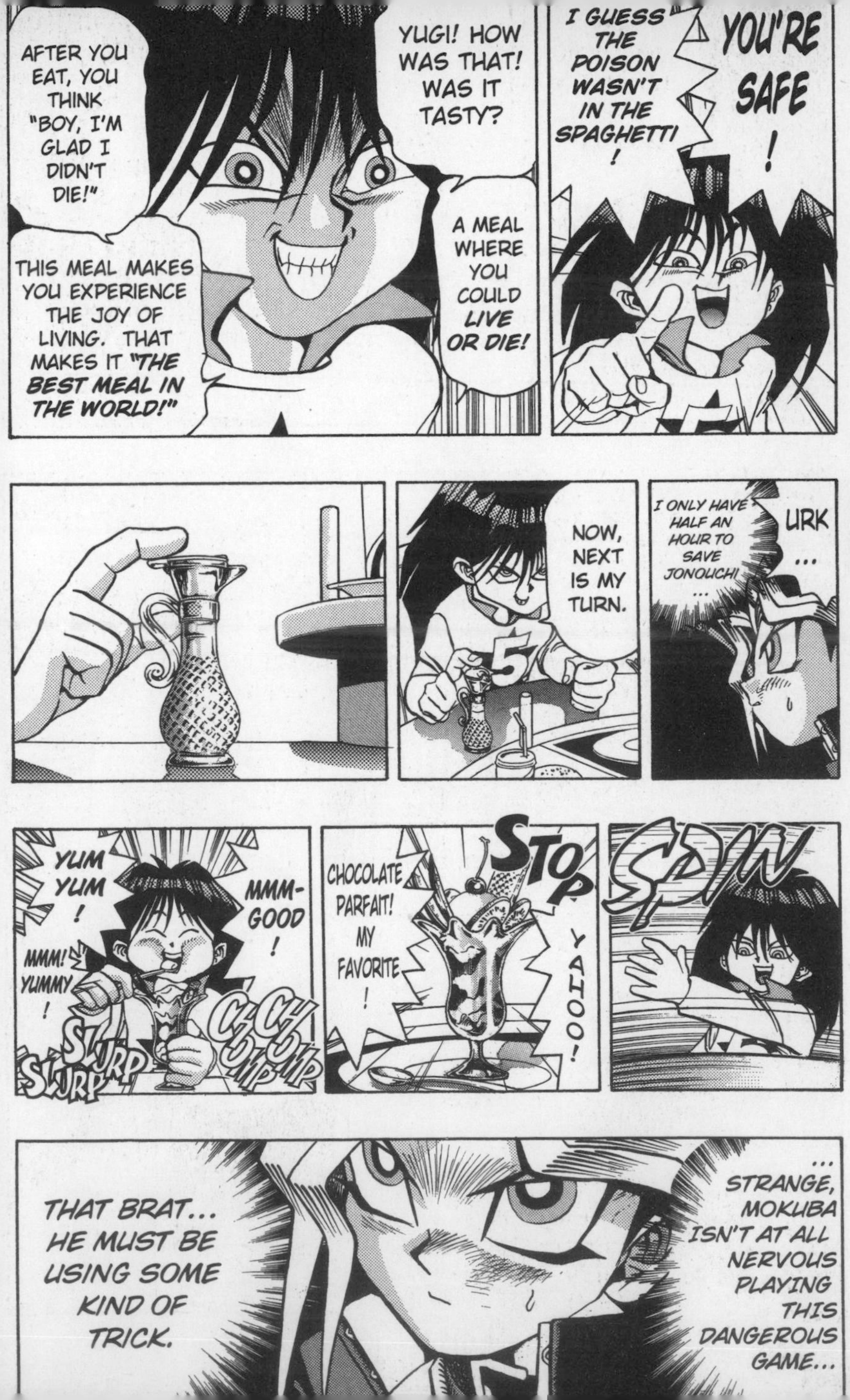
YOU'RE SAFE!
I GUESS THE POISON WASN'T IN THE SPAGHETTI!
YUGI! HOW WAS THAT! WAS IT TASTY?
A MEAL WHERE YOU COULD LIVE OR DIE!
AFTER YOU EAT, YOU THINK "BOY, I'M GLAD I DIDN'T DIE!"
THIS MEAL MAKES YOU EXPERIENCE THE JOY OF LIVING. THAT MAKES IT "THE BEST MEAL IN THE WORLD!"
URK...
I ONLY HAVE HALF AN HOUR TO SAVE JONOUCHI...
NOW, NEXT IS MY TURN.
SPIN
STOP
YAHOO!
CHOCOLATE PARFAIT! MY FAVORITE!
MMM-GOOD!
YUM YUM!
MMM! YUMMY!
CHOMP CHOMP
SLURP SLURP
...STRANGE, MOKUBA ISN'T AT ALL NERVOUS PLAYING THIS DANGEROUS GAME...
THAT BRAT... HE MUST BE USING SOME KIND OF TRICK.

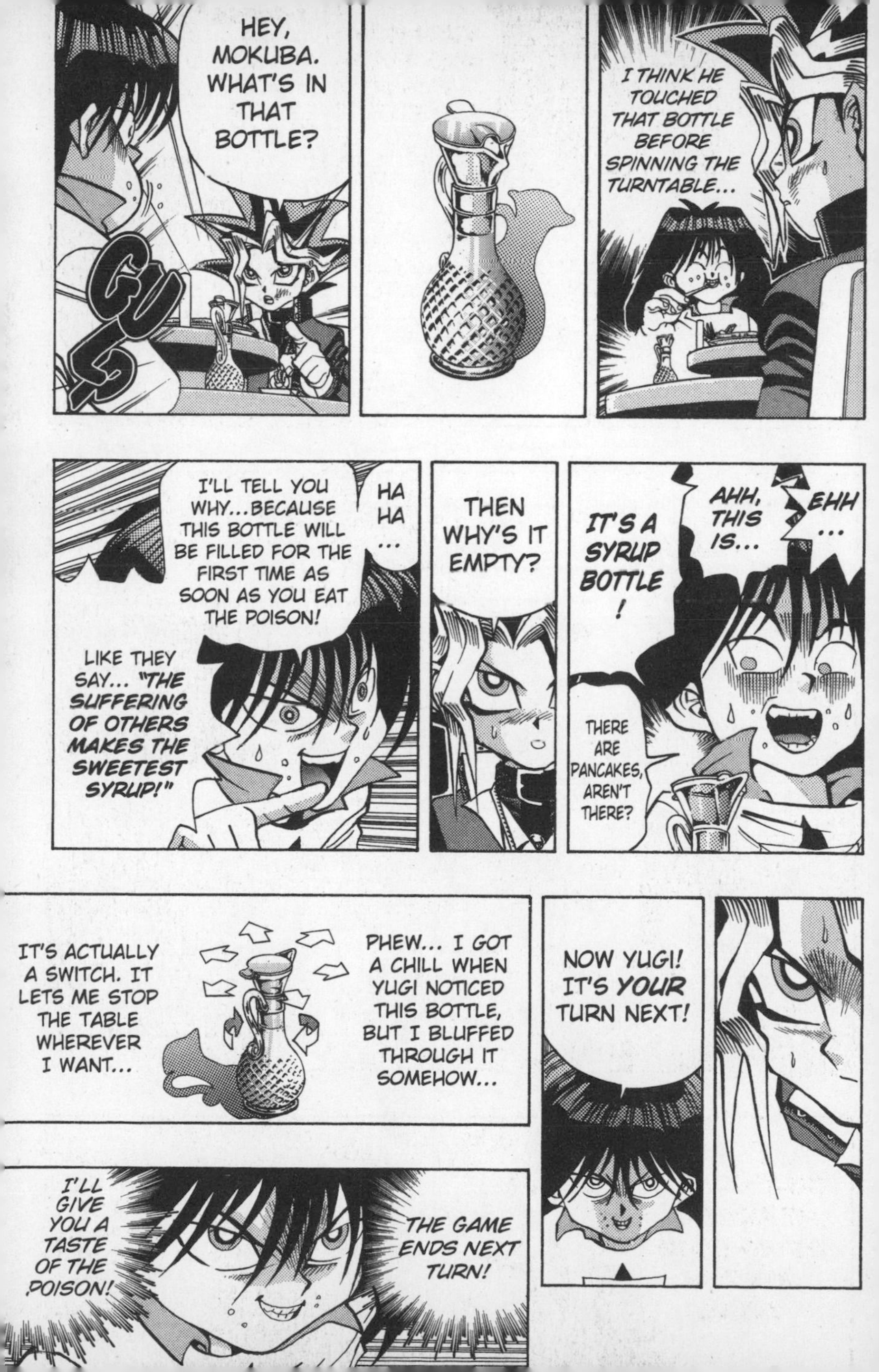
I THINK HE TOUCHED THAT BOTTLE BEFORE SPINNING THE TURNTABLE...
HEY, MOKUBA. WHAT'S IN THAT BOTTLE?
GU
EHH...
AHH, THIS IS...
IT'S A SYRUP BOTTLE!
THERE ARE PANCAKES, AREN'T THERE?
THEN WHY'S IT EMPTY?
HA HA...
I'LL TELL YOU WHY...BECAUSE THIS BOTTLE WILL BE FILLED FOR THE FIRST TIME AS SOON AS YOU EAT THE POISON!
LIKE THEY SAY... "THE SUFFERING OF OTHERS MAKES THE SWEETEST SYRUP!"
NOW YUGI! IT'S YOUR TURN NEXT!
PHEW... I GOT A CHILL WHEN YUGI NOTICED THIS BOTTLE, BUT I BLUFFED THROUGH IT SOMEHOW...
IT'S ACTUALLY A SWITCH. IT LETS ME STOP THE TABLE WHEREVER I WANT...
THE GAME ENDS NEXT TURN!
I'LL GIVE YOU A TASTE OF THE POISON!

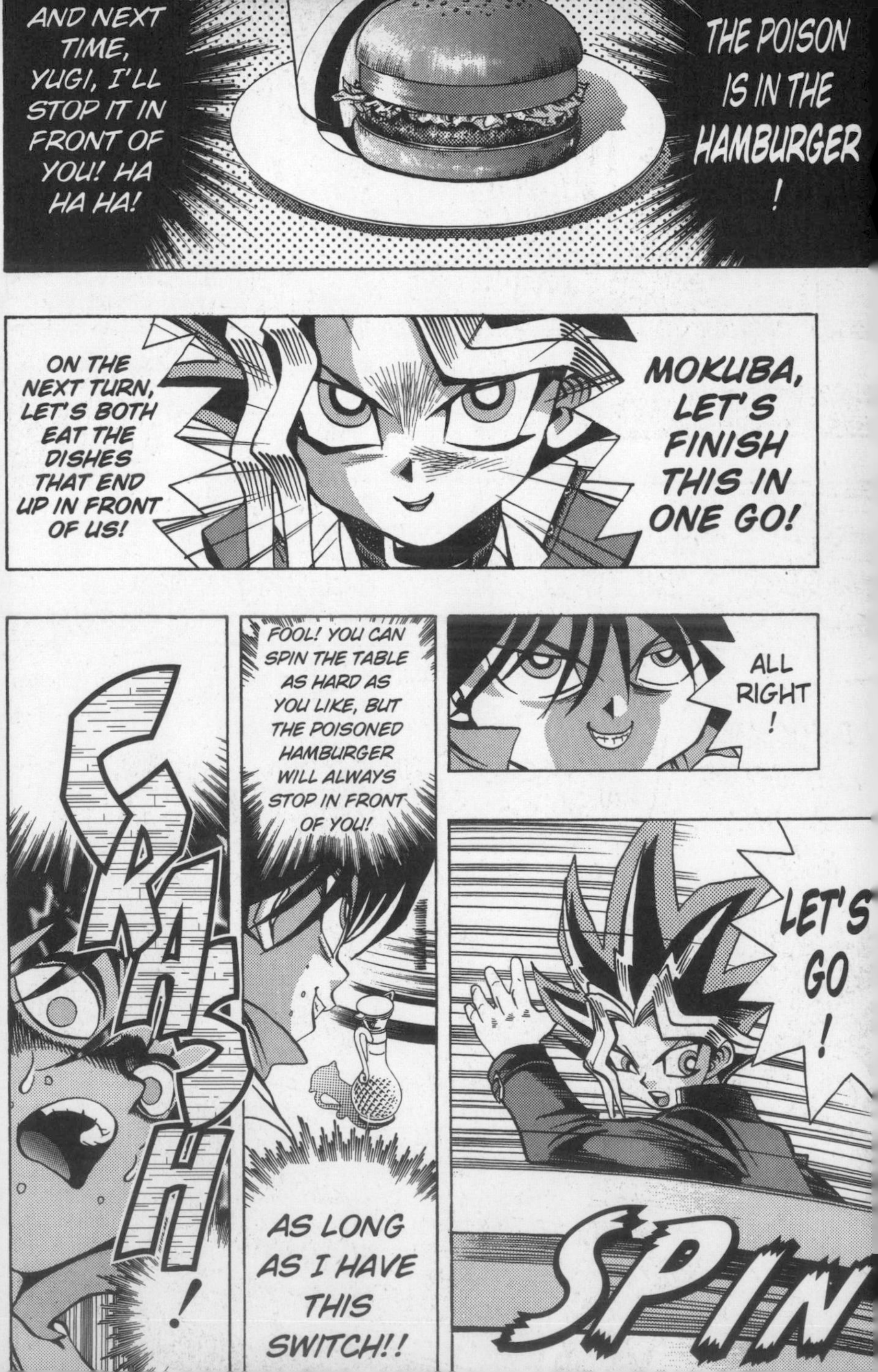
THE POISON IS IN THE HAMBURGER !
AND NEXT TIME, YUGI, I'LL STOP IT IN FRONT OF YOU! HA HA HA!
MOKUBA, LET'S FINISH THIS IN ONE GO!
ON THE NEXT TURN, LET'S BOTH EAT THE DISHES THAT END UP IN FRONT OF US!
ALL RIGHT !
LET'S GO !
SPIN
FOOL! YOU CAN SPIN THE TABLE AS HARD AS YOU LIKE, BUT THE POISONED HAMBURGER WILL ALWAYS STOP IN FRONT OF YOU!
AS LONG AS I HAVE THIS SWITCH!!

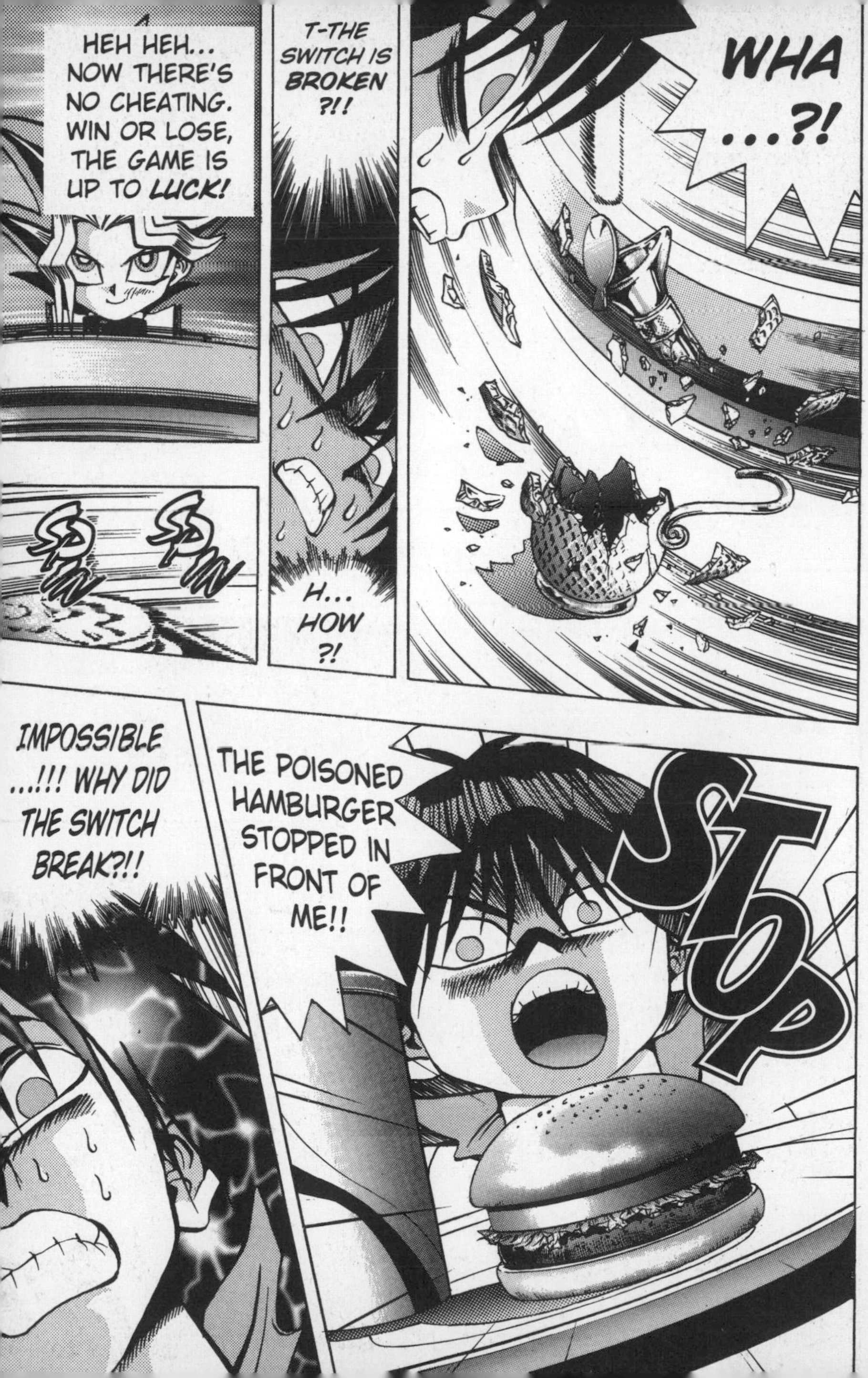
WHA ...?!
T-THE SWITCH IS BROKEN ?!!
H... HOW ?!
HEH HEH... NOW THERE'S NO CHEATING. WIN OR LOSE, THE GAME IS UP TO *LUCK!*
SPIN
SPIN
STOP
THE POISONED HAMBURGER STOPPED IN FRONT OF ME!!
IMPOSSIBLE ...!!! WHY DID THE SWITCH BREAK?!!

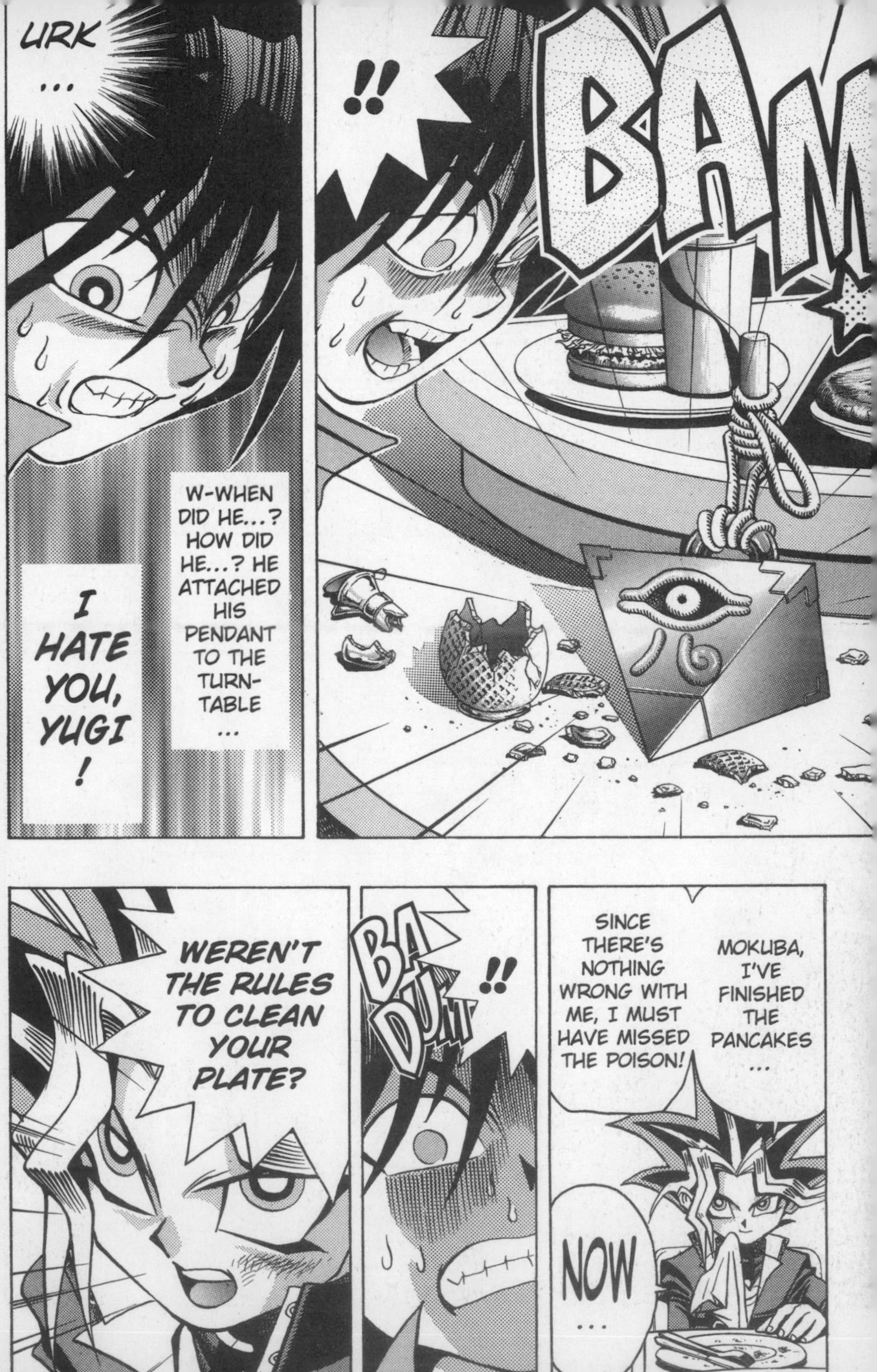
BAM
!!
URK ...
W-WHEN DID HE...? HOW DID HE...? HE ATTACHED HIS PENDANT TO THE TURN-TABLE ...
I HATE YOU, YUGI!
MOKUBA, I'VE FINISHED THE PANCAKES ...
SINCE THERE'S NOTHING WRONG WITH ME, I MUST HAVE MISSED THE POISON!
NOW ...
BA-DUMP
!!
WEREN'T THE RULES TO CLEAN YOUR PLATE?

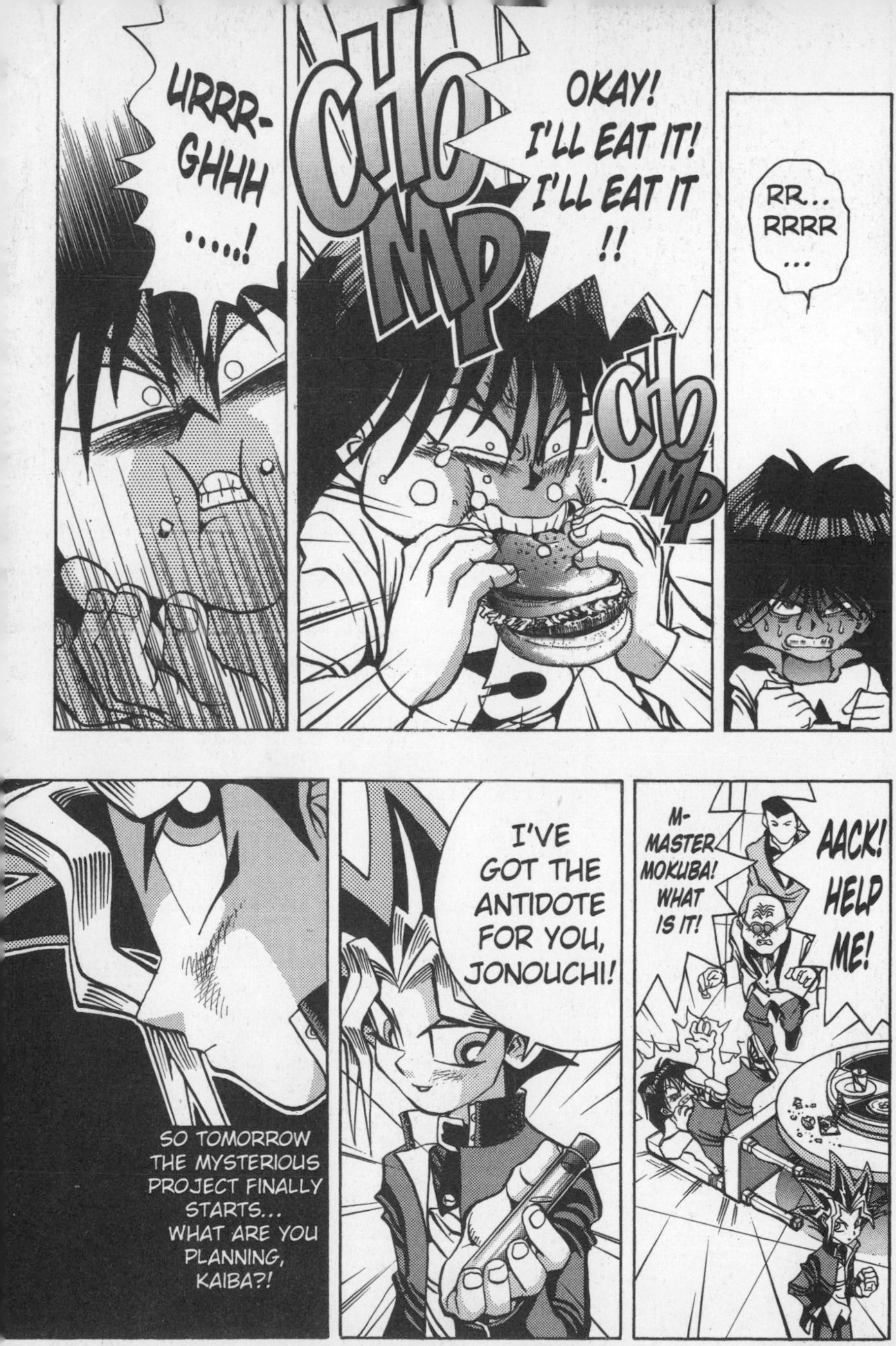
RR... RRRR ...
OKAY! I'LL EAT IT! I'LL EAT IT !!
CHOMP
CHOMP
URRR-GHHH .....!
AACK! HELP ME!
M-MASTER MOKUBA! WHAT IS IT!
I'VE GOT THE ANTIDOTE FOR YOU, JONOUCHI!
SO TOMORROW THE MYSTERIOUS PROJECT FINALLY STARTS... WHAT ARE YOU PLANNING, KAIBA?!

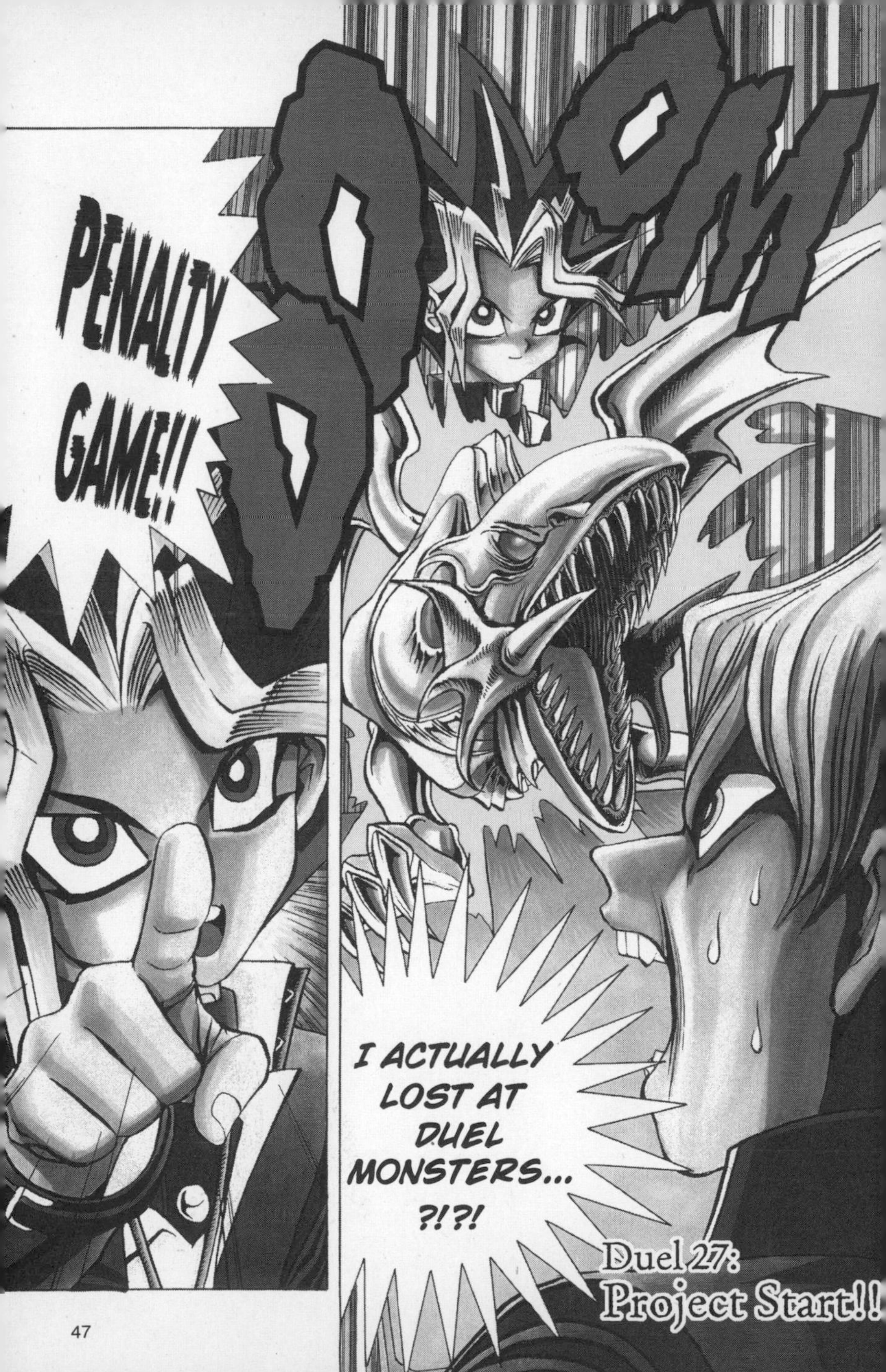
DOOM
I ACTUALLY LOST AT DUEL MONSTERS... ?!?!
Duel 27: Project Start!!
PENALTY GAME!!

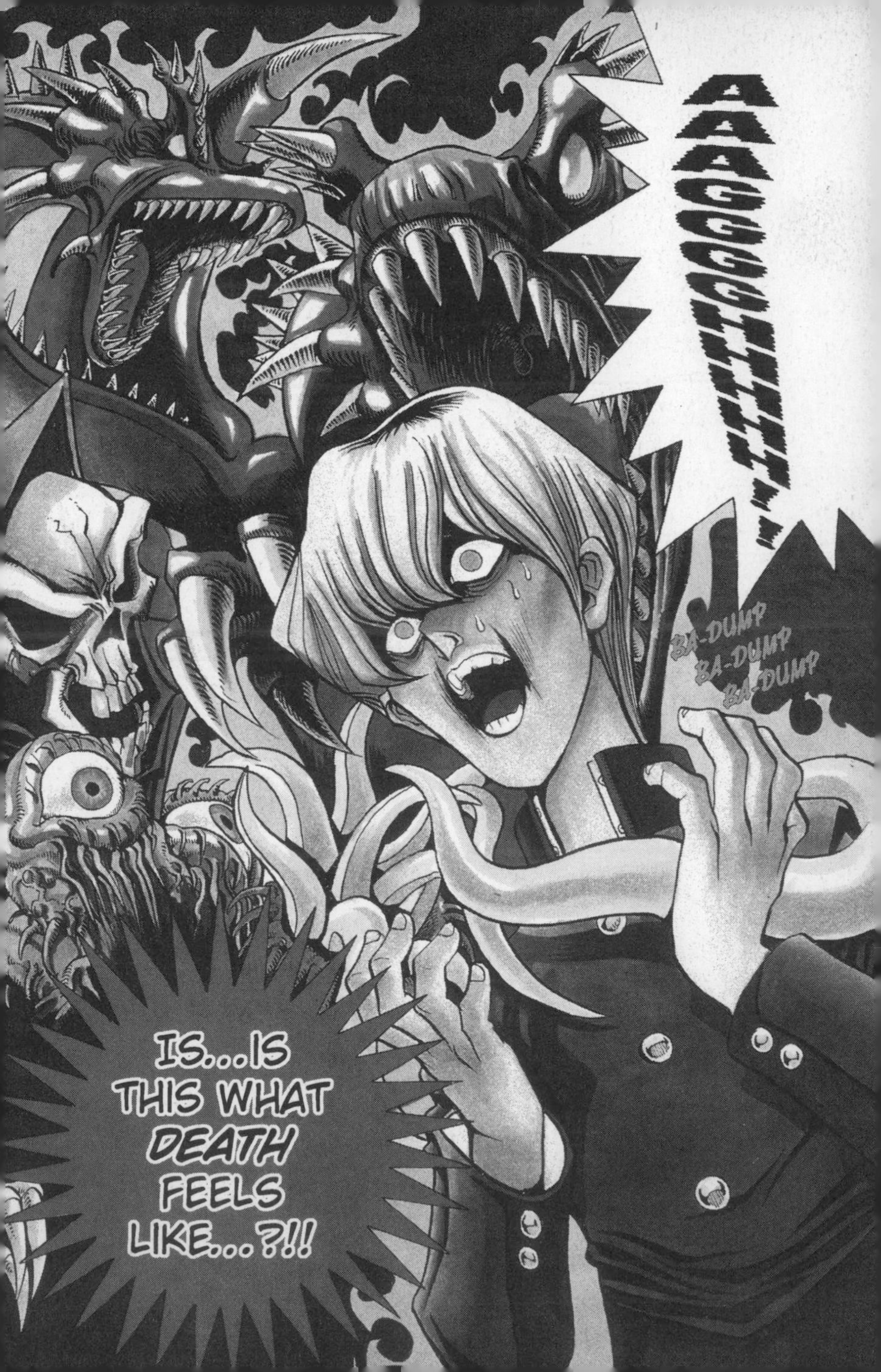
AAAGGGHHHH!!
BA-DUMP BA-DUMP BA-DUMP
IS...IS THIS WHAT DEATH FEELS LIKE...?!!

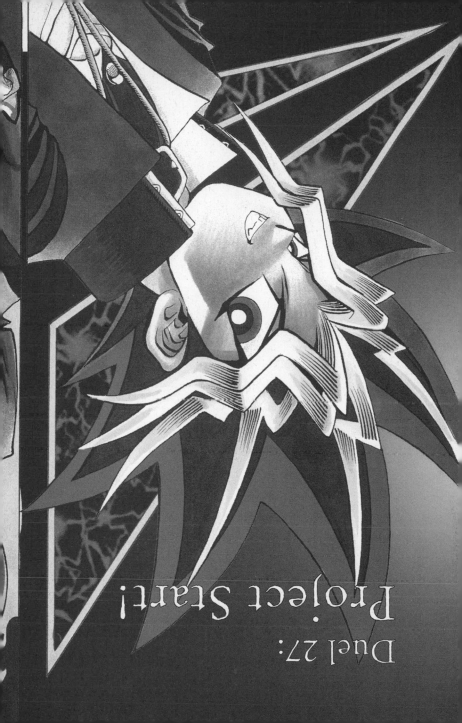

Duel 27: Project Start!

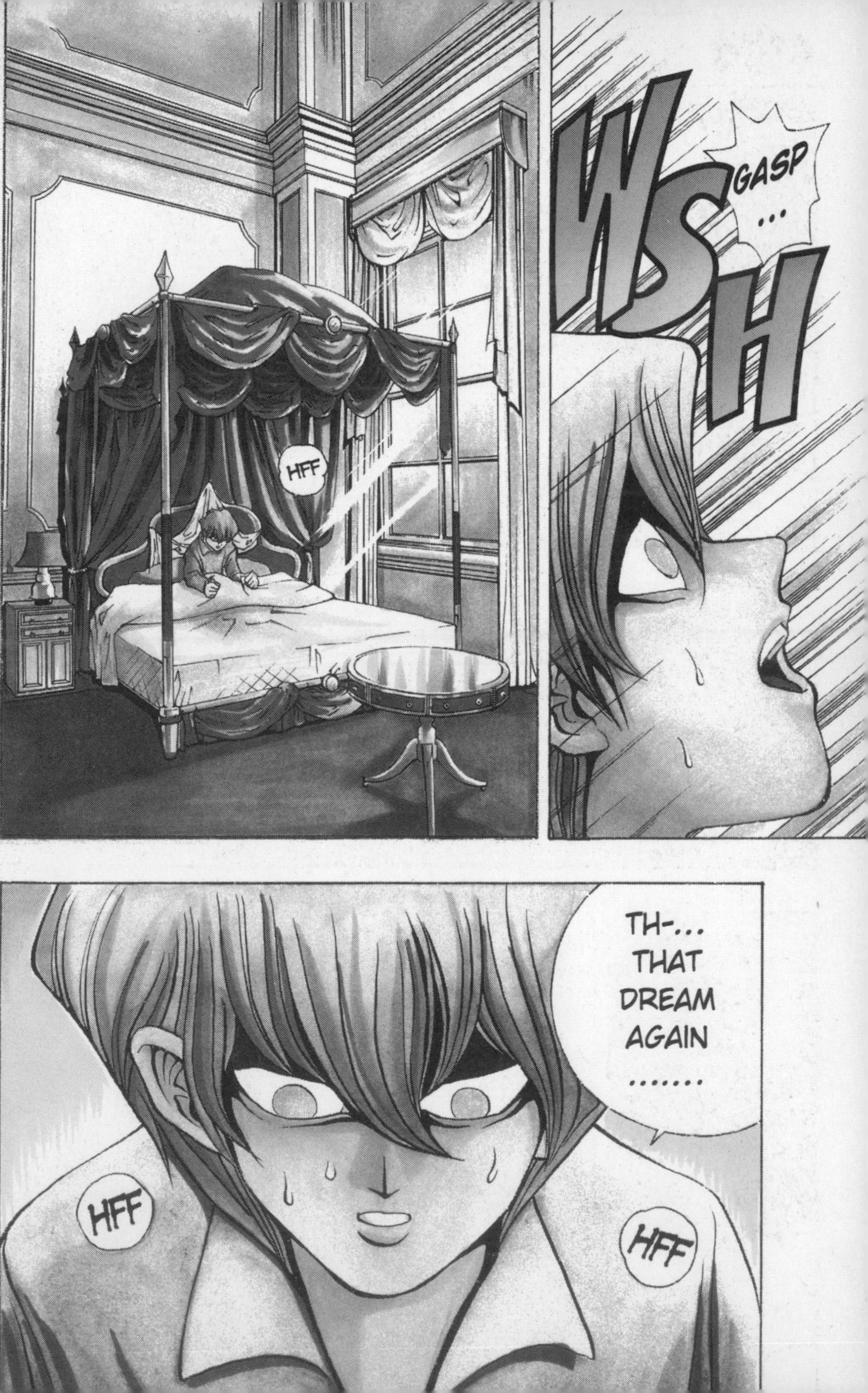
WSH
GASP ...
HFF
TH-... THAT DREAM AGAIN ....
HFF
HFF

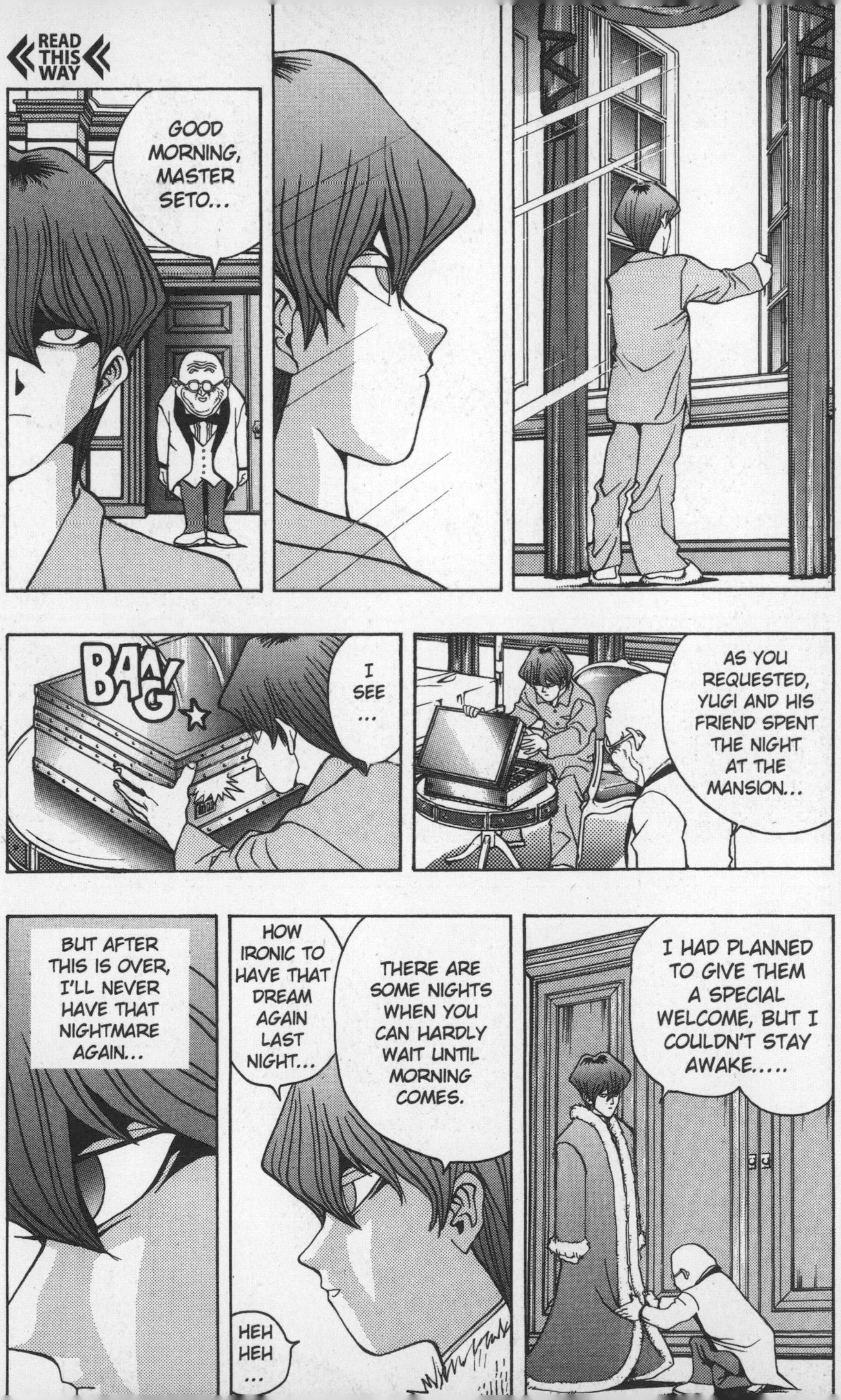
READ THIS WAY
GOOD MORNING, MASTER SETO...
AS YOU REQUESTED, YUGI AND HIS FRIEND SPENT THE NIGHT AT THE MANSION...
I SEE...
BAAG
I HAD PLANNED TO GIVE THEM A SPECIAL WELCOME, BUT I COULDN'T STAY AWAKE.....
THERE ARE SOME NIGHTS WHEN YOU CAN HARDLY WAIT UNTIL MORNING COMES.
HOW IRONIC TO HAVE THAT DREAM AGAIN LAST NIGHT...
HEH HEH...
BUT AFTER THIS IS OVER, I'LL NEVER HAVE THAT NIGHTMARE AGAIN...

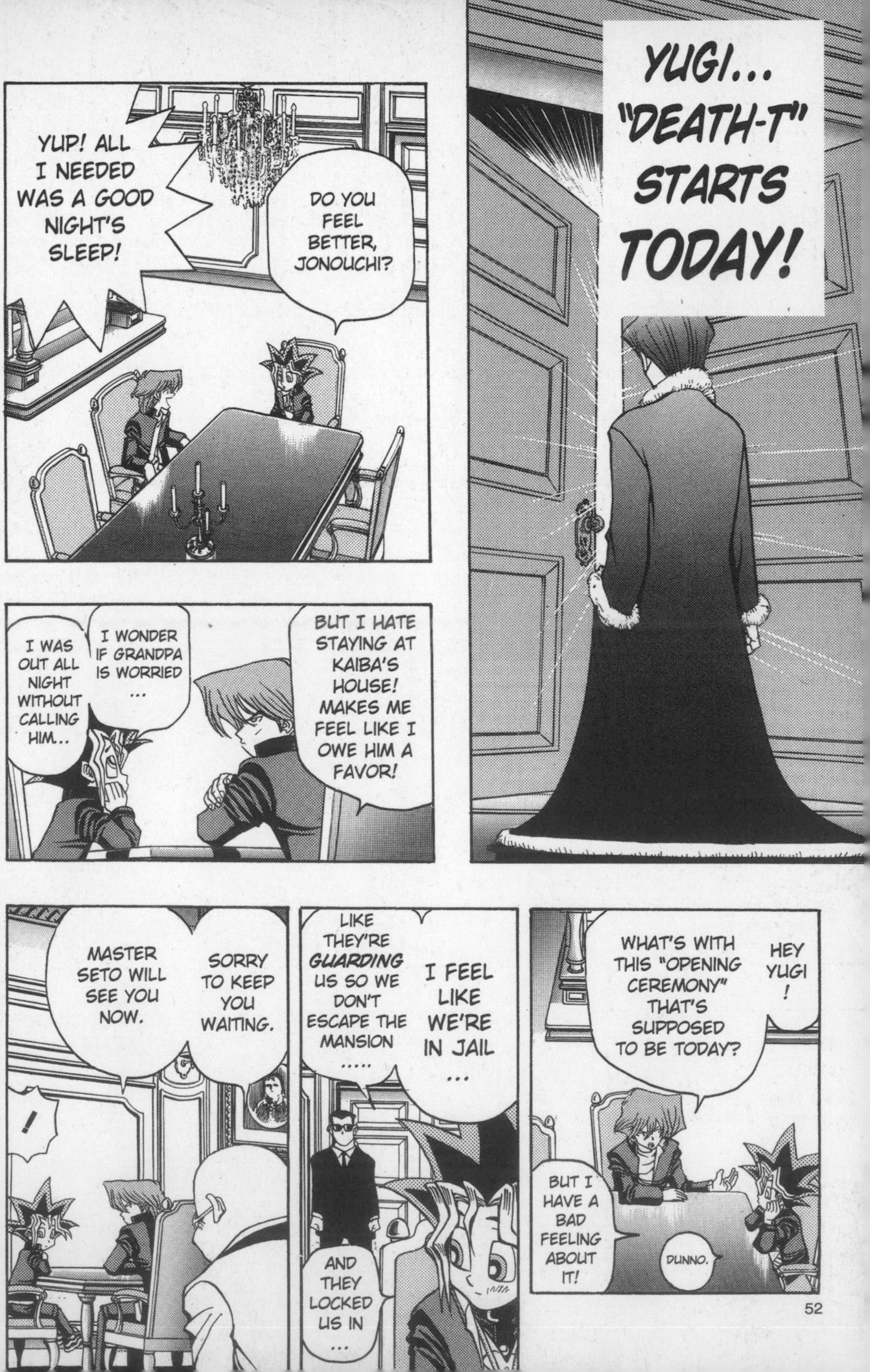
YUGI... "DEATH-T" STARTS TODAY!
DO YOU FEEL BETTER, JONOUCHI?
YUP! ALL I NEEDED WAS A GOOD NIGHT'S SLEEP!
BUT I HATE STAYING AT KAIBA'S HOUSE! MAKES ME FEEL LIKE I OWE HIM A FAVOR!
I WONDER IF GRANDPA IS WORRIED ...
I WAS OUT ALL NIGHT WITHOUT CALLING HIM...
HEY YUGI !
WHAT'S WITH THIS "OPENING CEREMONY" THAT'S SUPPOSED TO BE TODAY?
DUNNO.
BUT I HAVE A BAD FEELING ABOUT IT!
I FEEL LIKE WE'RE IN JAIL ...
LIKE THEY'RE *GUARDING* US SO WE DON'T ESCAPE THE MANSION .....
AND THEY LOCKED US IN ...
SORRY TO KEEP YOU WAITING.
MASTER SETO WILL SEE YOU NOW.
!

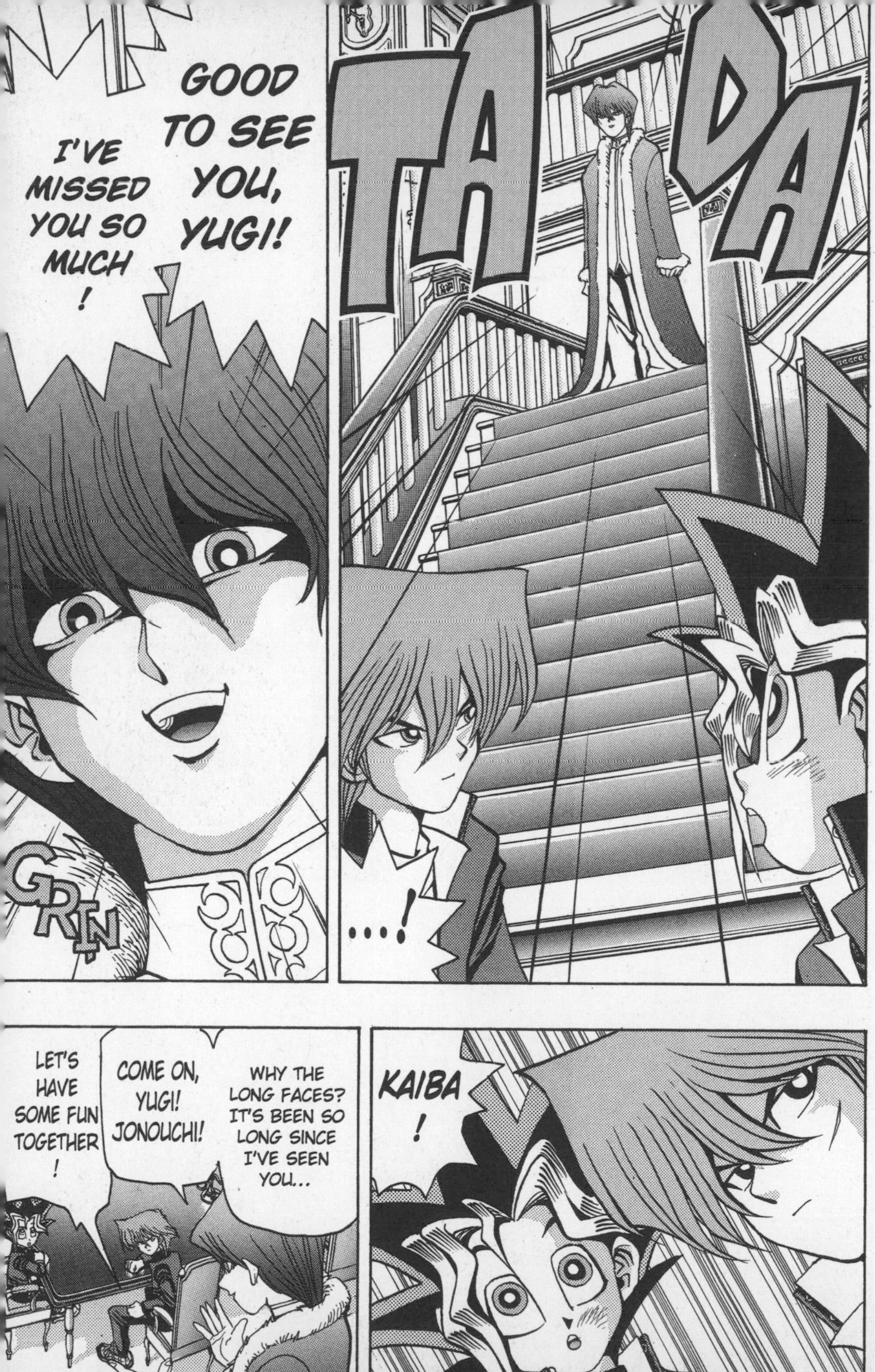
TA DA
...!
GOOD TO SEE YOU, YUGI!
I'VE MISSED YOU SO MUCH!
GRIN
KAIBA!
WHY THE LONG FACES? IT'S BEEN SO LONG SINCE I'VE SEEN YOU...
COME ON, YUGI! JONOUCHI!
LET'S HAVE SOME FUN TOGETHER!

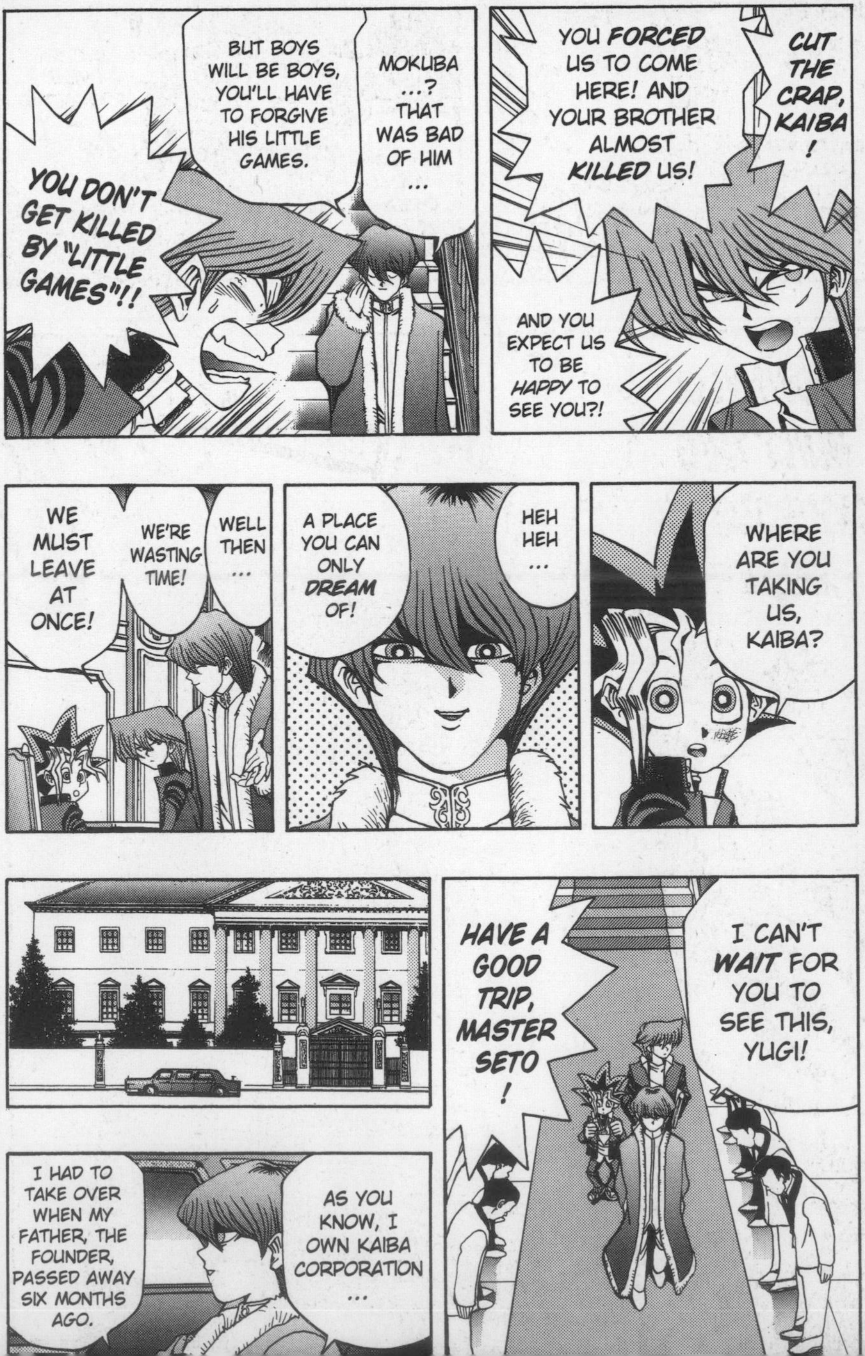
READ THIS WAY
CUT THE CRAP, KAIBA!
YOU FORCED US TO COME HERE! AND YOUR BROTHER ALMOST KILLED US!
AND YOU EXPECT US TO BE HAPPY TO SEE YOU?!
MOKUBA ...? THAT WAS BAD OF HIM ...
BUT BOYS WILL BE BOYS, YOU'LL HAVE TO FORGIVE HIS LITTLE GAMES.
YOU DON'T GET KILLED BY "LITTLE GAMES"!!
WHERE ARE YOU TAKING US, KAIBA?
HEH HEH ...
A PLACE YOU CAN ONLY DREAM OF!
WELL THEN ...
WE'RE WASTING TIME!
WE MUST LEAVE AT ONCE!
I CAN'T WAIT FOR YOU TO SEE THIS, YUGI!
HAVE A GOOD TRIP, MASTER SETO!
AS YOU KNOW, I OWN KAIBA CORPORATION ...
I HAD TO TAKE OVER WHEN MY FATHER, THE FOUNDER, PASSED AWAY SIX MONTHS AGO.

READ THIS WAY

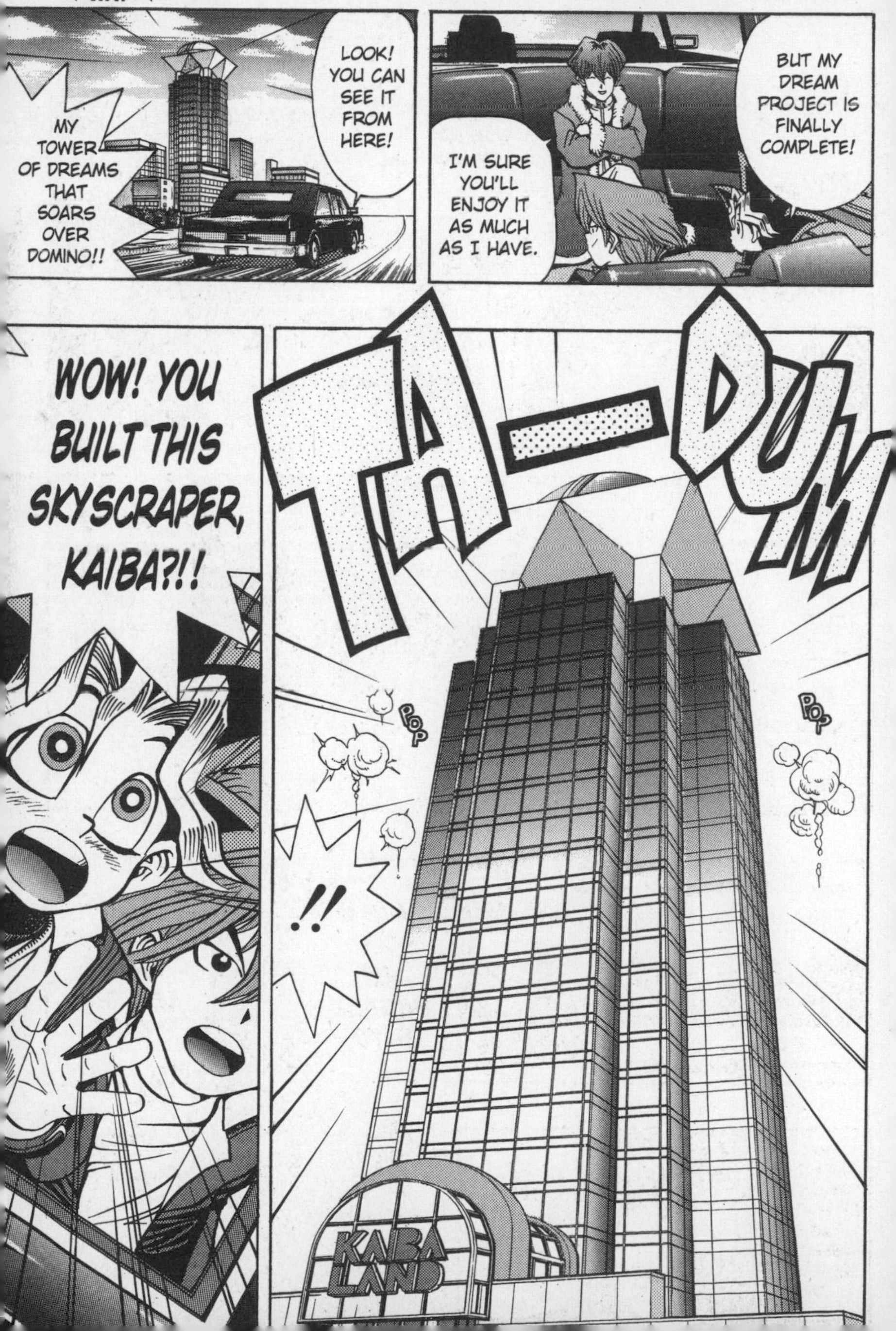
BUT MY DREAM PROJECT IS FINALLY COMPLETE!
I'M SURE YOU'LL ENJOY IT AS MUCH AS I HAVE.
LOOK! YOU CAN SEE IT FROM HERE!
MY TOWER OF DREAMS THAT SOARS OVER DOMINO!!
TA-DUM
POP
POP
!!
KAIBA LAND
WOW! YOU BUILT THIS SKYSCRAPER, KAIBA?!!

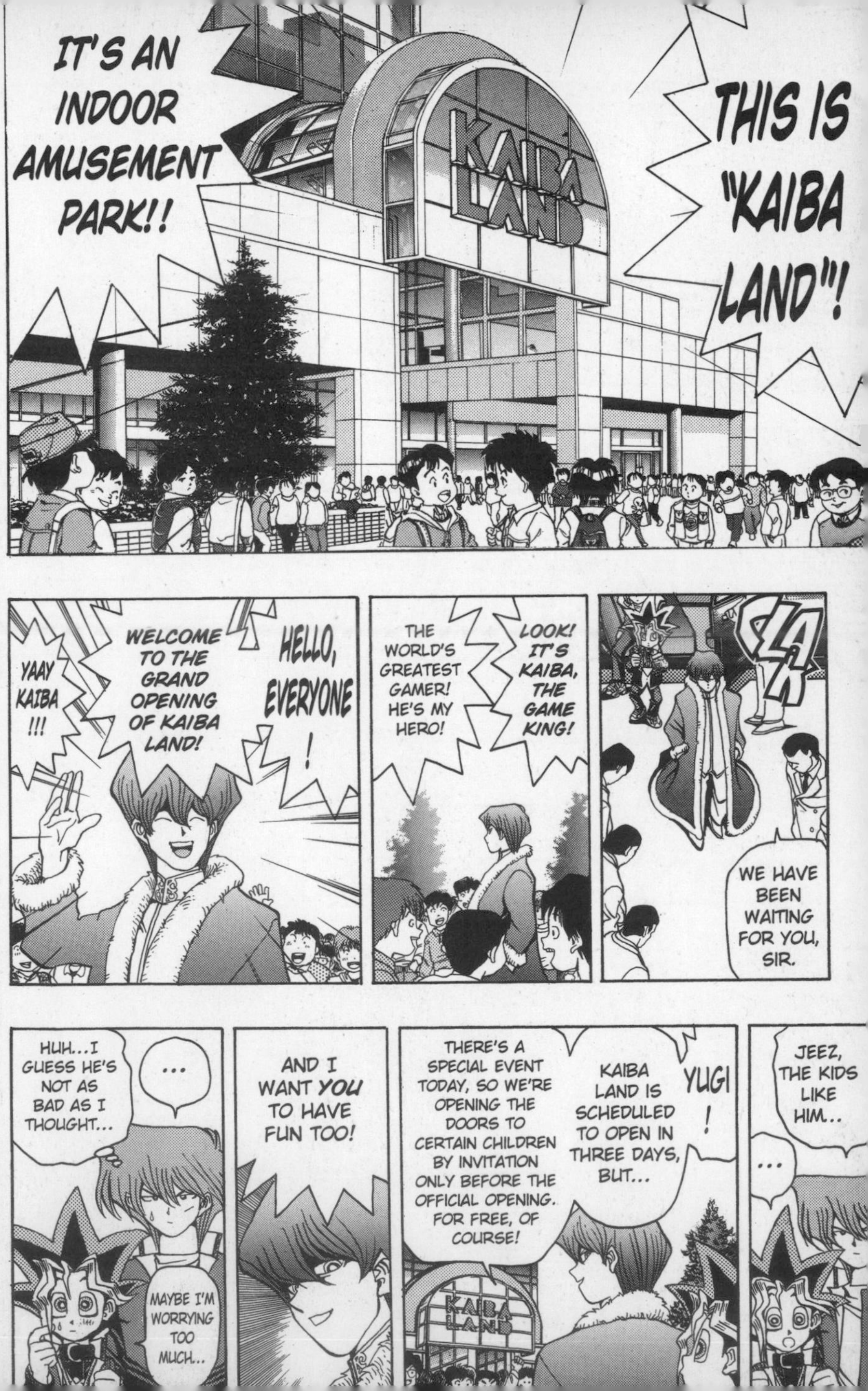
THIS IS "KAIBA LAND"!
IT'S AN INDOOR AMUSEMENT PARK!!
CLAK
WE HAVE BEEN WAITING FOR YOU, SIR.
LOOK! IT'S KAIBA, THE GAME KING!
THE WORLD'S GREATEST GAMER! HE'S MY HERO!
HELLO, EVERYONE!
WELCOME TO THE GRAND OPENING OF KAIBA LAND!
YAAY KAIBA!!!
JEEZ, THE KIDS LIKE HIM...
...
YUGI!
KAIBA LAND IS SCHEDULED TO OPEN IN THREE DAYS, BUT...
THERE'S A SPECIAL EVENT TODAY, SO WE'RE OPENING THE DOORS TO CERTAIN CHILDREN BY INVITATION ONLY BEFORE THE OFFICIAL OPENING. FOR FREE, OF COURSE!
AND I WANT YOU TO HAVE FUN TOO!
...
HUH...I GUESS HE'S NOT AS BAD AS I THOUGHT...
MAYBE I'M WORRYING TOO MUCH...

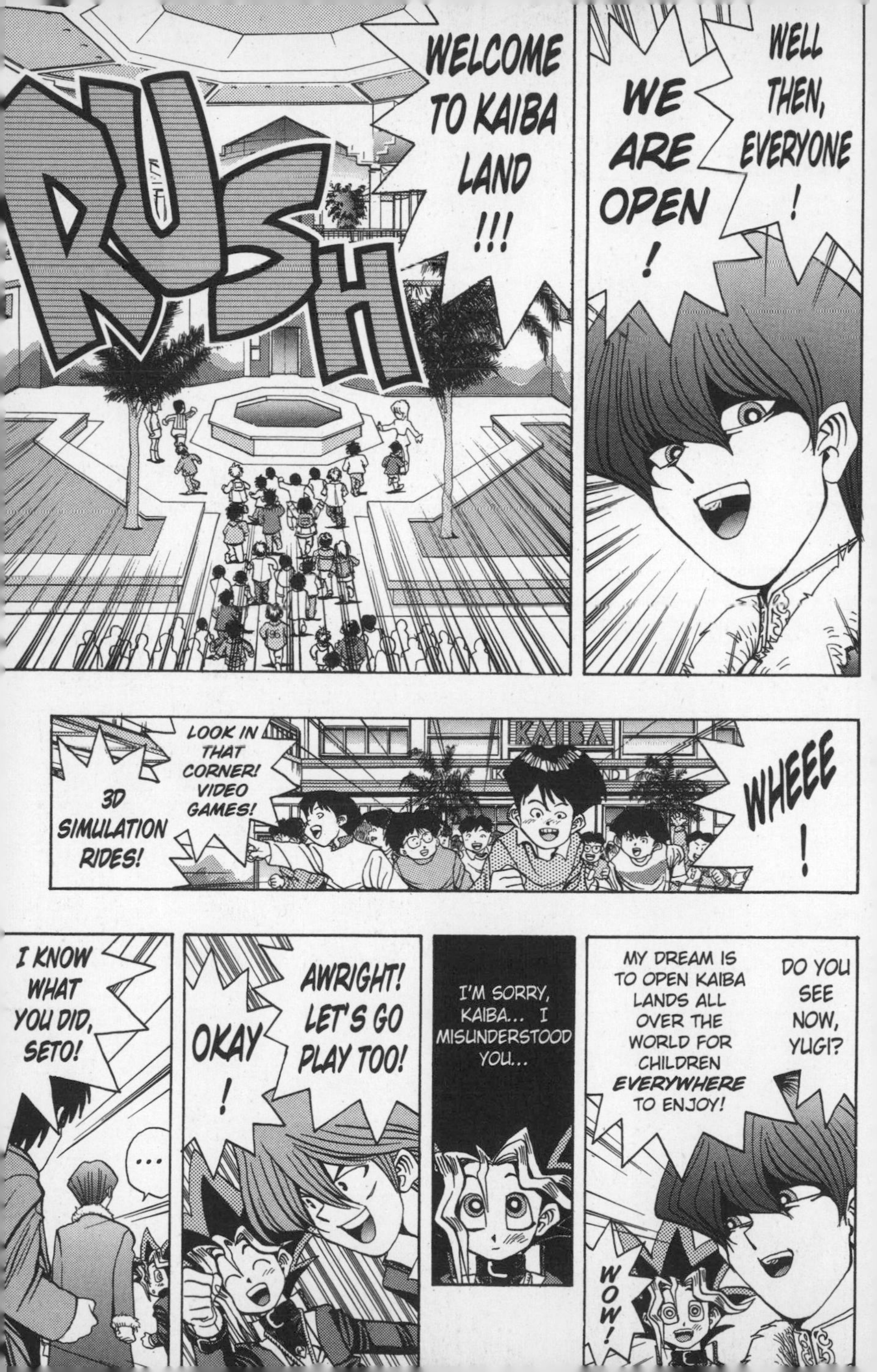
WELL THEN, EVERYONE !
WE ARE OPEN !
WELCOME TO KAIBA LAND !!!
RUSH
WHEEE !
LOOK IN THAT CORNER! VIDEO GAMES!
3D SIMULATION RIDES!
DO YOU SEE NOW, YUGI?
MY DREAM IS TO OPEN KAIBA LANDS ALL OVER THE WORLD FOR CHILDREN EVERYWHERE TO ENJOY!
WOW!
I'M SORRY, KAIBA... I MISUNDERSTOOD YOU...
AWRIGHT! LET'S GO PLAY TOO!
OKAY !
I KNOW WHAT YOU DID, SETO!
...

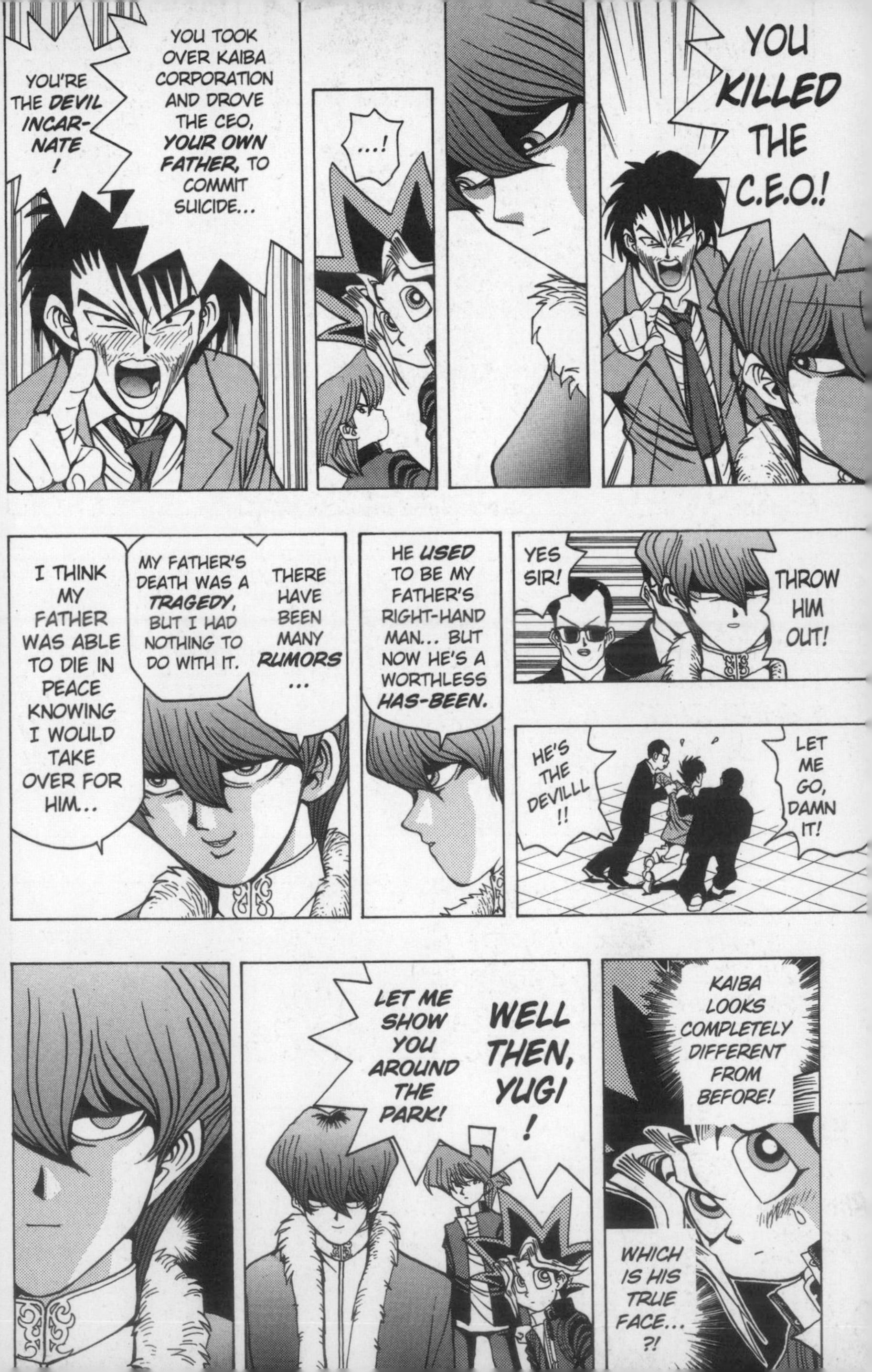
YOU KILLED THE C.E.O.!
...!
YOU TOOK OVER KAIBA CORPORATION AND DROVE THE CEO, YOUR OWN FATHER, TO COMMIT SUICIDE...
YOU'RE THE DEVIL INCARNATE!
THROW HIM OUT!
YES SIR!
LET ME GO, DAMN IT!
HE'S THE DEVILLL!!
HE USED TO BE MY FATHER'S RIGHT-HAND MAN... BUT NOW HE'S A WORTHLESS HAS-BEEN.
THERE HAVE BEEN MANY RUMORS...
MY FATHER'S DEATH WAS A TRAGEDY, BUT I HAD NOTHING TO DO WITH IT.
I THINK MY FATHER WAS ABLE TO DIE IN PEACE KNOWING I WOULD TAKE OVER FOR HIM...
KAIBA LOOKS COMPLETELY DIFFERENT FROM BEFORE!
WHICH IS HIS TRUE FACE...?!
WELL THEN, YUGI!
LET ME SHOW YOU AROUND THE PARK!

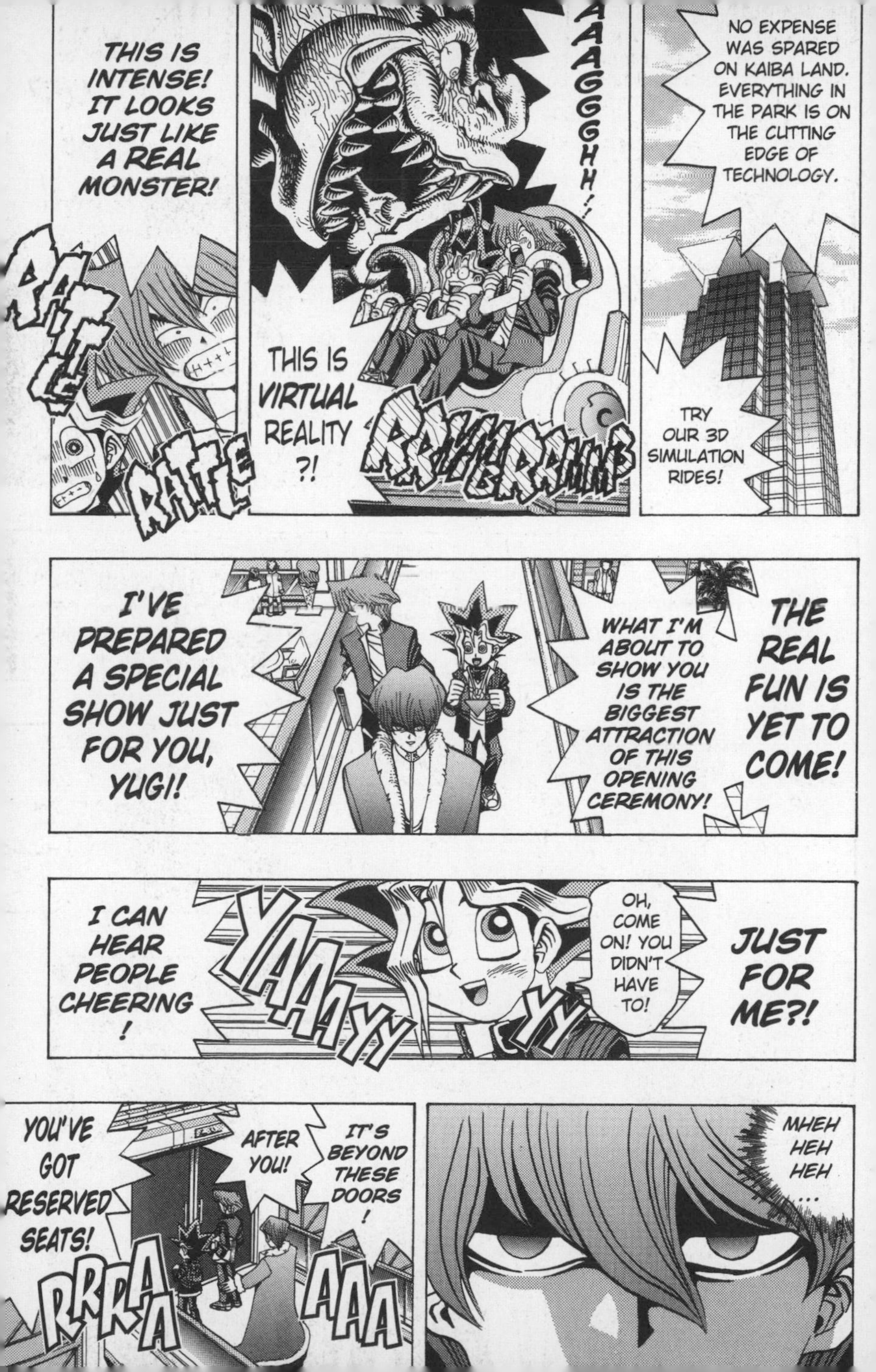
NO EXPENSE WAS SPARED ON KAIBA LAND. EVERYTHING IN THE PARK IS ON THE CUTTING EDGE OF TECHNOLOGY.
TRY OUR 3D SIMULATION RIDES!
AAAAGGGHH!!
THIS IS VIRTUAL REALITY ?!
THIS IS INTENSE! IT LOOKS JUST LIKE A REAL MONSTER!
RATTLE
THE REAL FUN IS YET TO COME!
WHAT I'M ABOUT TO SHOW YOU IS THE BIGGEST ATTRACTION OF THIS OPENING CEREMONY!
I'VE PREPARED A SPECIAL SHOW JUST FOR YOU, YUGI!
JUST FOR ME?!
OH, COME ON! YOU DIDN'T HAVE TO!
YAAAYY
I CAN HEAR PEOPLE CHEERING !
MHEH HEH HEH ...
IT'S BEYOND THESE DOORS !
AFTER YOU!
YOU'VE GOT RESERVED SEATS!
RRRAA AAA

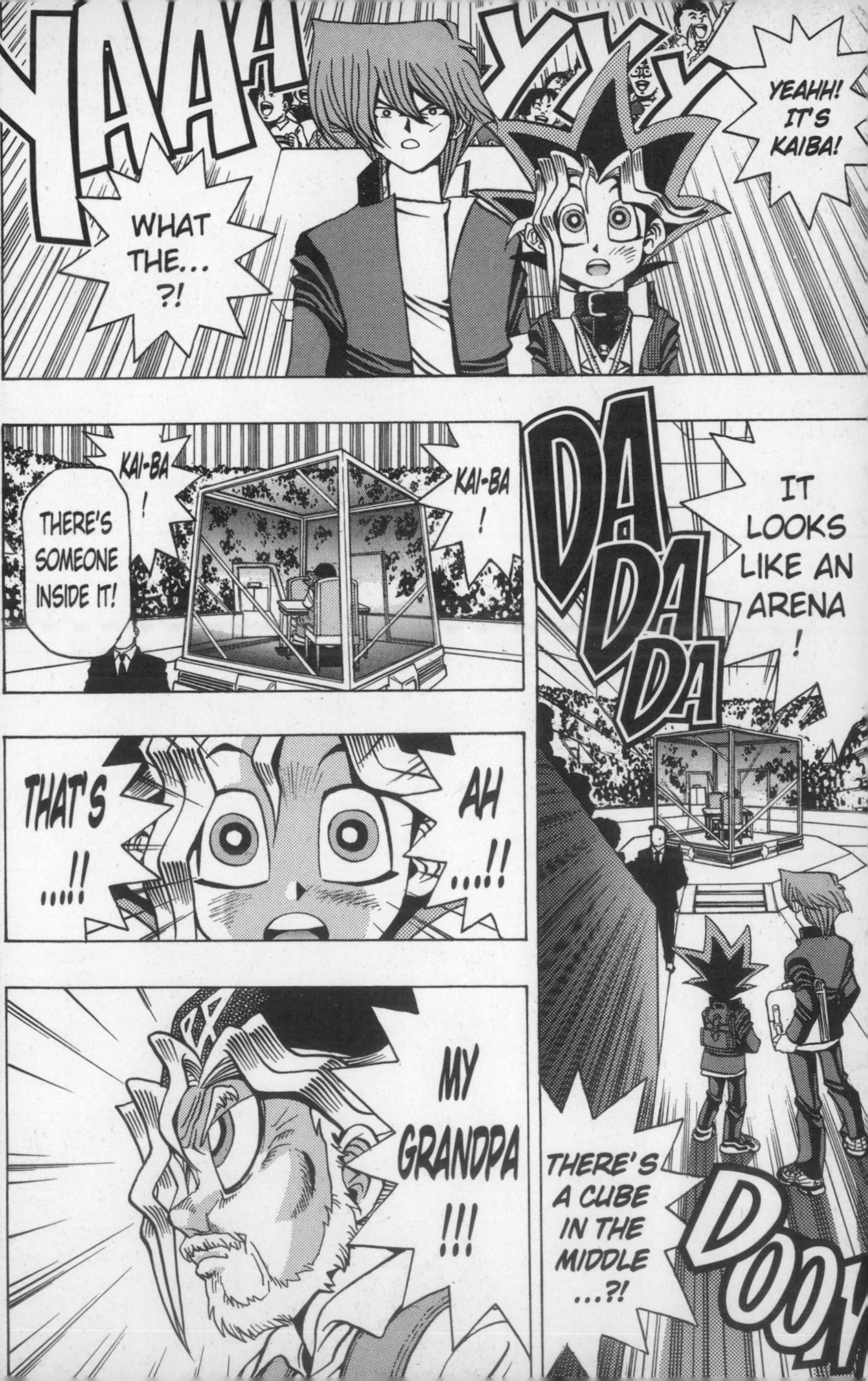
YEAHH! IT'S KAIBA!
YAAAYYY
WHAT THE... ?!
IT LOOKS LIKE AN ARENA!
DA DA DA DA
THERE'S A CUBE IN THE MIDDLE ...?!
DOOM
KAI-BA!
KAI-BA!
THERE'S SOMEONE INSIDE IT!
AH ...!!
THAT'S ...!!
MY GRANDPA!!!

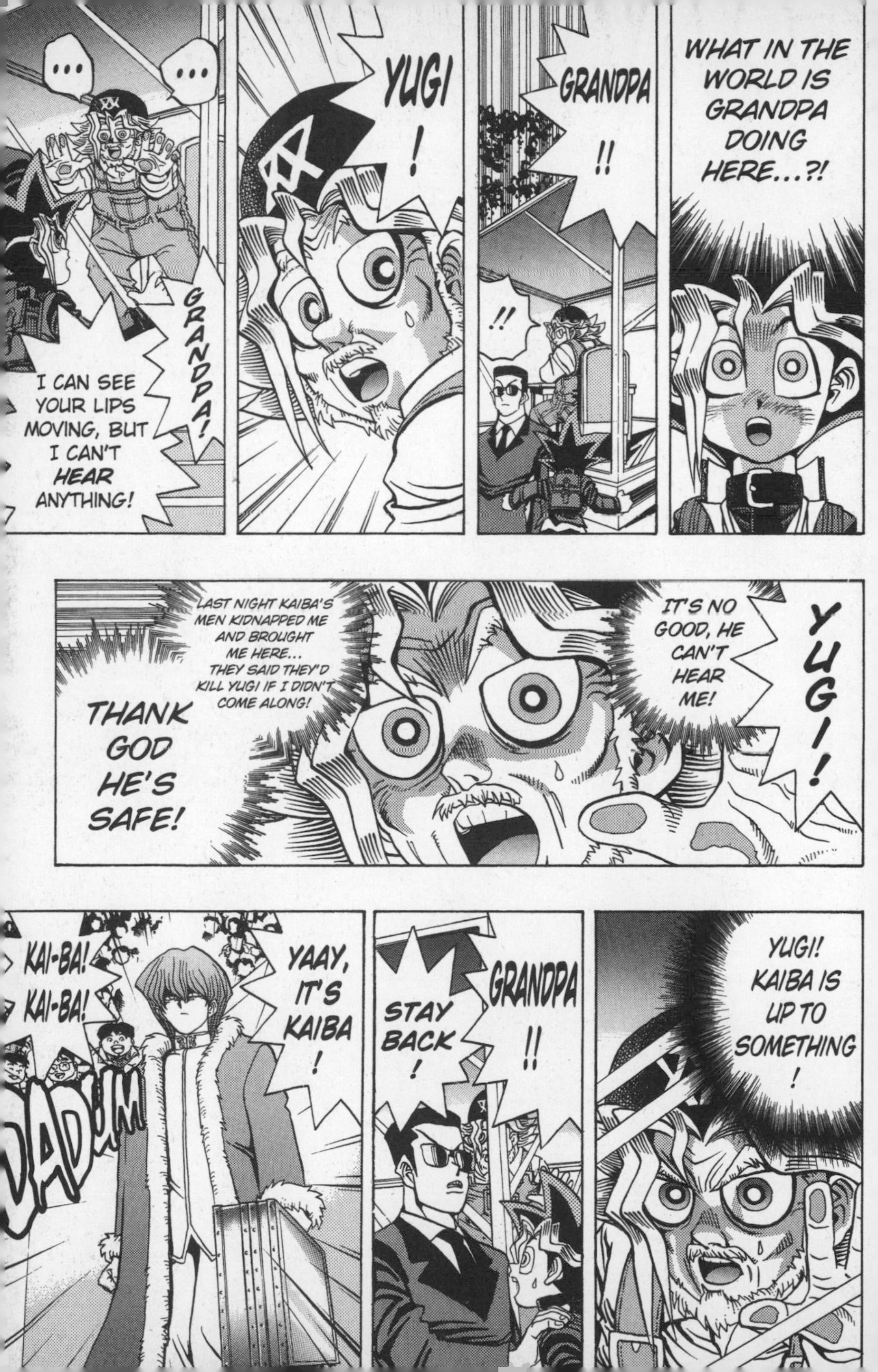
WHAT IN THE WORLD IS GRANDPA DOING HERE...?!
GRANDPA !!
!!
YUGI !
...
...
GRANDPA!
I CAN SEE YOUR LIPS MOVING, BUT I CAN'T HEAR ANYTHING!
YUGI!
IT'S NO GOOD, HE CAN'T HEAR ME!
LAST NIGHT KAIBA'S MEN KIDNAPPED ME AND BROUGHT ME HERE... THEY SAID THEY'D KILL YUGI IF I DIDN'T COME ALONG!
THANK GOD HE'S SAFE!
YUGI! KAIBA IS UP TO SOMETHING !
GRANDPA !!
STAY BACK !
YAAY, IT'S KAIBA !
KAI-BA! KAI-BA!

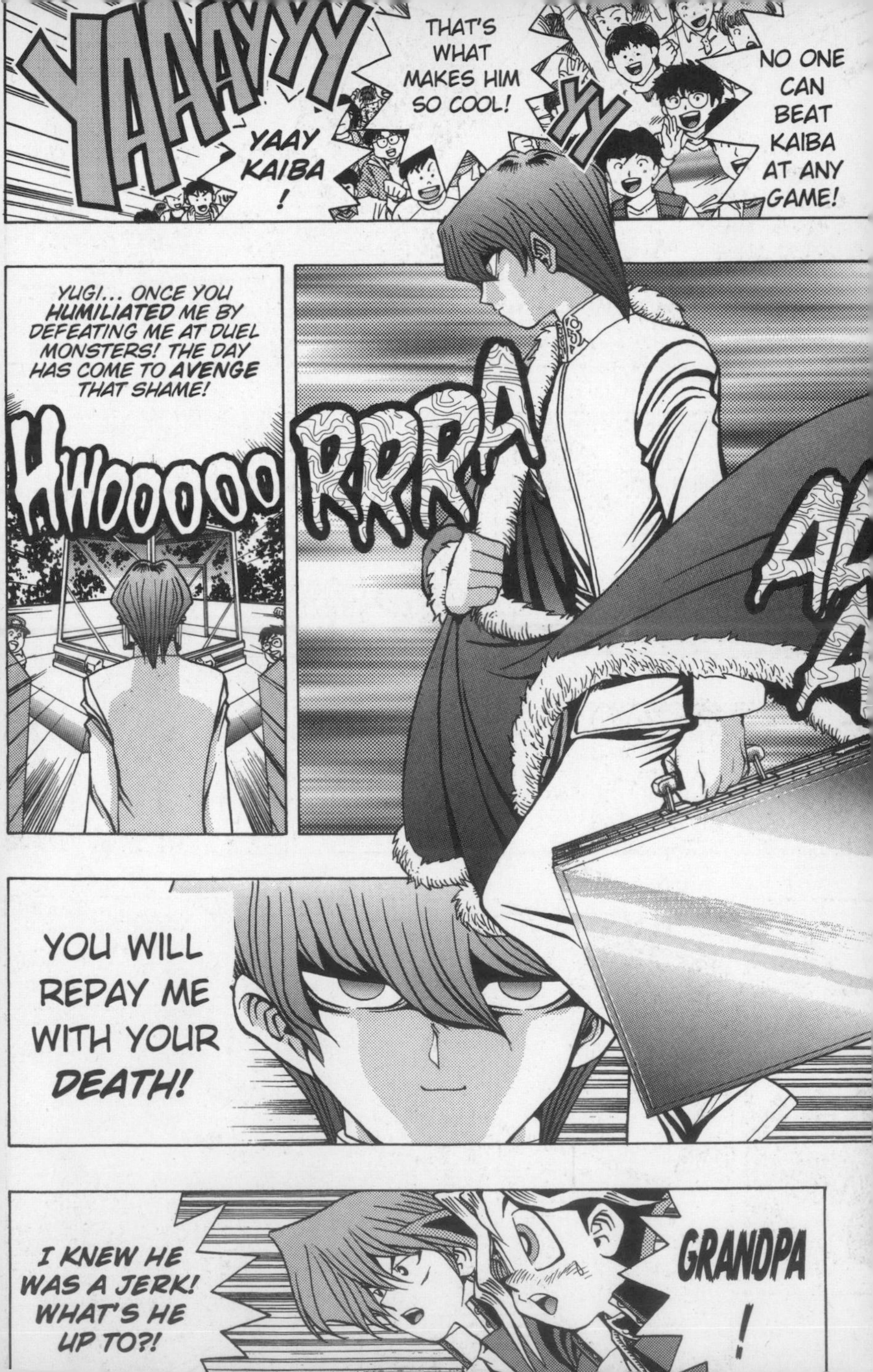
NO ONE CAN BEAT KAIBA AT ANY GAME!
YY
THAT'S WHAT MAKES HIM SO COOL!
YAAAYYY
YAAY KAIBA !
YUGI... ONCE YOU HUMILIATED ME BY DEFEATING ME AT DUEL MONSTERS! THE DAY HAS COME TO AVENGE THAT SHAME!
HWOOOOO RRRA
YOU WILL REPAY ME WITH YOUR DEATH!
GRANDPA !
I KNEW HE WAS A JERK! WHAT'S HE UP TO?!

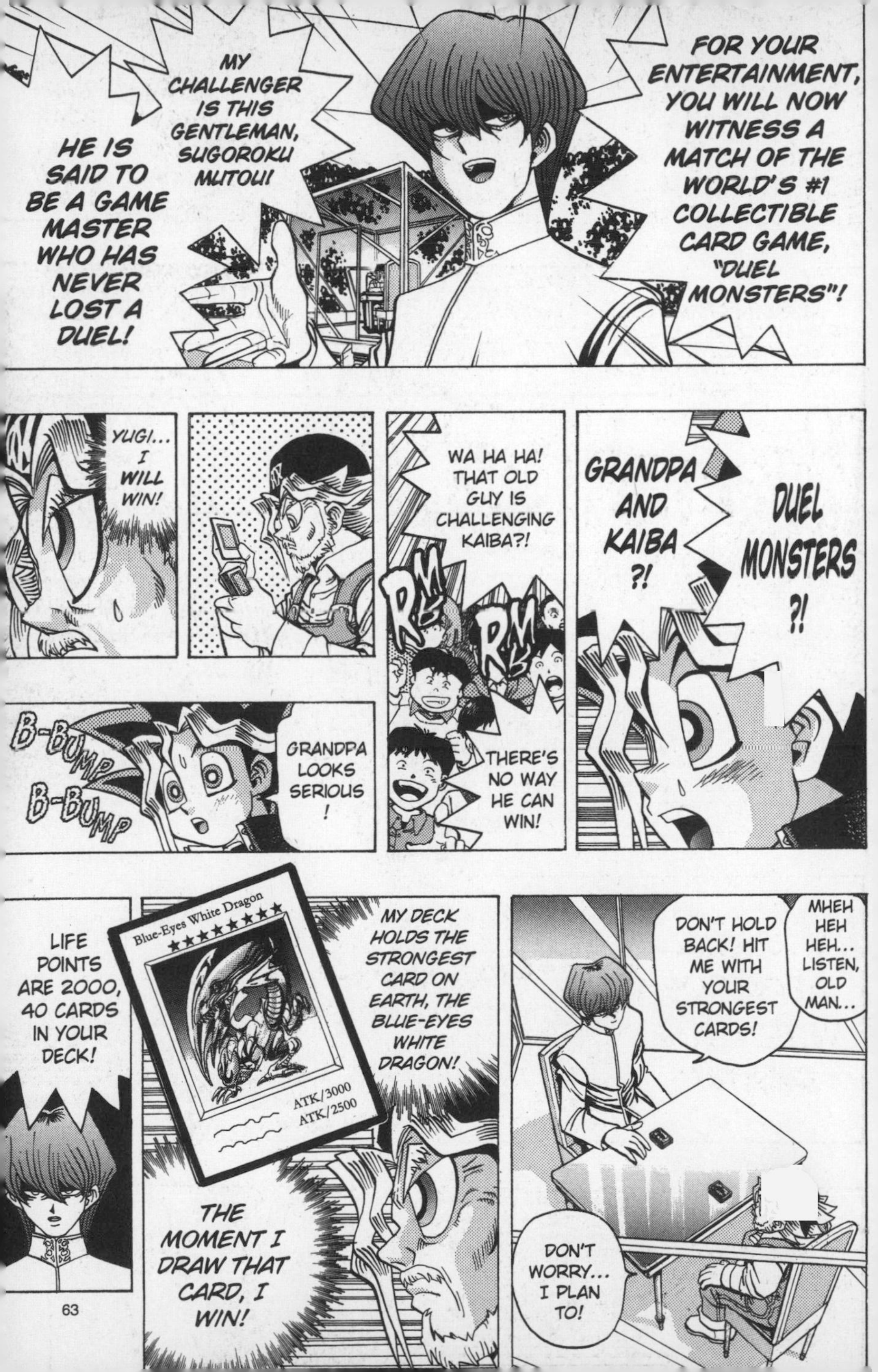
FOR YOUR ENTERTAINMENT, YOU WILL NOW WITNESS A MATCH OF THE WORLD'S #1 COLLECTIBLE CARD GAME, "DUEL MONSTERS"!
MY CHALLENGER IS THIS GENTLEMAN, SUGOROKU MUTOU!
HE IS SAID TO BE A GAME MASTER WHO HAS NEVER LOST A DUEL!
DUEL MONSTERS ?!
GRANDPA AND KAIBA ?!
WA HA HA! THAT OLD GUY IS CHALLENGING KAIBA?!
RM RM
THERE'S NO WAY HE CAN WIN!
YUGI... I WILL WIN!
GRANDPA LOOKS SERIOUS !
B-BUMP B-BUMP
MHEH HEH HEH... LISTEN, OLD MAN...
DON'T HOLD BACK! HIT ME WITH YOUR STRONGEST CARDS!
DON'T WORRY... I PLAN TO!
MY DECK HOLDS THE STRONGEST CARD ON EARTH, THE BLUE-EYES WHITE DRAGON!
Blue-Eyes White Dragon
ATK/3000
ATK/2500
THE MOMENT I DRAW THAT CARD, I WIN!
LIFE POINTS ARE 2000, 40 CARDS IN YOUR DECK!

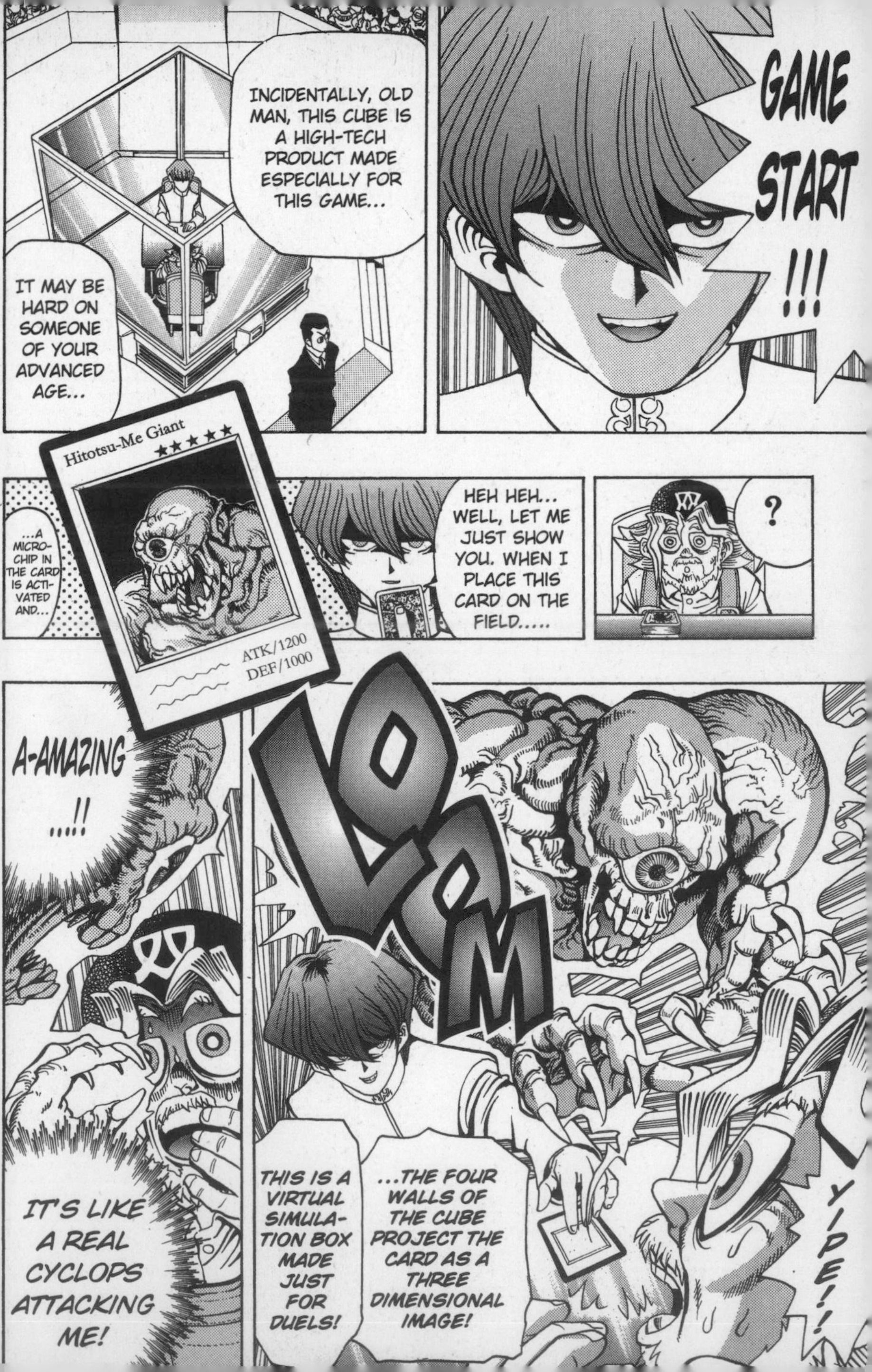
GAME START!!!
INCIDENTALLY, OLD MAN, THIS CUBE IS A HIGH-TECH PRODUCT MADE ESPECIALLY FOR THIS GAME...
IT MAY BE HARD ON SOMEONE OF YOUR ADVANCED AGE...
?
HEH HEH... WELL, LET ME JUST SHOW YOU. WHEN I PLACE THIS CARD ON THE FIELD.....
...A MICRO-CHIP IN THE CARD IS ACTI-VATED AND...
Hitotsu-Me Giant
ATK/1200
DEF/1000
LOOM
YIPE!!
...THE FOUR WALLS OF THE CUBE PROJECT THE CARD AS A THREE DIMENSIONAL IMAGE!
THIS IS A VIRTUAL SIMULA-TION BOX MADE JUST FOR DUELS!
A-AMAZING.....!!
IT'S LIKE A REAL CYCLOPS ATTACKING ME!

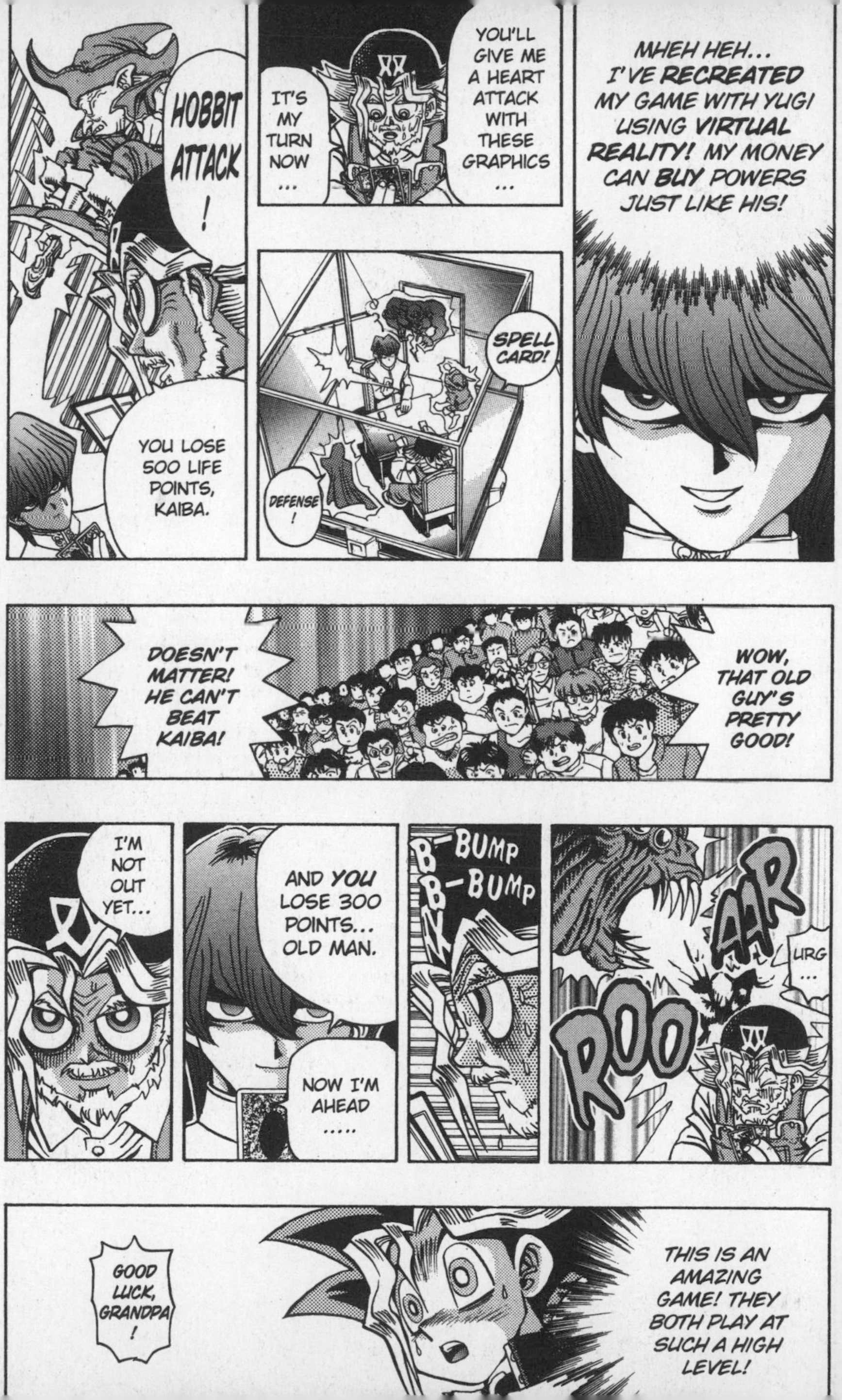
MHEH HEH... I'VE RECREATED MY GAME WITH YUGI USING VIRTUAL REALITY! MY MONEY CAN BUY POWERS JUST LIKE HIS!
YOU'LL GIVE ME A HEART ATTACK WITH THESE GRAPHICS...
IT'S MY TURN NOW...
SPELL CARD!
DEFENSE!
HOBBIT ATTACK!
YOU LOSE 500 LIFE POINTS, KAIBA.
WOW, THAT OLD GUY'S PRETTY GOOD!
DOESN'T MATTER! HE CAN'T BEAT KAIBA!
AAR
ROO
URG...
B-BUMP
B-BUMP
AND YOU LOSE 300 POINTS... OLD MAN.
NOW I'M AHEAD .....
I'M NOT OUT YET...
THIS IS AN AMAZING GAME! THEY BOTH PLAY AT SUCH A HIGH LEVEL!
GOOD LUCK, GRANDPA!

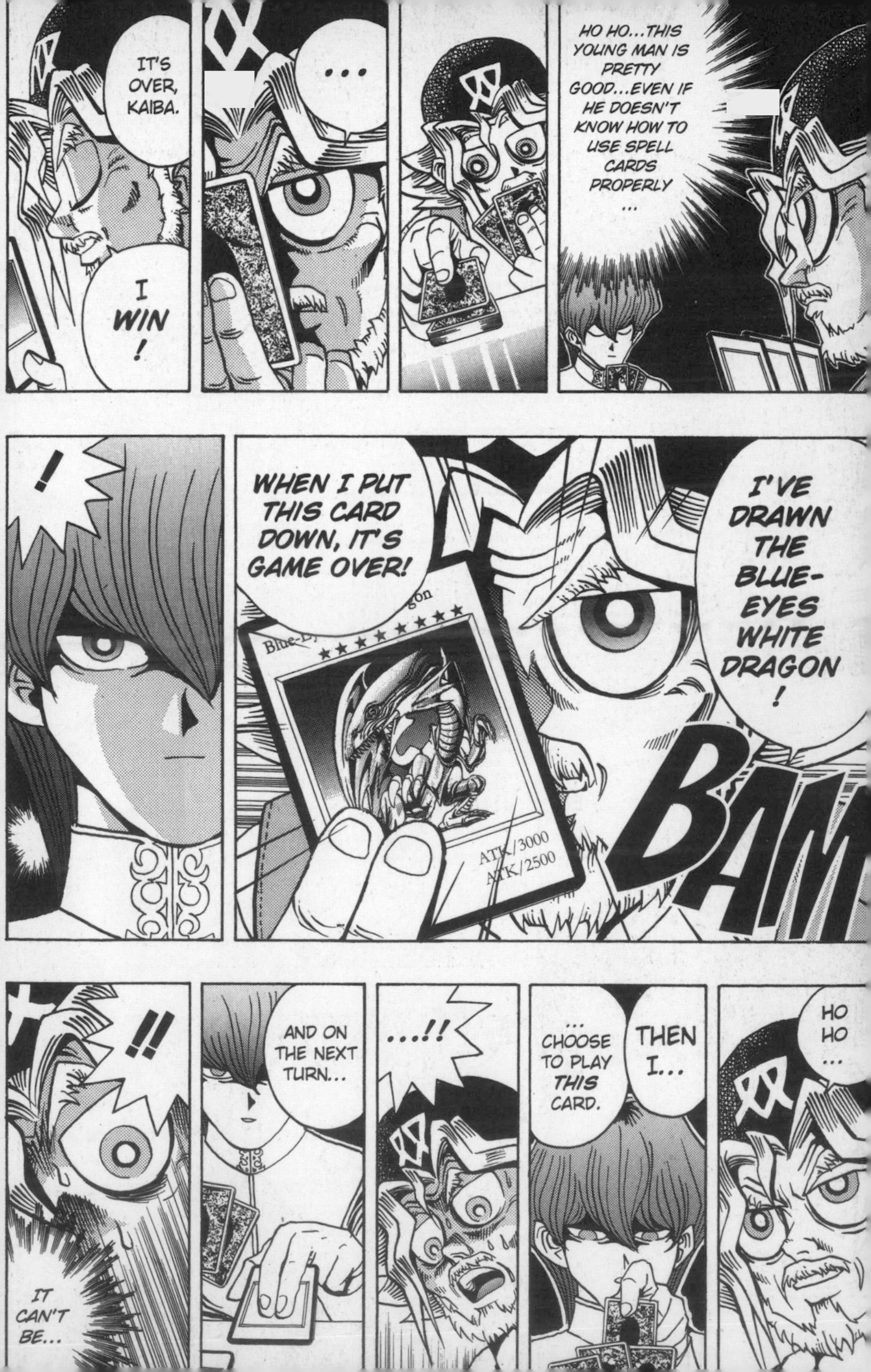
HO HO...THIS YOUNG MAN IS PRETTY GOOD...EVEN IF HE DOESN'T KNOW HOW TO USE SPELL CARDS PROPERLY ...
...
IT'S OVER, KAIBA.
I WIN !
I'VE DRAWN THE BLUE-EYES WHITE DRAGON !
WHEN I PUT THIS CARD DOWN, IT'S GAME OVER!
ATK/3000
ATK/2500
BAM
!
HO HO ...
THEN I...
... CHOOSE TO PLAY THIS CARD.
...!!
AND ON THE NEXT TURN...
!!
IT CAN'T BE...

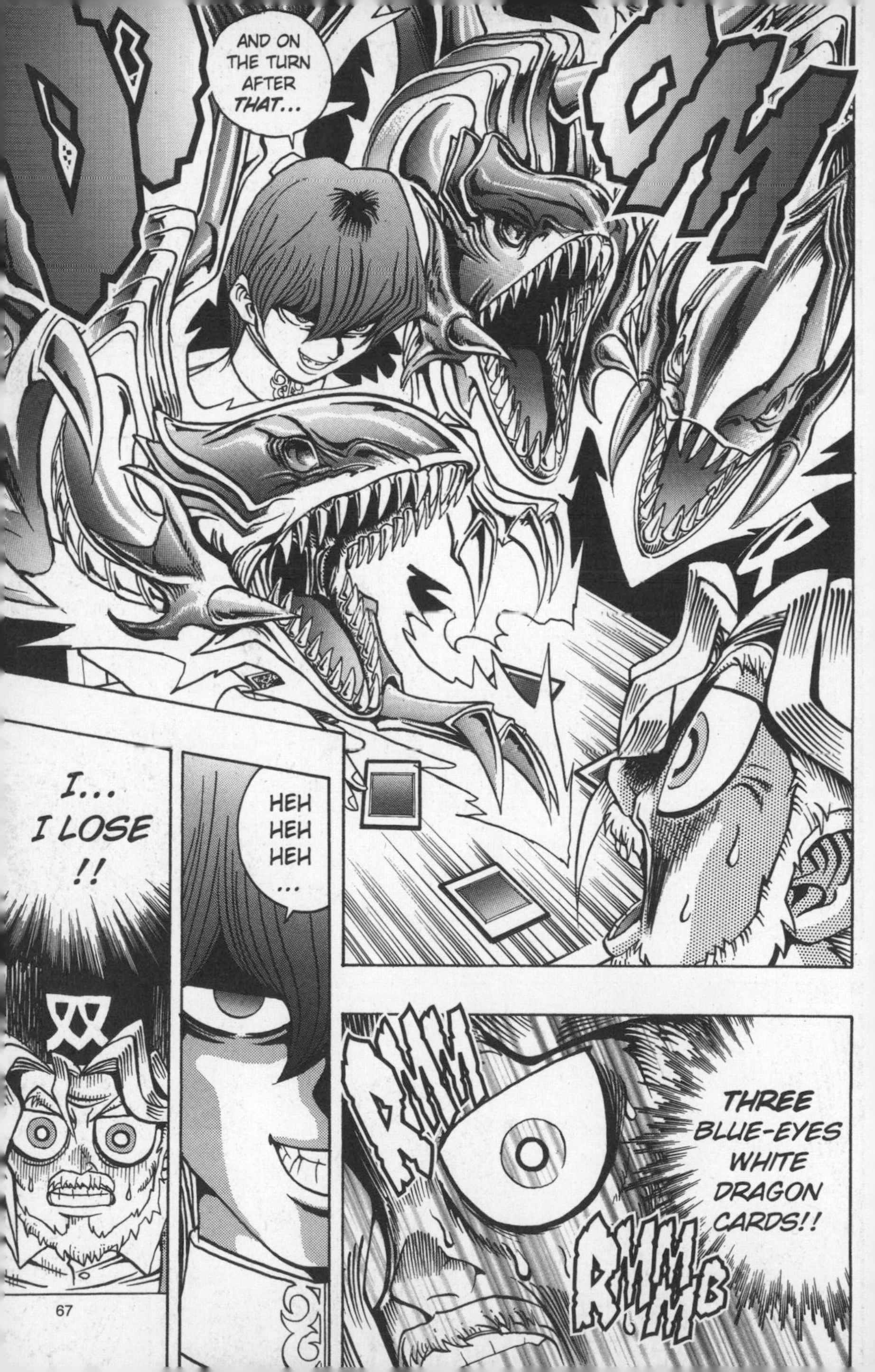
AND ON THE TURN AFTER THAT...
THREE BLUE-EYES WHITE DRAGON CARDS!!
HEH HEH HEH ...
I... I LOSE !!

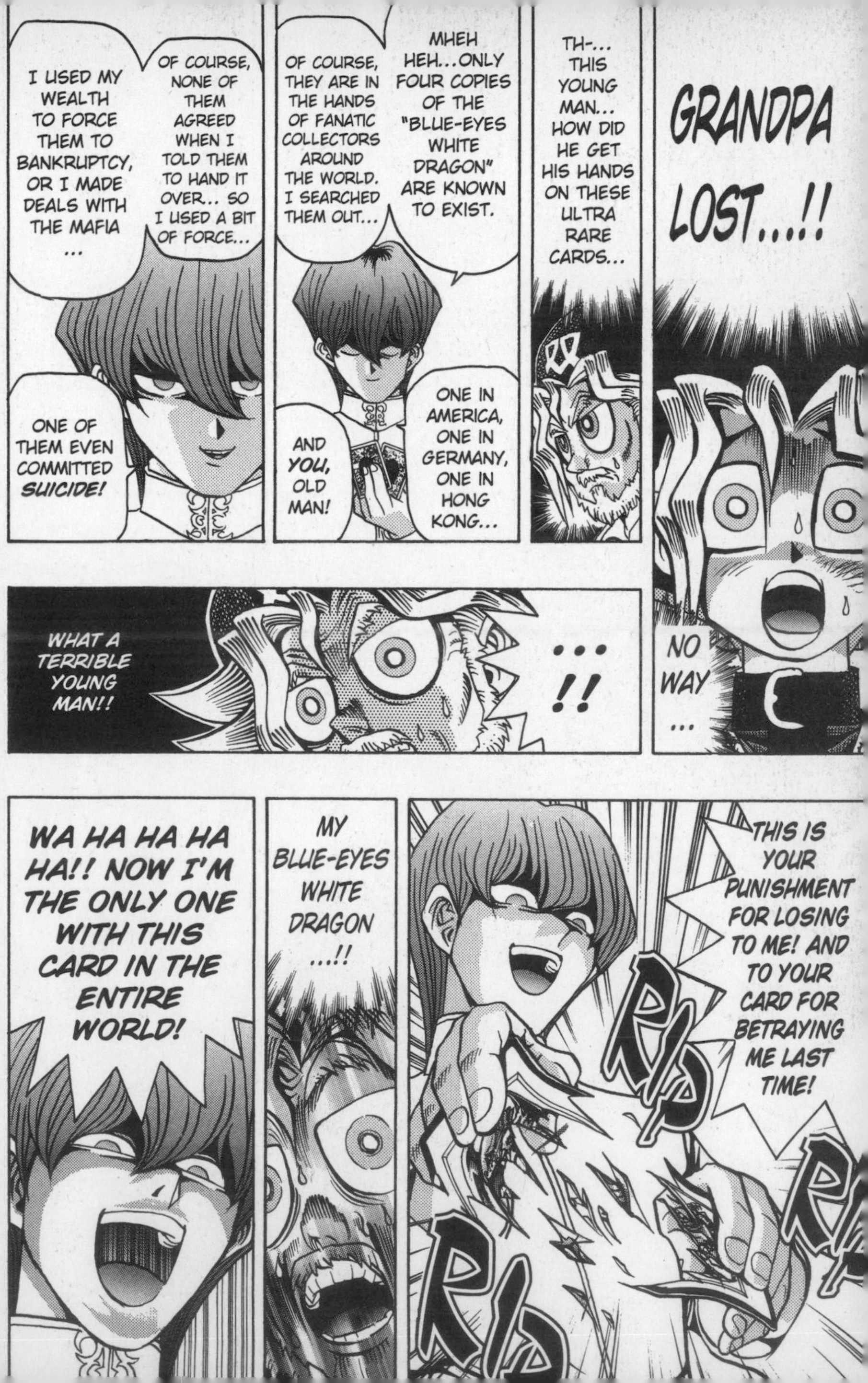
GRANDPA LOST.....!!
NO WAY ...
TH-... THIS YOUNG MAN... HOW DID HE GET HIS HANDS ON THESE ULTRA RARE CARDS...
MHEH HEH...ONLY FOUR COPIES OF THE "BLUE-EYES WHITE DRAGON" ARE KNOWN TO EXIST.
OF COURSE, THEY ARE IN THE HANDS OF FANATIC COLLECTORS AROUND THE WORLD. I SEARCHED THEM OUT...
ONE IN AMERICA, ONE IN GERMANY, ONE IN HONG KONG...
AND YOU, OLD MAN!
OF COURSE, NONE OF THEM AGREED WHEN I TOLD THEM TO HAND IT OVER... SO I USED A BIT OF FORCE...
I USED MY WEALTH TO FORCE THEM TO BANKRUPTCY, OR I MADE DEALS WITH THE MAFIA ...
ONE OF THEM EVEN COMMITTED SUICIDE!
...!!
WHAT A TERRIBLE YOUNG MAN!!
THIS IS YOUR PUNISHMENT FOR LOSING TO ME! AND TO YOUR CARD FOR BETRAYING ME LAST TIME!
RIP
RIP
RIP
MY BLUE-EYES WHITE DRAGON ...!!
WA HA HA HA HA!! NOW I'M THE ONLY ONE WITH THIS CARD IN THE ENTIRE WORLD!

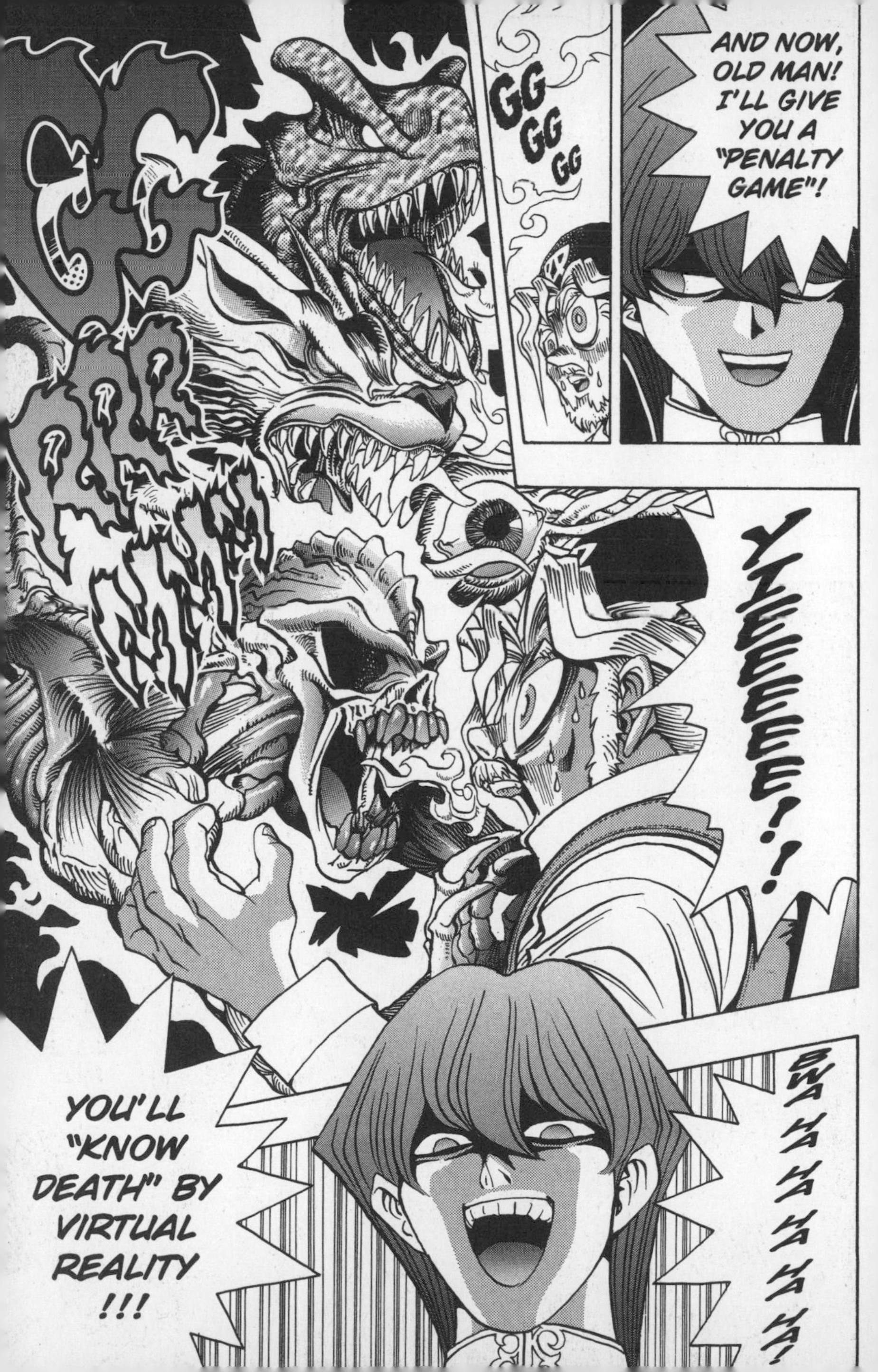
AND NOW, OLD MAN! I'LL GIVE YOU A "PENALTY GAME"!
GG GG GG
YIEEEEEE!!
BWA HA HA HA HA HA HA!
YOU'LL "KNOW DEATH" BY VIRTUAL REALITY!!!

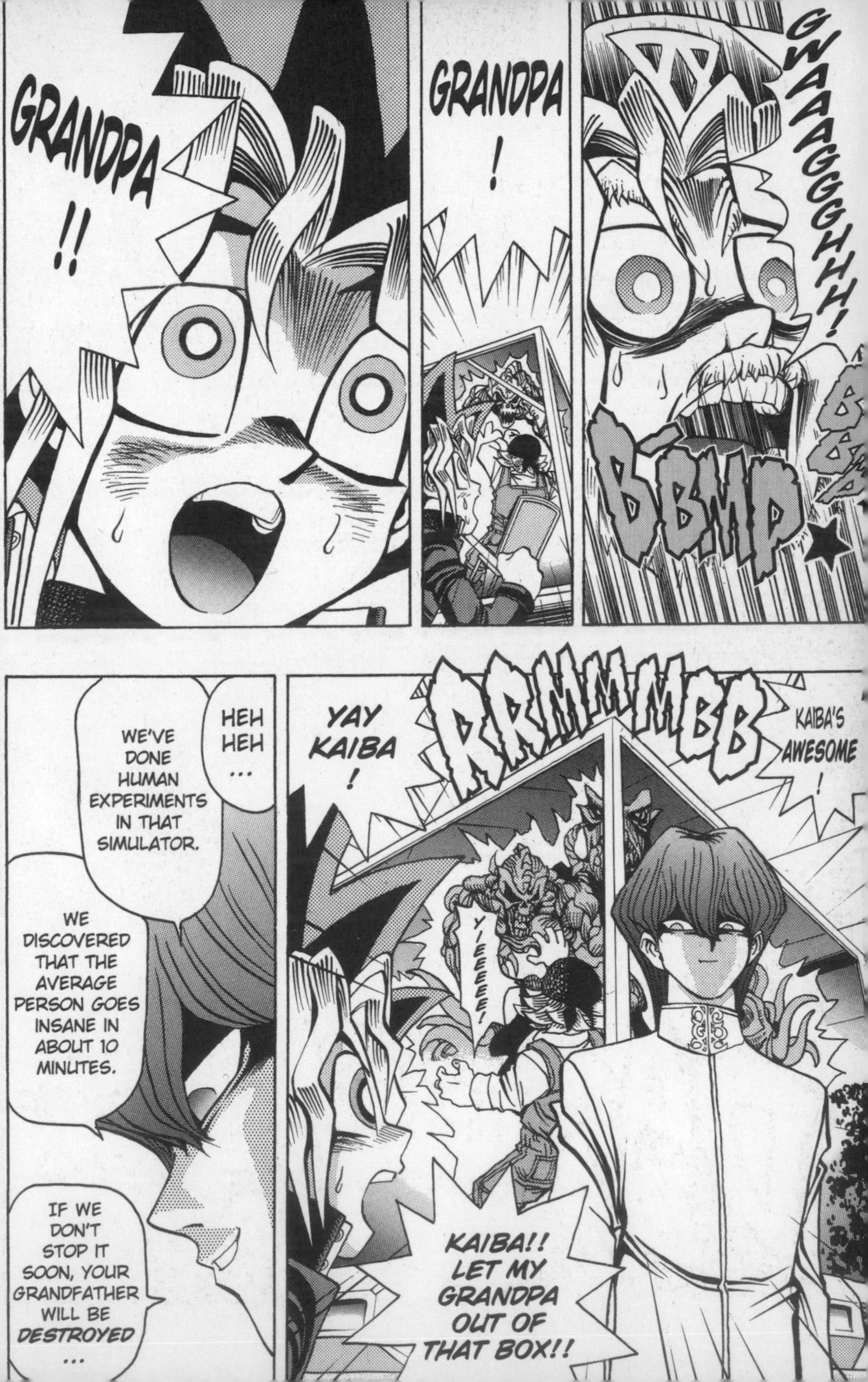
GWAAAGGGHHHH!
BBMP
BB
GRANDPA!
GRANDPA!!
KAIBA'S AWESOME!
RRMMMBB
YAY KAIBA!
Y/IEEEEE!
KAIBA!! LET MY GRANDPA OUT OF THAT BOX!!
HEH HEH...
WE'VE DONE HUMAN EXPERIMENTS IN THAT SIMULATOR.
WE DISCOVERED THAT THE AVERAGE PERSON GOES INSANE IN ABOUT 10 MINUTES.
IF WE DON'T STOP IT SOON, YOUR GRANDFATHER WILL BE DESTROYED...

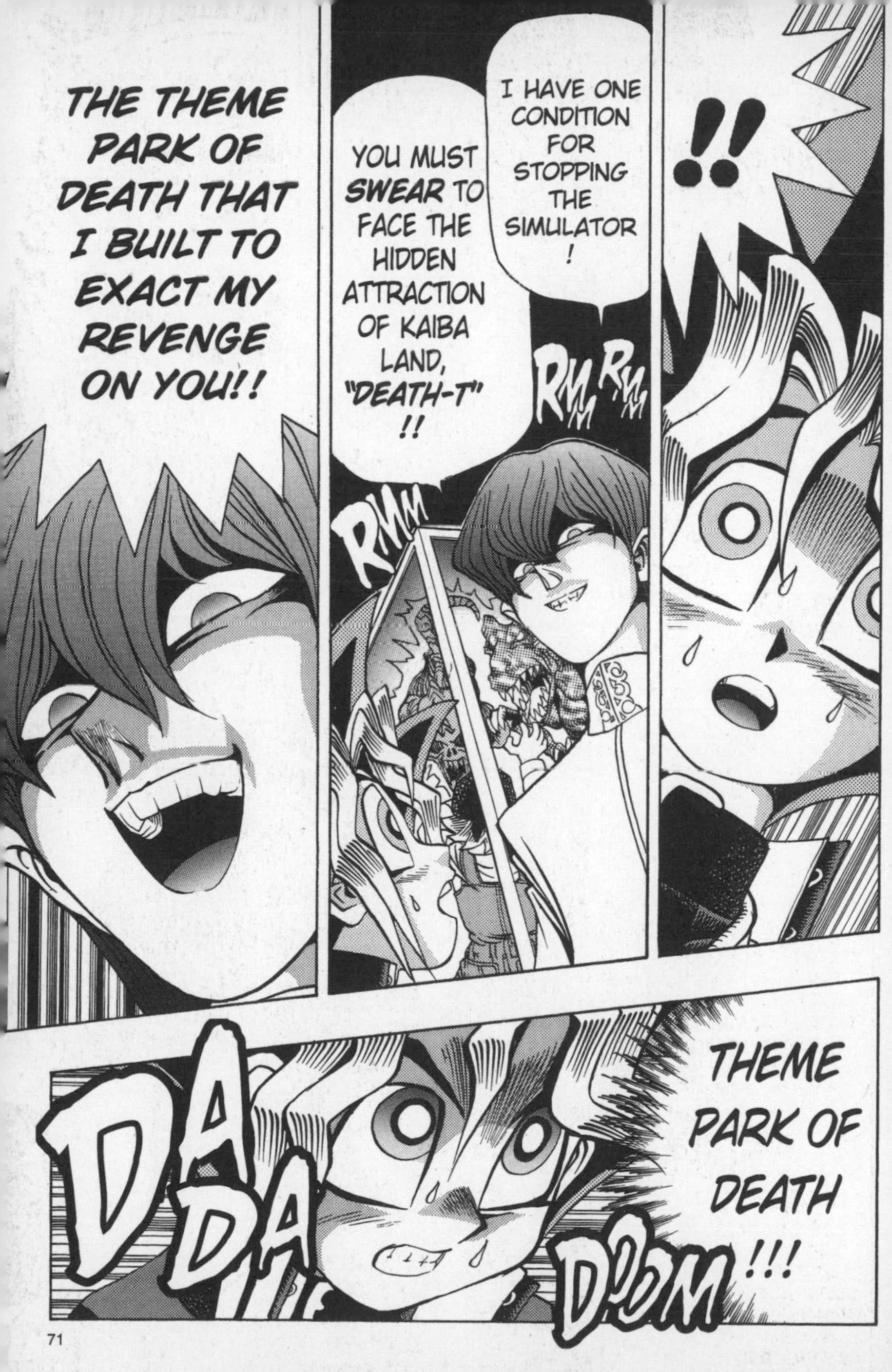
!!
I HAVE ONE CONDITION FOR STOPPING THE SIMULATOR!
RM RM
YOU MUST SWEAR TO FACE THE HIDDEN ATTRACTION OF KAIBA LAND, "DEATH-T"!!
RMM
THE THEME PARK OF DEATH THAT I BUILT TO EXACT MY REVENGE ON YOU!!
THEME PARK OF DEATH!!!
D'DM
DA DA

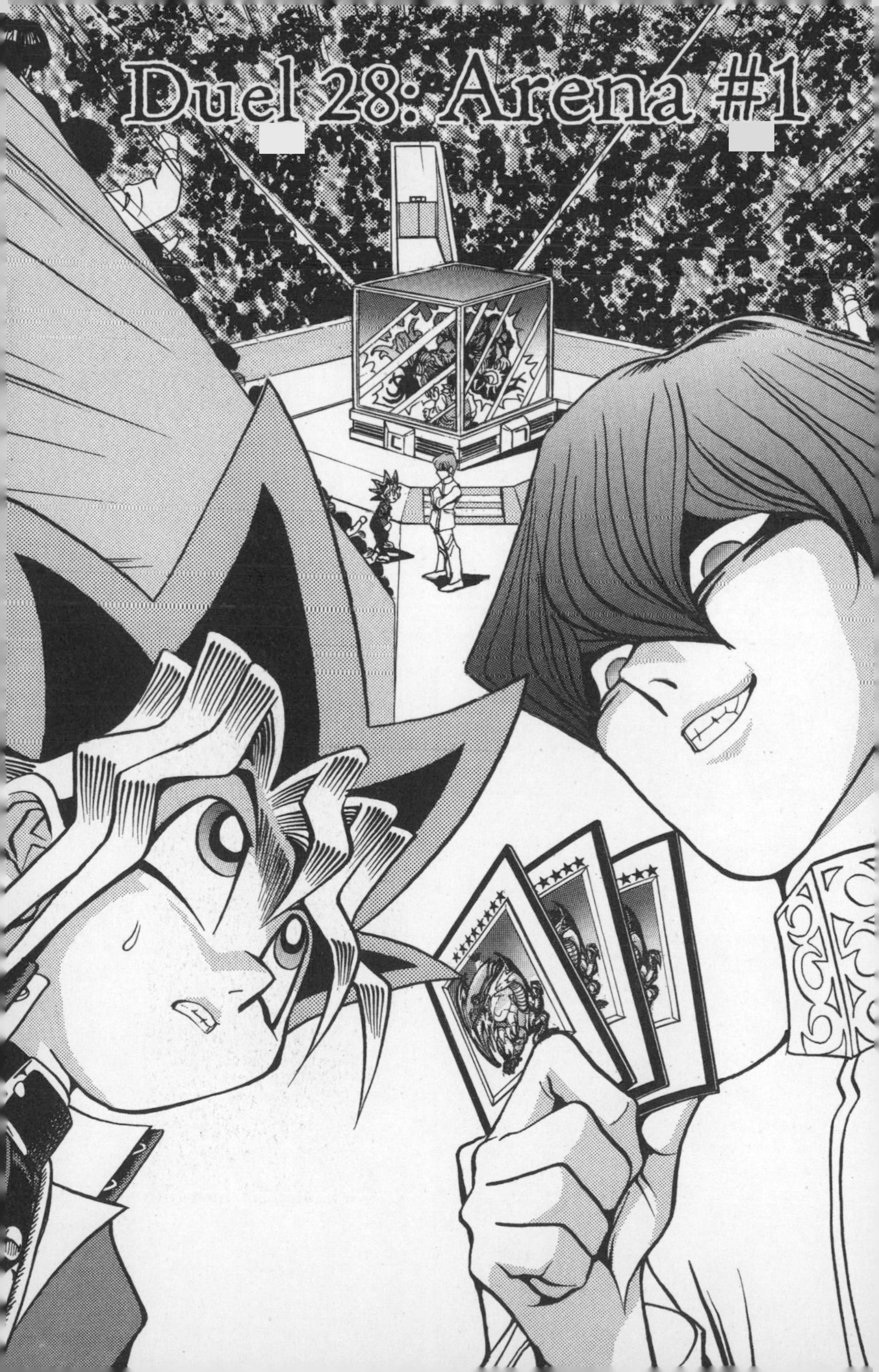
Duel 28: Arena #1

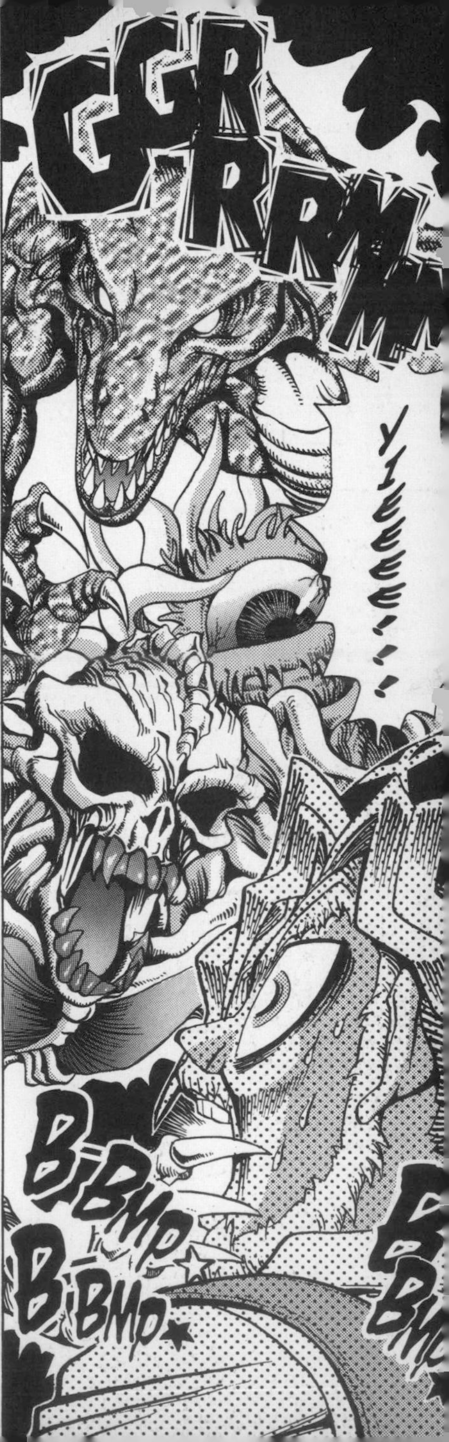
GGRRRM
YIIEEEE!!!
B-BMP
B-BMP
BMP

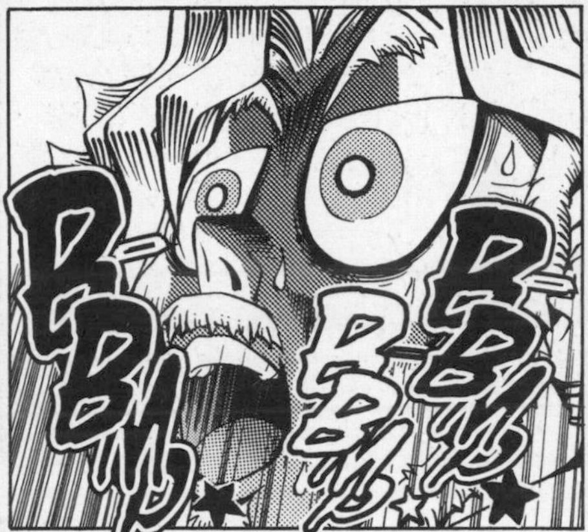
B-BMP
B-BMP
B-BMP

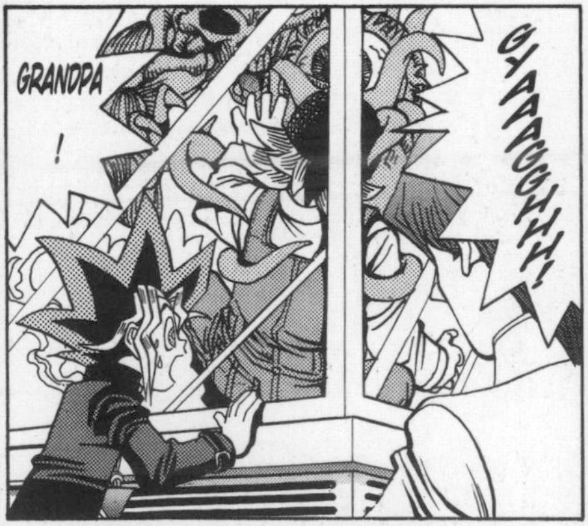
GYAAAGGHHH!
GRANDPA
!

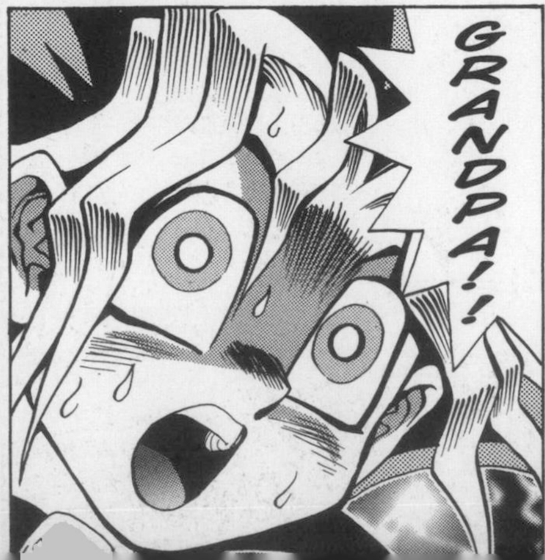
GRANDPA!!

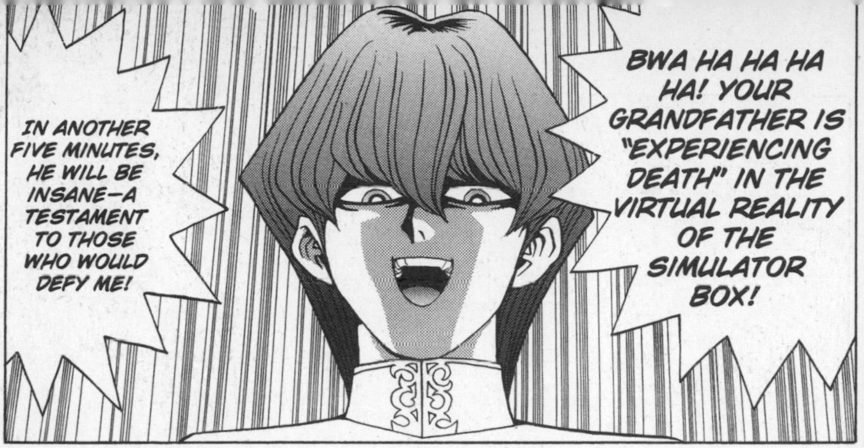
BWA HA HA HA HA! YOUR GRANDFATHER IS "EXPERIENCING DEATH" IN THE VIRTUAL REALITY OF THE SIMULATOR BOX!
IN ANOTHER FIVE MINUTES, HE WILL BE INSANE—A TESTAMENT TO THOSE WHO WOULD DEFY ME!

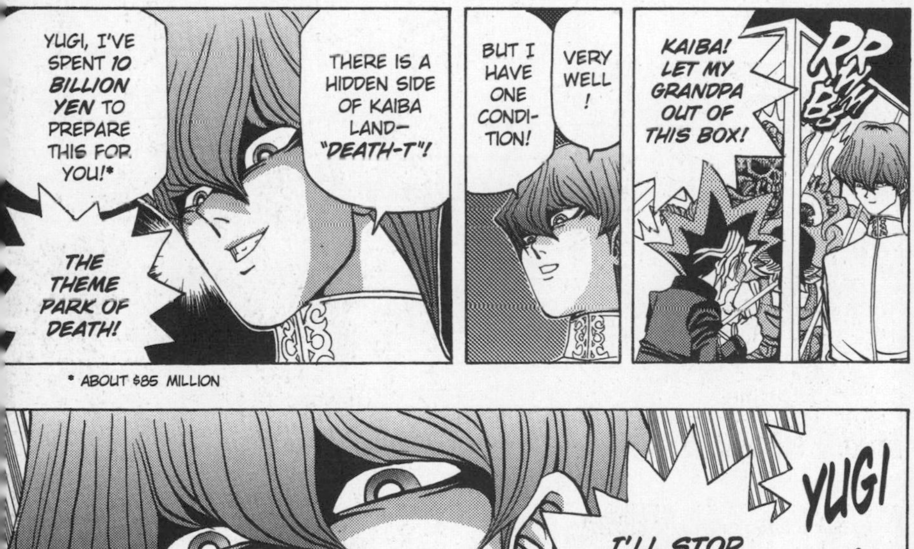
PRRMB
KAIBA! LET MY GRANDPA OUT OF THIS BOX!
VERY WELL!
BUT I HAVE ONE CONDITION!
THERE IS A HIDDEN SIDE OF KAIBA LAND—"DEATH-T"!
YUGI, I'VE SPENT 10 BILLION YEN TO PREPARE THIS FOR YOU!*
THE THEME PARK OF DEATH!

* ABOUT $85 MILLION

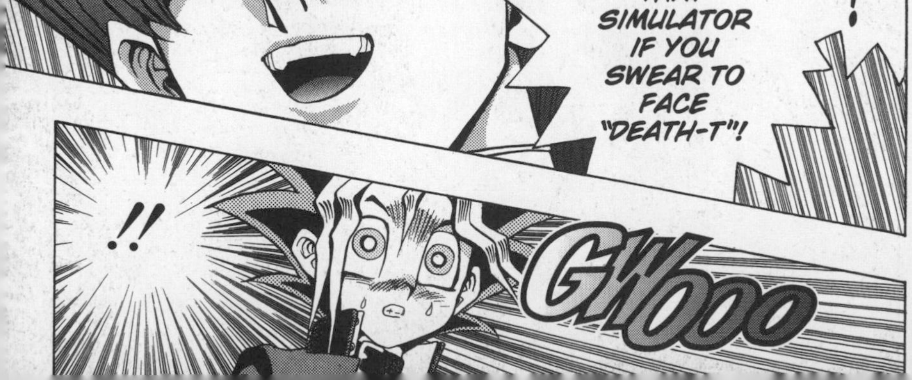
YUGI!
I'LL STOP THAT SIMULATOR IF YOU SWEAR TO FACE "DEATH-T"!
!!
GYOOO

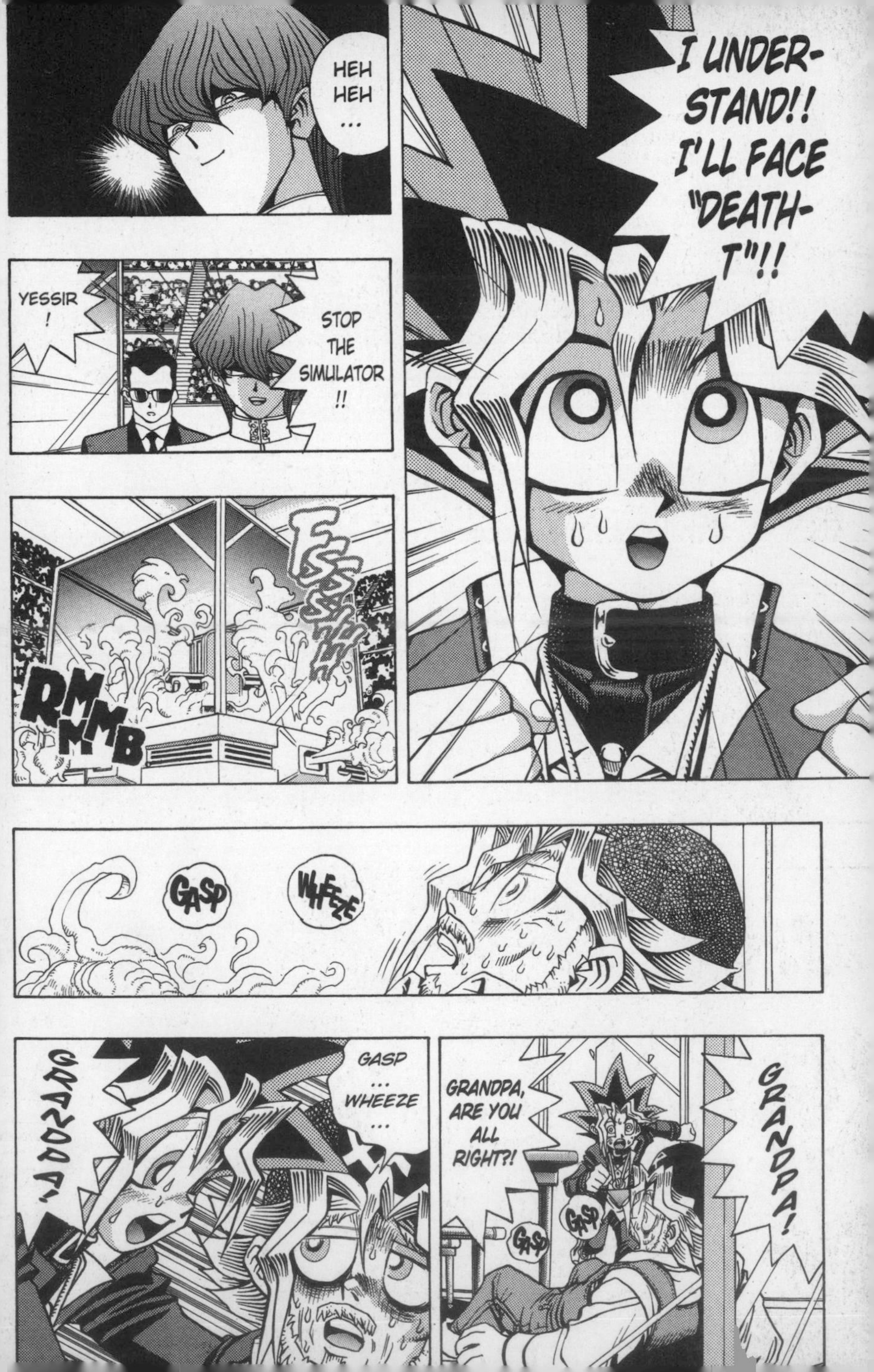
I UNDER-STAND!! I'LL FACE "DEATH-T"!!
HEH HEH ...
STOP THE SIMULATOR !!
YESSIR !
FSSSHH
RMMMB
GASP
WHEEZE
GRANDPA!
GRANDPA, ARE YOU ALL RIGHT?!
GASP
GASP
GASP ... WHEEZE ...
GRANDPA!

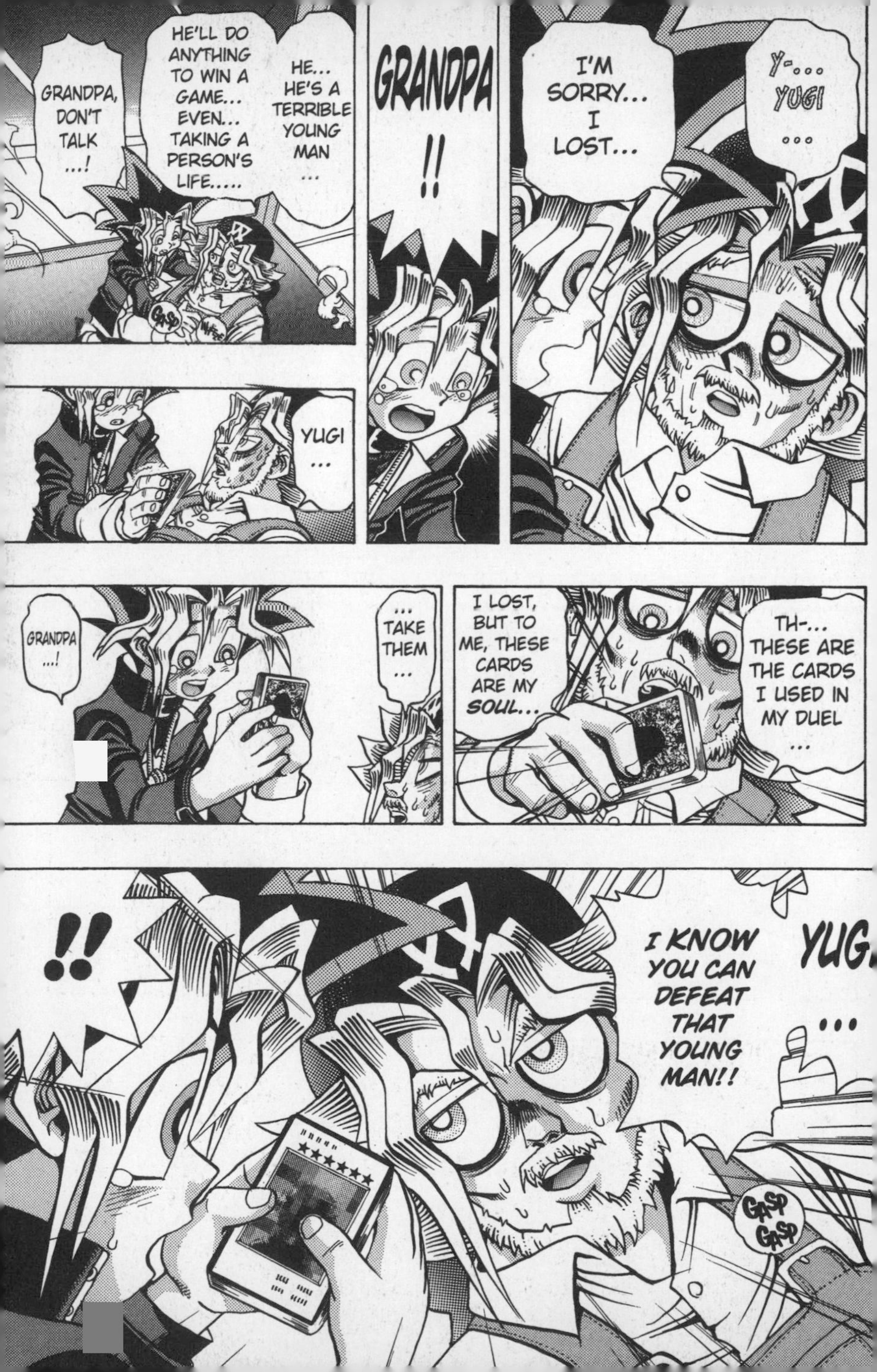
Y-... YUGI ...
I'M SORRY... I LOST...
GRANDPA!!
HE... HE'S A TERRIBLE YOUNG MAN ...
HE'LL DO ANYTHING TO WIN A GAME... EVEN... TAKING A PERSON'S LIFE.....
GRANDPA, DON'T TALK ...!
GASP
YUGI ...
TH-... THESE ARE THE CARDS I USED IN MY DUEL ...
I LOST, BUT TO ME, THESE CARDS ARE MY SOUL...
... TAKE THEM ...
GRANDPA ...!
YUG...
...
I KNOW YOU CAN DEFEAT THAT YOUNG MAN!!
GASP GASP
!!

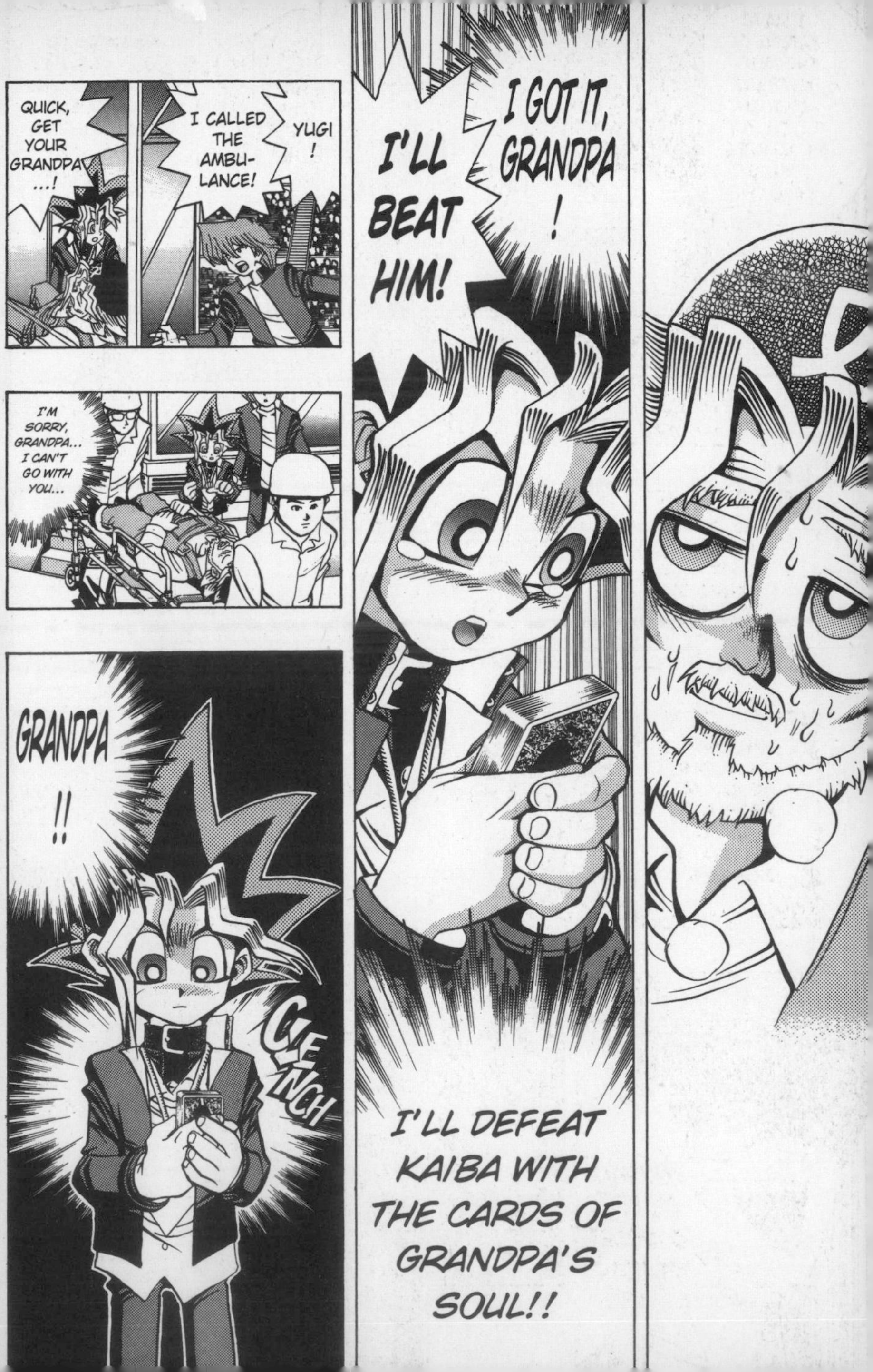
I GOT IT, GRANDPA!
I'LL BEAT HIM!
I'LL DEFEAT KAIBA WITH THE CARDS OF GRANDPA'S SOUL!!
YUGI!
I CALLED THE AMBU-LANCE!
QUICK, GET YOUR GRANDPA...!
I'M SORRY, GRANDPA... I CAN'T GO WITH YOU...
GRANDPA!!
CLENCH

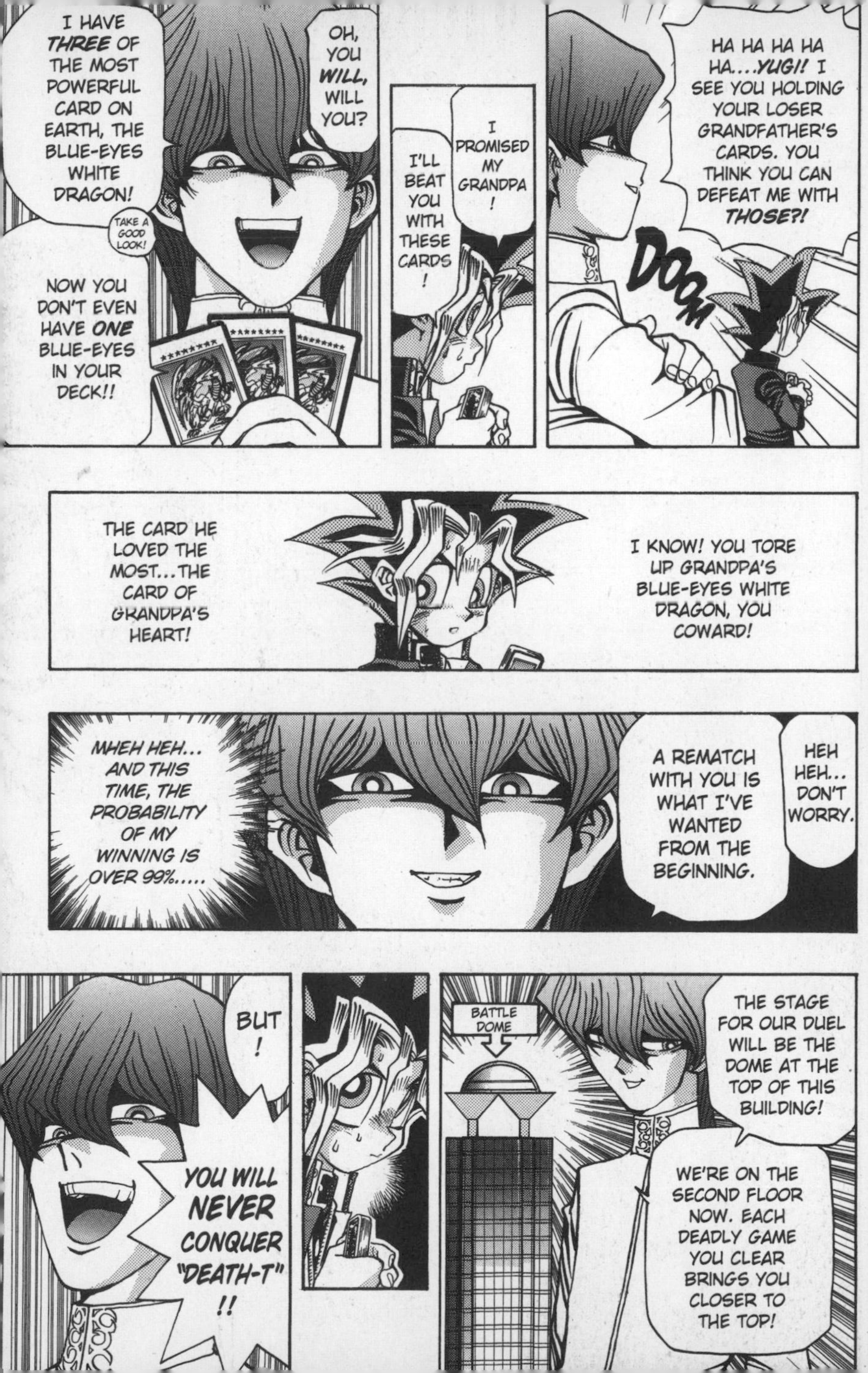
HA HA HA HA HA....YUGI!! I SEE YOU HOLDING YOUR LOSER GRANDFATHER'S CARDS. YOU THINK YOU CAN DEFEAT ME WITH THOSE?!
DOOM
I PROMISED MY GRANDPA!
I'LL BEAT YOU WITH THESE CARDS!
OH, YOU WILL, WILL YOU?
I HAVE THREE OF THE MOST POWERFUL CARD ON EARTH, THE BLUE-EYES WHITE DRAGON!
TAKE A GOOD LOOK!
NOW YOU DON'T EVEN HAVE ONE BLUE-EYES IN YOUR DECK!!
I KNOW! YOU TORE UP GRANDPA'S BLUE-EYES WHITE DRAGON, YOU COWARD!
THE CARD HE LOVED THE MOST...THE CARD OF GRANDPA'S HEART!
HEH HEH... DON'T WORRY.
A REMATCH WITH YOU IS WHAT I'VE WANTED FROM THE BEGINNING.
MHEH HEH... AND THIS TIME, THE PROBABILITY OF MY WINNING IS OVER 99%.....
THE STAGE FOR OUR DUEL WILL BE THE DOME AT THE TOP OF THIS BUILDING!
BATTLE DOME
WE'RE ON THE SECOND FLOOR NOW. EACH DEADLY GAME YOU CLEAR BRINGS YOU CLOSER TO THE TOP!
BUT!
YOU WILL NEVER CONQUER "DEATH-T"!!

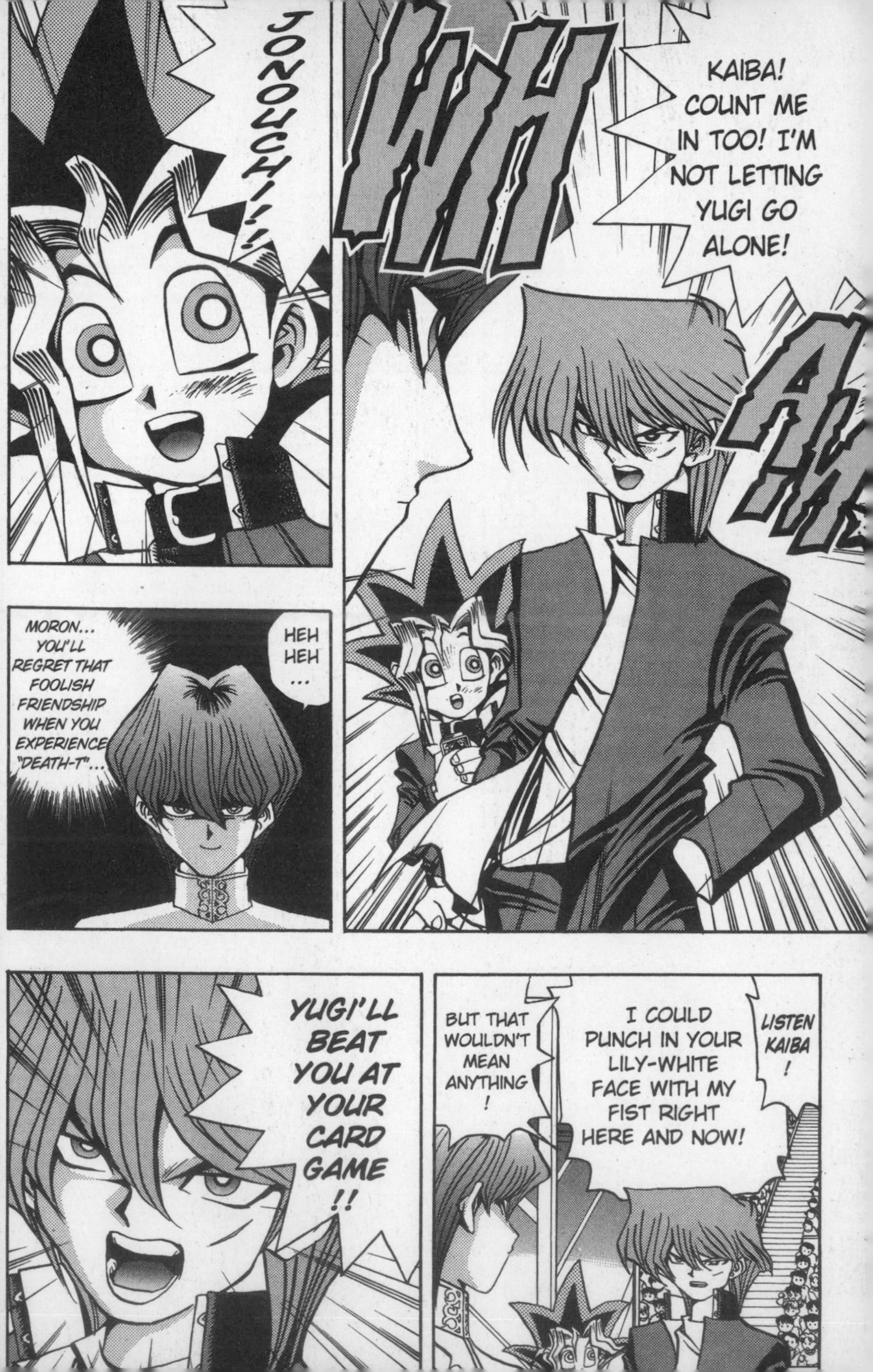
KAIBA! COUNT ME IN TOO! I'M NOT LETTING YUGI GO ALONE!
WHA
JONOUCHI!!!
HEH HEH ...
MORON... YOU'LL REGRET THAT FOOLISH FRIENDSHIP WHEN YOU EXPERIENCE "DEATH-T"...
LISTEN KAIBA!
I COULD PUNCH IN YOUR LILY-WHITE FACE WITH MY FIST RIGHT HERE AND NOW!
BUT THAT WOULDN'T MEAN ANYTHING!
YUGI'LL BEAT YOU AT YOUR CARD GAME!!

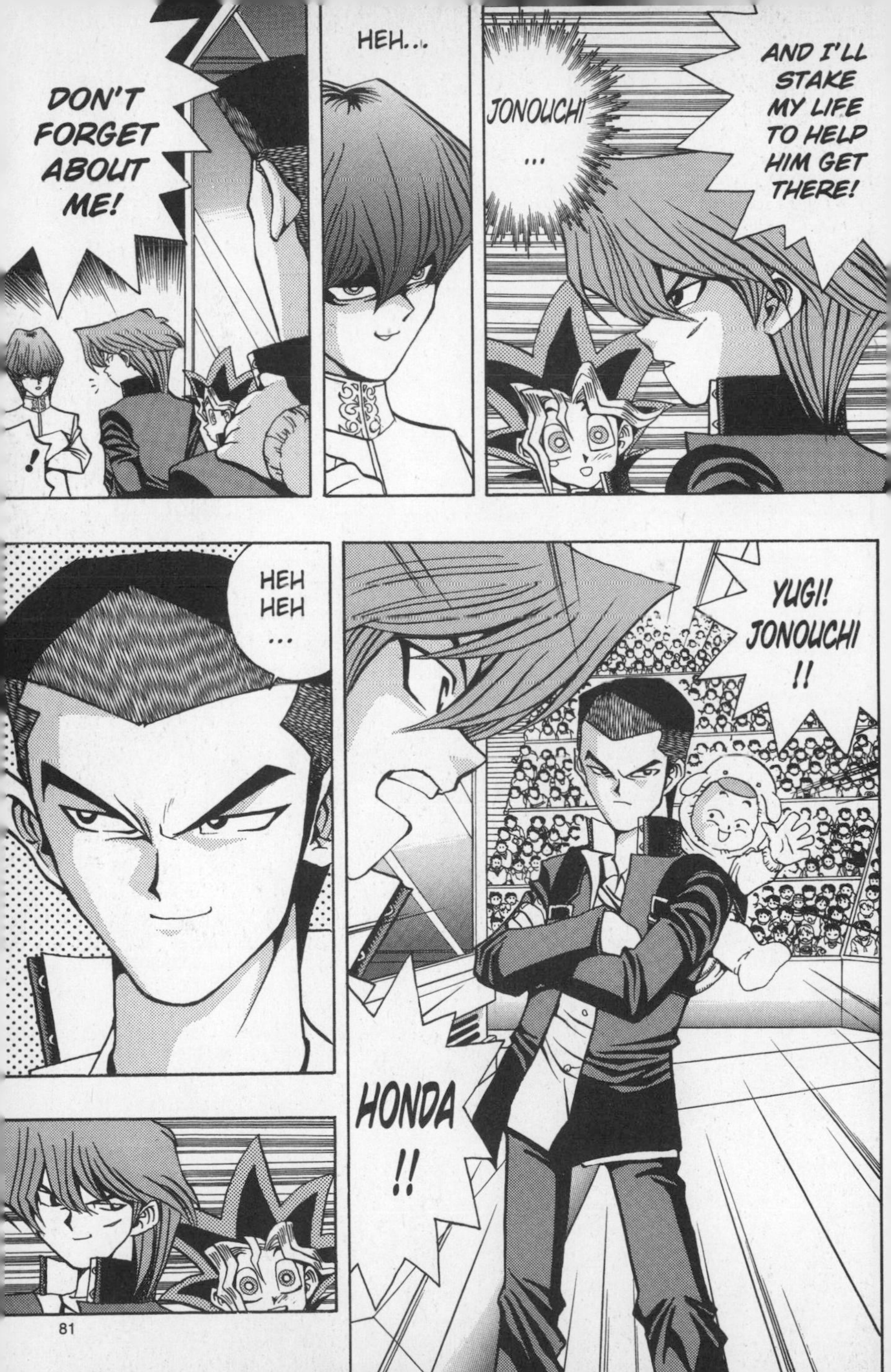
AND I'LL STAKE MY LIFE TO HELP HIM GET THERE!
JONOUCHI ...
HEH...
DON'T FORGET ABOUT ME!
!
YUGI! JONOUCHI !!
HONDA !!
HEH HEH ...

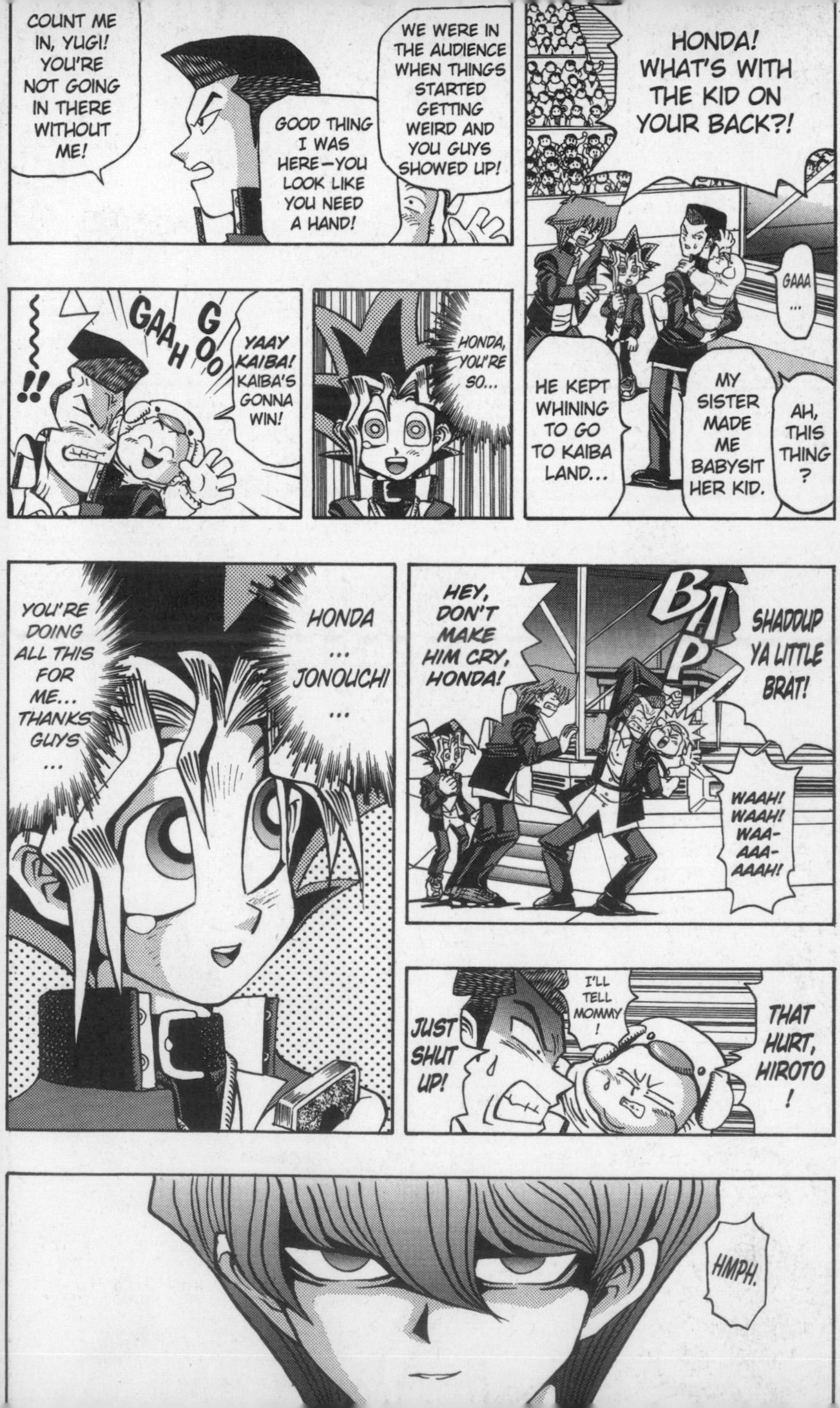
HONDA! WHAT'S WITH THE KID ON YOUR BACK?!
GAAA ...
AH, THIS THING ?
MY SISTER MADE ME BABYSIT HER KID.
HE KEPT WHINING TO GO TO KAIBA LAND...
WE WERE IN THE AUDIENCE WHEN THINGS STARTED GETTING WEIRD AND YOU GUYS SHOWED UP!
GOOD THING I WAS HERE—YOU LOOK LIKE YOU NEED A HAND!
COUNT ME IN, YUGI! YOU'RE NOT GOING IN THERE WITHOUT ME!
HONDA, YOU'RE SO...
YAAY KAIBA! KAIBA'S GONNA WIN!
GOO
GAAH
!!
SHADDUP YA LITTLE BRAT!
BAP
HEY, DON'T MAKE HIM CRY, HONDA!
WAAH! WAAH! WAA-AAA-AAAH!
THAT HURT, HIROTO !
I'LL TELL MOMMY !
JUST SHUT UP!
HONDA ... JONOUCHI ...
YOU'RE DOING ALL THIS FOR ME... THANKS GUYS ...
HMPH.

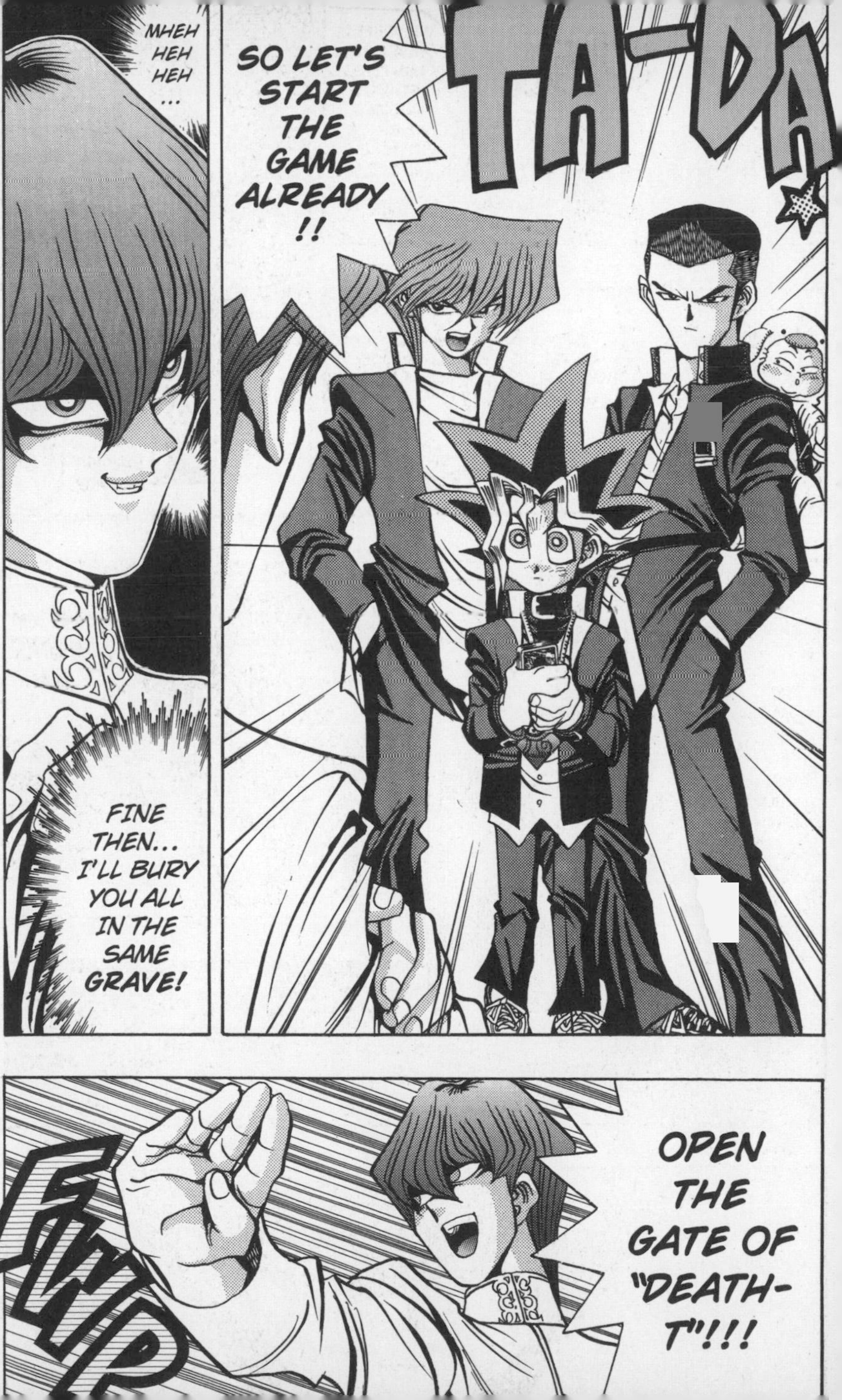
TA-DA
SO LET'S START THE GAME ALREADY !!
MHEH HEH HEH ...
FINE THEN... I'LL BURY YOU ALL IN THE SAME GRAVE!
OPEN THE GATE OF "DEATH-T"!!!

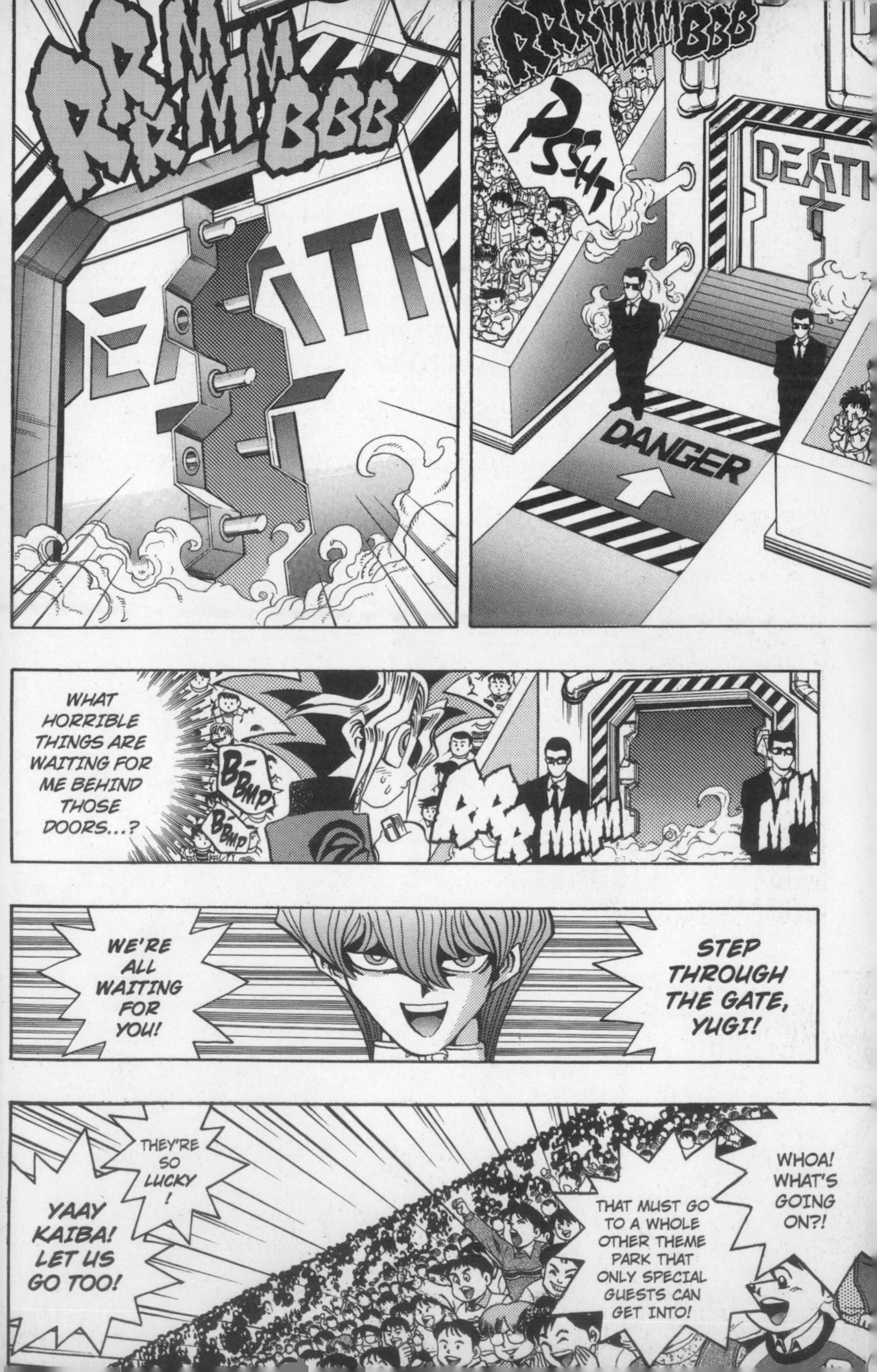
RRRMMMBBB
PSSHT
DANGER
DEATH T
RRRMMMBBB
DEATH T
WHAT HORRIBLE THINGS ARE WAITING FOR ME BEHIND THOSE DOORS...?
B-BMP
B-BMP
RRRMMM
MM
STEP THROUGH THE GATE, YUGI!
WE'RE ALL WAITING FOR YOU!
WHOA! WHAT'S GOING ON?!
THAT MUST GO TO A WHOLE OTHER THEME PARK THAT ONLY SPECIAL GUESTS CAN GET INTO!
THEY'RE SO LUCKY!
YAAY KAIBA! LET US GO TOO!

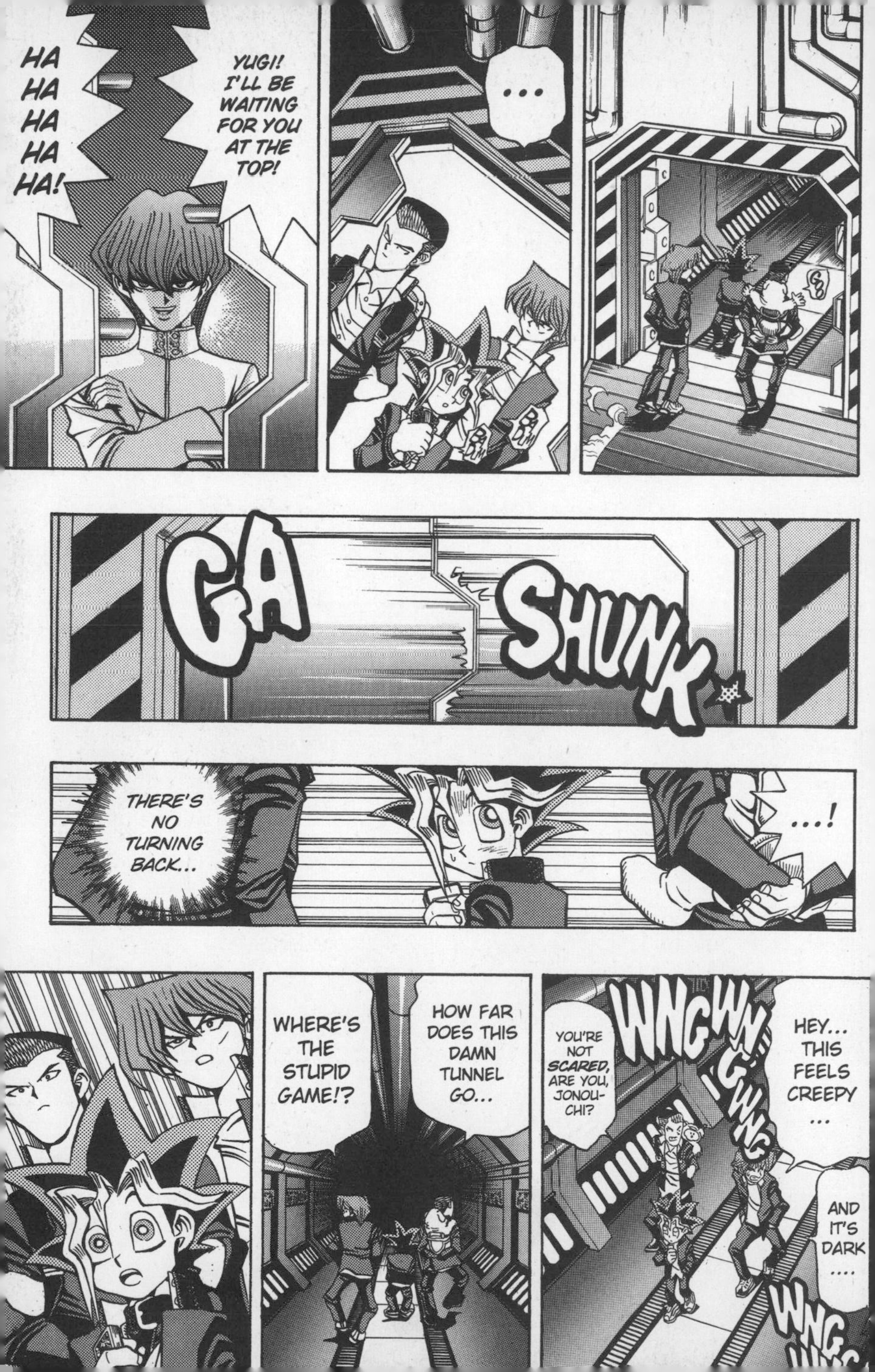
...
YUGI! I'LL BE WAITING FOR YOU AT THE TOP!
HA HA HA HA HA!
GA
SHUNK
...!
THERE'S NO TURNING BACK...
HEY... THIS FEELS CREEPY...
AND IT'S DARK....
WNGWN GWNG
YOU'RE NOT SCARED, ARE YOU, JONOU-CHI?
WNG
HOW FAR DOES THIS DAMN TUNNEL GO...
WHERE'S THE STUPID GAME!?

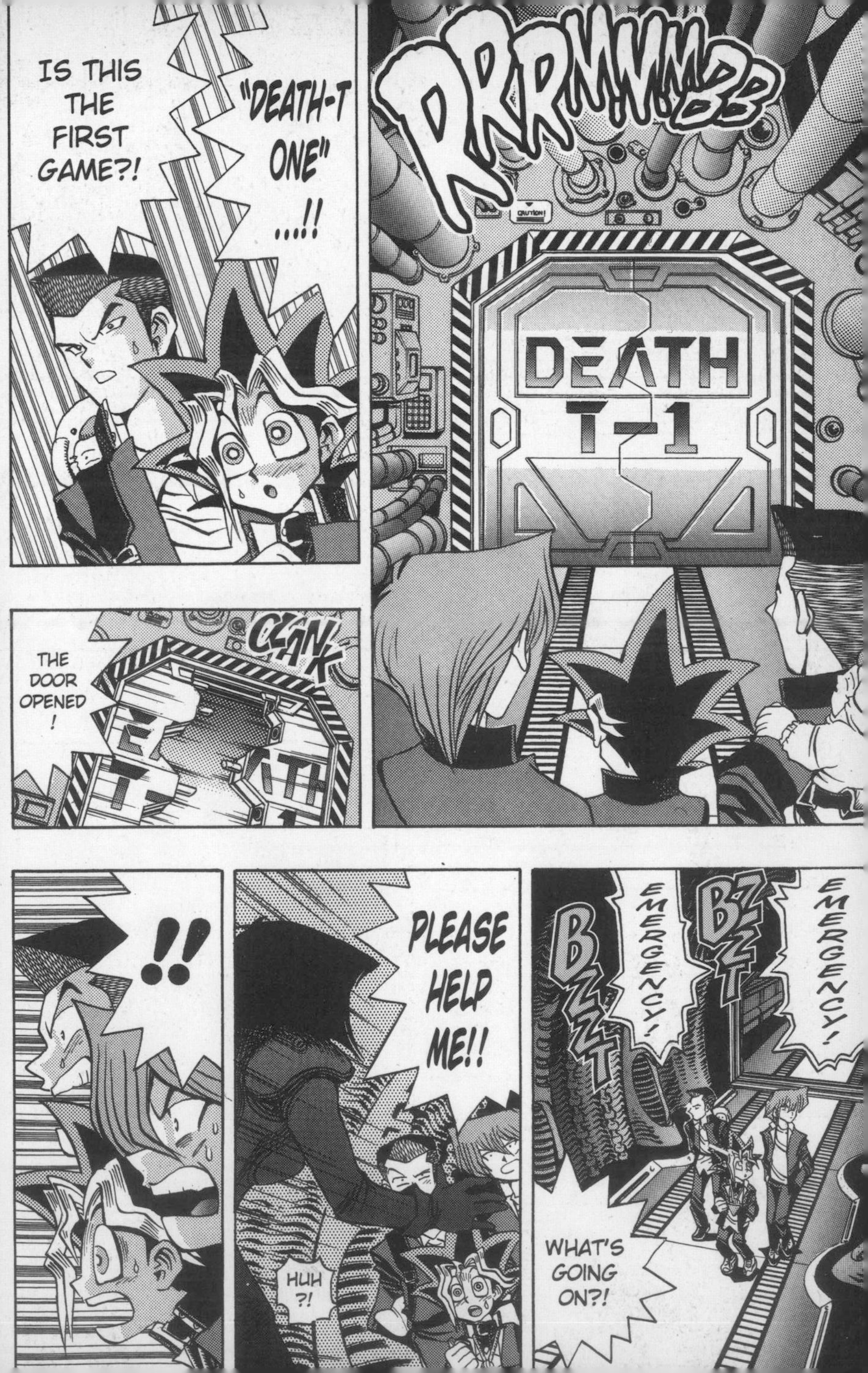
RRRMMMBB
CAUTION!
DEATH T-1
IS THIS THE FIRST GAME?!
"DEATH-T ONE" ...!!
THE DOOR OPENED!
CLANK
EMERGENCY!
BZZT
BZZT
EMERGENCY!
WHAT'S GOING ON?!
PLEASE HELP ME!!
HUH ?!
!!

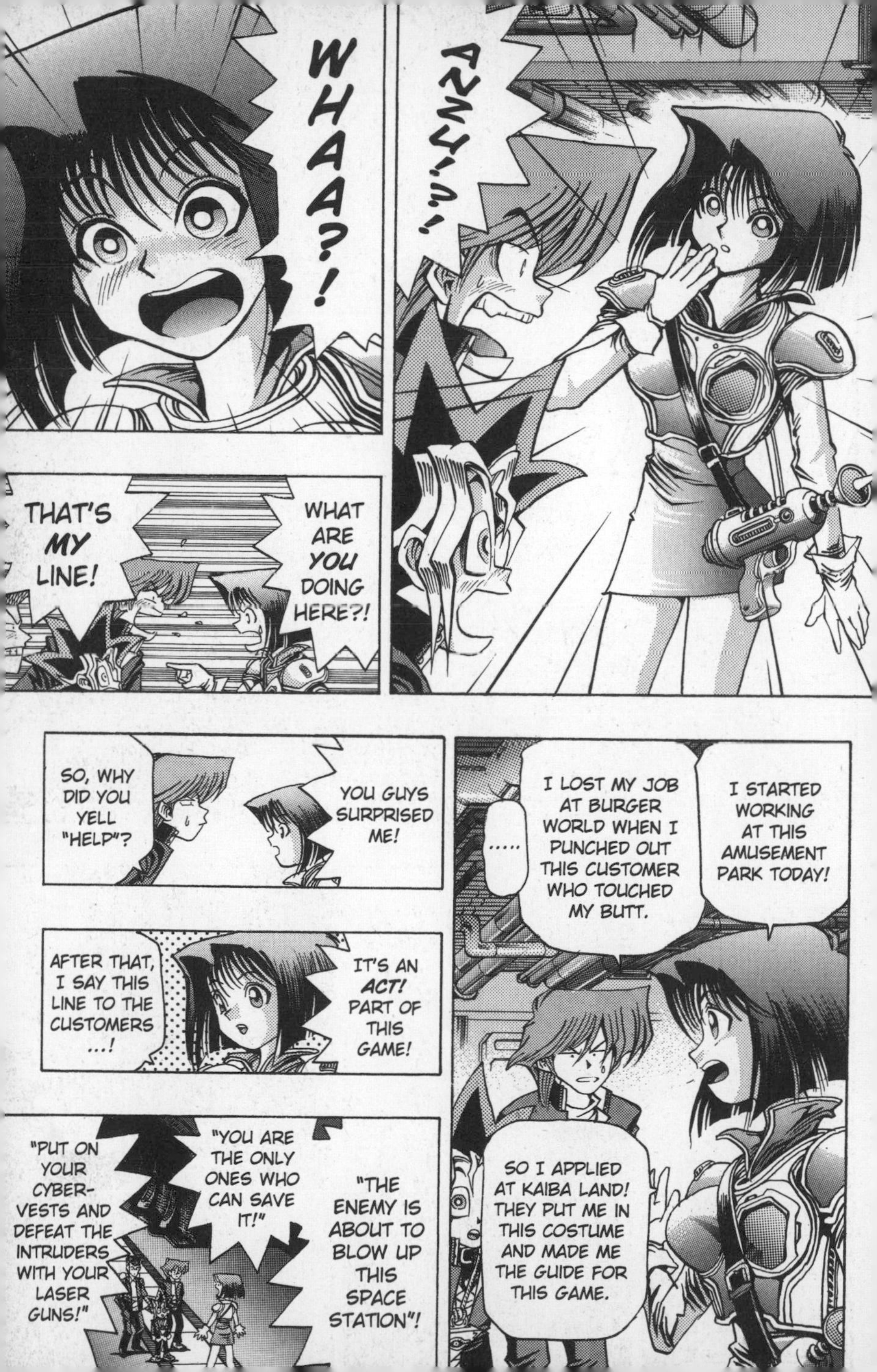
ANZU!?!
WHAAA?!
WHAT ARE *YOU* DOING HERE?!
THAT'S *MY* LINE!
I STARTED WORKING AT THIS AMUSEMENT PARK TODAY!
I LOST MY JOB AT BURGER WORLD WHEN I PUNCHED OUT THIS CUSTOMER WHO TOUCHED MY BUTT.
.....
SO I APPLIED AT KAIBA LAND! THEY PUT ME IN THIS COSTUME AND MADE ME THE GUIDE FOR THIS GAME.
YOU GUYS SURPRISED ME!
SO, WHY DID YOU YELL "HELP"?
IT'S AN *ACT!* PART OF THIS GAME!
AFTER THAT, I SAY THIS LINE TO THE CUSTOMERS ...!
"THE ENEMY IS ABOUT TO BLOW UP THIS SPACE STATION"!
"YOU ARE THE ONLY ONES WHO CAN SAVE IT!"
"PUT ON YOUR CYBER-VESTS AND DEFEAT THE INTRUDERS WITH YOUR LASER GUNS!"

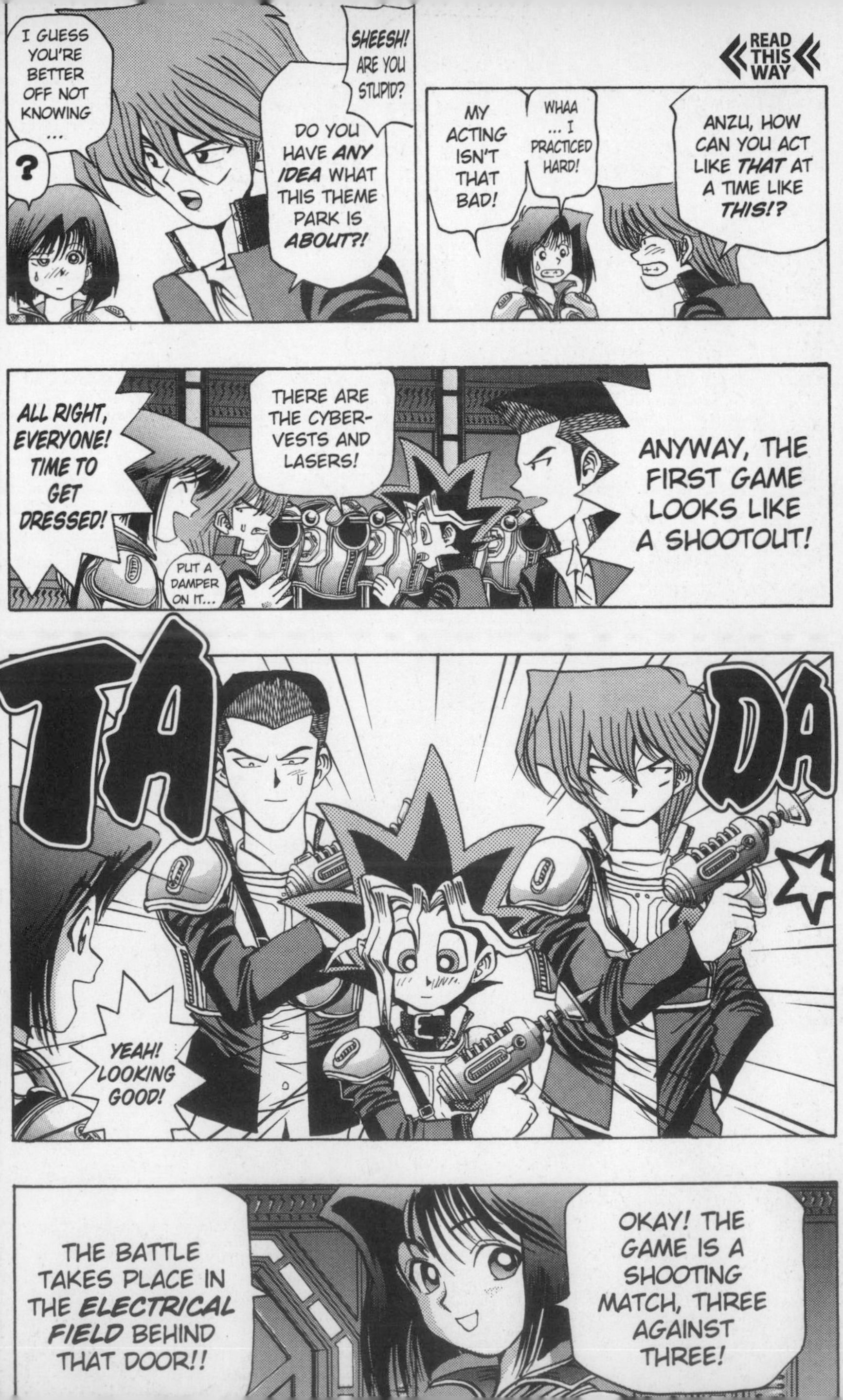
READ THIS WAY
ANZU, HOW CAN YOU ACT LIKE THAT AT A TIME LIKE THIS!?
WHAA ... I PRACTICED HARD!
MY ACTING ISN'T THAT BAD!
SHEESH! ARE YOU STUPID?
DO YOU HAVE ANY IDEA WHAT THIS THEME PARK IS ABOUT?!
I GUESS YOU'RE BETTER OFF NOT KNOWING ...
?
ANYWAY, THE FIRST GAME LOOKS LIKE A SHOOTOUT!
THERE ARE THE CYBER-VESTS AND LASERS!
ALL RIGHT, EVERYONE! TIME TO GET DRESSED!
PUT A DAMPER ON IT...
DA
TA
YEAH! LOOKING GOOD!
OKAY! THE GAME IS A SHOOTING MATCH, THREE AGAINST THREE!
THE BATTLE TAKES PLACE IN THE ELECTRICAL FIELD BEHIND THAT DOOR!!

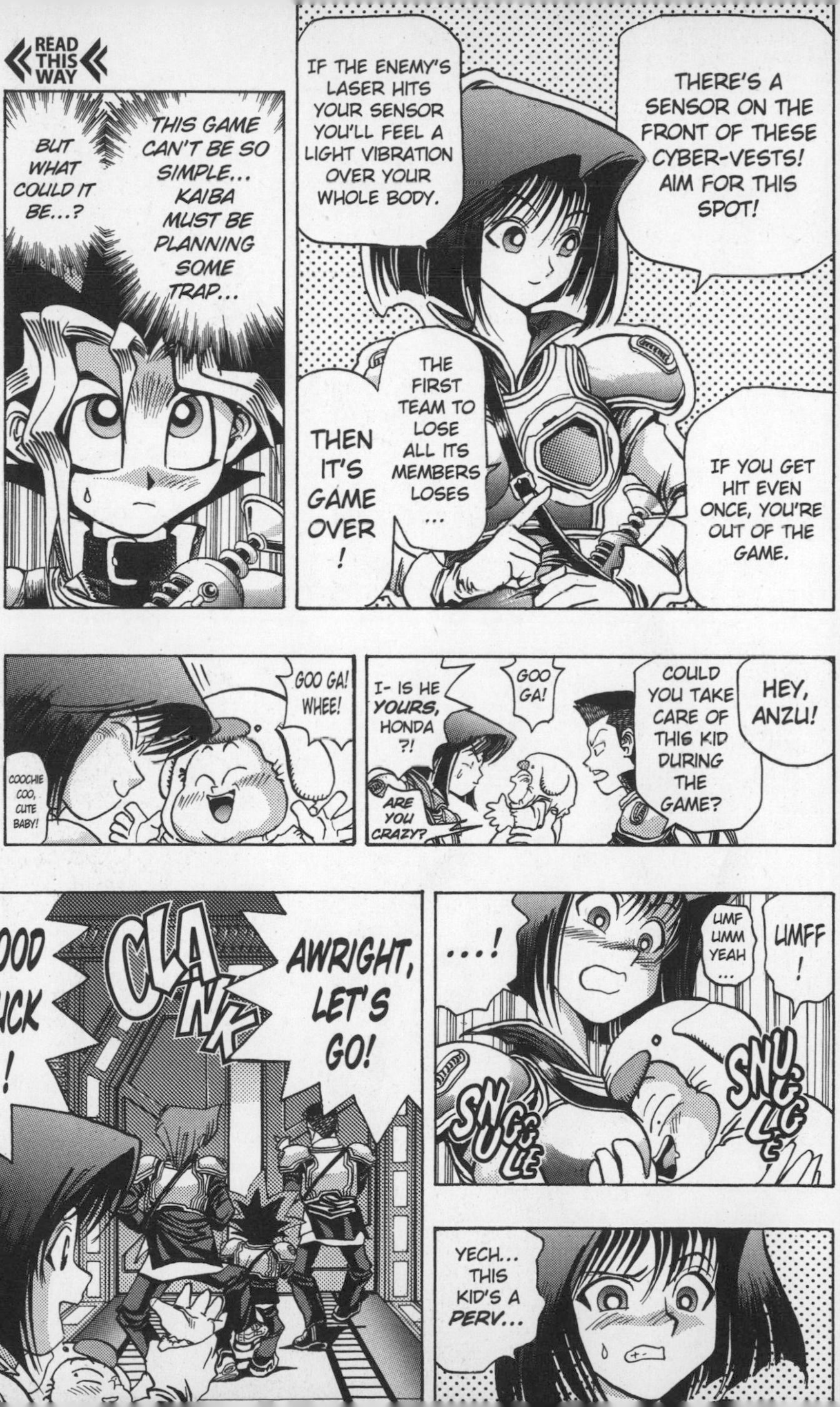
READ THIS WAY
THERE'S A SENSOR ON THE FRONT OF THESE CYBER-VESTS! AIM FOR THIS SPOT!
IF THE ENEMY'S LASER HITS YOUR SENSOR YOU'LL FEEL A LIGHT VIBRATION OVER YOUR WHOLE BODY.
IF YOU GET HIT EVEN ONCE, YOU'RE OUT OF THE GAME.
THE FIRST TEAM TO LOSE ALL ITS MEMBERS LOSES ...
THEN IT'S GAME OVER !
THIS GAME CAN'T BE SO SIMPLE... KAIBA MUST BE PLANNING SOME TRAP...
BUT WHAT COULD IT BE...?
HEY, ANZU!
COULD YOU TAKE CARE OF THIS KID DURING THE GAME?
GOO GA!
I- IS HE YOURS, HONDA ?!
ARE YOU CRAZY?
GOO GA! WHEE!
COOCHIE COO, CUTE BABY!
UMFF !
UMF UMM YEAH ...
...!
SNUGGLE
SNUGGLE
YECH... THIS KID'S A PERV...
AWRIGHT, LET'S GO!
CLANK
GOOD LUCK !

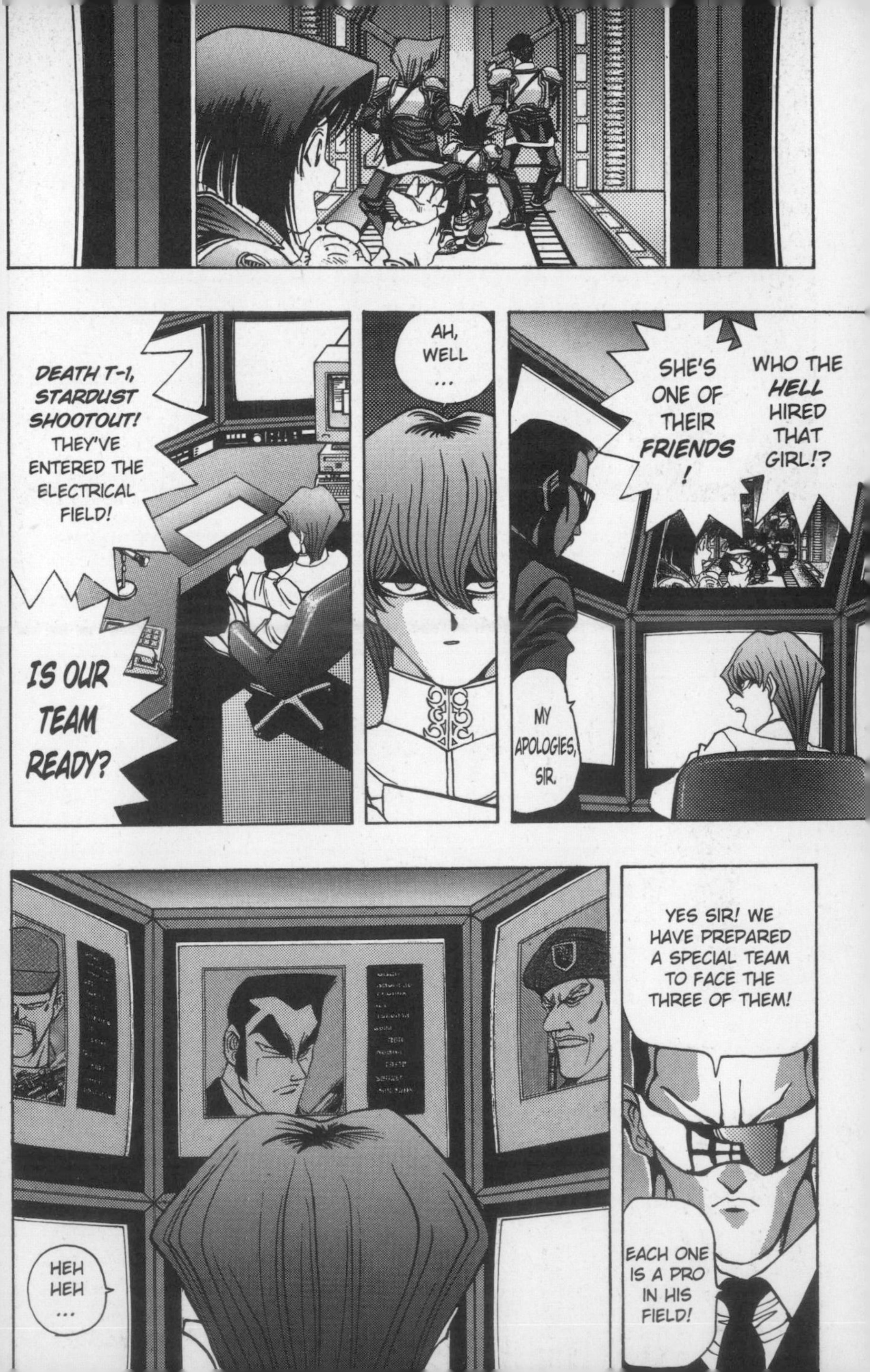
WHO THE HELL HIRED THAT GIRL!?
SHE'S ONE OF THEIR FRIENDS!
MY APOLOGIES, SIR.
AH, WELL ...
DEATH T-1, STARDUST SHOOTOUT! THEY'VE ENTERED THE ELECTRICAL FIELD!
IS OUR TEAM READY?
YES SIR! WE HAVE PREPARED A SPECIAL TEAM TO FACE THE THREE OF THEM!
EACH ONE IS A PRO IN HIS FIELD!
HEH HEH ...

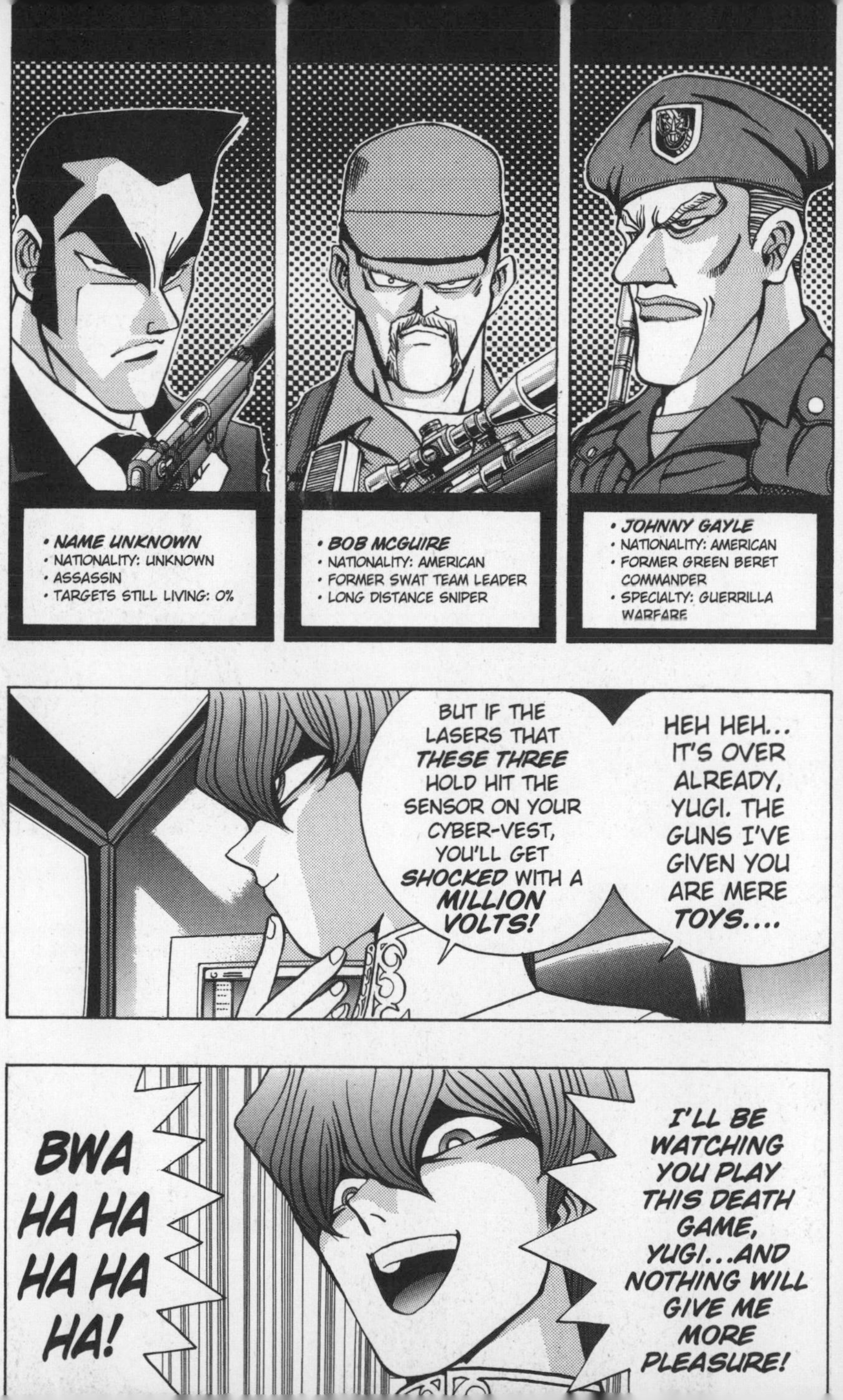
• JOHNNY GAYLE
• NATIONALITY: AMERICAN
• FORMER GREEN BERET COMMANDER
• SPECIALTY: GUERRILLA WARFARE
• BOB MCGUIRE
• NATIONALITY: AMERICAN
• FORMER SWAT TEAM LEADER
• LONG DISTANCE SNIPER
• NAME UNKNOWN
• NATIONALITY: UNKNOWN
• ASSASSIN
• TARGETS STILL LIVING: 0%
HEH HEH... IT'S OVER ALREADY, YUGI. THE GUNS I'VE GIVEN YOU ARE MERE TOYS....
BUT IF THE LASERS THAT THESE THREE HOLD HIT THE SENSOR ON YOUR CYBER-VEST, YOU'LL GET SHOCKED WITH A MILLION VOLTS!
I'LL BE WATCHING YOU PLAY THIS DEATH GAME, YUGI...AND NOTHING WILL GIVE ME MORE PLEASURE!
BWA HA HA HA HA HA!

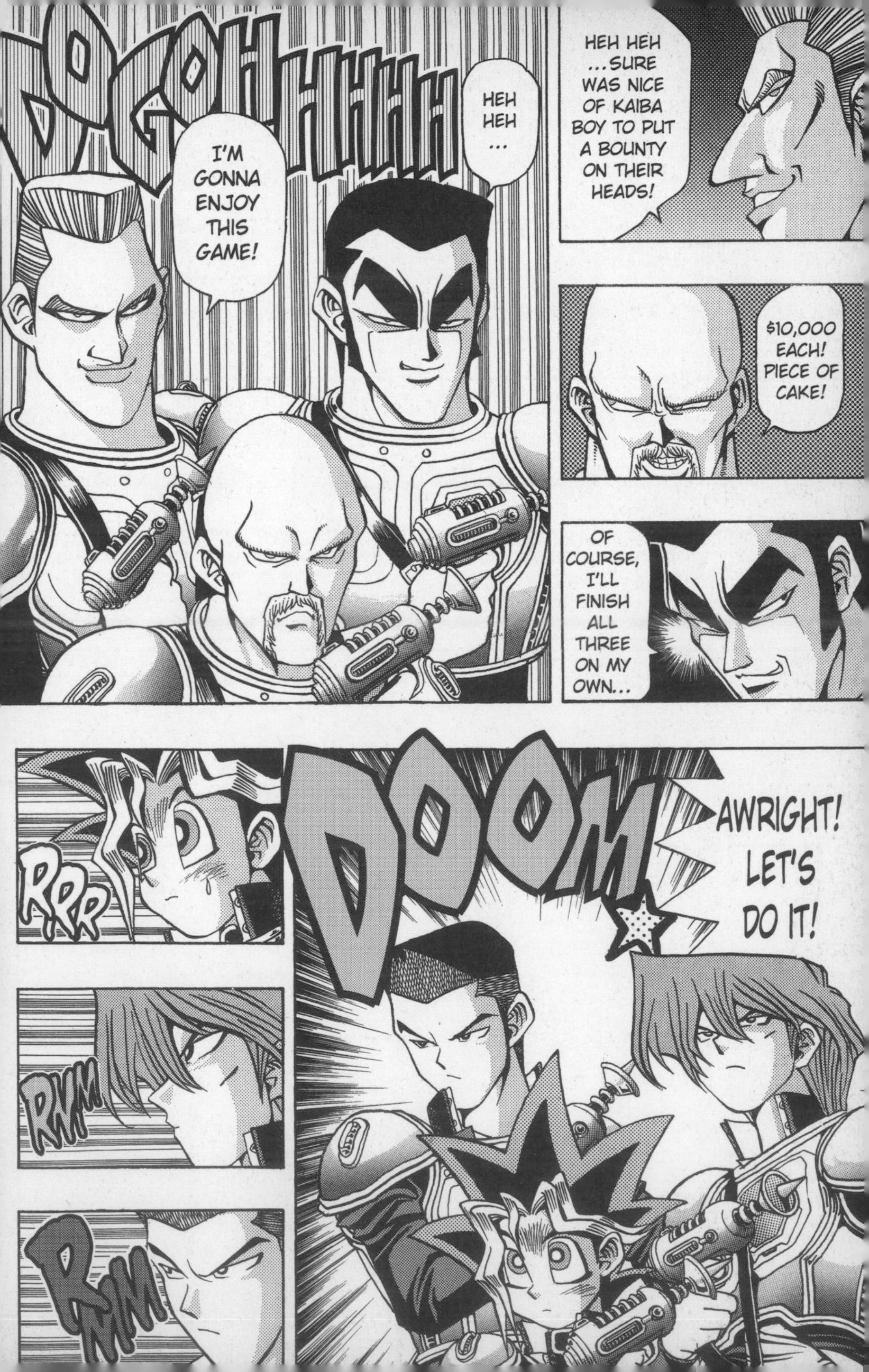
HEH HEH ...SURE WAS NICE OF KAIBA BOY TO PUT A BOUNTY ON THEIR HEADS!
$10,000 EACH! PIECE OF CAKE!
OF COURSE, I'LL FINISH ALL THREE ON MY OWN...
HEH HEH ...
I'M GONNA ENJOY THIS GAME!
GOHHHHH
AWRIGHT! LET'S DO IT!
DOOM
RPP
RMM
RMM

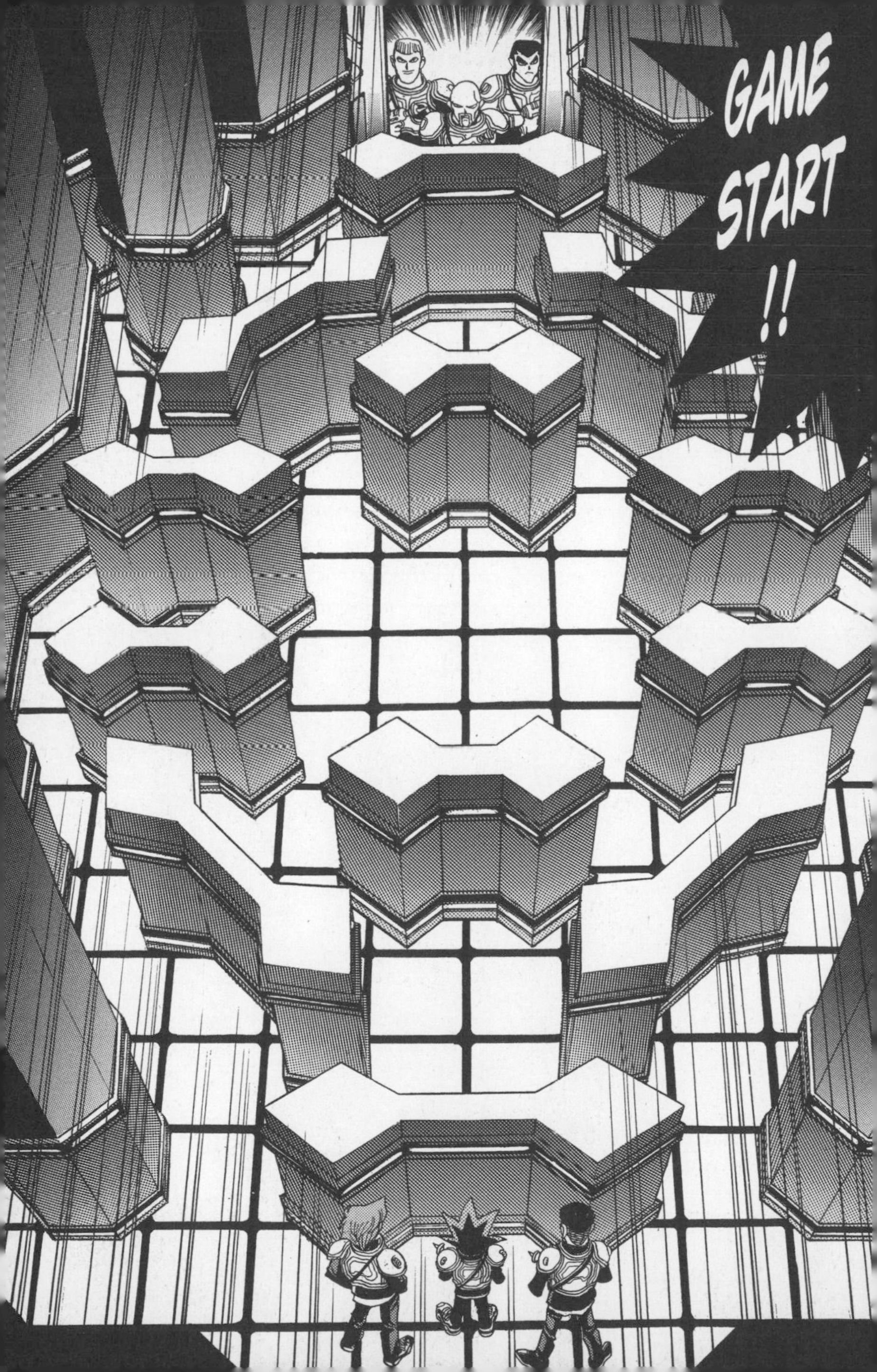
GAME START!!

Duel 29: Shooting Stardust

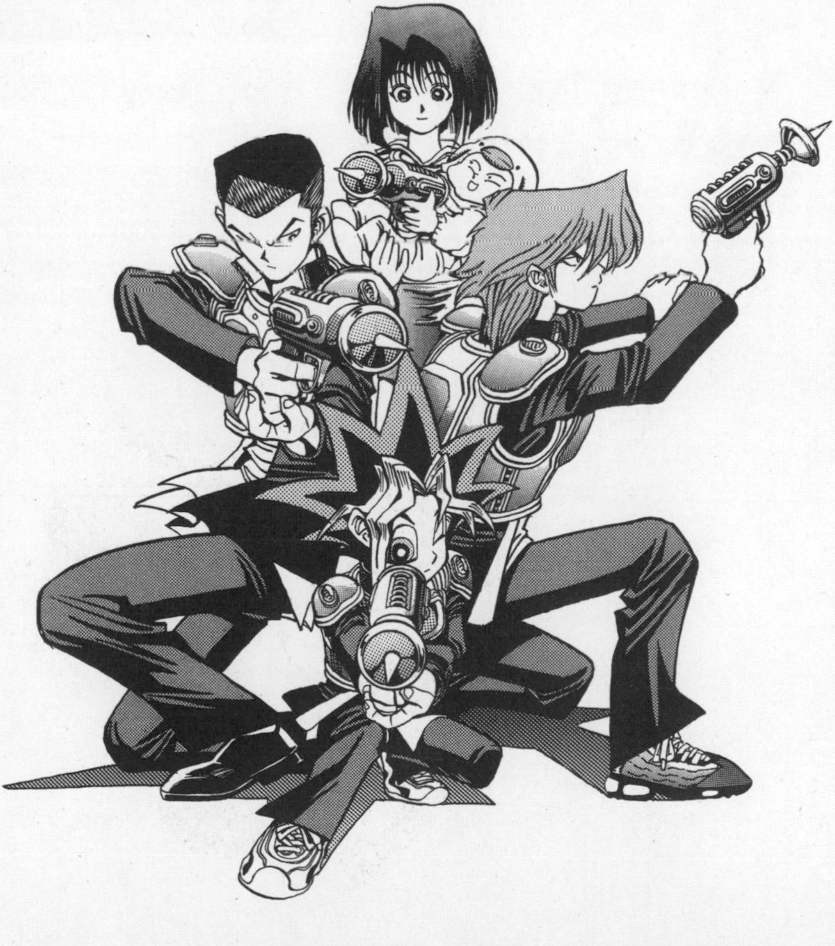

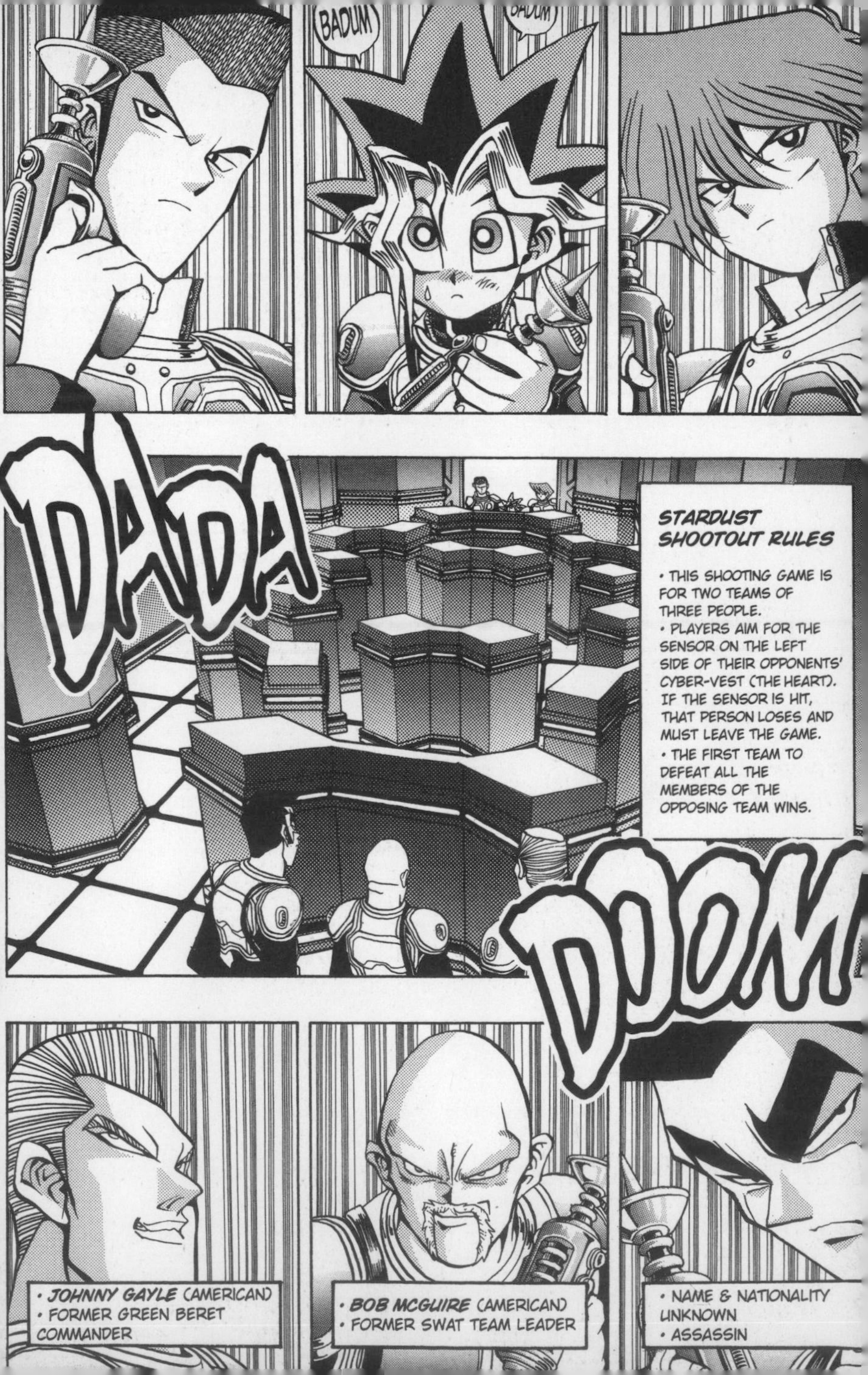
BADUM
BADUM
STARDUST SHOOTOUT RULES
• THIS SHOOTING GAME IS FOR TWO TEAMS OF THREE PEOPLE.
• PLAYERS AIM FOR THE SENSOR ON THE LEFT SIDE OF THEIR OPPONENTS' CYBER-VEST (THE HEART). IF THE SENSOR IS HIT, THAT PERSON LOSES AND MUST LEAVE THE GAME.
• THE FIRST TEAM TO DEFEAT ALL THE MEMBERS OF THE OPPOSING TEAM WINS.
DADA
DOOM
• NAME & NATIONALITY UNKNOWN
• ASSASSIN
• BOB MCGUIRE (AMERICAN)
• FORMER SWAT TEAM LEADER
• JOHNNY GAYLE (AMERICAN)
• FORMER GREEN BERET COMMANDER

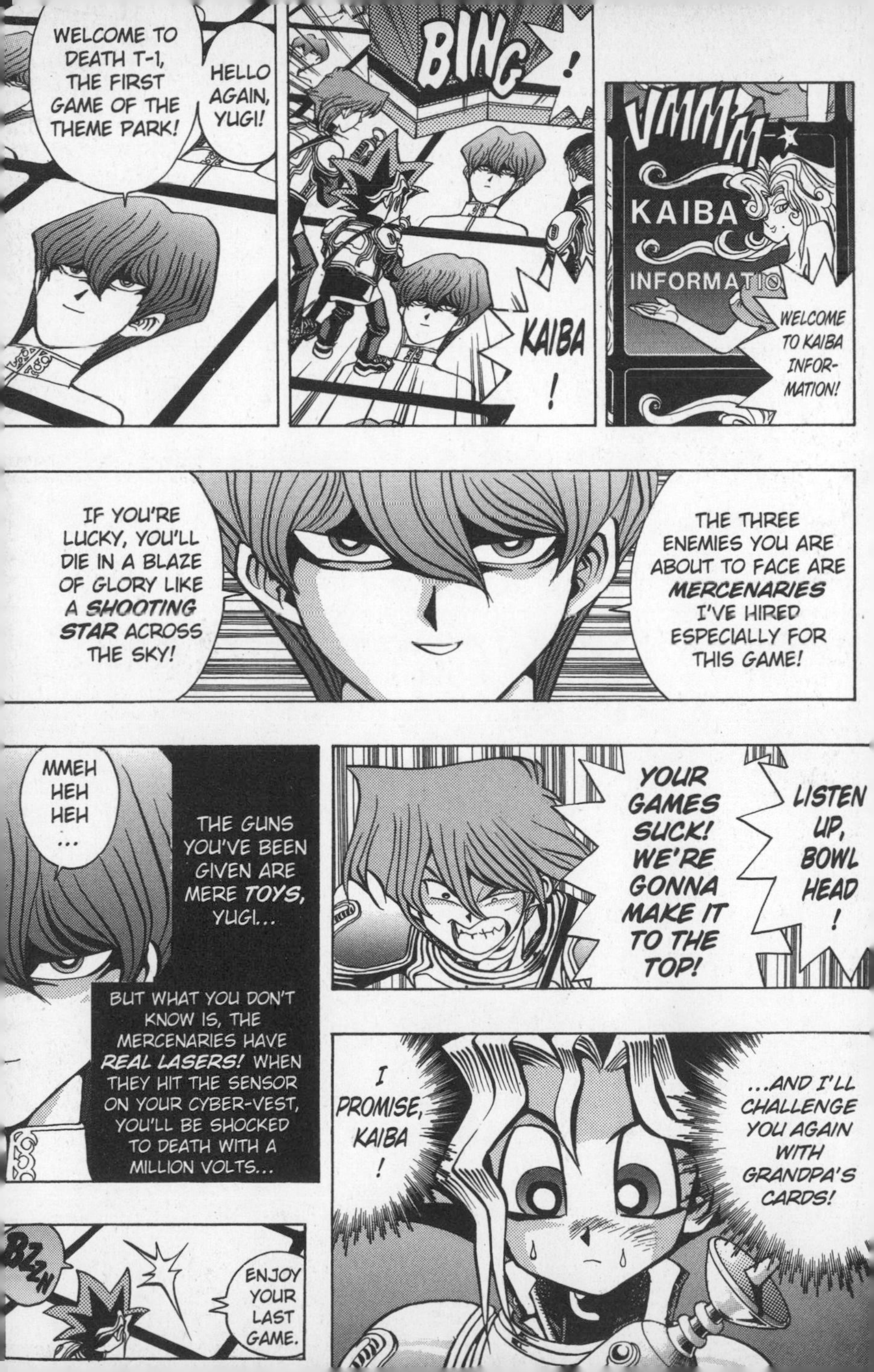
VMMMM
KAIBA
INFORMATIO
WELCOME TO KAIBA INFORMATION!
BING!
KAIBA!
HELLO AGAIN, YUGI!
WELCOME TO DEATH T-1, THE FIRST GAME OF THE THEME PARK!
THE THREE ENEMIES YOU ARE ABOUT TO FACE ARE MERCENARIES I'VE HIRED ESPECIALLY FOR THIS GAME!
IF YOU'RE LUCKY, YOU'LL DIE IN A BLAZE OF GLORY LIKE A SHOOTING STAR ACROSS THE SKY!
LISTEN UP, BOWL HEAD!
YOUR GAMES SUCK! WE'RE GONNA MAKE IT TO THE TOP!
...AND I'LL CHALLENGE YOU AGAIN WITH GRANDPA'S CARDS!
I PROMISE, KAIBA!
MMEH HEH HEH...
THE GUNS YOU'VE BEEN GIVEN ARE MERE TOYS, YUGI...
BUT WHAT YOU DON'T KNOW IS, THE MERCENARIES HAVE REAL LASERS! WHEN THEY HIT THE SENSOR ON YOUR CYBER-VEST, YOU'LL BE SHOCKED TO DEATH WITH A MILLION VOLTS...
BZZN
ENJOY YOUR LAST GAME.

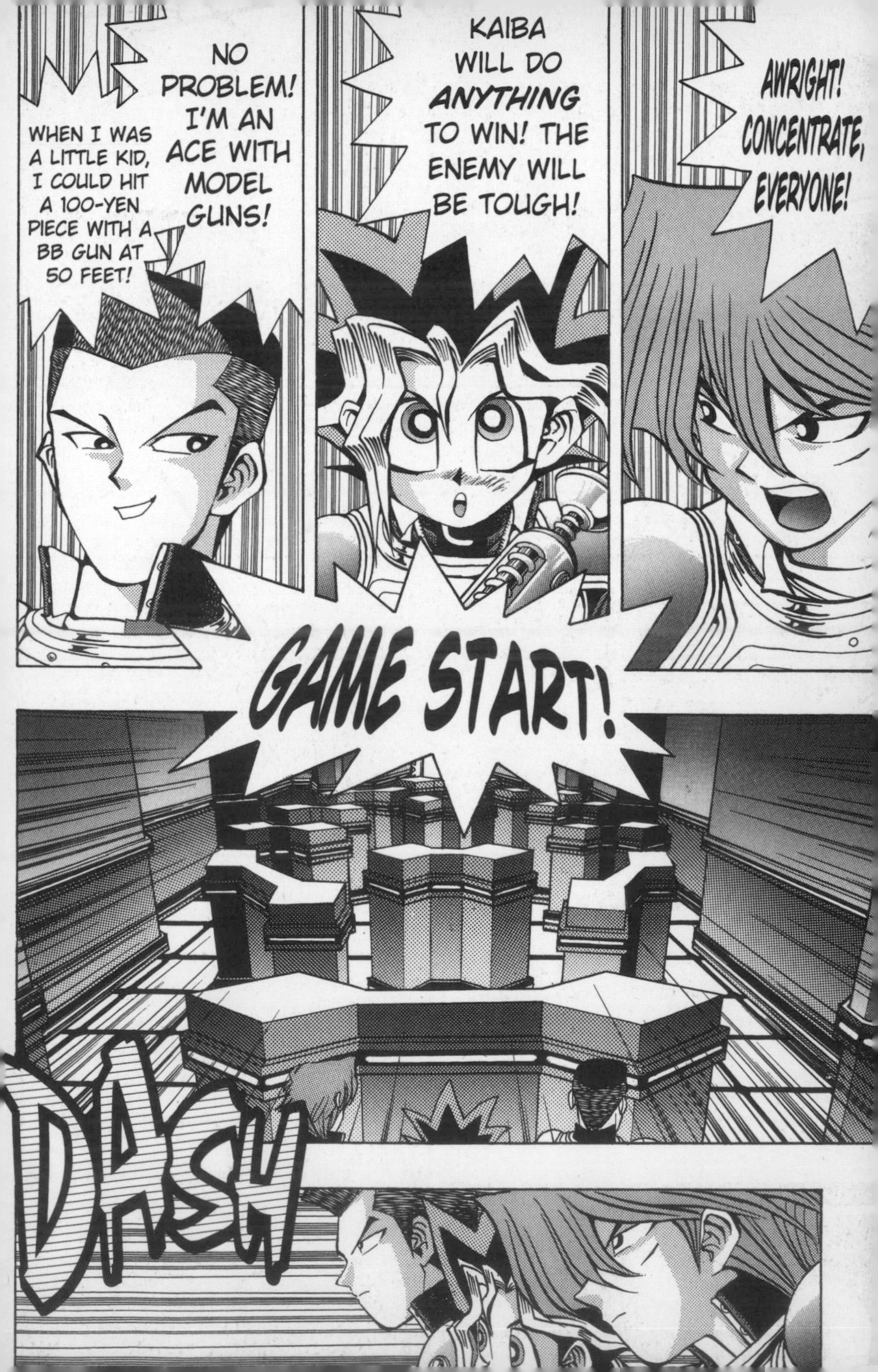
AWRIGHT! CONCENTRATE, EVERYONE!
KAIBA WILL DO *ANYTHING* TO WIN! THE ENEMY WILL BE TOUGH!
NO PROBLEM! I'M AN ACE WITH MODEL GUNS!
WHEN I WAS A LITTLE KID, I COULD HIT A 100-YEN PIECE WITH A BB GUN AT 50 FEET!
GAME START!
DASH

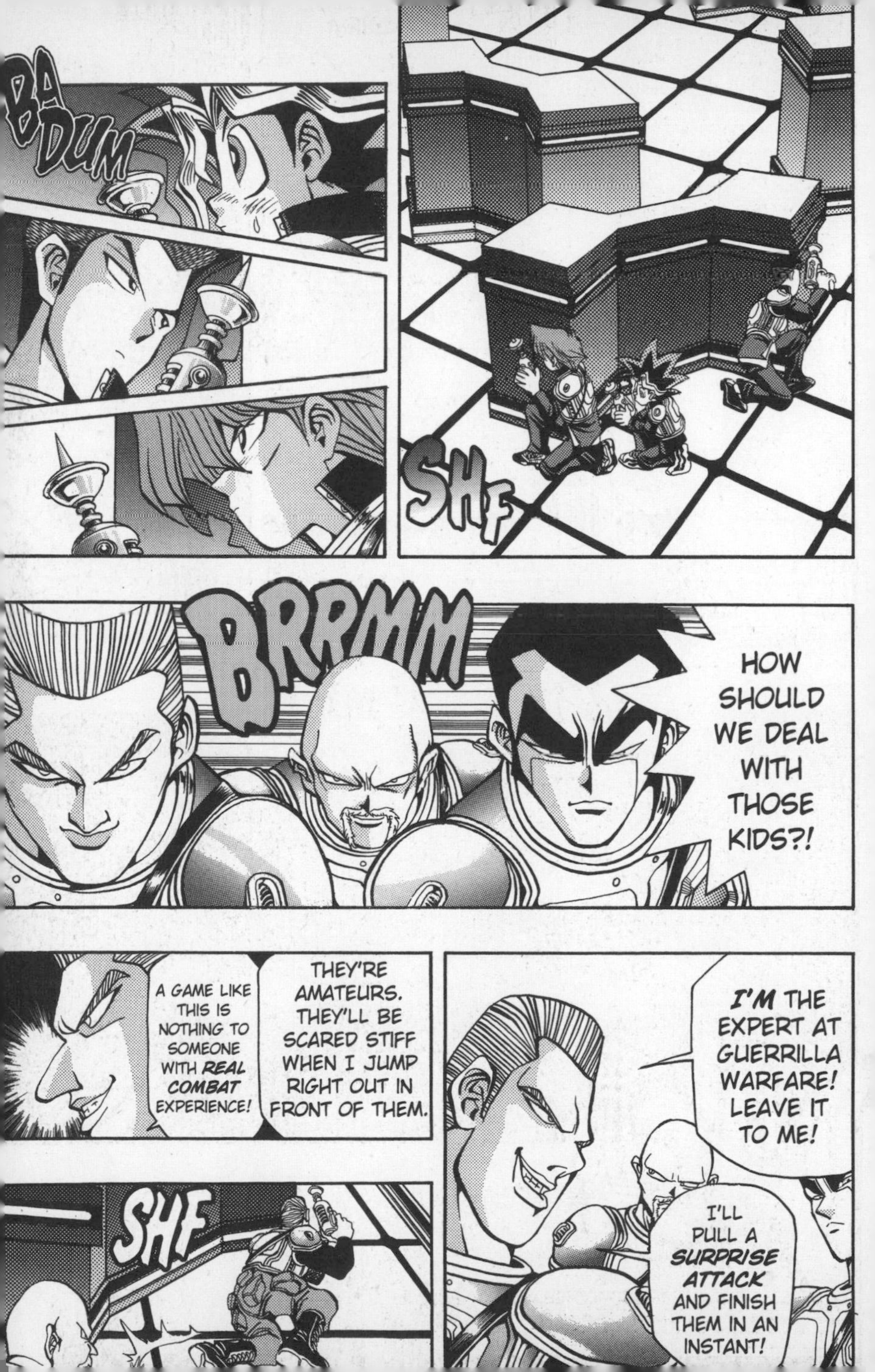
SHF
BA DUM
BRRMM
HOW SHOULD WE DEAL WITH THOSE KIDS?!
I'M THE EXPERT AT GUERRILLA WARFARE! LEAVE IT TO ME!
I'LL PULL A SURPRISE ATTACK AND FINISH THEM IN AN INSTANT!
THEY'RE AMATEURS. THEY'LL BE SCARED STIFF WHEN I JUMP RIGHT OUT IN FRONT OF THEM.
A GAME LIKE THIS IS NOTHING TO SOMEONE WITH REAL COMBAT EXPERIENCE!
SHF

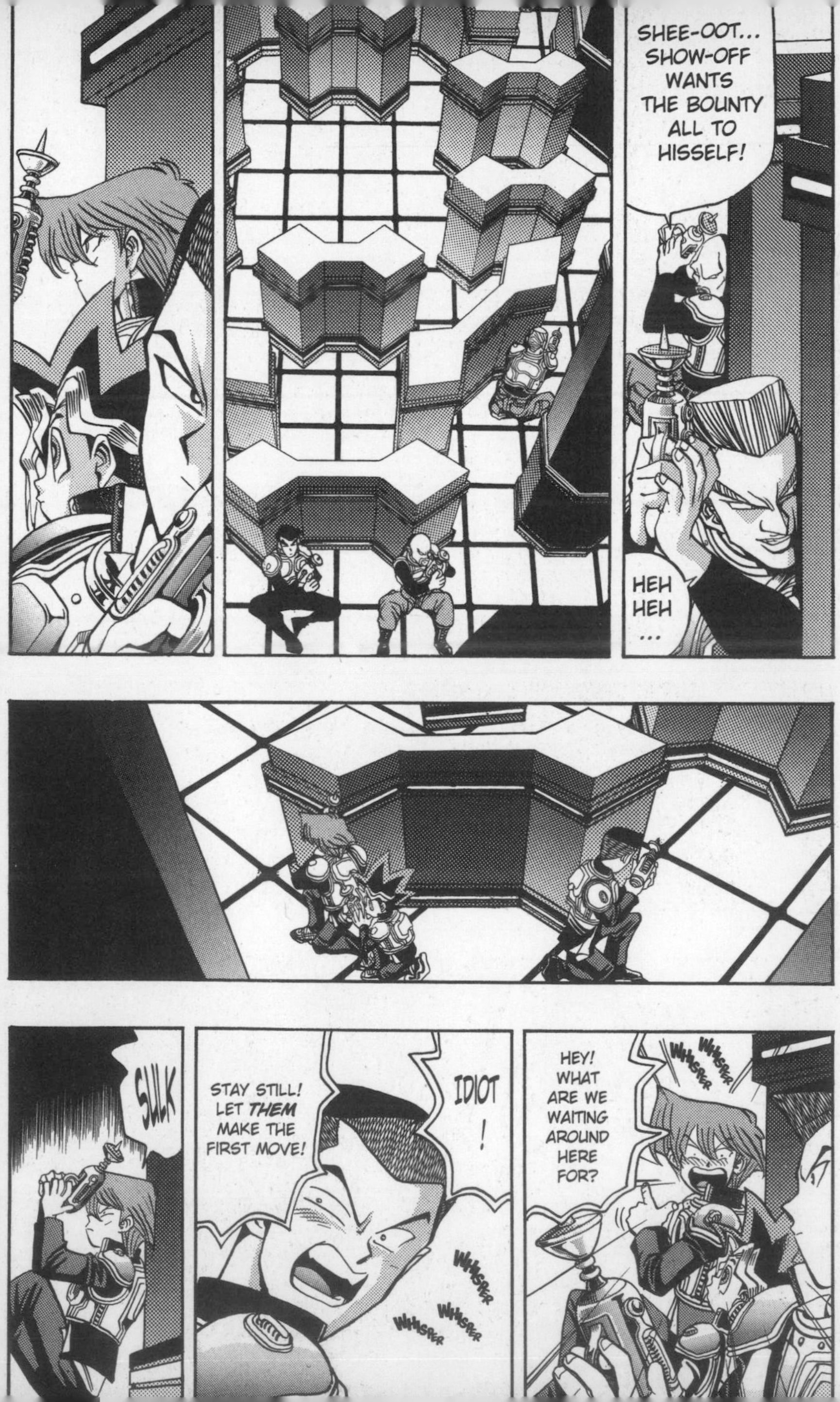
SHEE-OOT... SHOW-OFF WANTS THE BOUNTY ALL TO HISSELF!
HEH HEH ...
HEY! WHAT ARE WE WAITING AROUND HERE FOR?
WHISPER WHISPER
IDIOT !
STAY STILL! LET *THEM* MAKE THE FIRST MOVE!
WHISPER WHISPER WHISPER
SULK

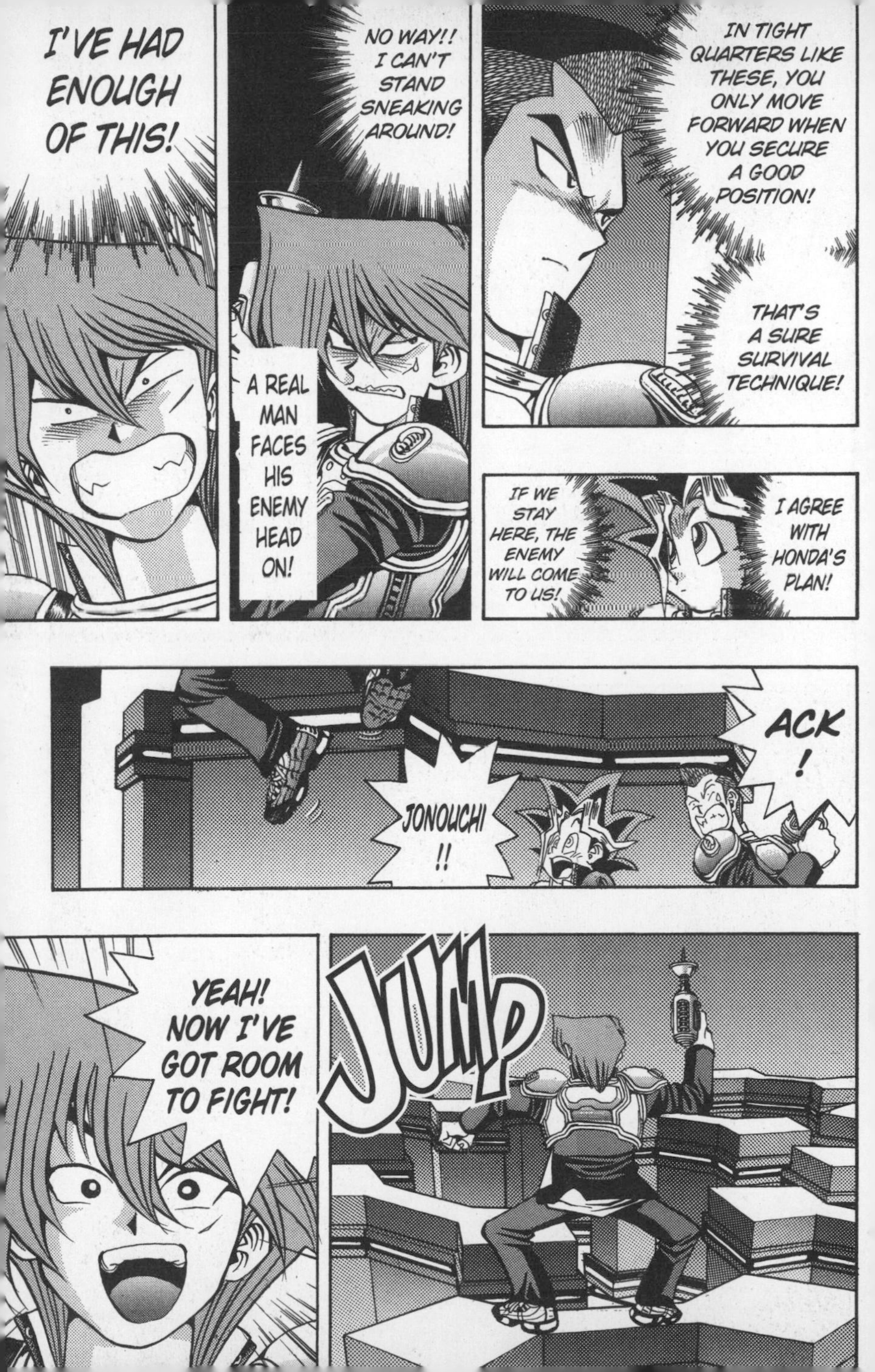
IN TIGHT QUARTERS LIKE THESE, YOU ONLY MOVE FORWARD WHEN YOU SECURE A GOOD POSITION!
THAT'S A SURE SURVIVAL TECHNIQUE!
I AGREE WITH HONDA'S PLAN!
IF WE STAY HERE, THE ENEMY WILL COME TO US!
NO WAY!! I CAN'T STAND SNEAKING AROUND!
A REAL MAN FACES HIS ENEMY HEAD ON!
I'VE HAD ENOUGH OF THIS!
ACK!
JONOUCHI!!
JUMP
YEAH! NOW I'VE GOT ROOM TO FIGHT!

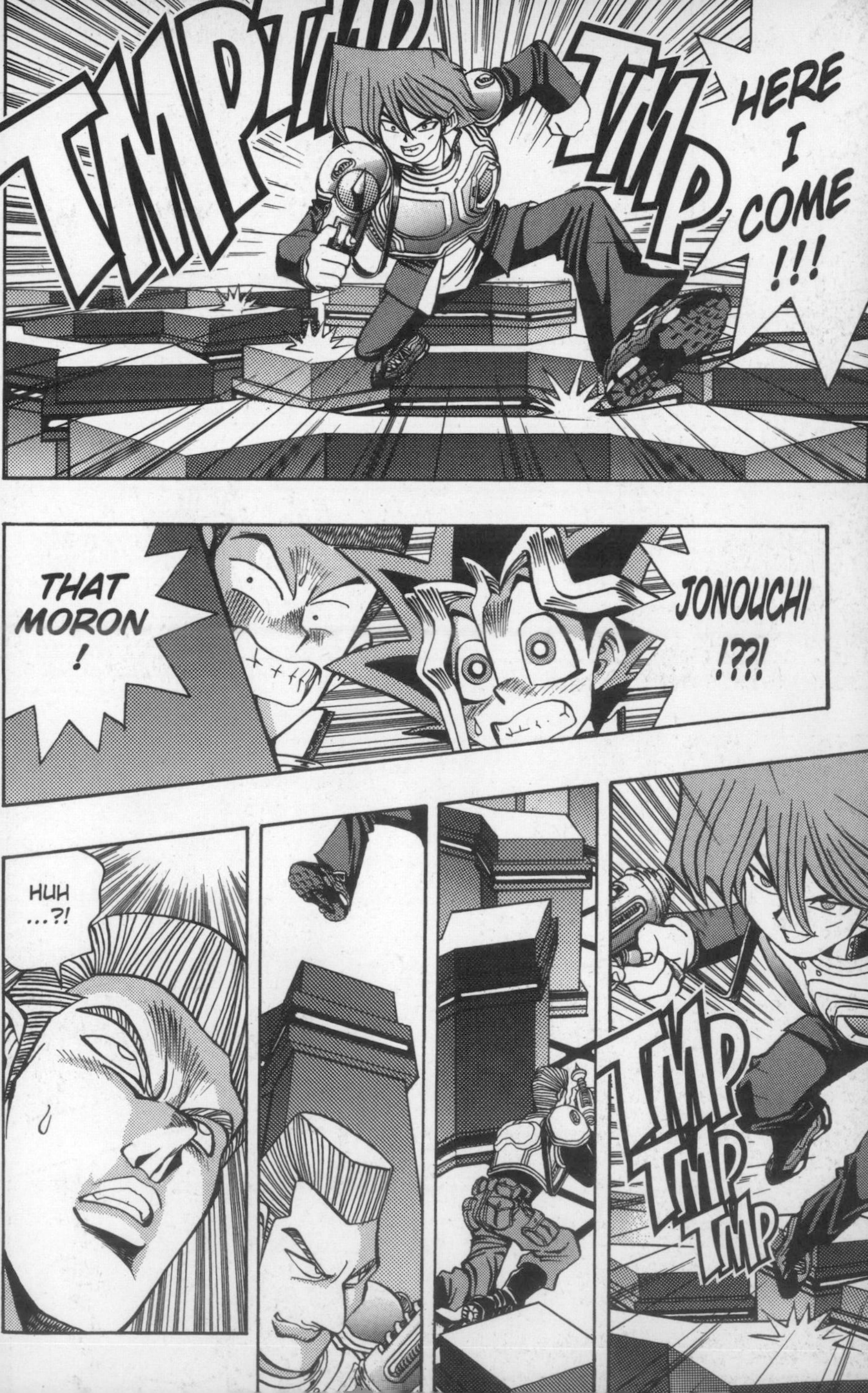
HERE I COME !!!
TMP
TMP TMP
JONOUCHI !??!
THAT MORON !
TMP TMP TMP TMP
HUH ...?!

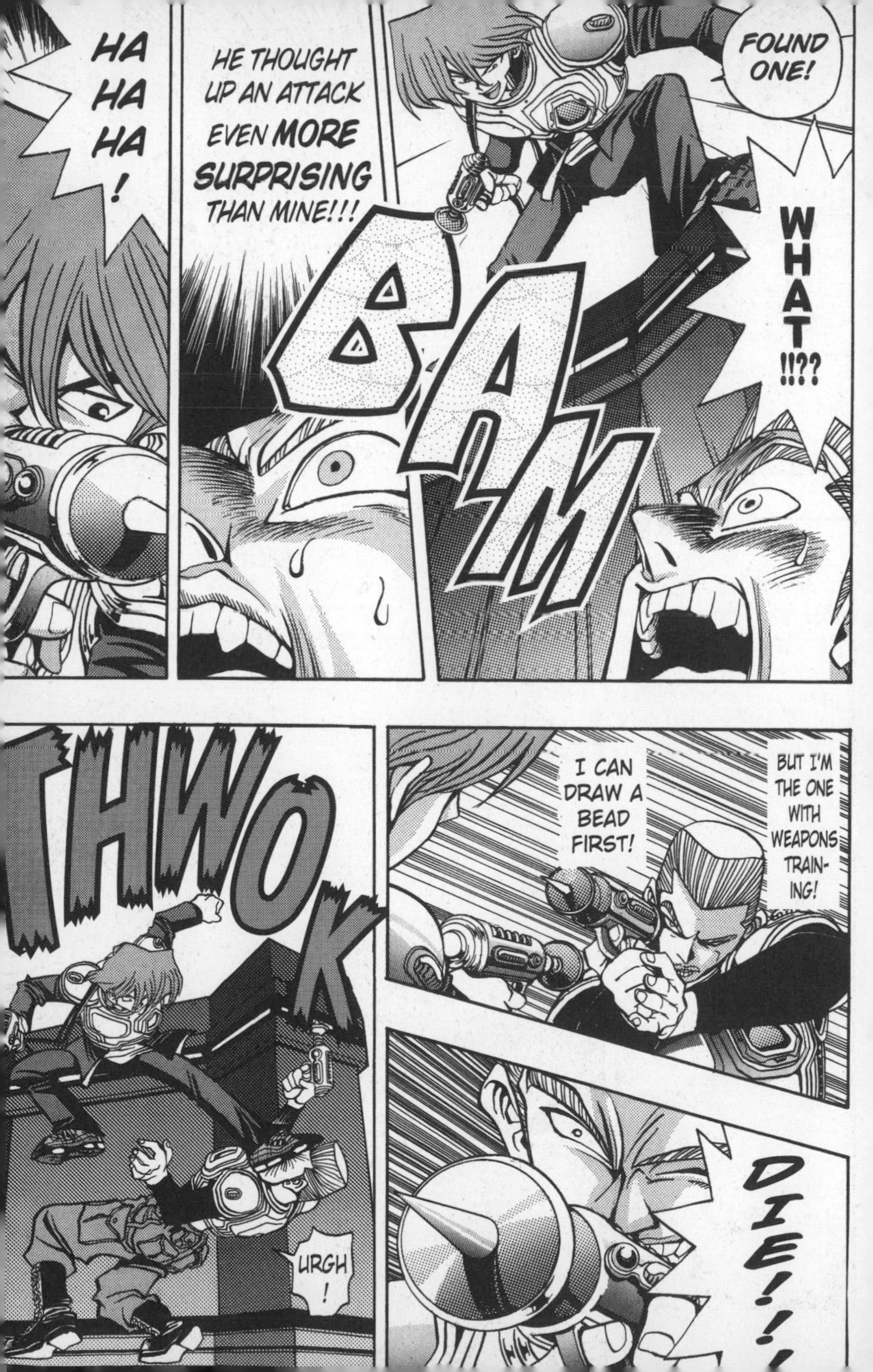
FOUND ONE!
WHAT!!??
BAM
HE THOUGHT UP AN ATTACK EVEN MORE SURPRISING THAN MINE!!!
HA HA HA!
BUT I'M THE ONE WITH WEAPONS TRAIN-ING!
I CAN DRAW A BEAD FIRST!
DIE!!!
THWOK
URGH!

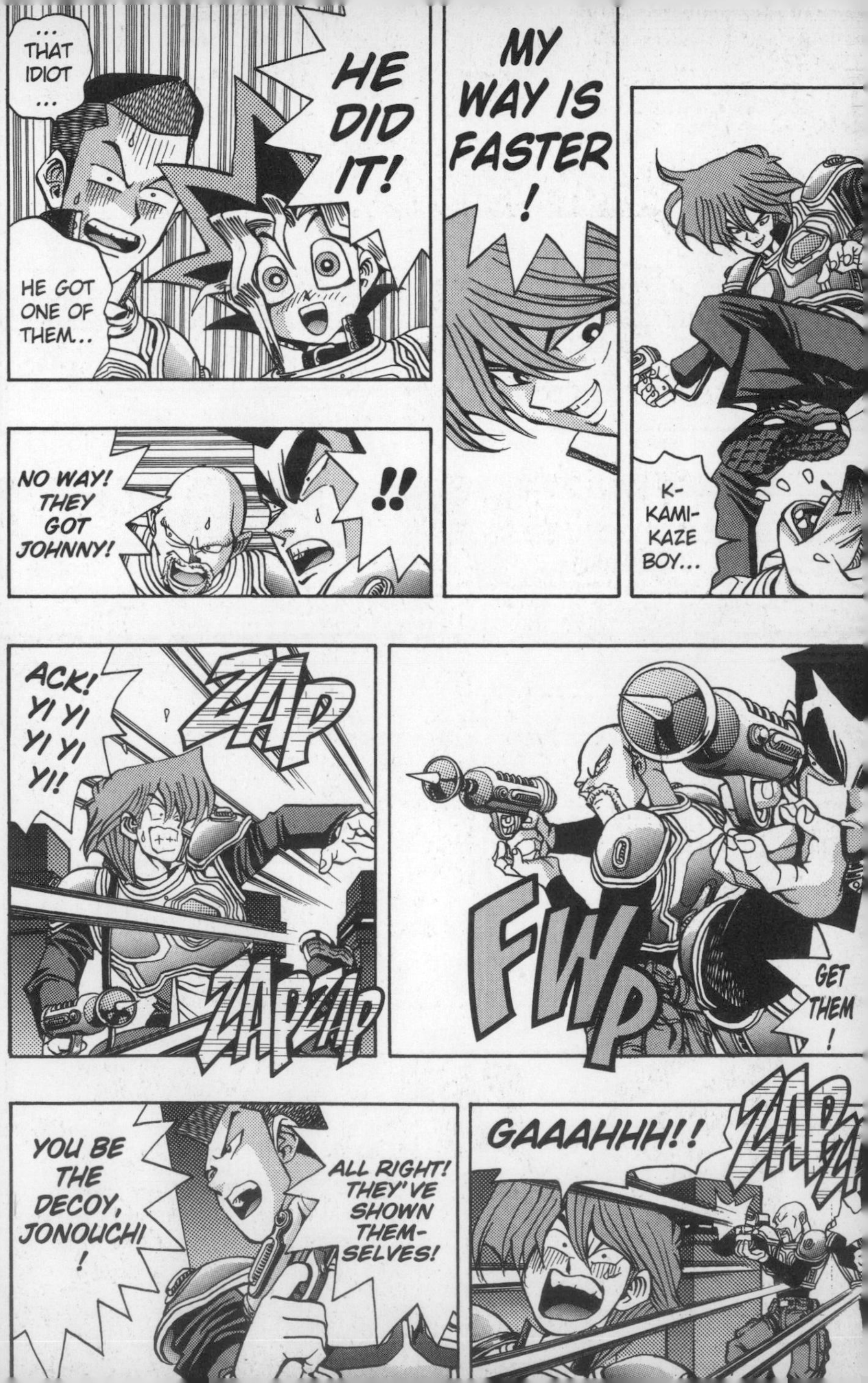
K-KAMIKAZE BOY...
MY WAY IS FASTER!
HE DID IT!
... THAT IDIOT ...
HE GOT ONE OF THEM...
!!
NO WAY! THEY GOT JOHNNY!
GET THEM!
FWP
ACK! YI YI YI YI YI!
ZAP
ZAPZAP
ZAP
GAAAHHH!!
ALL RIGHT! THEY'VE SHOWN THEMSELVES!
YOU BE THE DECOY, JONOUCHI!

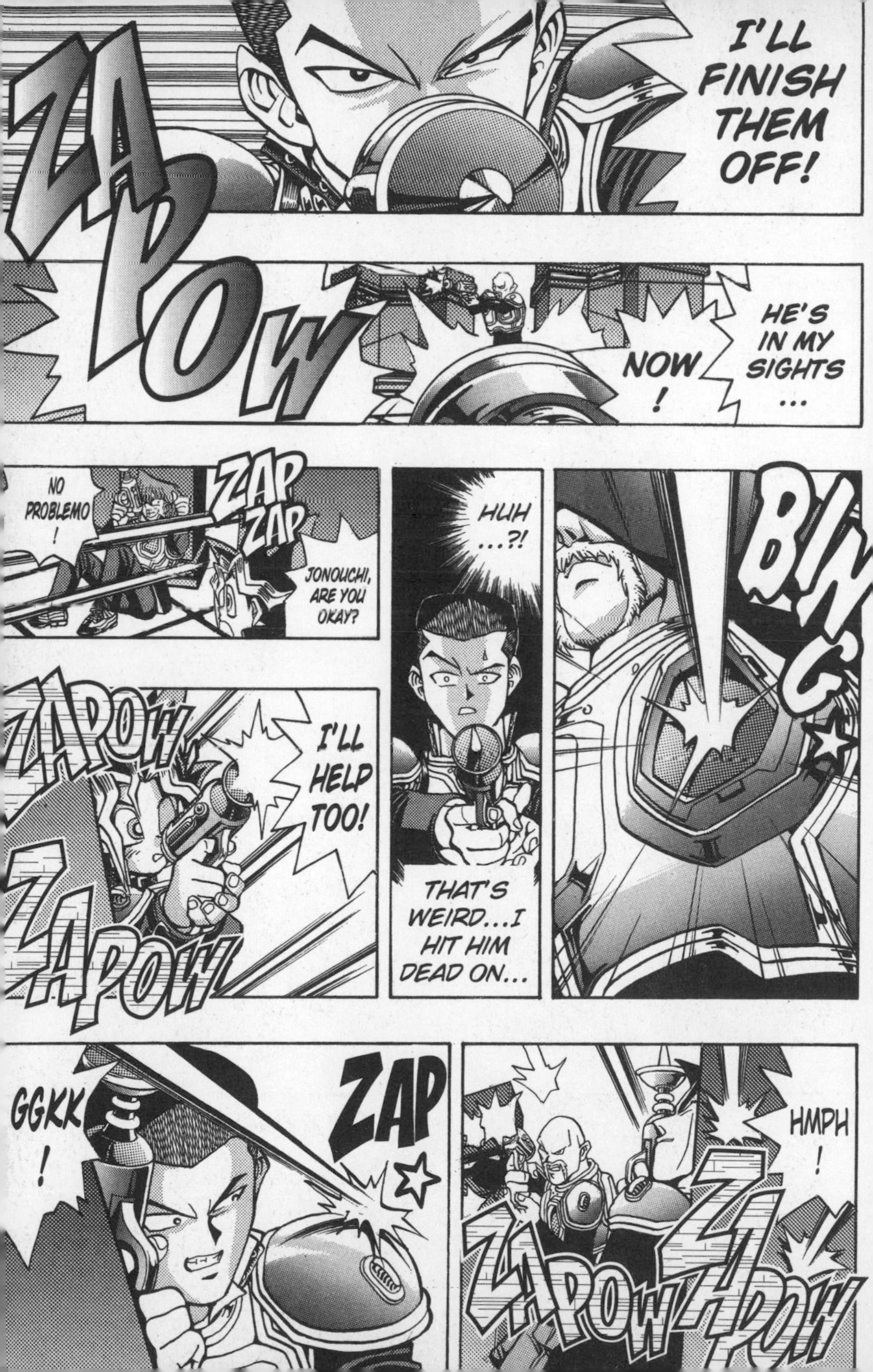
I'LL FINISH THEM OFF!
ZAPOW
HE'S IN MY SIGHTS ...
NOW !
BING
HUH ...?!
THAT'S WEIRD...I HIT HIM DEAD ON...
ZAP ZAP
NO PROBLEMO !
JONOUCHI, ARE YOU OKAY?
I'LL HELP TOO!
ZAPOW
ZAPOW
HMPH !
ZAPOW ZAPOW
ZAP
GGKK !

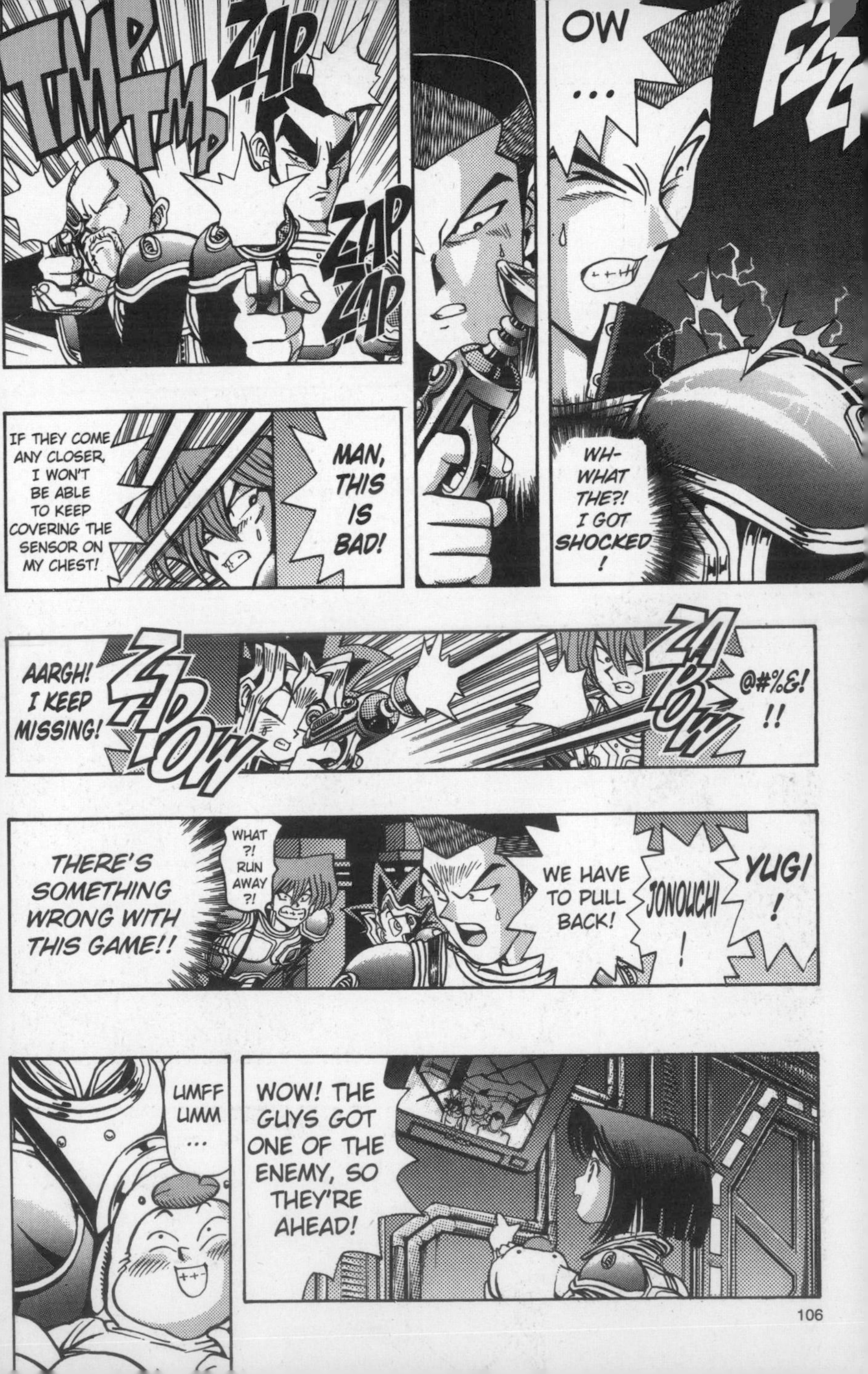
FZZ
OW
...
WH-WHAT THE?! I GOT SHOCKED!
TMP TMP
ZAP
ZAP ZAP
MAN, THIS IS BAD!
IF THEY COME ANY CLOSER, I WON'T BE ABLE TO KEEP COVERING THE SENSOR ON MY CHEST!
@#%&!!!
ZAPOW
ZAPOW
AARGH! I KEEP MISSING!
YUGI!
JONOUCHI!
WE HAVE TO PULL BACK!
WHAT?! RUN AWAY?!
THERE'S SOMETHING WRONG WITH THIS GAME!!
WOW! THE GUYS GOT ONE OF THE ENEMY, SO THEY'RE AHEAD!
UMFF UMM ...

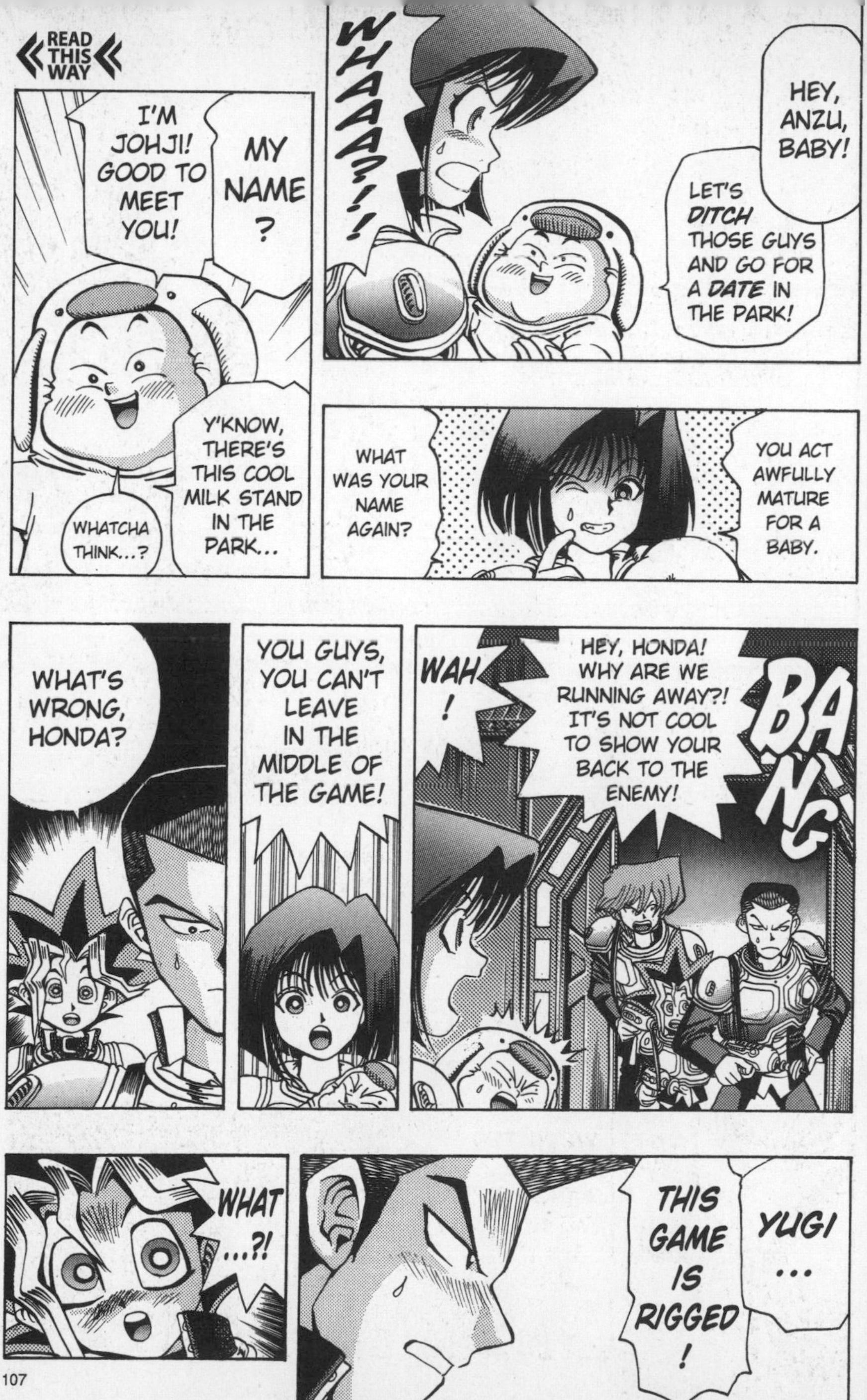
READ THIS WAY
HEY, ANZU, BABY!
LET'S *DITCH* THOSE GUYS AND GO FOR A *DATE* IN THE PARK!
WHAAAA?!!
MY NAME ?
I'M JOHJI! GOOD TO MEET YOU!
YOU ACT AWFULLY MATURE FOR A BABY.
WHAT WAS YOUR NAME AGAIN?
Y'KNOW, THERE'S THIS COOL MILK STAND IN THE PARK...
WHATCHA THINK...?
BANG
HEY, HONDA! WHY ARE WE RUNNING AWAY?! IT'S NOT COOL TO SHOW YOUR BACK TO THE ENEMY!
WAH!
YOU GUYS, YOU CAN'T LEAVE IN THE MIDDLE OF THE GAME!
WHAT'S WRONG, HONDA?
YUGI...
THIS GAME IS RIGGED!
WHAT...?!

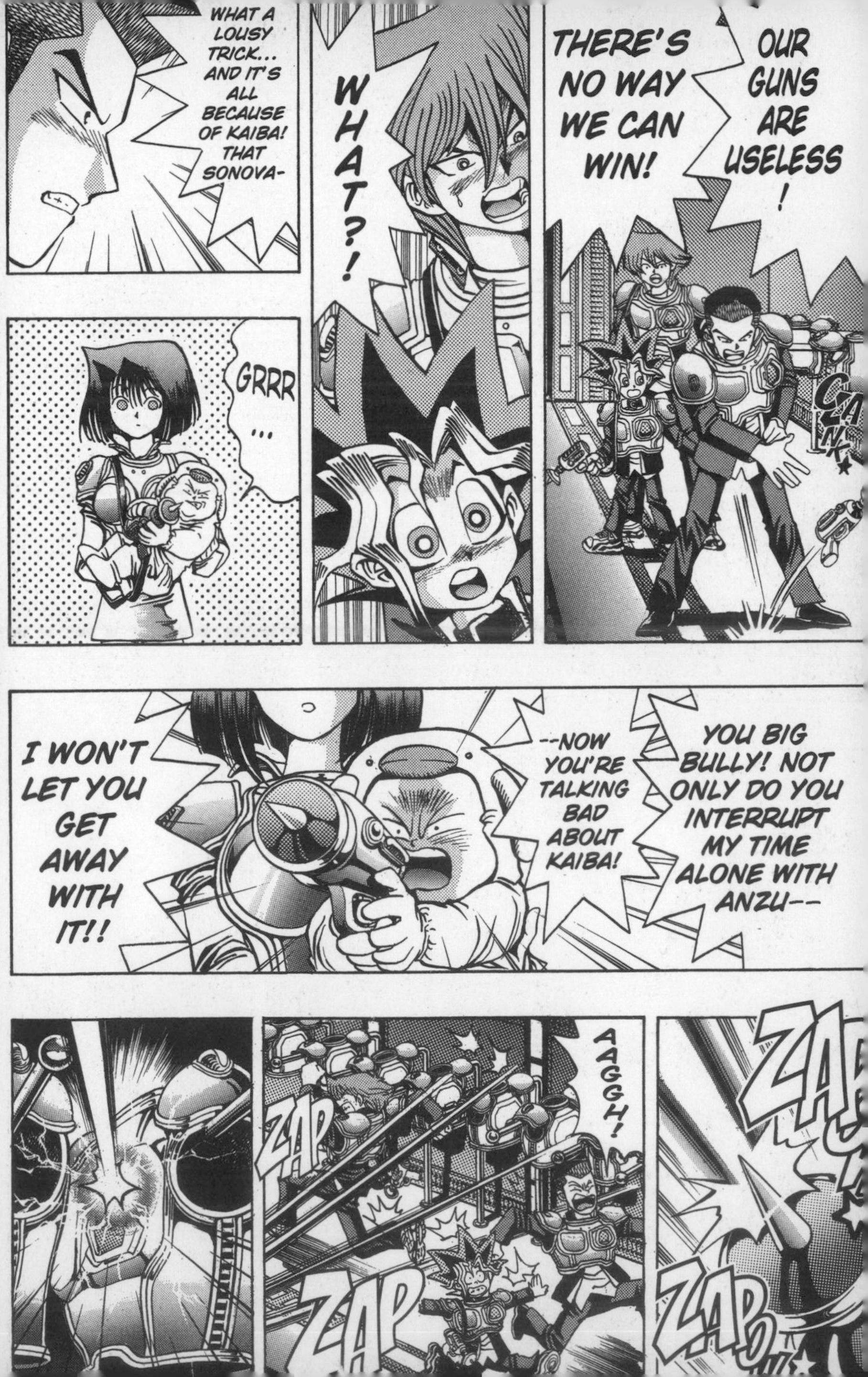
THERE'S NO WAY WE CAN WIN!
OUR GUNS ARE USELESS!
WHAT?!
WHAT A LOUSY TRICK... AND IT'S ALL BECAUSE OF KAIBA! THAT SONOVA-
GRRR...
YOU BIG BULLY! NOT ONLY DO YOU INTERRUPT MY TIME ALONE WITH ANZU--
--NOW YOU'RE TALKING BAD ABOUT KAIBA!
I WON'T LET YOU GET AWAY WITH IT!!
ZAP
AAGGH!
ZAP
ZAP

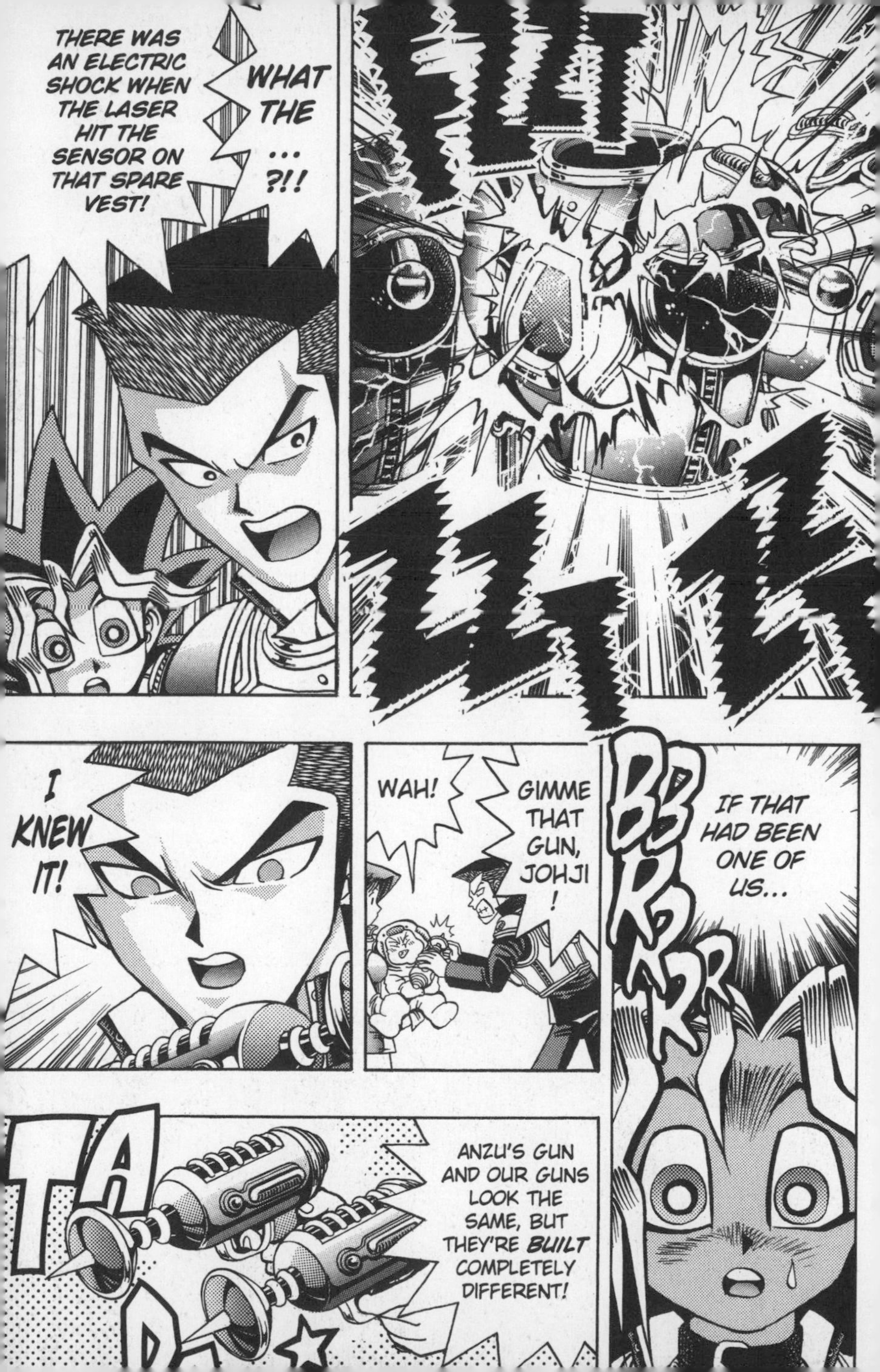
WHAT THE ...?!!
THERE WAS AN ELECTRIC SHOCK WHEN THE LASER HIT THE SENSOR ON THAT SPARE VEST!
BBRRRR
IF THAT HAD BEEN ONE OF US...
GIMME THAT GUN, JOHJI!
WAH!
I KNEW IT!
ANZU'S GUN AND OUR GUNS LOOK THE SAME, BUT THEY'RE *BUILT* COMPLETELY DIFFERENT!
TA

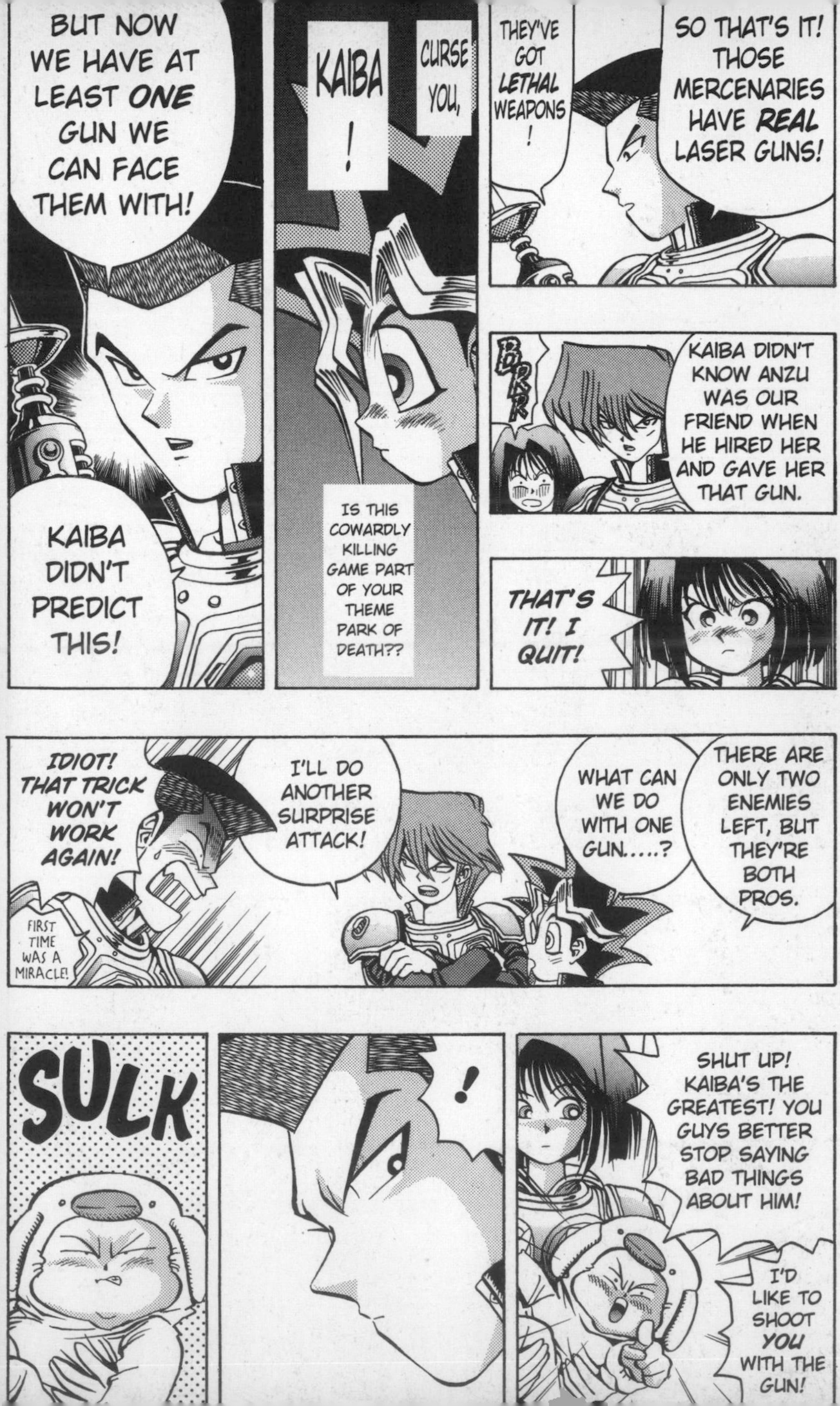
SO THAT'S IT! THOSE MERCENARIES HAVE *REAL* LASER GUNS!
THEY'VE GOT *LETHAL* WEAPONS!
KAIBA DIDN'T KNOW ANZU WAS OUR FRIEND WHEN HE HIRED HER AND GAVE HER THAT GUN.
BRRR
THAT'S IT! I QUIT!
CURSE YOU,
KAIBA!
IS THIS COWARDLY KILLING GAME PART OF YOUR THEME PARK OF DEATH??
BUT NOW WE HAVE AT LEAST *ONE* GUN WE CAN FACE THEM WITH!
KAIBA DIDN'T PREDICT THIS!
THERE ARE ONLY TWO ENEMIES LEFT, BUT THEY'RE BOTH PROS.
WHAT CAN WE DO WITH ONE GUN.....?
I'LL DO ANOTHER SURPRISE ATTACK!
IDIOT! THAT TRICK WON'T WORK AGAIN!
FIRST TIME WAS A MIRACLE!
SHUT UP! KAIBA'S THE GREATEST! YOU GUYS BETTER STOP SAYING BAD THINGS ABOUT HIM!
I'D LIKE TO SHOOT *YOU* WITH THE GUN!
!
SULK

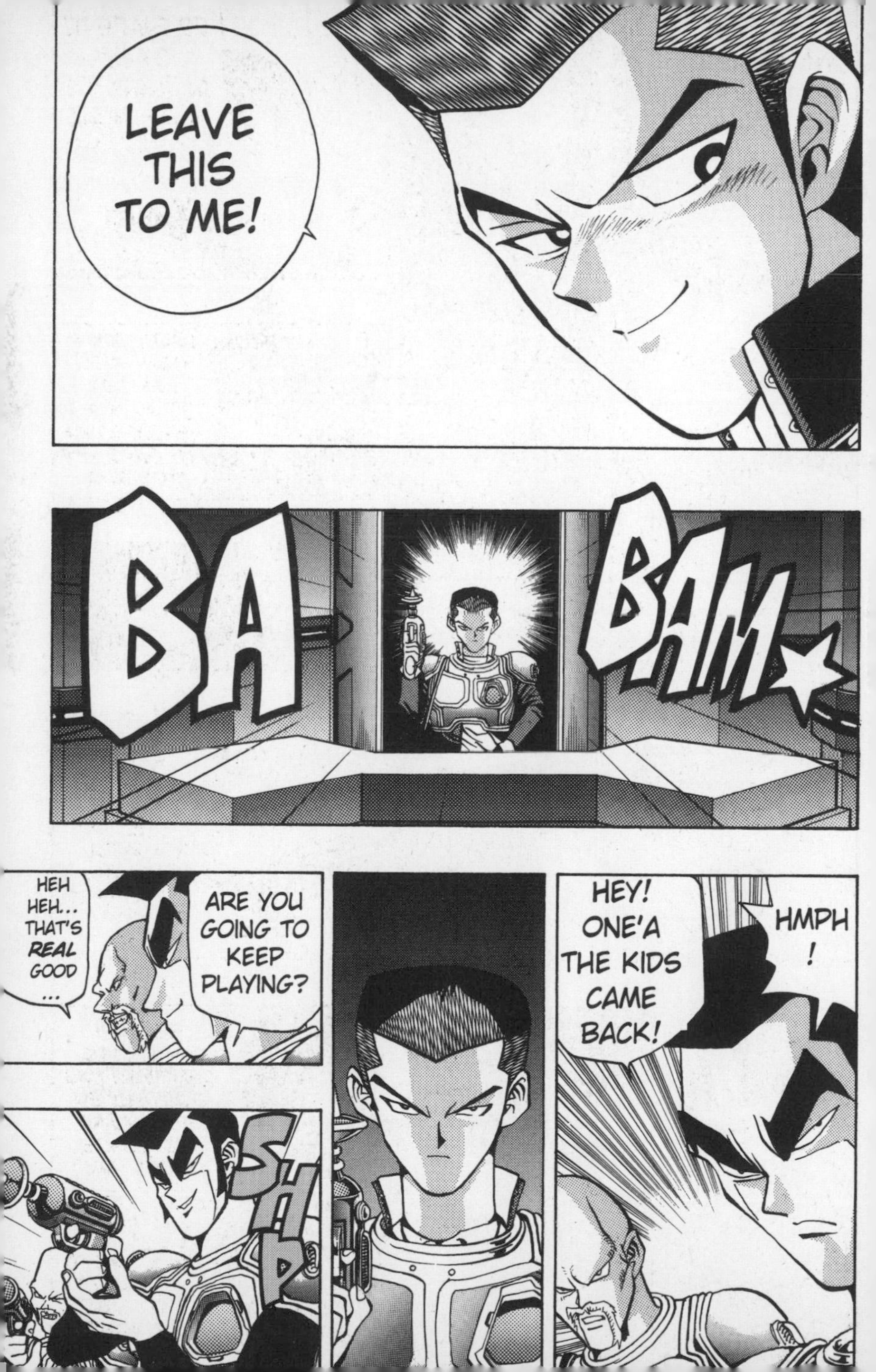
LEAVE THIS TO ME!
BA BAM
HMPH!
HEY! ONE'A THE KIDS CAME BACK!
ARE YOU GOING TO KEEP PLAYING?
HEH HEH... THAT'S *REAL* GOOD...
SHP

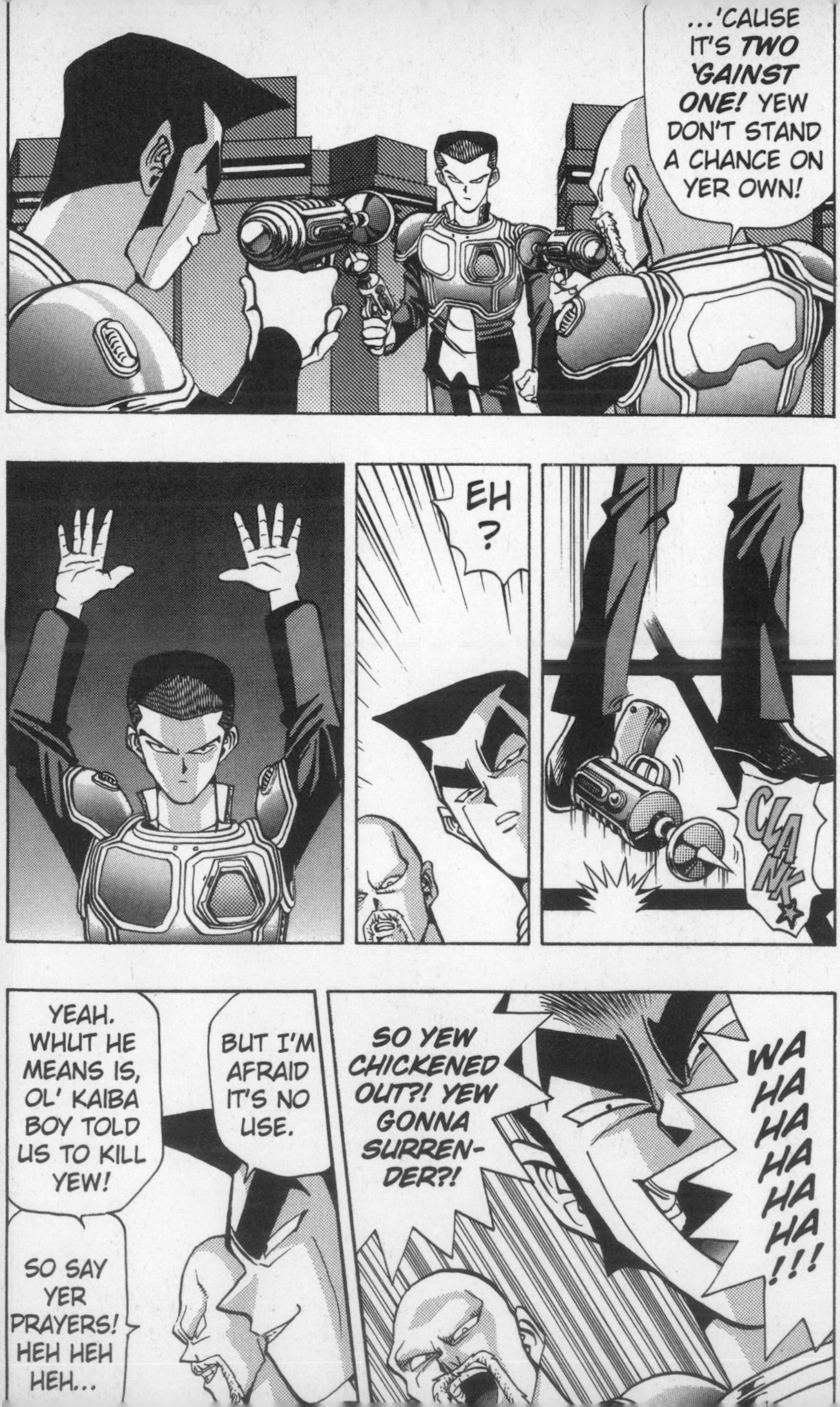
...'CAUSE IT'S TWO 'GAINST ONE! YEW DON'T STAND A CHANCE ON YER OWN!
CLANK
EH ?
WA HA HA HA HA HA HA!!!
SO YEW CHICKENED OUT?! YEW GONNA SURREN-DER?!
BUT I'M AFRAID IT'S NO USE.
YEAH. WHUT HE MEANS IS, OL' KAIBA BOY TOLD US TO KILL YEW!
SO SAY YER PRAYERS! HEH HEH HEH...

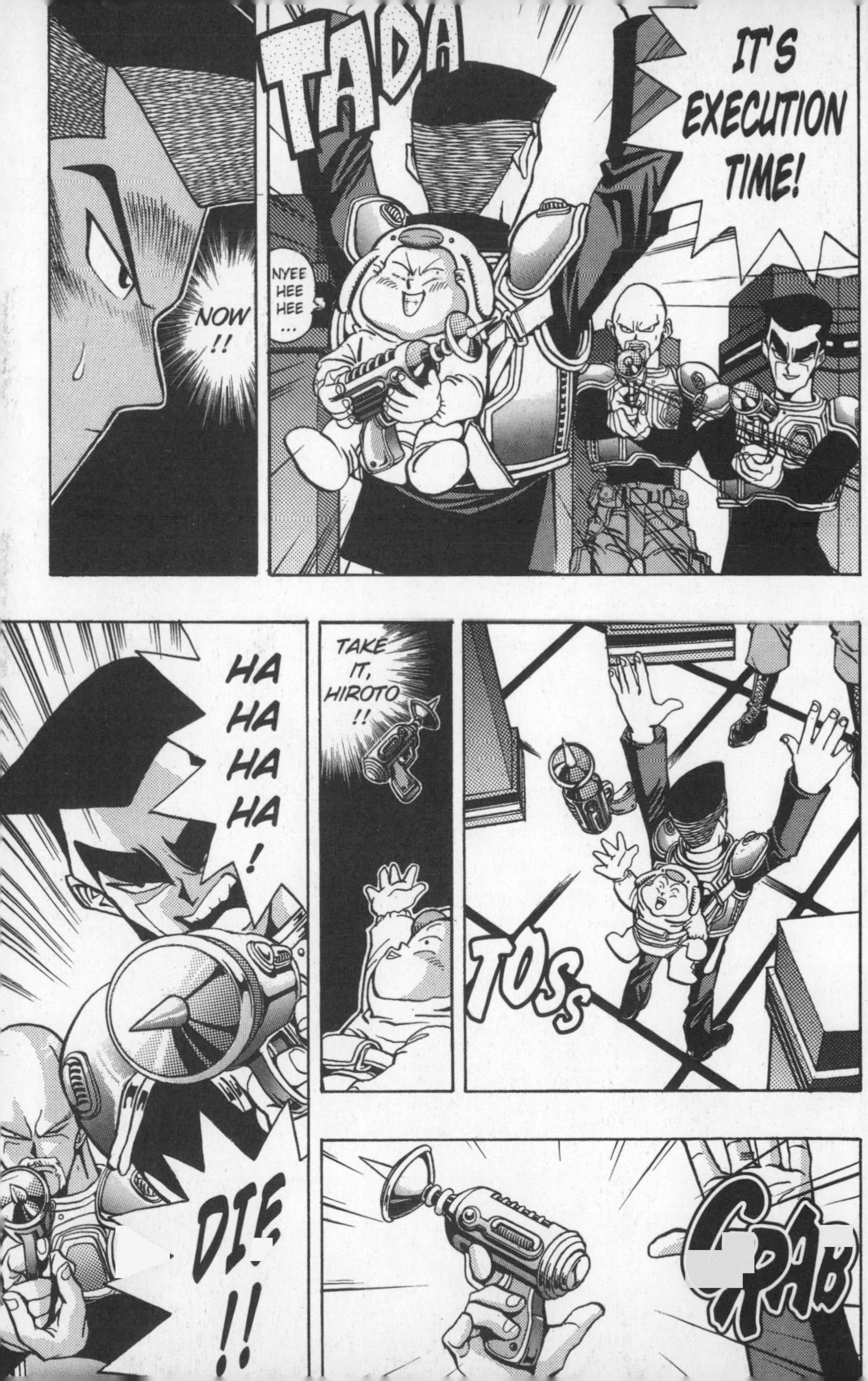
TADA
IT'S EXECUTION TIME!
NYEE HEE HEE ...
NOW !!
TOSS
TAKE IT, HIROTO !!
GRAB
HA HA HA HA !
DIE !!

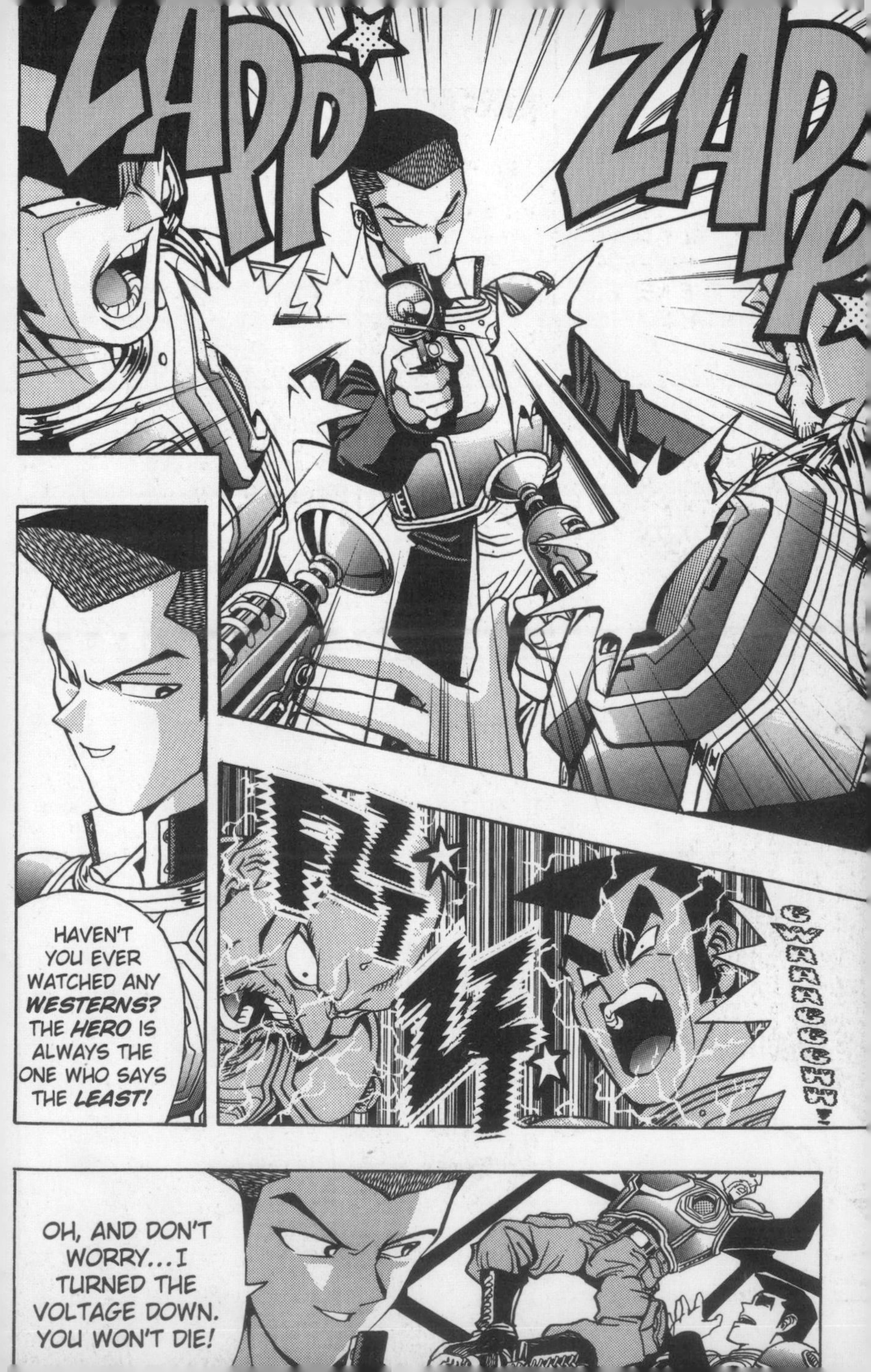
ZAPP
ZAPP
FZZT
GWAAAGGHH!
HAVEN'T YOU EVER WATCHED ANY ***WESTERNS?*** THE ***HERO*** IS ALWAYS THE ONE WHO SAYS THE ***LEAST!***
OH, AND DON'T WORRY...I TURNED THE VOLTAGE DOWN. YOU WON'T DIE!

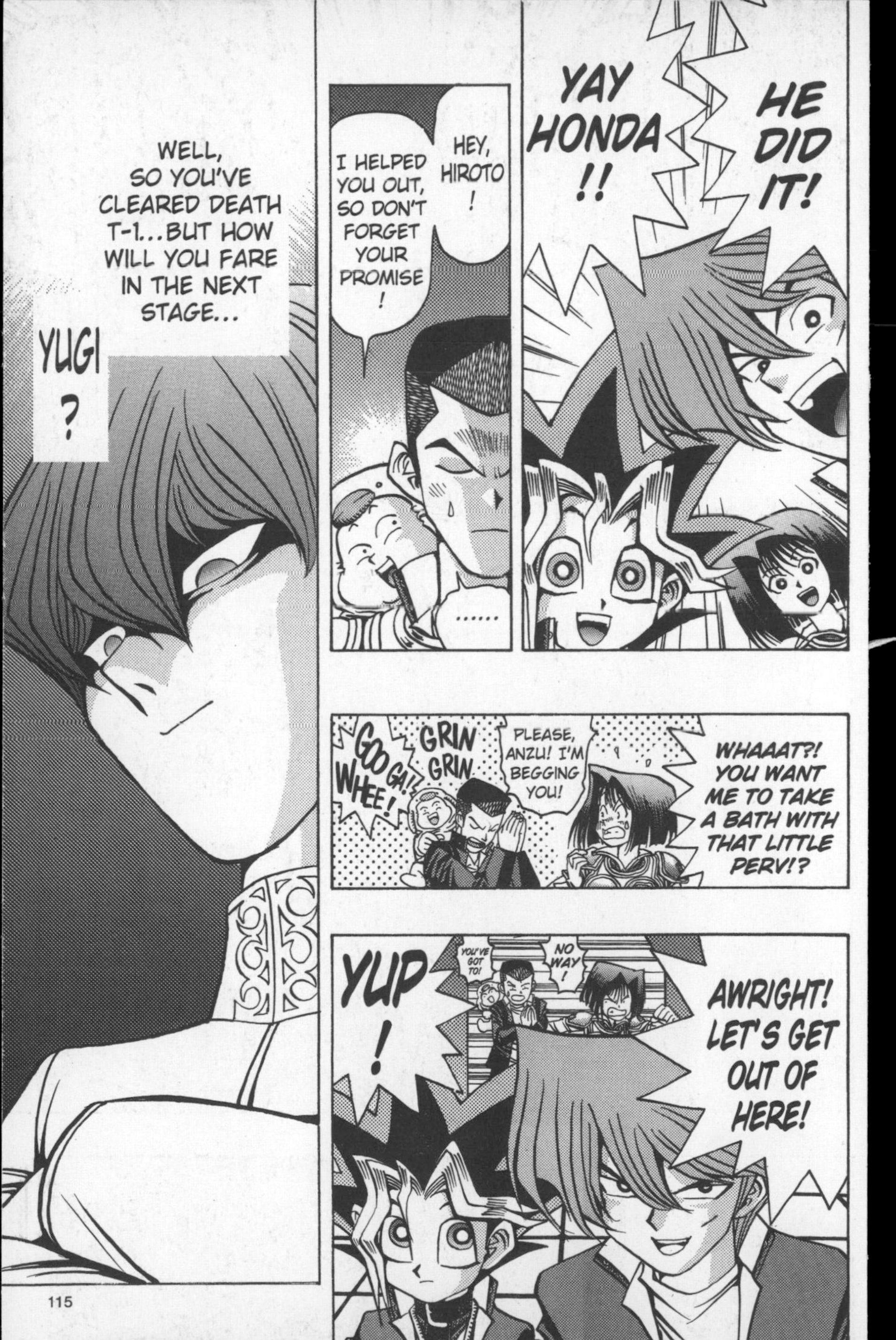
HE DID IT!
YAY HONDA !!
HEY, HIROTO !
I HELPED YOU OUT, SO DON'T FORGET YOUR PROMISE !
......
WHAAAT?! YOU WANT ME TO TAKE A BATH WITH THAT LITTLE PERV!?
PLEASE, ANZU! I'M BEGGING YOU!
GRIN GRIN
GOO GA! WHEE!
AWRIGHT! LET'S GET OUT OF HERE!
NO WAY !
YOU'VE GOT TO!
YUP !
WELL, SO YOU'VE CLEARED DEATH T-1...BUT HOW WILL YOU FARE IN THE NEXT STAGE...
YUGI ?

Duel 30:
Don't Make a Sound!

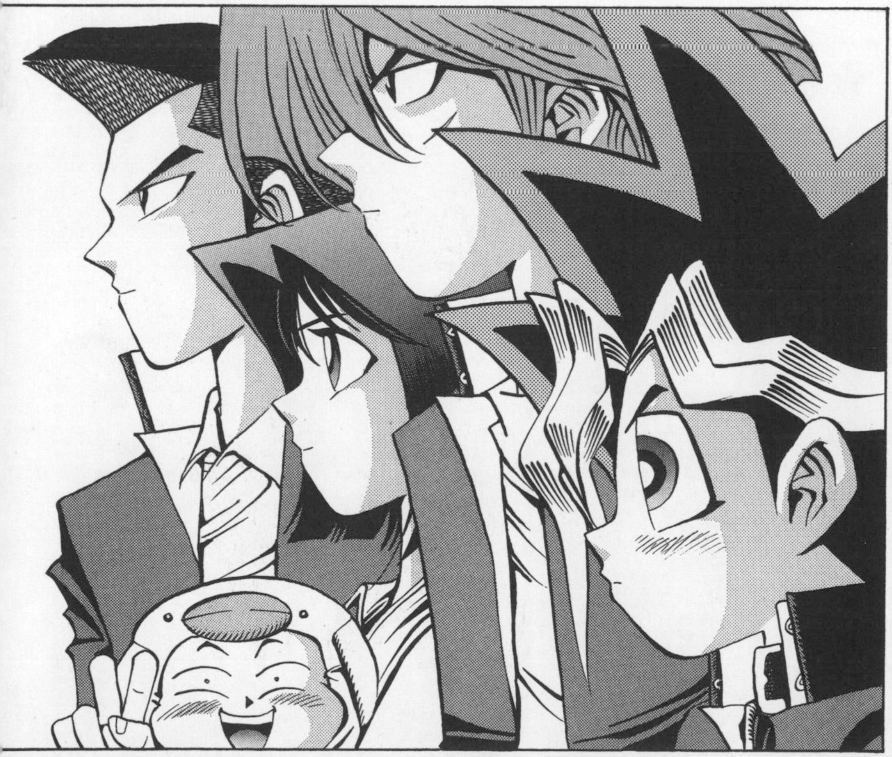

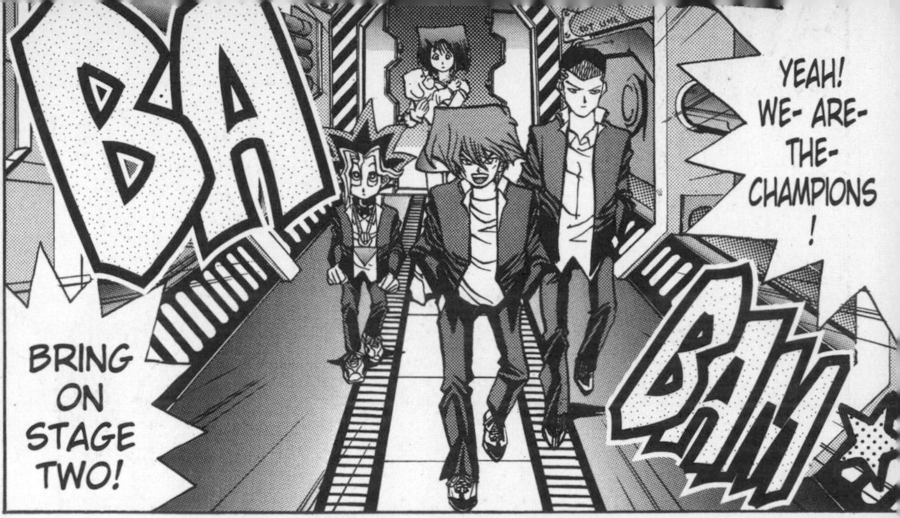
YEAH! WE- ARE- THE- CHAMPIONS !
BA
BAM
BRING ON STAGE TWO!

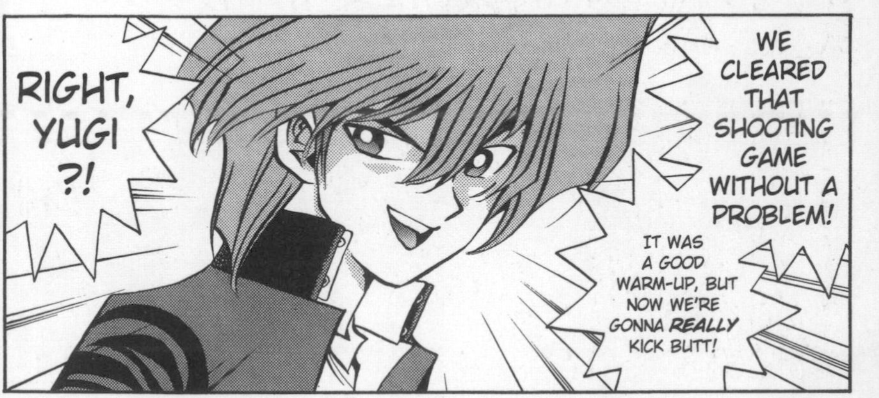
WE CLEARED THAT SHOOTING GAME WITHOUT A PROBLEM!
IT WAS A GOOD WARM-UP, BUT NOW WE'RE GONNA ***REALLY*** KICK BUTT!
RIGHT, YUGI ?!

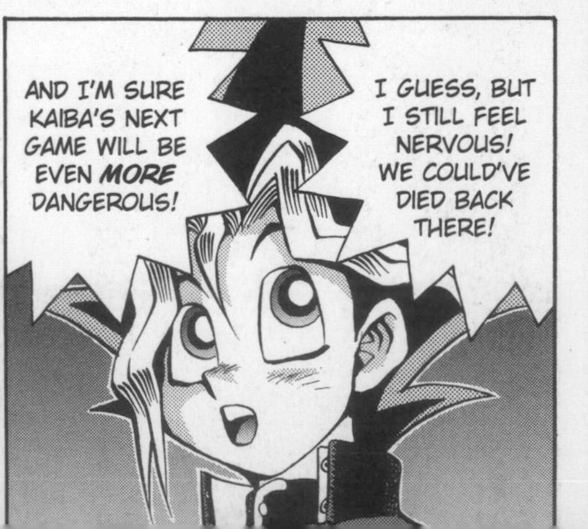
I GUESS, BUT I STILL FEEL NERVOUS! WE COULD'VE DIED BACK THERE!
AND I'M SURE KAIBA'S NEXT GAME WILL BE EVEN ***MORE*** DANGEROUS!

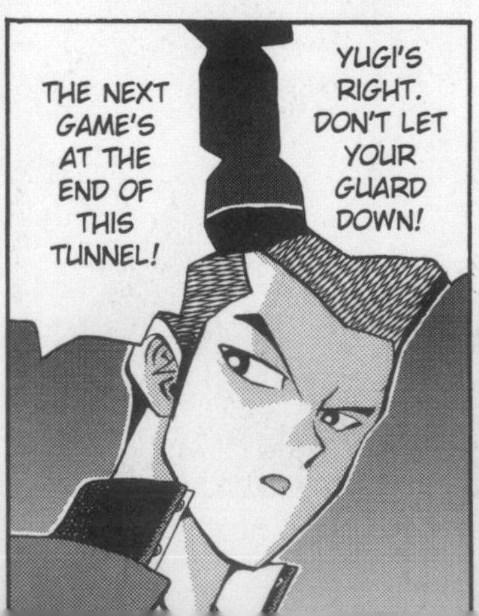
YUGI'S RIGHT. DON'T LET YOUR GUARD DOWN!
THE NEXT GAME'S AT THE END OF THIS TUNNEL!

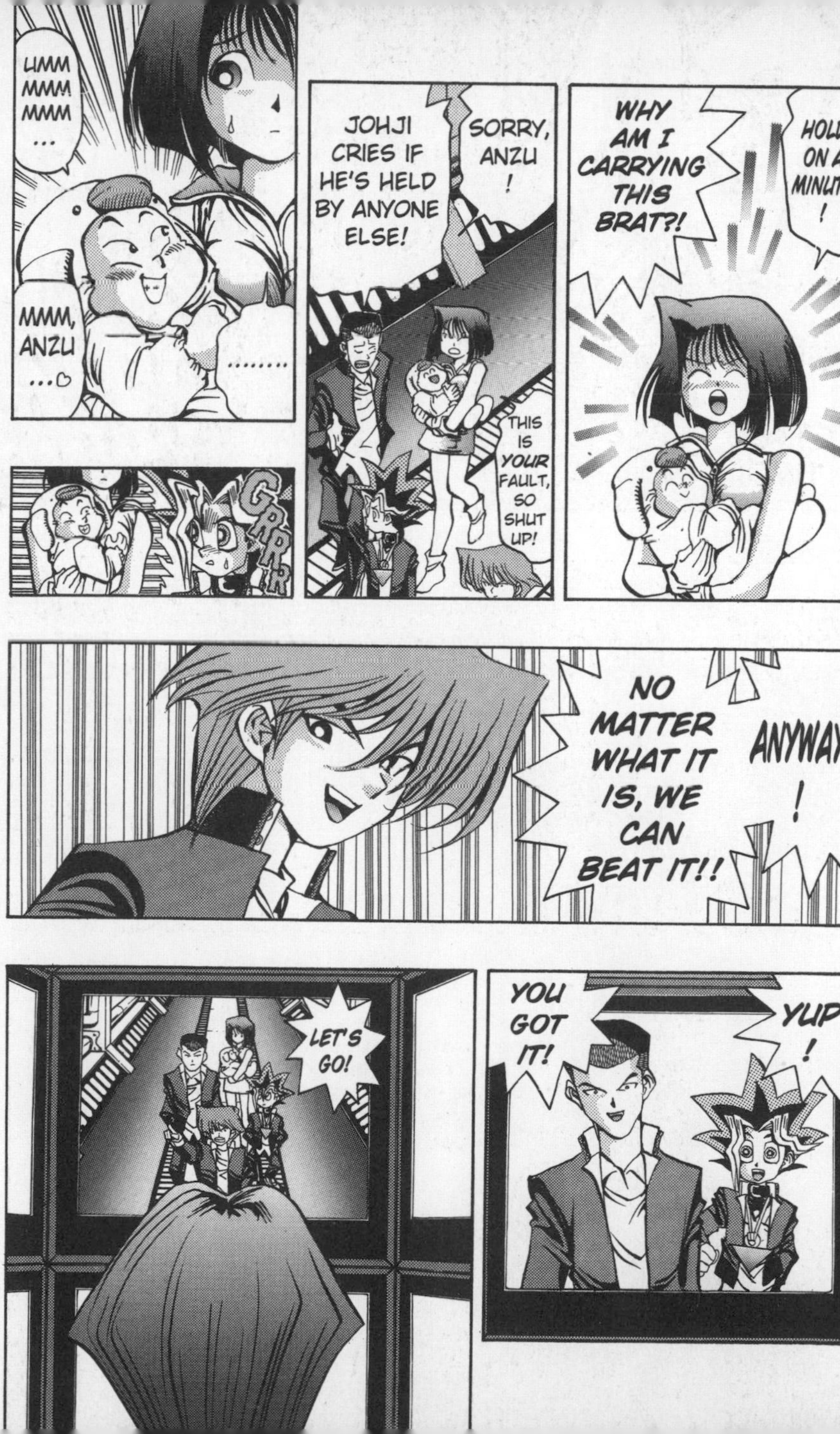
HOLD ON A MINUTE!
WHY AM I CARRYING THIS BRAT?!
SORRY, ANZU!
JOHJI CRIES IF HE'S HELD BY ANYONE ELSE!
THIS IS YOUR FAULT, SO SHUT UP!
UMMMMMMMMM...
MMM, ANZU...♡
....
GRRR
ANYWAY!
NO MATTER WHAT IT IS, WE CAN BEAT IT!!
YUP!
YOU GOT IT!
LET'S GO!

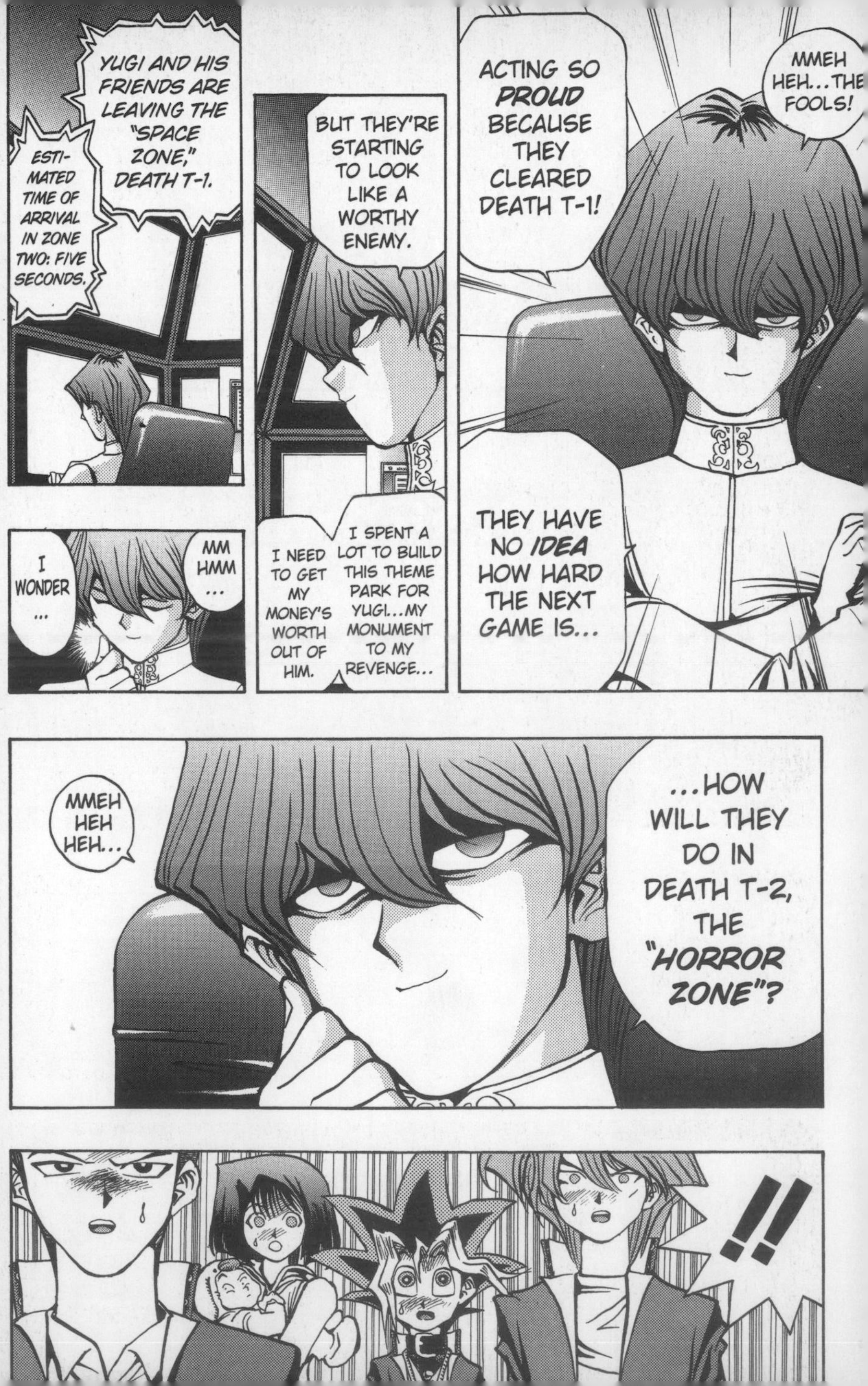
MMEH HEH...THE FOOLS!
ACTING SO *PROUD* BECAUSE THEY CLEARED DEATH T-1!
THEY HAVE NO *IDEA* HOW HARD THE NEXT GAME IS...
BUT THEY'RE STARTING TO LOOK LIKE A WORTHY ENEMY.
I SPENT A LOT TO BUILD THIS THEME PARK FOR YUGI...MY MONUMENT TO MY REVENGE...
I NEED TO GET MY MONEY'S WORTH OUT OF HIM.
YUGI AND HIS FRIENDS ARE LEAVING THE "SPACE ZONE," DEATH T-1.
ESTIMATED TIME OF ARRIVAL IN ZONE TWO: FIVE SECONDS.
MM HMM ...
I WONDER ...
...HOW WILL THEY DO IN DEATH T-2, THE "*HORROR ZONE*"?
MMEH HEH HEH...
!!

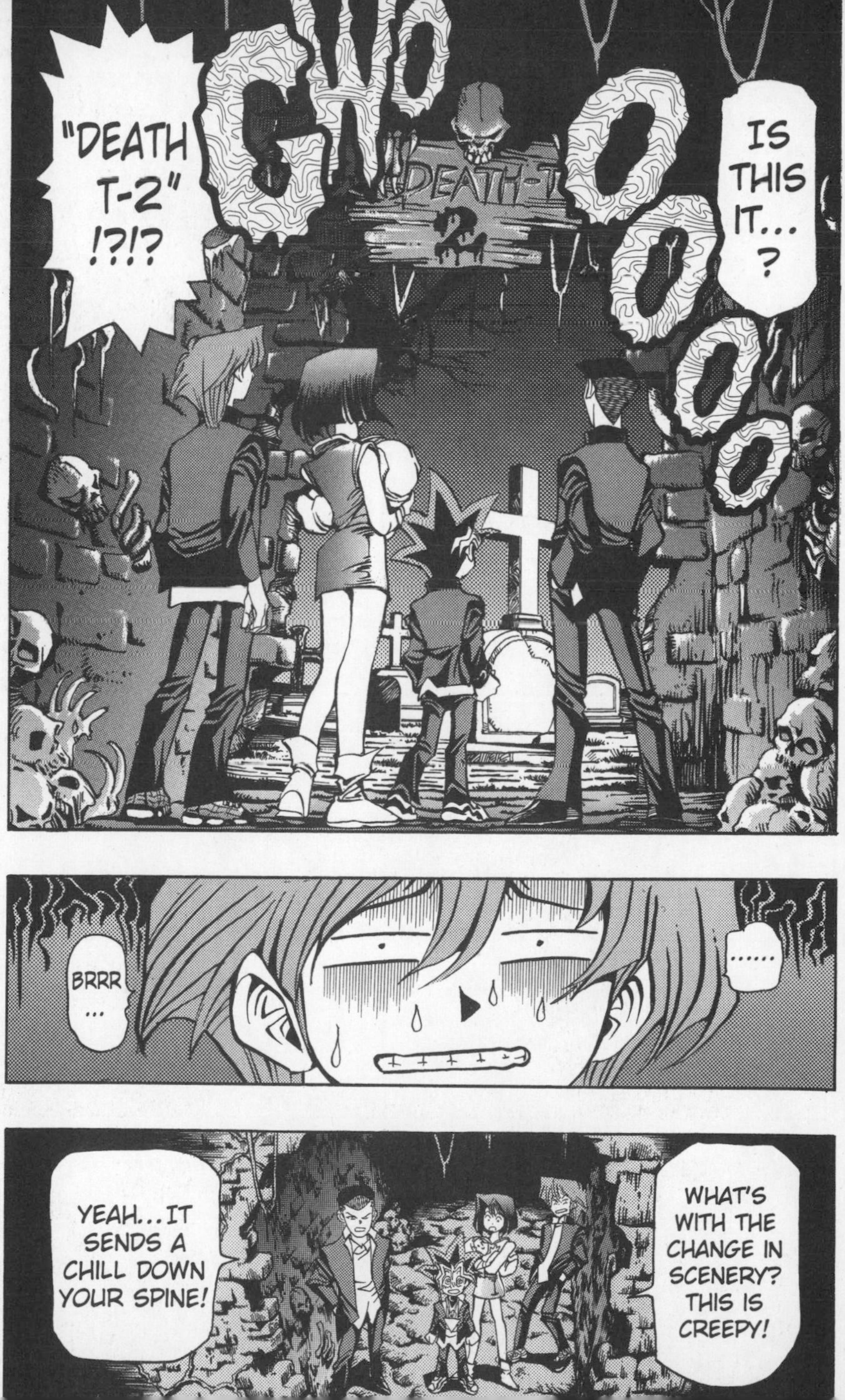
IS THIS IT...?
"DEATH T-2" !?!?
DEATH-T 2
......
BRRR ...
WHAT'S WITH THE CHANGE IN SCENERY? THIS IS CREEPY!
YEAH...IT SENDS A CHILL DOWN YOUR SPINE!

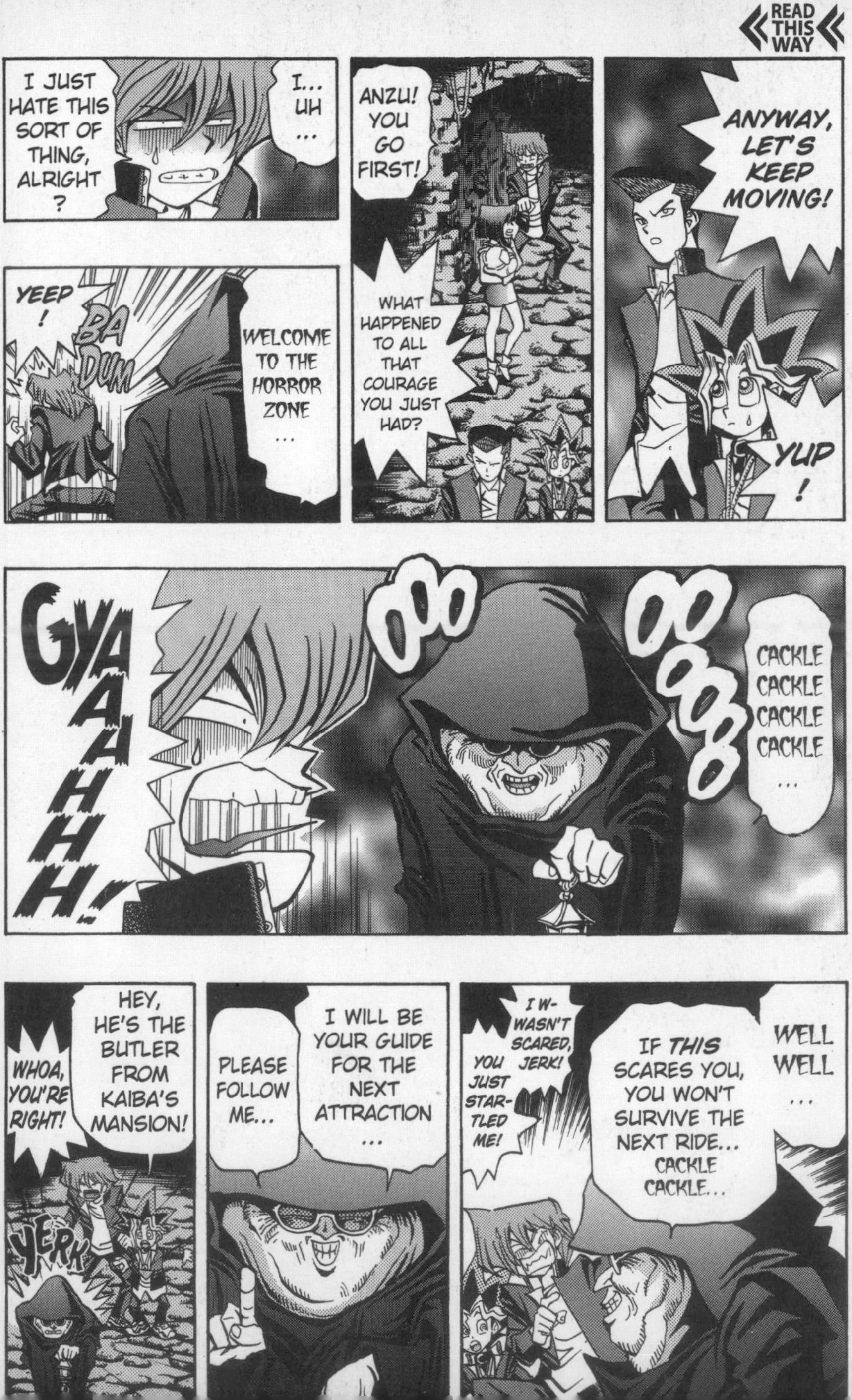
READ THIS WAY
ANYWAY, LET'S KEEP MOVING!
YUP!
ANZU! YOU GO FIRST!
WHAT HAPPENED TO ALL THAT COURAGE YOU JUST HAD?
I... UH ...
I JUST HATE THIS SORT OF THING, ALRIGHT?
WELCOME TO THE HORROR ZONE ...
BA DUM
YEEP!
CACKLE CACKLE CACKLE CACKLE ...
OOOOOOOO
GYAAAHHHH!
WELL WELL ...
IF THIS SCARES YOU, YOU WON'T SURVIVE THE NEXT RIDE... CACKLE CACKLE...
I W-WASN'T SCARED, JERK!
YOU JUST STAR-TLED ME!
I WILL BE YOUR GUIDE FOR THE NEXT ATTRACTION ...
PLEASE FOLLOW ME...
HEY, HE'S THE BUTLER FROM KAIBA'S MANSION!
WHOA, YOU'RE RIGHT!
YERK

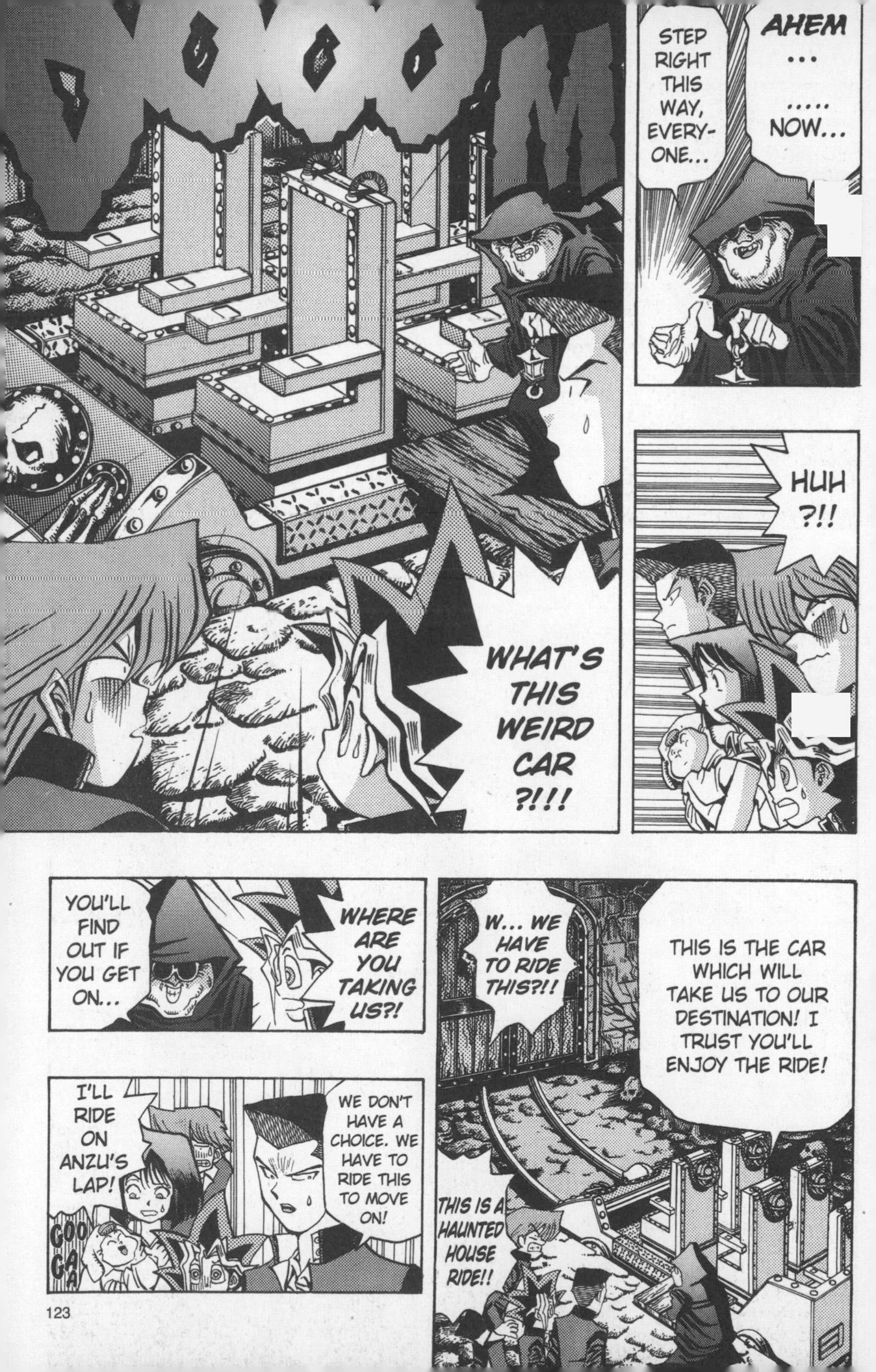
AHEM ... . NOW...
STEP RIGHT THIS WAY, EVERY-ONE...
HUH ?!!
WHAT'S THIS WEIRD CAR ?!!!
THIS IS THE CAR WHICH WILL TAKE US TO OUR DESTINATION! I TRUST YOU'LL ENJOY THE RIDE!
W... WE HAVE TO RIDE THIS?!!
THIS IS A HAUNTED HOUSE RIDE!!
WHERE ARE YOU TAKING US?!
YOU'LL FIND OUT IF YOU GET ON...
WE DON'T HAVE A CHOICE. WE HAVE TO RIDE THIS TO MOVE ON!
I'LL RIDE ON ANZU'S LAP!
GOO GAA

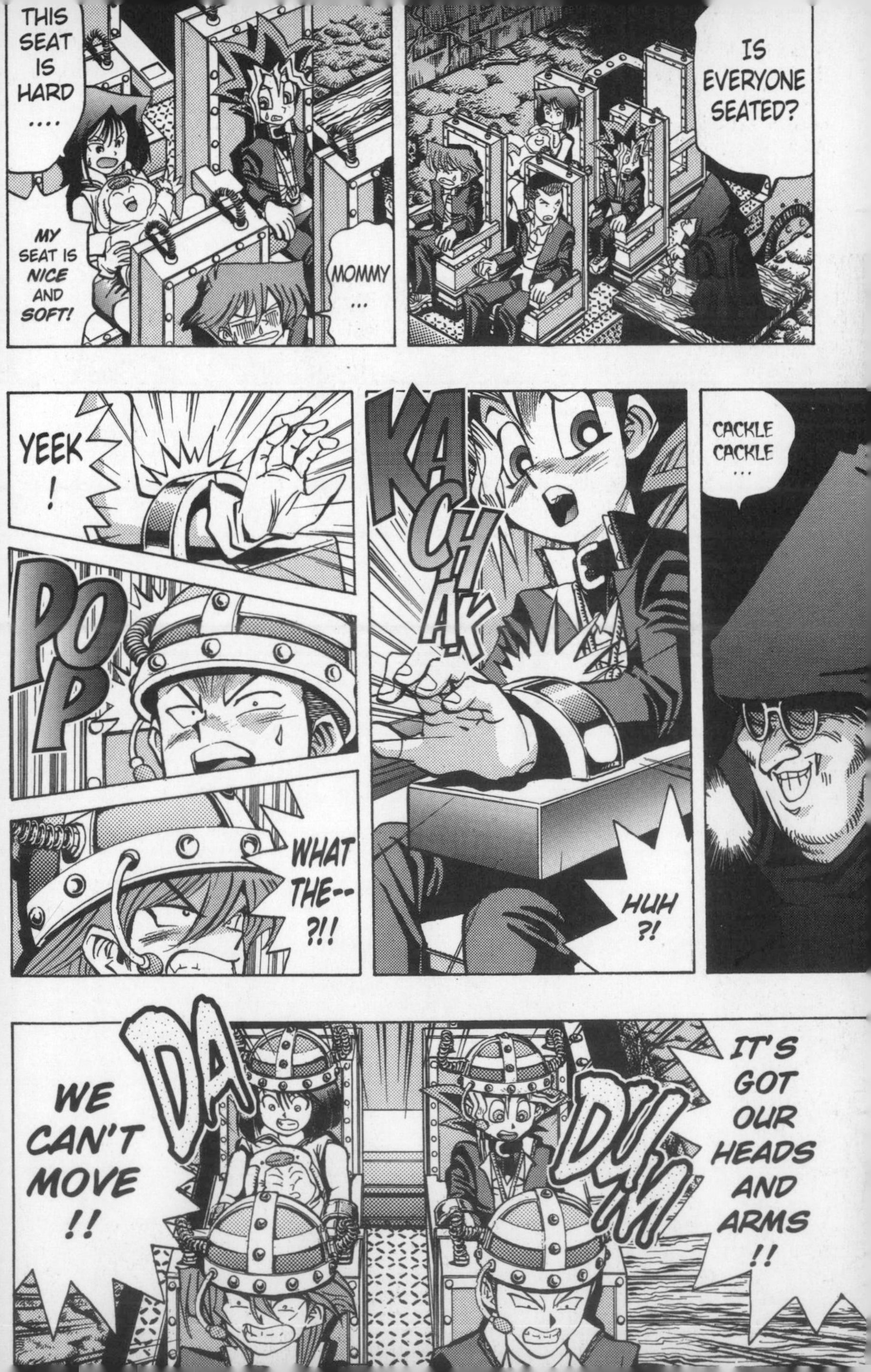
IS EVERYONE SEATED?
THIS SEAT IS HARD ....
MY SEAT IS NICE AND SOFT!
MOMMY ...
CACKLE CACKLE ...
KACHAK
HUH ?!
YEEK !
POP
WHAT THE-- ?!!
IT'S GOT OUR HEADS AND ARMS !!
DUM
DA
WE CAN'T MOVE !!

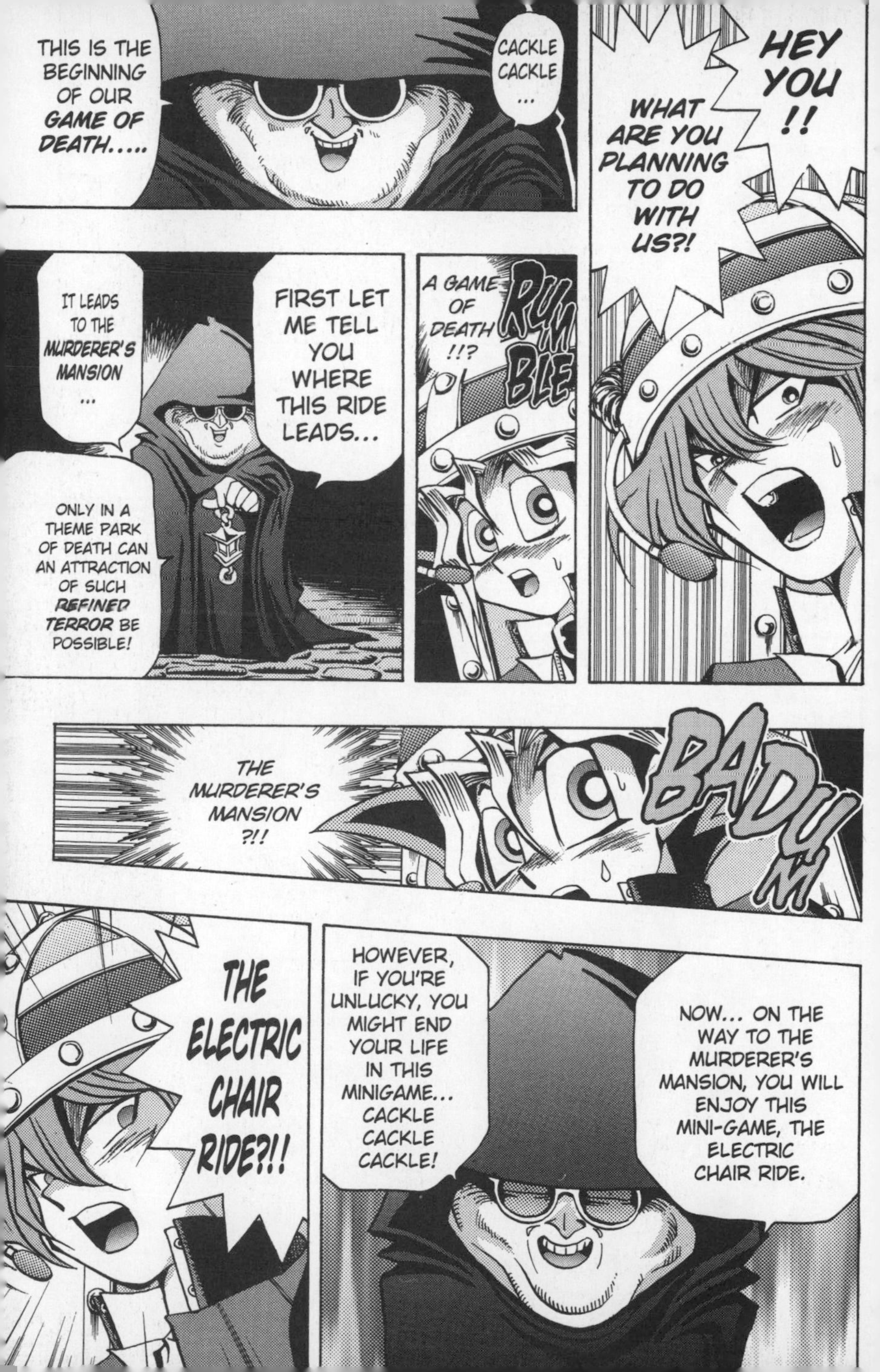
HEY YOU !!
WHAT ARE YOU PLANNING TO DO WITH US?!
CACKLE CACKLE ...
THIS IS THE BEGINNING OF OUR GAME OF DEATH.....
A GAME OF DEATH !!?
RUMBLE
FIRST LET ME TELL YOU WHERE THIS RIDE LEADS...
IT LEADS TO THE MURDERER'S MANSION ...
ONLY IN A THEME PARK OF DEATH CAN AN ATTRACTION OF SUCH REFINED TERROR BE POSSIBLE!
BADUM
THE MURDERER'S MANSION ?!!
NOW... ON THE WAY TO THE MURDERER'S MANSION, YOU WILL ENJOY THIS MINI-GAME, THE ELECTRIC CHAIR RIDE.
HOWEVER, IF YOU'RE UNLUCKY, YOU MIGHT END YOUR LIFE IN THIS MINIGAME... CACKLE CACKLE CACKLE!
THE ELECTRIC CHAIR RIDE?!!

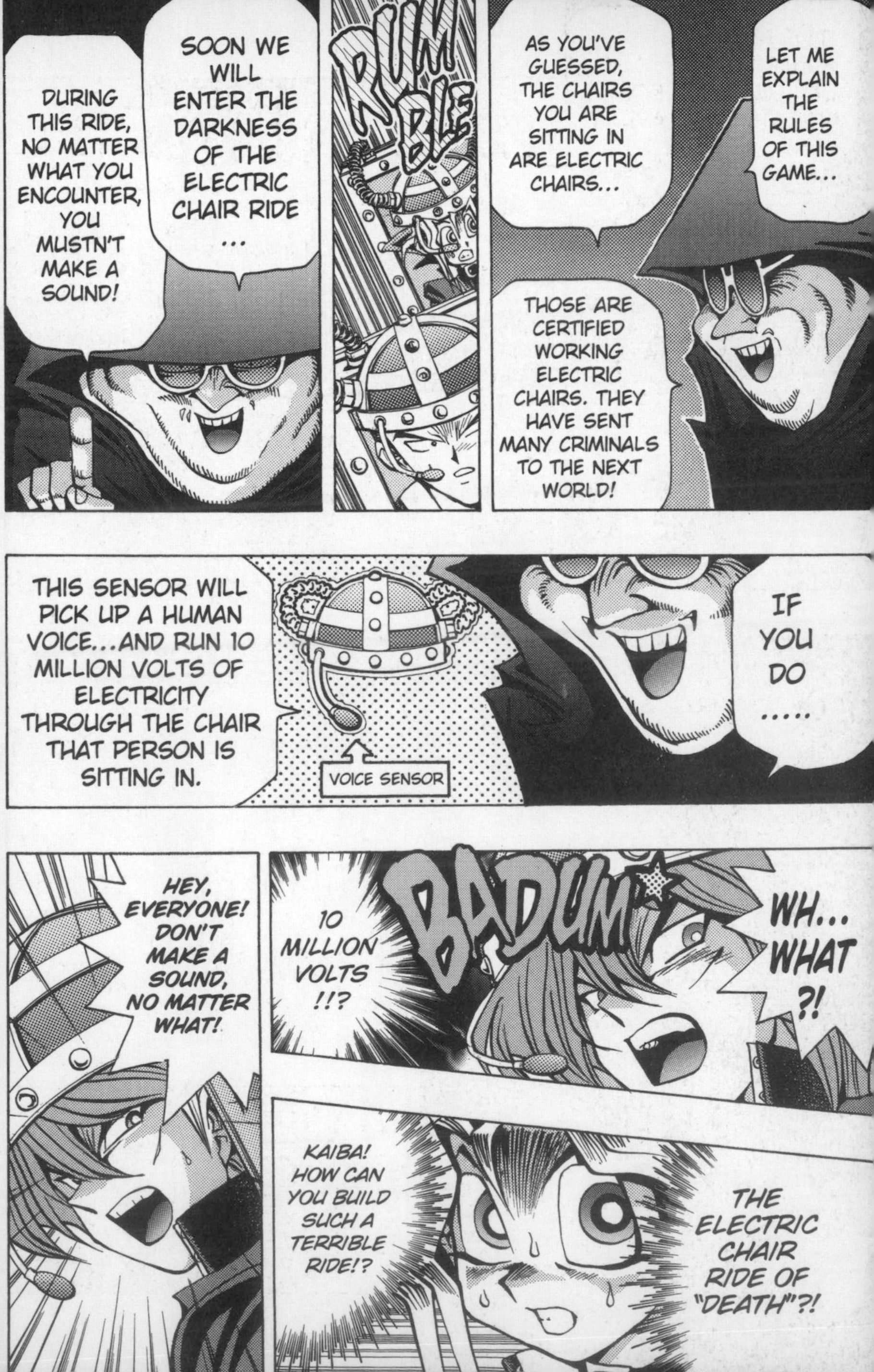
LET ME EXPLAIN THE RULES OF THIS GAME...
AS YOU'VE GUESSED, THE CHAIRS YOU ARE SITTING IN ARE ELECTRIC CHAIRS...
THOSE ARE CERTIFIED WORKING ELECTRIC CHAIRS. THEY HAVE SENT MANY CRIMINALS TO THE NEXT WORLD!
RUMBLE
SOON WE WILL ENTER THE DARKNESS OF THE ELECTRIC CHAIR RIDE ...
DURING THIS RIDE, NO MATTER WHAT YOU ENCOUNTER, YOU MUSTN'T MAKE A SOUND!
IF YOU DO .....
THIS SENSOR WILL PICK UP A HUMAN VOICE...AND RUN 10 MILLION VOLTS OF ELECTRICITY THROUGH THE CHAIR THAT PERSON IS SITTING IN.
VOICE SENSOR
WH... WHAT ?!
BADUM
10 MILLION VOLTS !!?
THE ELECTRIC CHAIR RIDE OF "DEATH"?!
KAIBA! HOW CAN YOU BUILD SUCH A TERRIBLE RIDE!?
HEY, EVERYONE! DON'T MAKE A SOUND, NO MATTER WHAT!

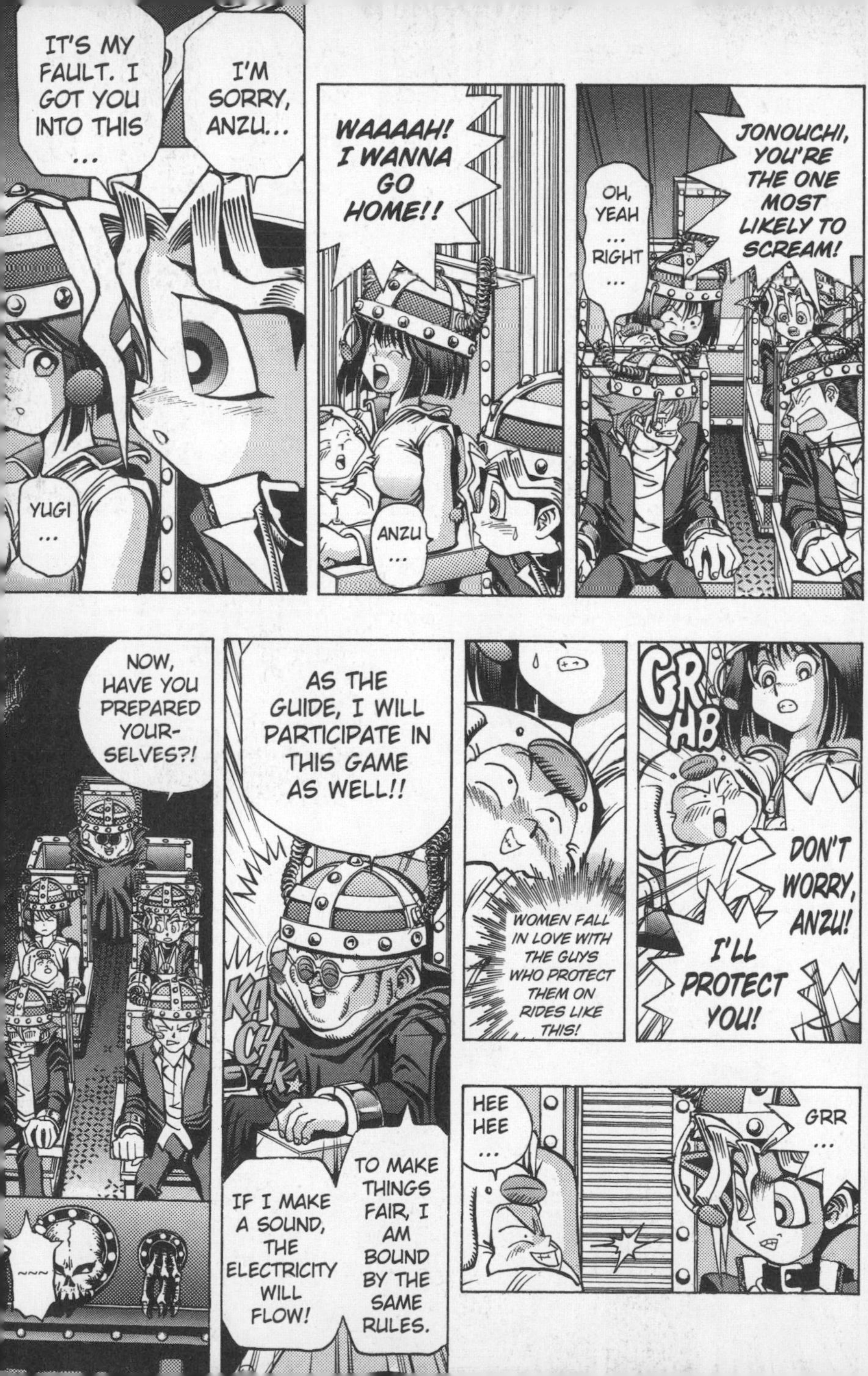
JONOUCHI, YOU'RE THE ONE MOST LIKELY TO SCREAM!
OH, YEAH ... RIGHT ...
WAAAAH! I WANNA GO HOME!!
ANZU ...
I'M SORRY, ANZU...
IT'S MY FAULT. I GOT YOU INTO THIS ...
YUGI ...
GRAB
DON'T WORRY, ANZU!
I'LL PROTECT YOU!
WOMEN FALL IN LOVE WITH THE GUYS WHO PROTECT THEM ON RIDES LIKE THIS!
GRR ...
HEE HEE ...
AS THE GUIDE, I WILL PARTICIPATE IN THIS GAME AS WELL!!
KA CHIK
TO MAKE THINGS FAIR, I AM BOUND BY THE SAME RULES.
IF I MAKE A SOUND, THE ELECTRICITY WILL FLOW!
NOW, HAVE YOU PREPARED YOUR-SELVES?!
~~~
~~~

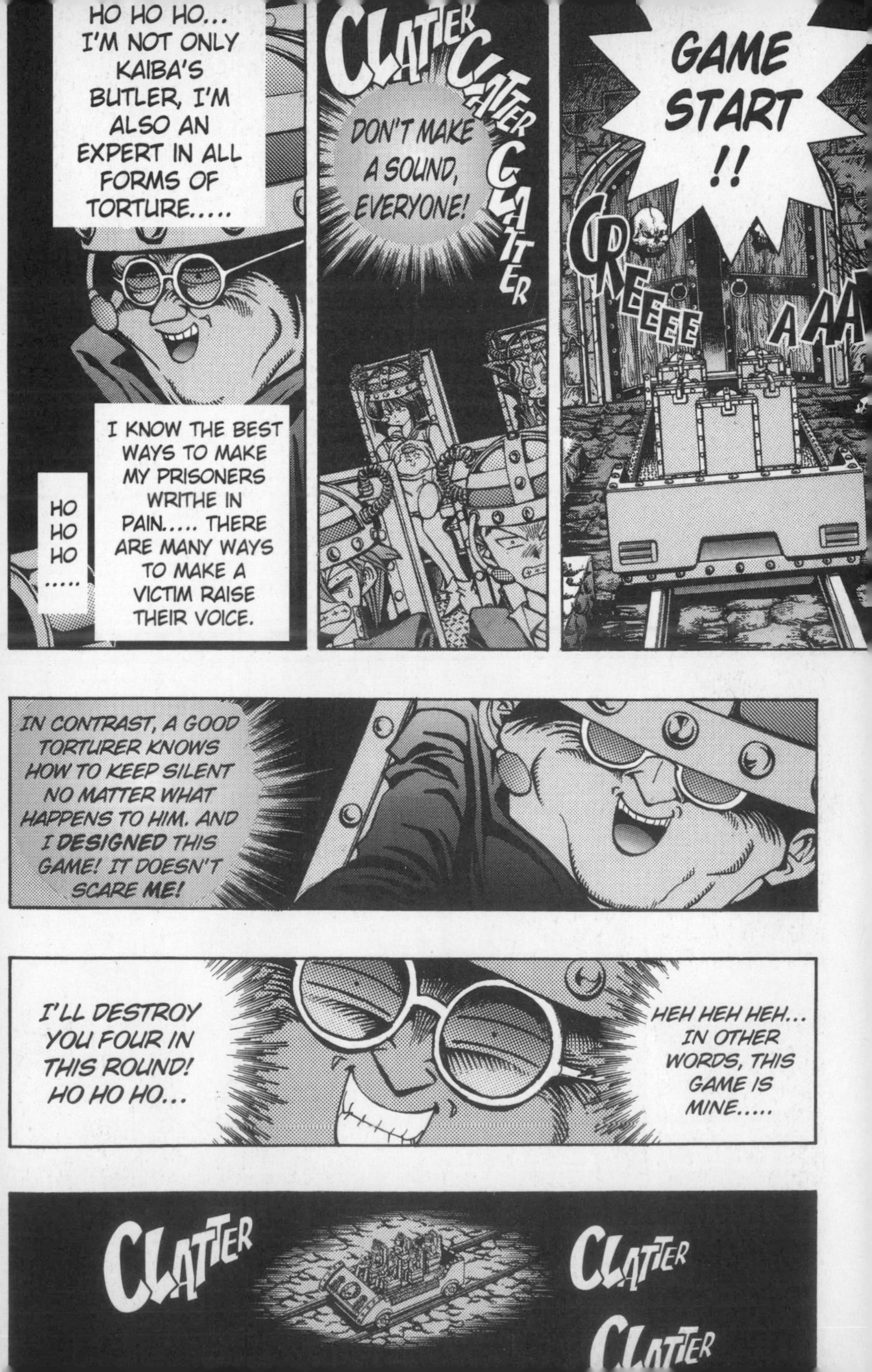
GAME START !!
CREEEEE
AAA
CLATTER CLATTER CLATTER
DON'T MAKE A SOUND, EVERYONE!
HO HO HO... I'M NOT ONLY KAIBA'S BUTLER, I'M ALSO AN EXPERT IN ALL FORMS OF TORTURE.....
I KNOW THE BEST WAYS TO MAKE MY PRISONERS WRITHE IN PAIN..... THERE ARE MANY WAYS TO MAKE A VICTIM RAISE THEIR VOICE.
HO HO HO .....
IN CONTRAST, A GOOD TORTURER KNOWS HOW TO KEEP SILENT NO MATTER WHAT HAPPENS TO HIM. AND I DESIGNED THIS GAME! IT DOESN'T SCARE ME!
HEH HEH HEH... IN OTHER WORDS, THIS GAME IS MINE.....
I'LL DESTROY YOU FOUR IN THIS ROUND! HO HO HO...
CLATTER
CLATTER
CLATTER

NOW WITNESS
THE FIRST
TERROR...

HO HO
HO...

CLATTER

CLATTER

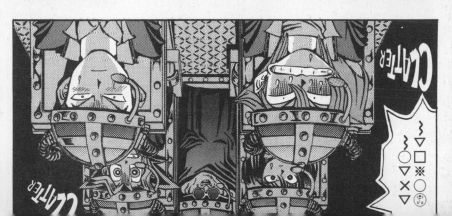

CLATTER

CLATTER

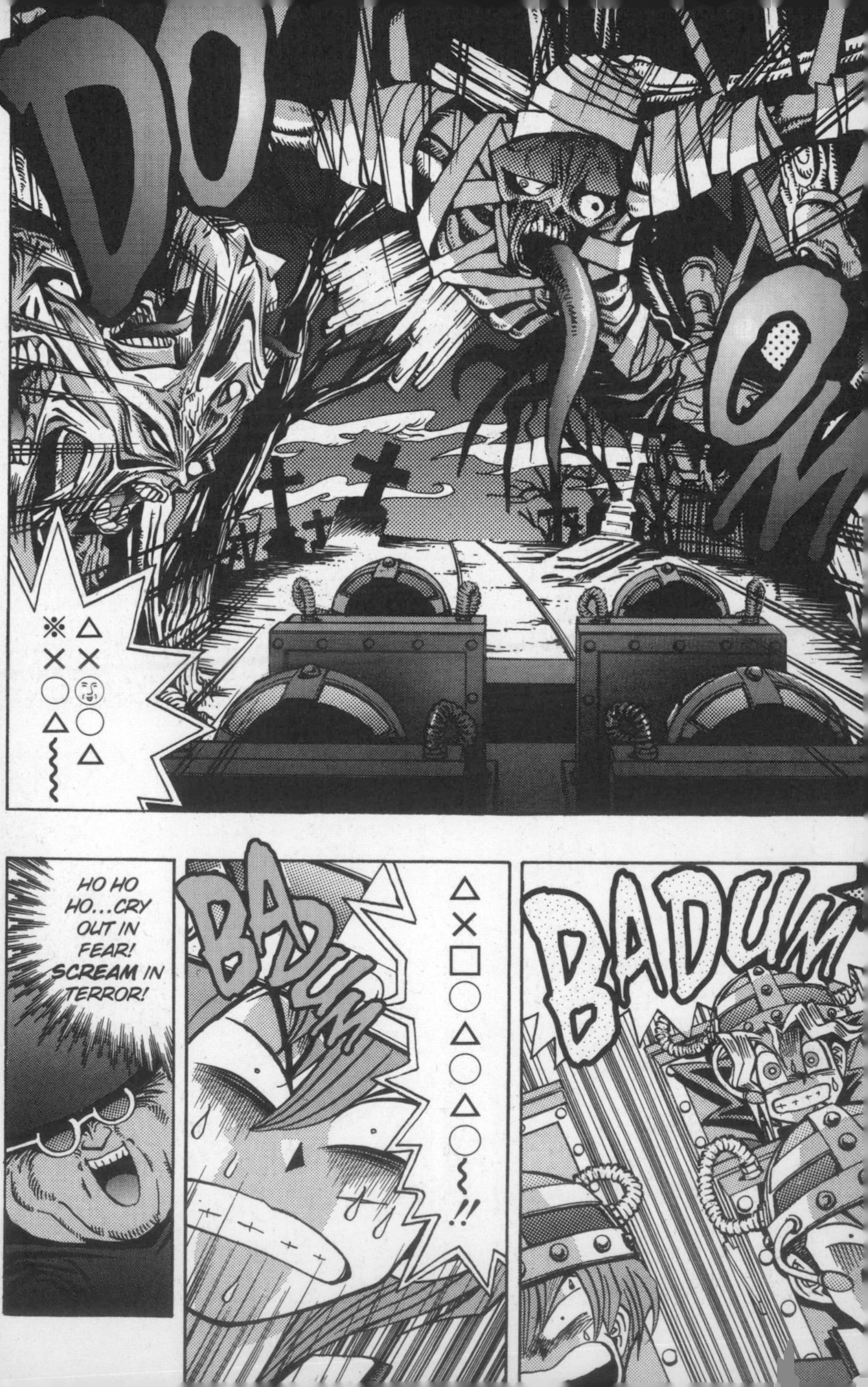
DOOM
△×○△～
※×○△
BADUM
△×□○△○△○～!!
BADUM
HO HO HO...CRY OUT IN FEAR! SCREAM IN TERROR!

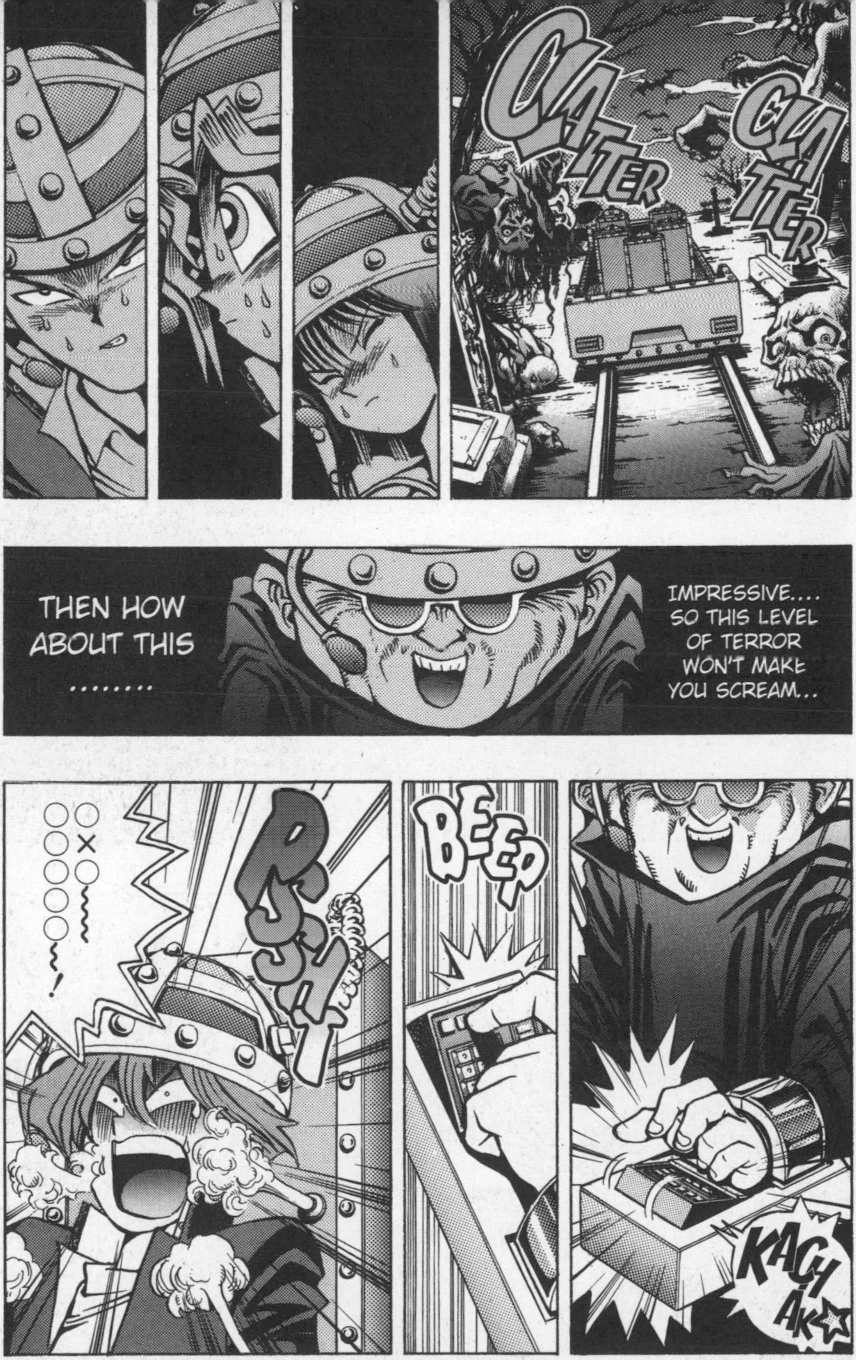
CLATTER
CLATTER
IMPRESSIVE.... SO THIS LEVEL OF TERROR WON'T MAKE YOU SCREAM...
THEN HOW ABOUT THIS ....
KACHAK
BEEP
PSSH
○○○○○
○×○~~~!

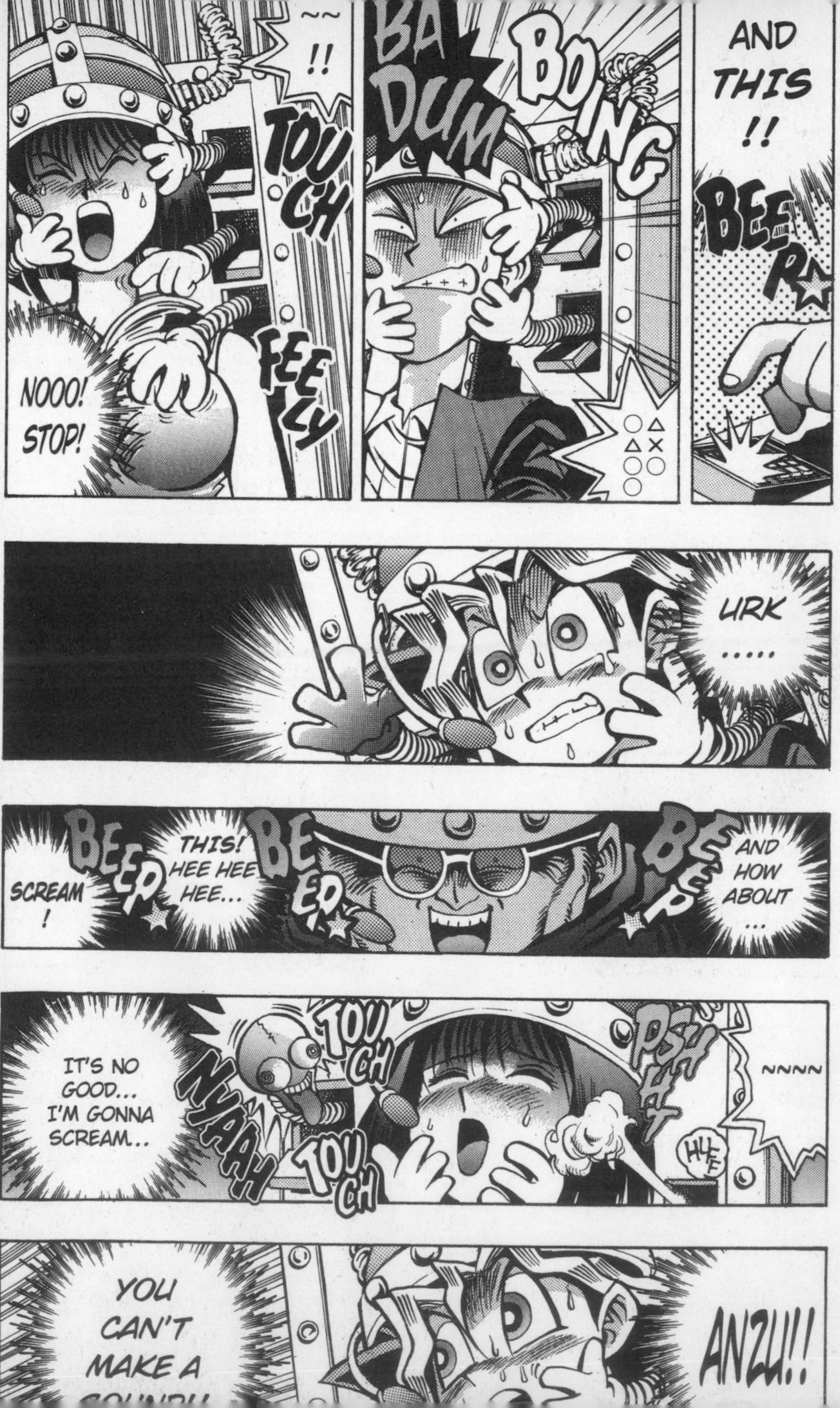
AND THIS !!
BEER
BA DUM
BOING
~~ !!
TOUCH
FEELY
NOOO! STOP!
URK .....
AND HOW ABOUT ...
BEEP
THIS! HEE HEE HEE...
BEEP
SCREAM !
NNNN
PSH HT
HUFF
TOUCH
TOUCH
NYAAH
IT'S NO GOOD... I'M GONNA SCREAM...
ANZU!!
YOU CAN'T MAKE A SOUND!!

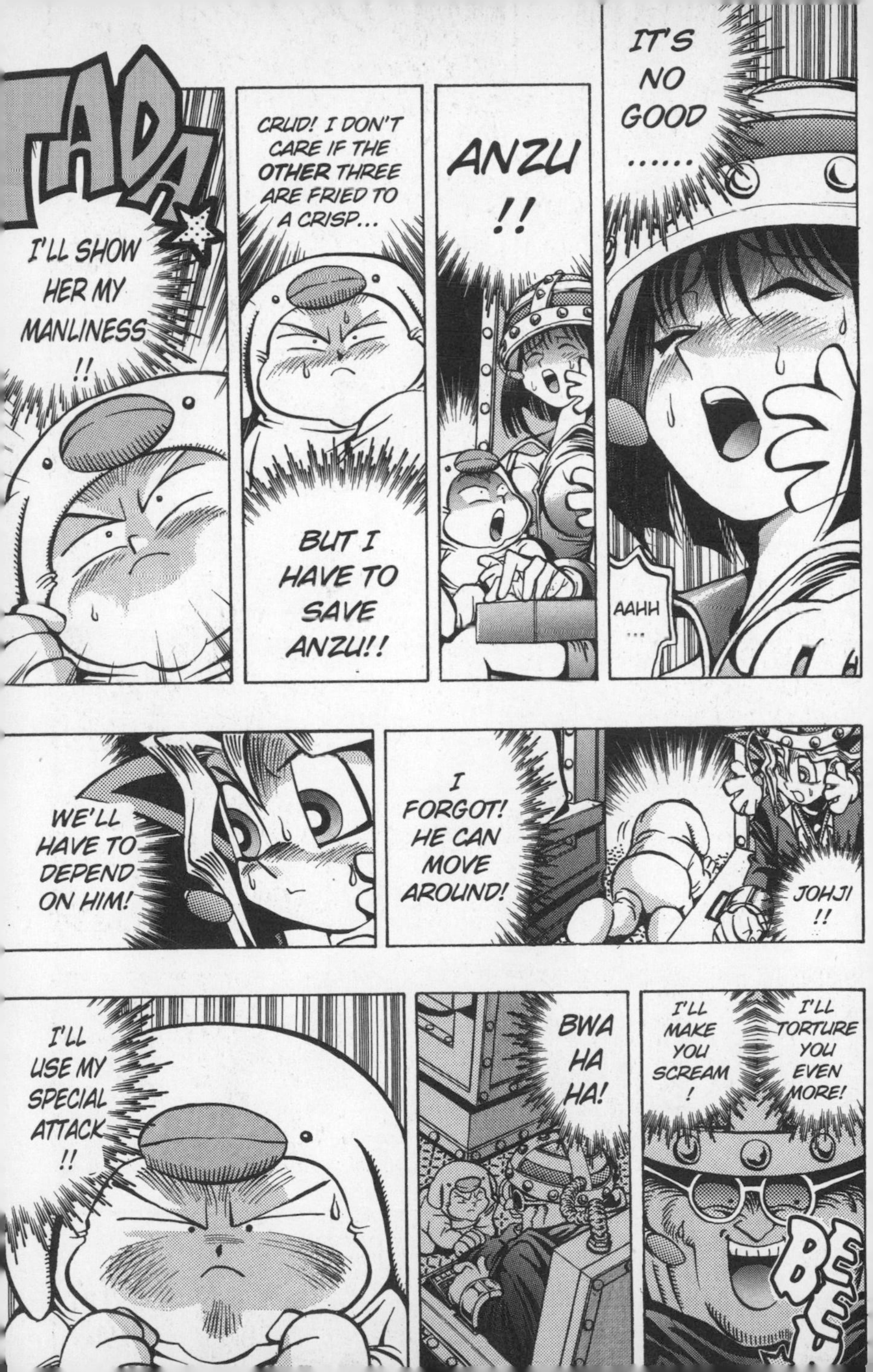
IT'S NO GOOD ......
AAHH ...
ANZU !!
CRUD! I DON'T CARE IF THE OTHER THREE ARE FRIED TO A CRISP...
BUT I HAVE TO SAVE ANZU!!
TADA
I'LL SHOW HER MY MANLINESS !!
JOHJI !!
I FORGOT! HE CAN MOVE AROUND!
WE'LL HAVE TO DEPEND ON HIM!
I'LL TORTURE YOU EVEN MORE!
I'LL MAKE YOU SCREAM !
BWA HA HA!
I'LL USE MY SPECIAL ATTACK !!

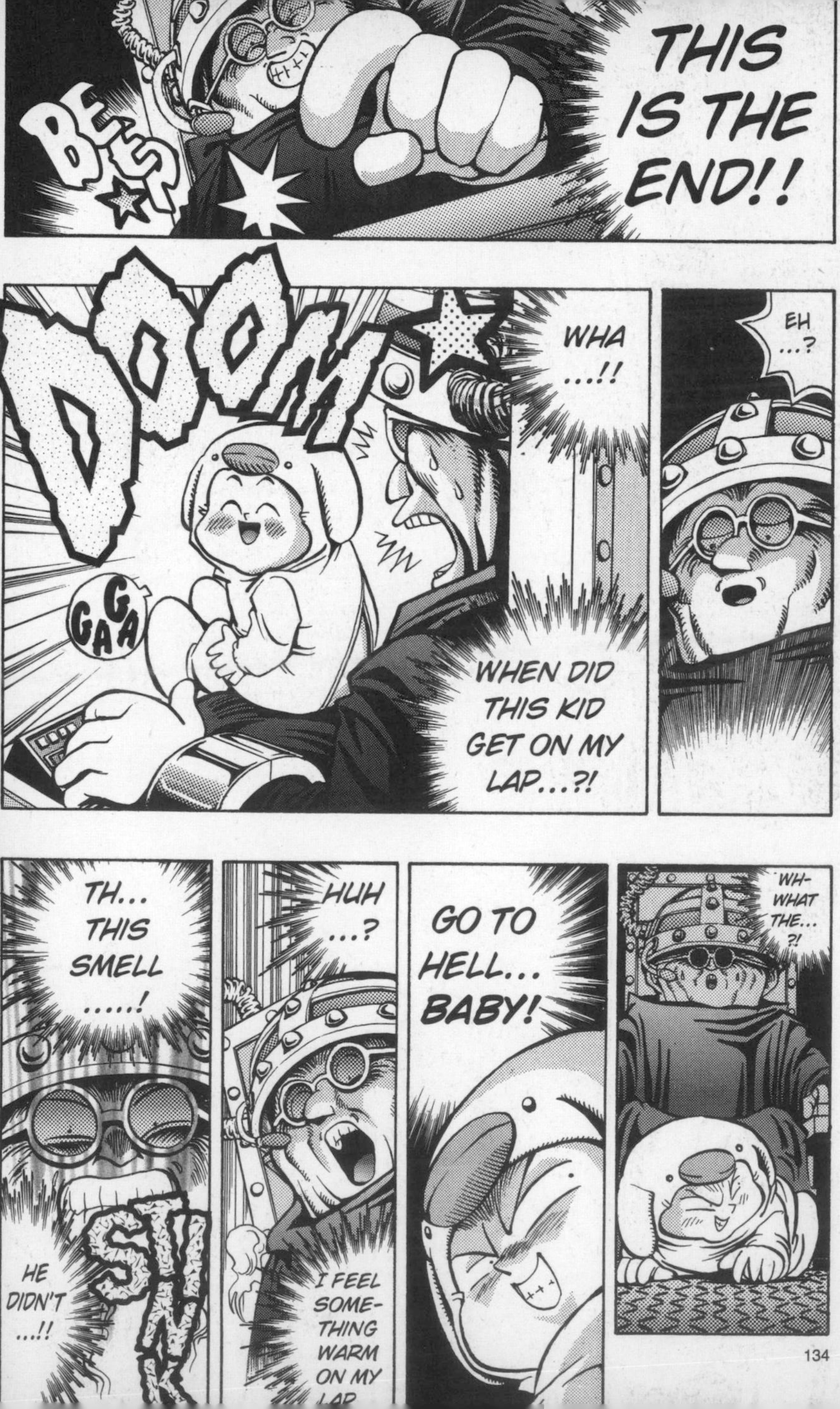
THIS IS THE END!!
BEEP
EH ...?
WHA ...!!
DOOM
GAGA
WHEN DID THIS KID GET ON MY LAP...?!
WH- WHAT THE... ?!
GO TO HELL... BABY!
HUH ...?
I FEEL SOME- THING WARM ON MY LAP
TH... THIS SMELL .....!
HE DIDN'T ...!!

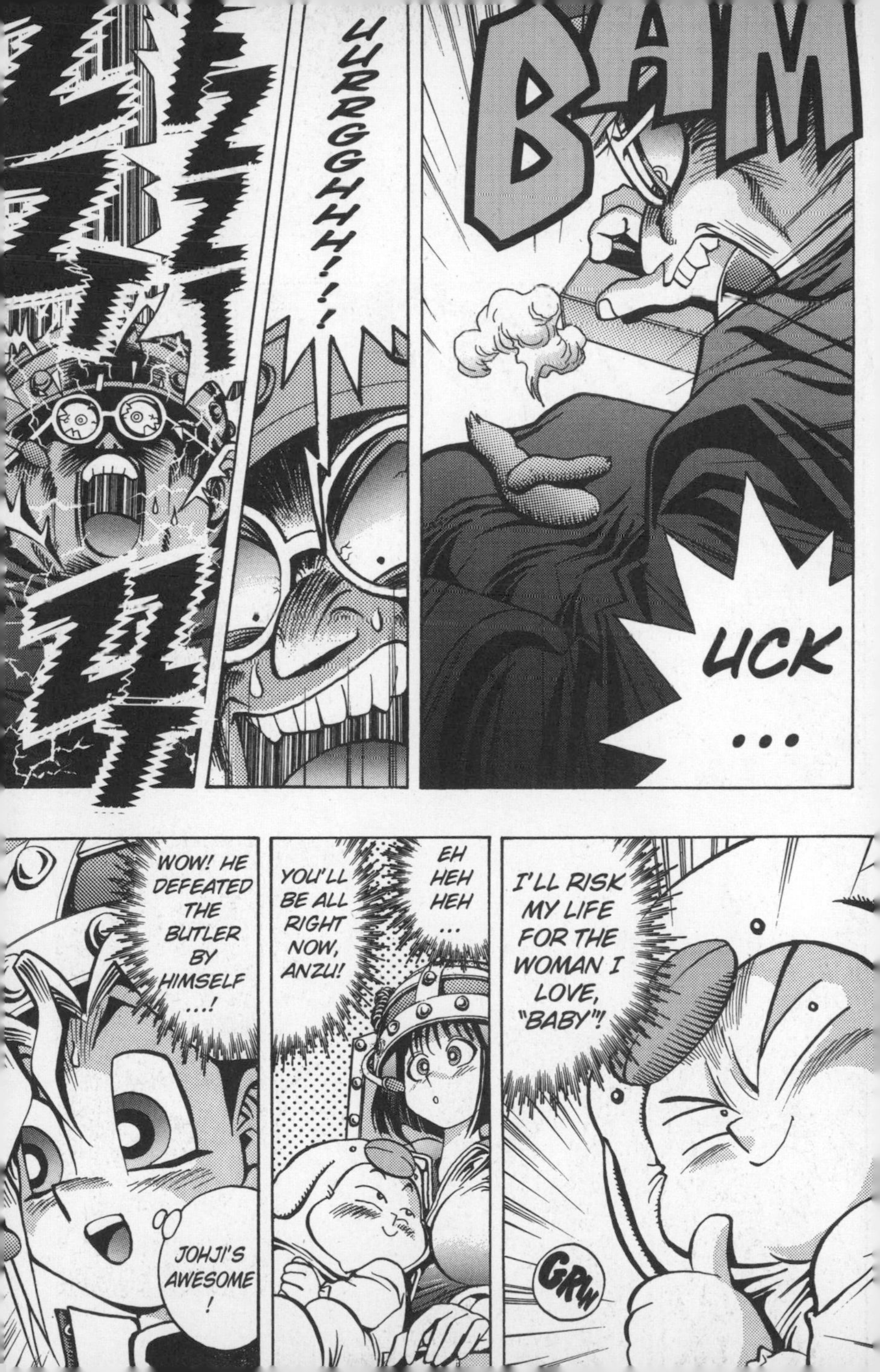
BAM
UCK
...
UURRGGHHHH!!!
I'LL RISK MY LIFE FOR THE WOMAN I LOVE, "BABY"!
GRW
EH HEH HEH ...
YOU'LL BE ALL RIGHT NOW, ANZU!
WOW! HE DEFEATED THE BUTLER BY HIMSELF ...!
JOHJI'S AWESOME !

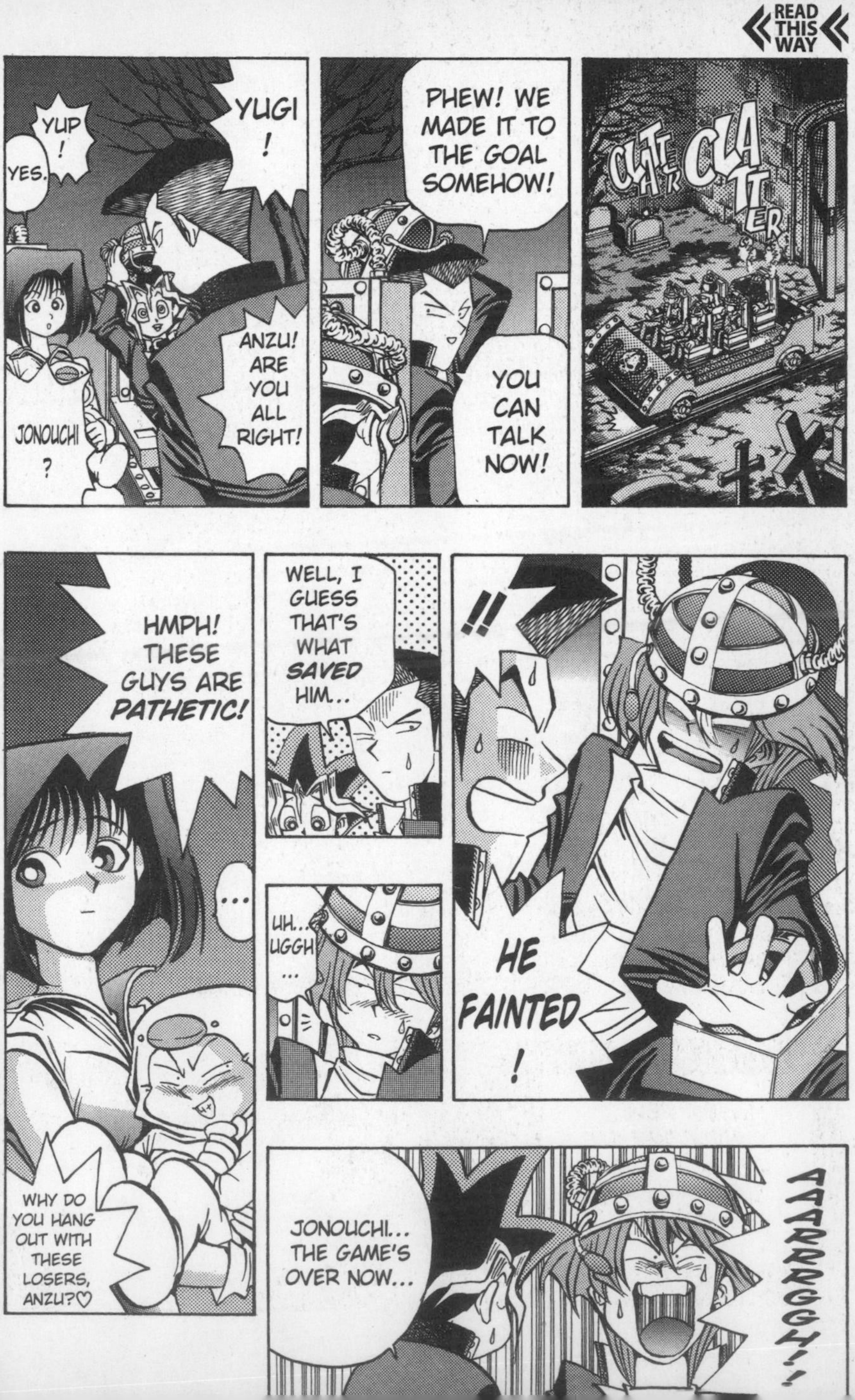
READ THIS WAY
CLATTER CLATTER
PHEW! WE MADE IT TO THE GOAL SOMEHOW!
YOU CAN TALK NOW!
YUGI!
ANZU! ARE YOU ALL RIGHT!
YUP!
YES.
JONOUCHI?
!!
HE FAINTED!
WELL, I GUESS THAT'S WHAT SAVED HIM...
UH... UGGH...
HMPH! THESE GUYS ARE PATHETIC!
...
WHY DO YOU HANG OUT WITH THESE LOSERS, ANZU?♡
AAARRRGGH!!
JONOUCHI... THE GAME'S OVER NOW...

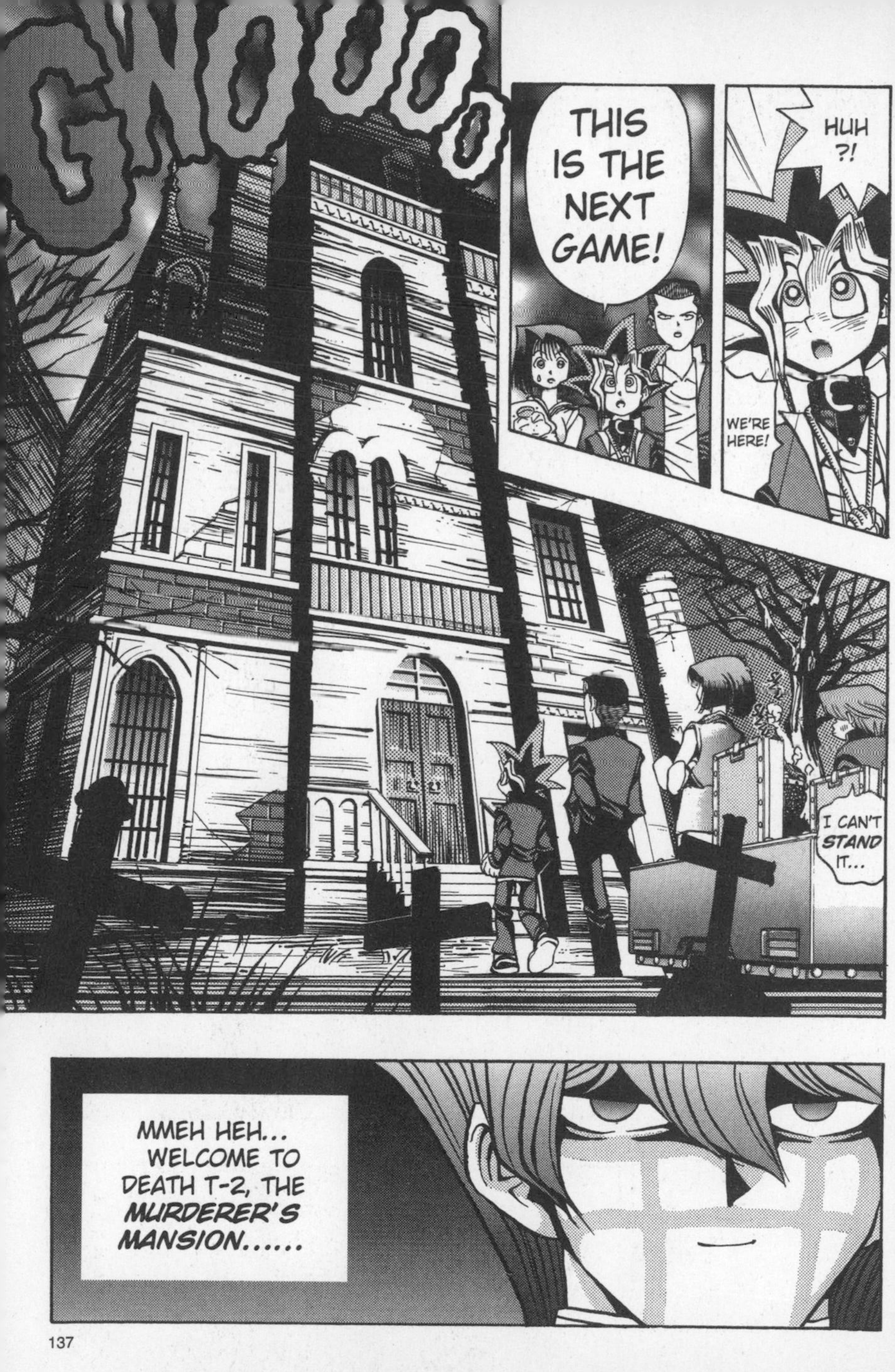
HUH ?!
WE'RE HERE!
THIS IS THE NEXT GAME!
GNOOOO
I CAN'T STAND IT...
MMEH HEH... WELCOME TO DEATH T-2, THE MURDERER'S MANSION......

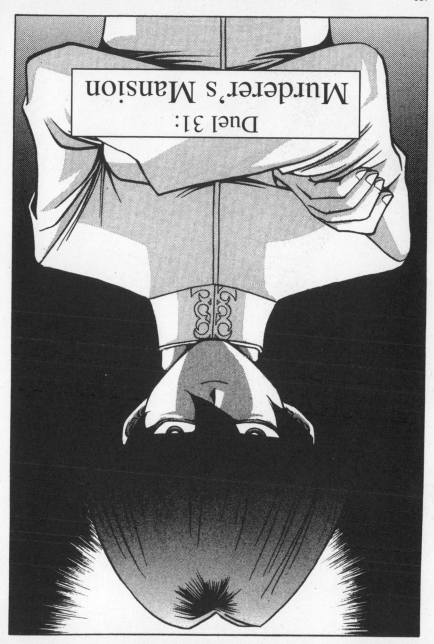

Duel 31:
Murderer's Mansion

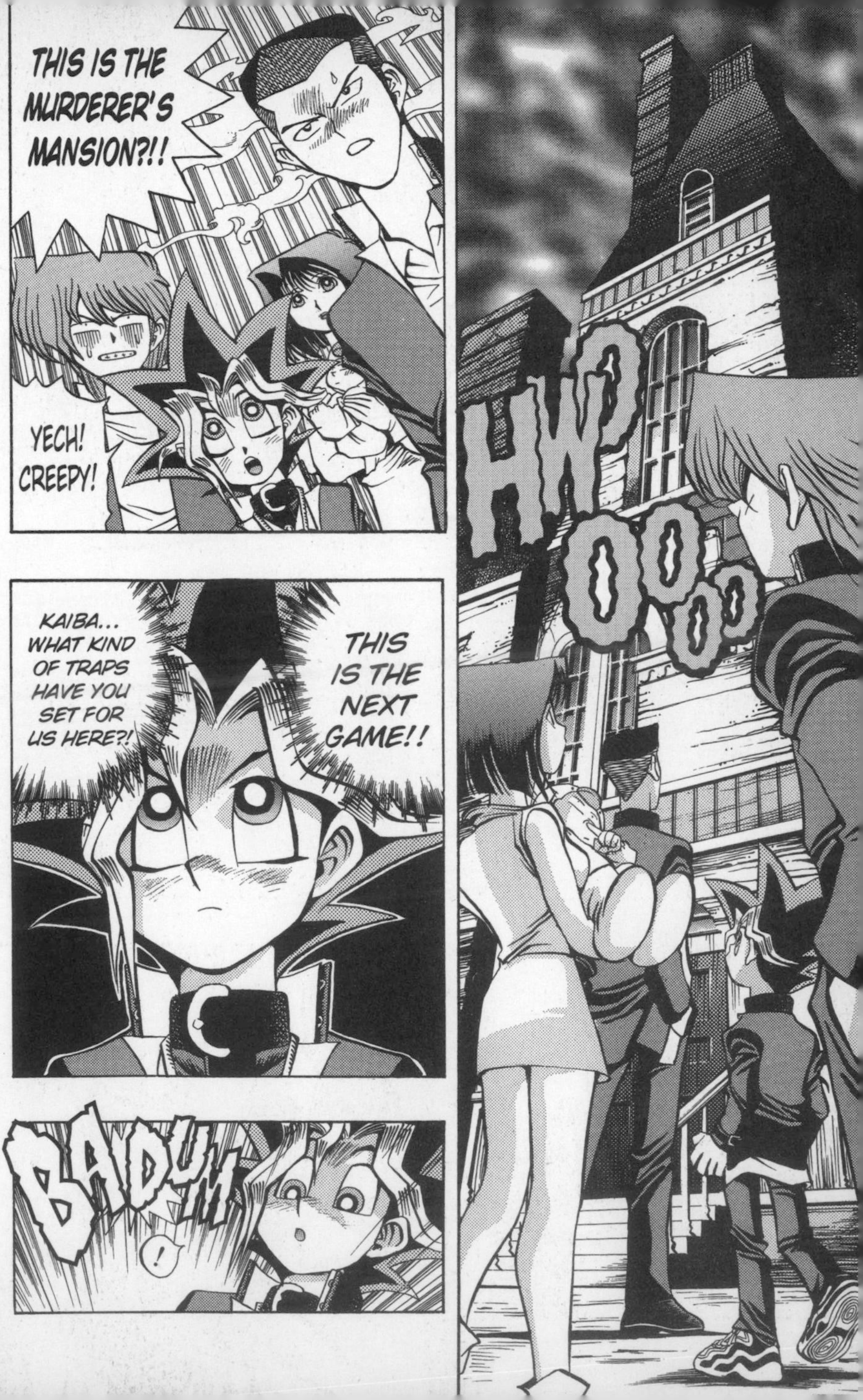
HWOOOO
THIS IS THE MURDERER'S MANSION?!!
YECH! CREEPY!
THIS IS THE NEXT GAME!!
KAIBA... WHAT KIND OF TRAPS HAVE YOU SET FOR US HERE?!
BADUM
!

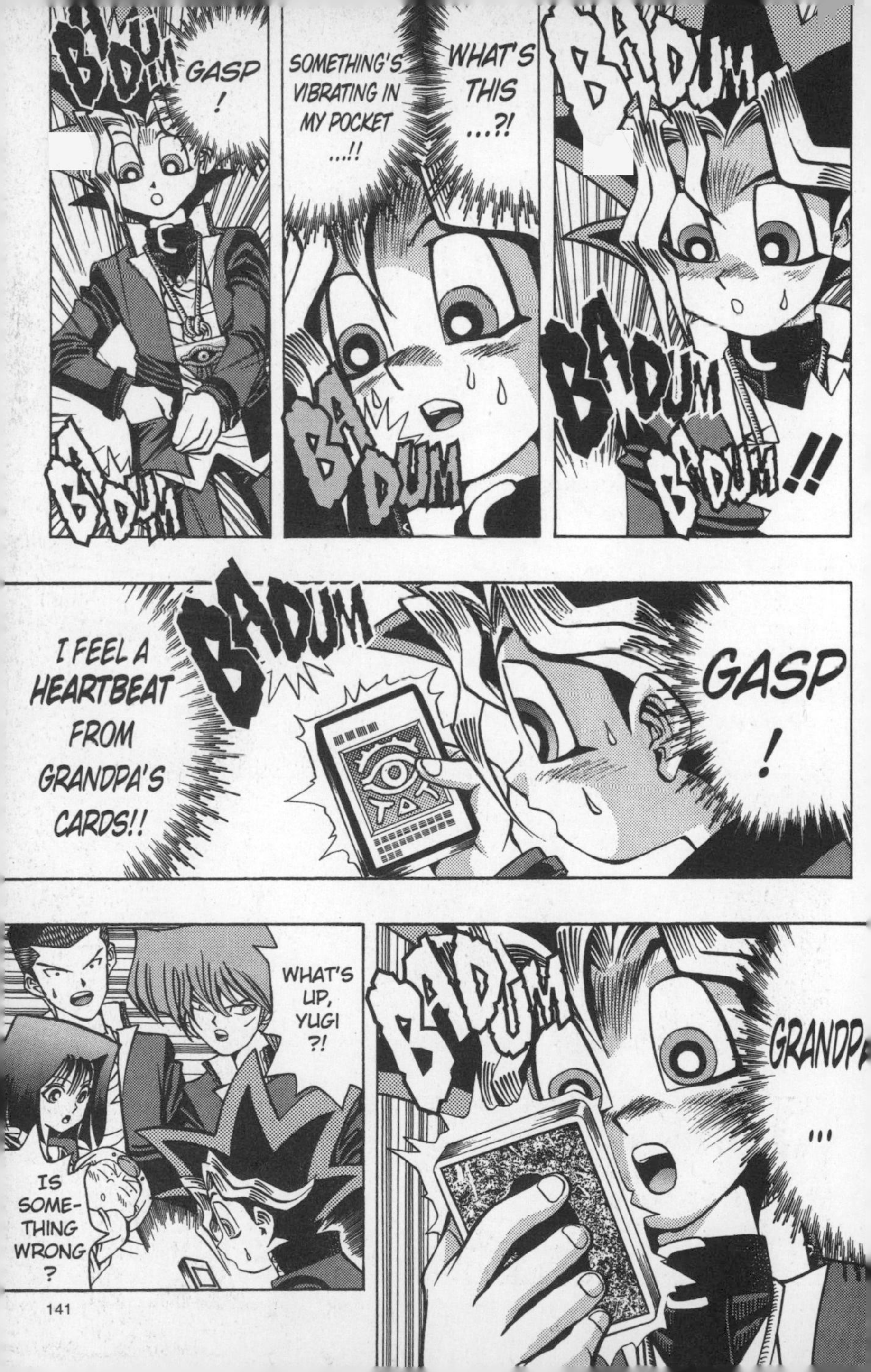
BADUM
BADUM
BADUM!!
WHAT'S THIS ...?!
SOMETHING'S VIBRATING IN MY POCKET ...!!
BADUM
BADUM
GASP !
BADUM
GASP !
BADUM
I FEEL A HEARTBEAT FROM GRANDPA'S CARDS!!
GRANDP
...
BADUM
WHAT'S UP, YUGI ?!
IS SOME-THING WRONG ?

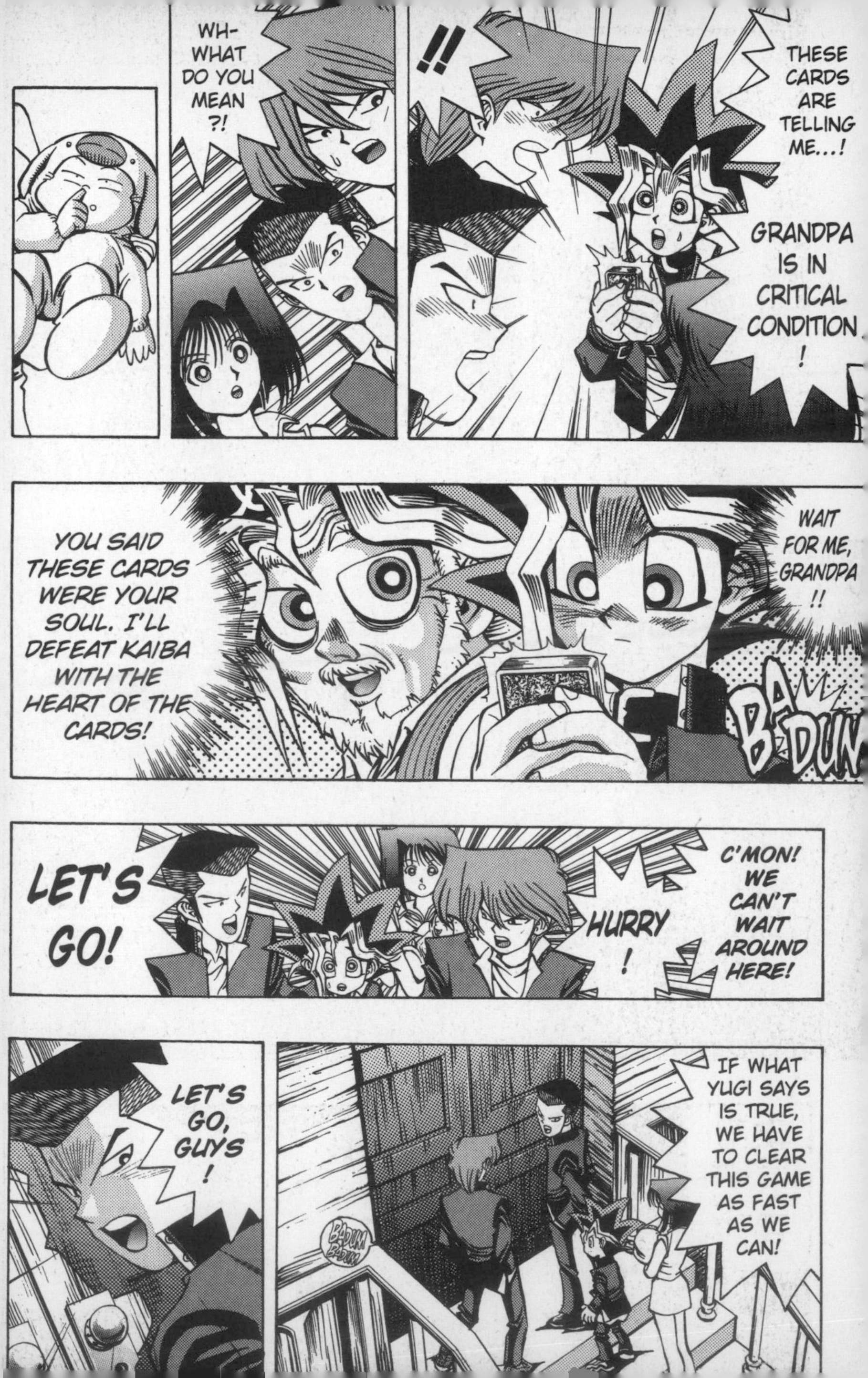
THESE CARDS ARE TELLING ME...!
GRANDPA IS IN CRITICAL CONDITION!
!!
WH-WHAT DO YOU MEAN?!
WAIT FOR ME, GRANDPA!!
BA-DUN
YOU SAID THESE CARDS WERE YOUR SOUL. I'LL DEFEAT KAIBA WITH THE HEART OF THE CARDS!
C'MON! WE CAN'T WAIT AROUND HERE!
HURRY!
LET'S GO!
IF WHAT YUGI SAYS IS TRUE, WE HAVE TO CLEAR THIS GAME AS FAST AS WE CAN!
BADUM BADUM
LET'S GO, GUYS!

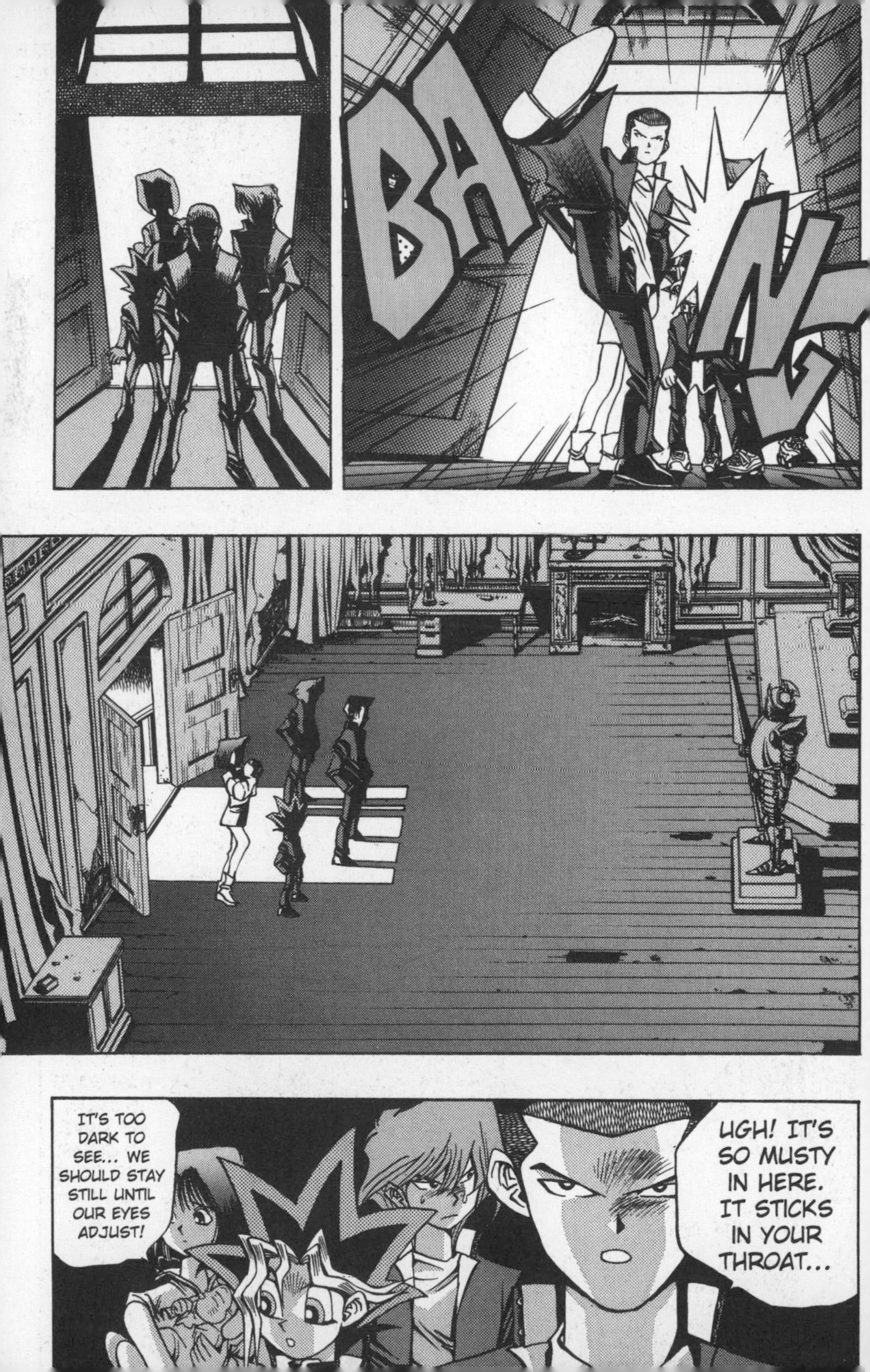
BAN
UGH! IT'S SO MUSTY IN HERE. IT STICKS IN YOUR THROAT...
IT'S TOO DARK TO SEE... WE SHOULD STAY STILL UNTIL OUR EYES ADJUST!

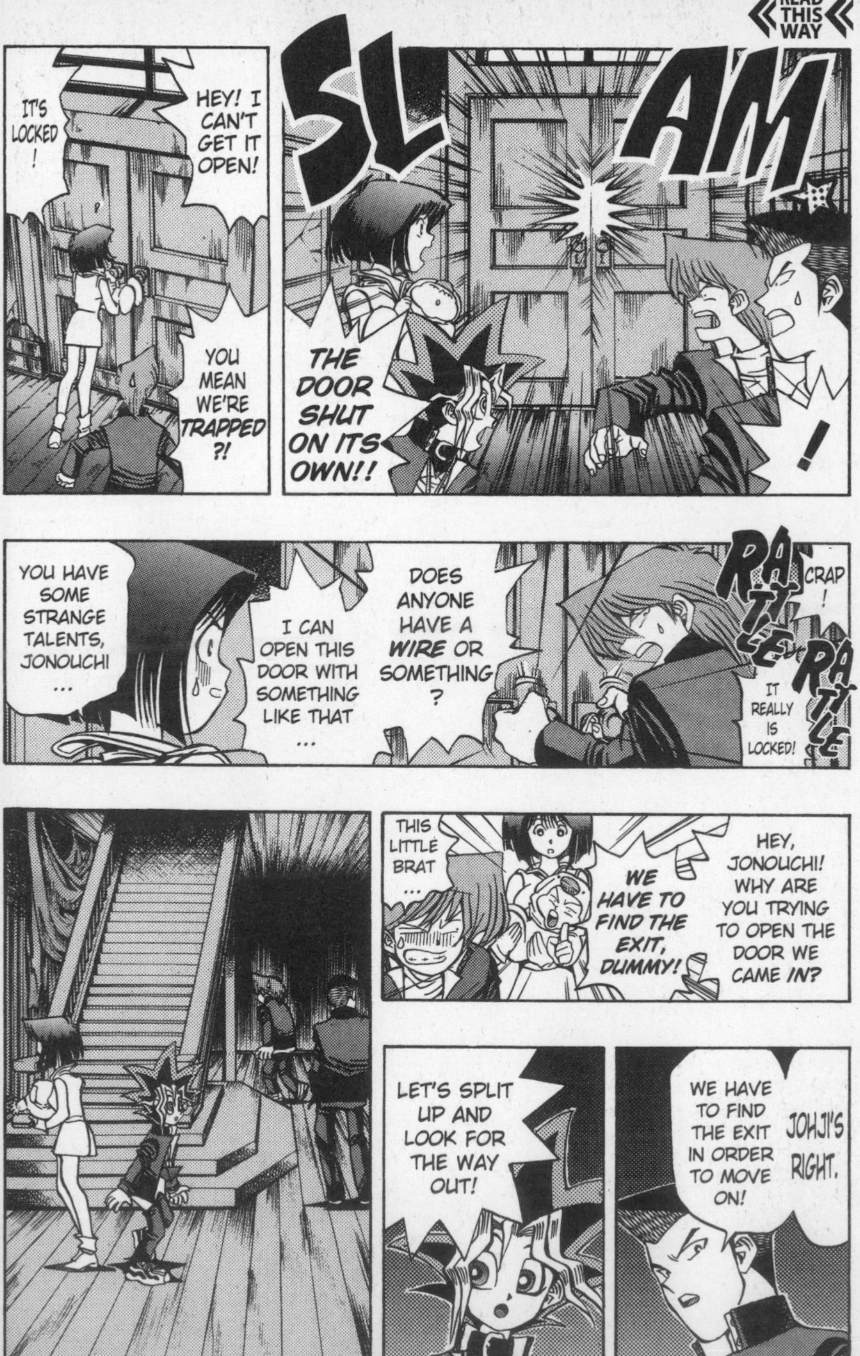
READ THIS WAY
SLAM
THE DOOR SHUT ON ITS OWN!!
!
HEY! I CAN'T GET IT OPEN!
IT'S LOCKED!
YOU MEAN WE'RE TRAPPED?!
RATTLE RATTLE
CRAP!
IT REALLY IS LOCKED!
DOES ANYONE HAVE A WIRE OR SOMETHING?
I CAN OPEN THIS DOOR WITH SOMETHING LIKE THAT...
YOU HAVE SOME STRANGE TALENTS, JONOUCHI...
HEY, JONOUCHI! WHY ARE YOU TRYING TO OPEN THE DOOR WE CAME IN?
WE HAVE TO FIND THE EXIT, DUMMY!
THIS LITTLE BRAT...
JOHJI'S RIGHT.
WE HAVE TO FIND THE EXIT IN ORDER TO MOVE ON!
LET'S SPLIT UP AND LOOK FOR THE WAY OUT!

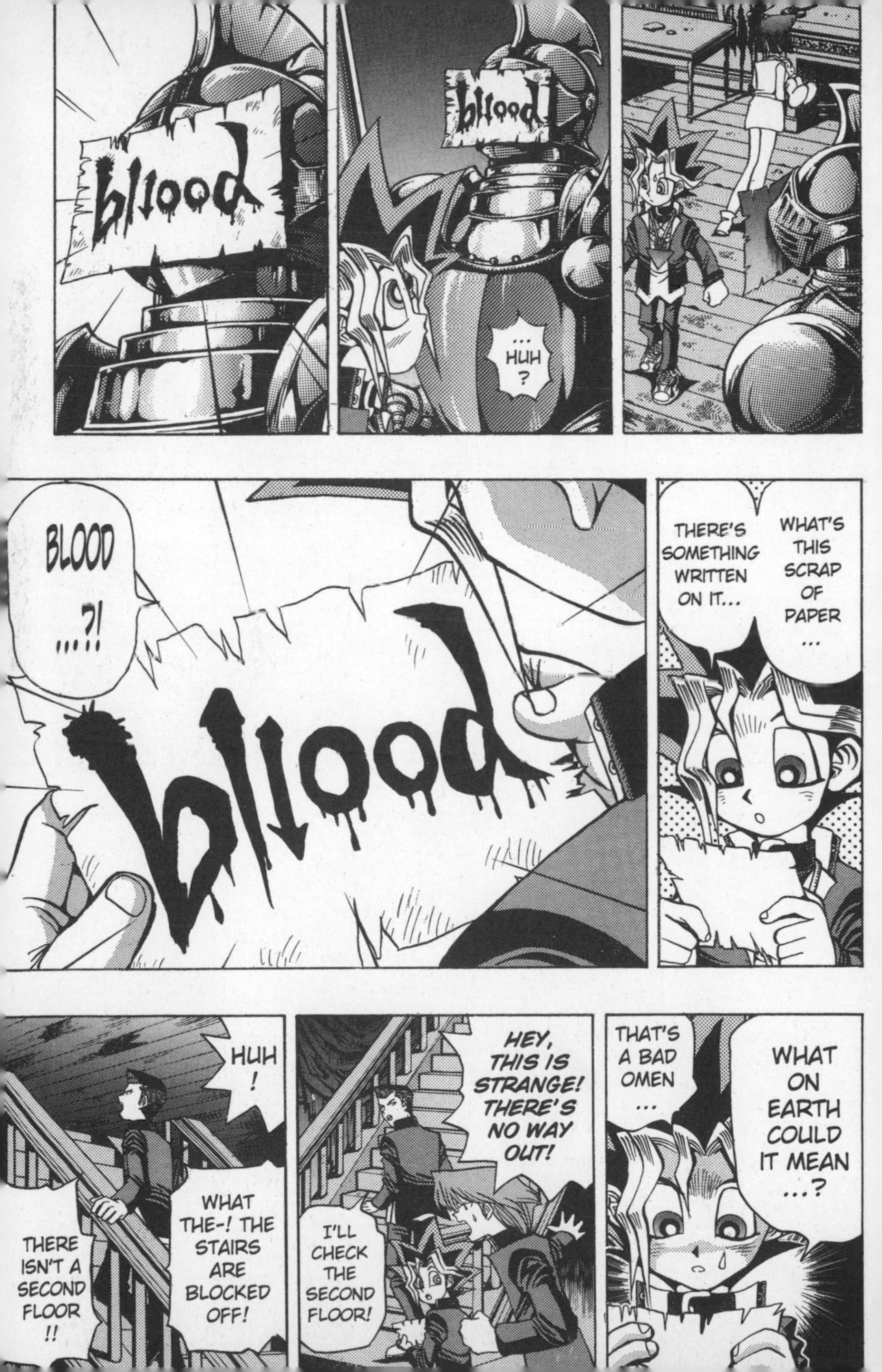

blood
... HUH ?
blood
WHAT'S THIS SCRAP OF PAPER ...
THERE'S SOMETHING WRITTEN ON IT...
BLOOD ...?!
blood
WHAT ON EARTH COULD IT MEAN ...?
THAT'S A BAD OMEN ...
HEY, THIS IS STRANGE! THERE'S NO WAY OUT!
I'LL CHECK THE SECOND FLOOR!
HUH !
WHAT THE-! THE STAIRS ARE BLOCKED OFF!
THERE ISN'T A SECOND FLOOR !!

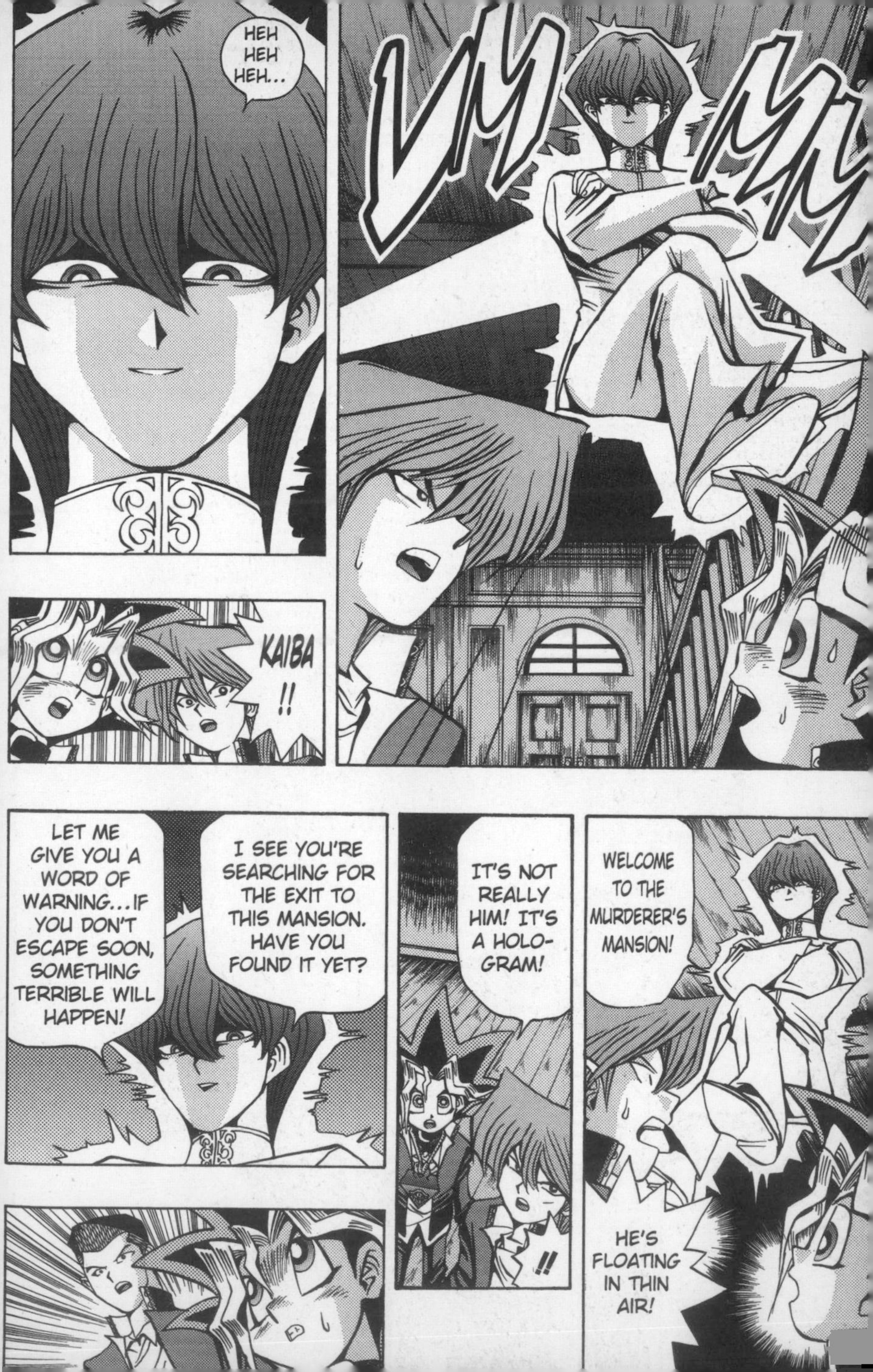
VM MM
HEH HEH HEH...
KAIBA !!
WELCOME TO THE MURDERER'S MANSION!
HE'S FLOATING IN THIN AIR!
IT'S NOT REALLY HIM! IT'S A HOLO-GRAM!
!!
I SEE YOU'RE SEARCHING FOR THE EXIT TO THIS MANSION. HAVE YOU FOUND IT YET?
LET ME GIVE YOU A WORD OF WARNING...IF YOU DON'T ESCAPE SOON, SOMETHING TERRIBLE WILL HAPPEN!

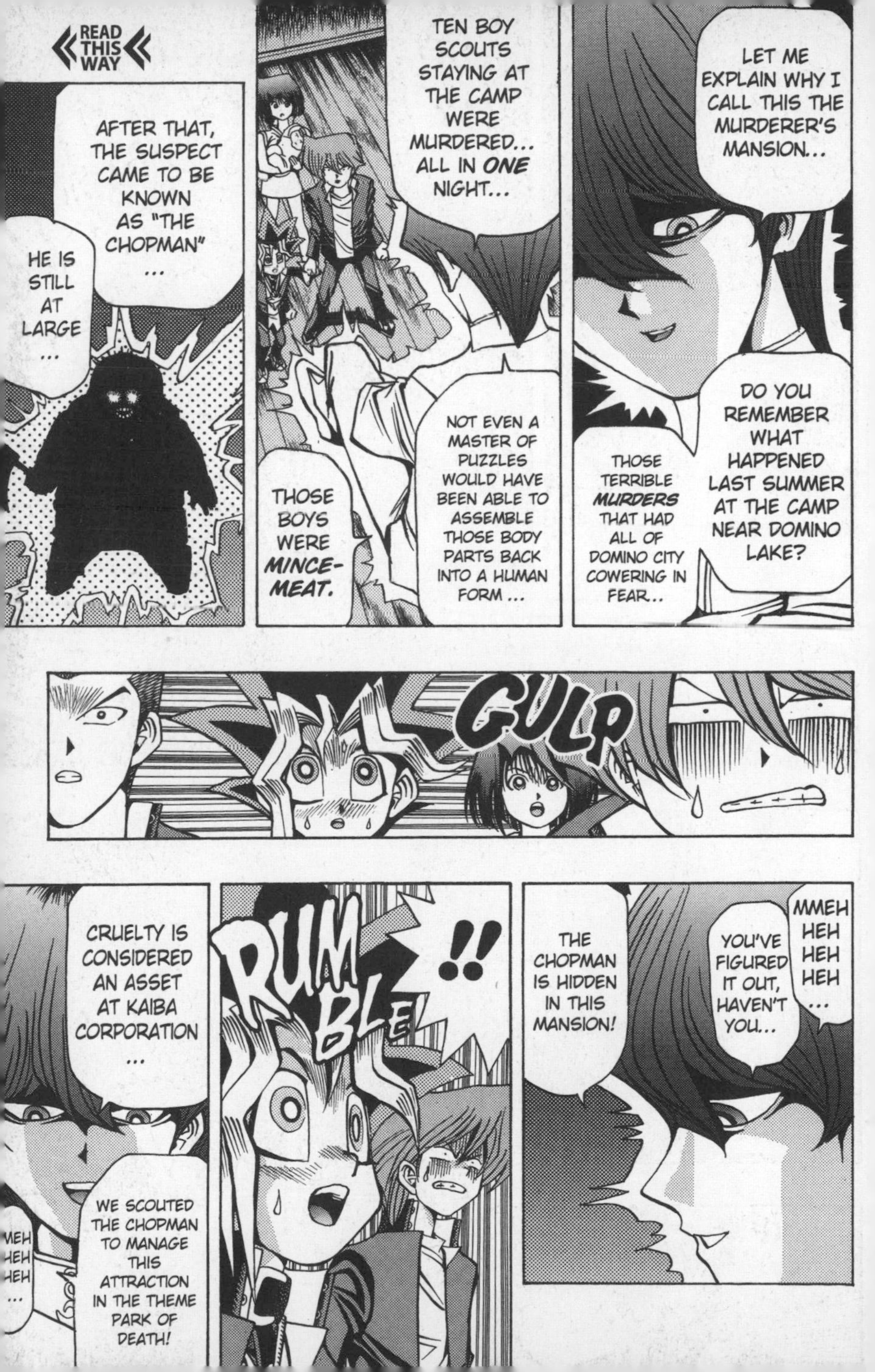
READ THIS WAY
LET ME EXPLAIN WHY I CALL THIS THE MURDERER'S MANSION...
DO YOU REMEMBER WHAT HAPPENED LAST SUMMER AT THE CAMP NEAR DOMINO LAKE?
THOSE TERRIBLE *MURDERS* THAT HAD ALL OF DOMINO CITY COWERING IN FEAR...
TEN BOY SCOUTS STAYING AT THE CAMP WERE MURDERED... ALL IN *ONE* NIGHT...
NOT EVEN A MASTER OF PUZZLES WOULD HAVE BEEN ABLE TO ASSEMBLE THOSE BODY PARTS BACK INTO A HUMAN FORM...
THOSE BOYS WERE *MINCE-MEAT.*
AFTER THAT, THE SUSPECT CAME TO BE KNOWN AS "THE CHOPMAN" ...
HE IS STILL AT LARGE ...
GULP
MMEH HEH HEH HEH ...
YOU'VE FIGURED IT OUT, HAVEN'T YOU...
THE CHOPMAN IS HIDDEN IN THIS MANSION!
RUMBLE
!!
CRUELTY IS CONSIDERED AN ASSET AT KAIBA CORPORATION ...
WE SCOUTED THE CHOPMAN TO MANAGE THIS ATTRACTION IN THE THEME PARK OF DEATH!
MEH HEH HEH ...

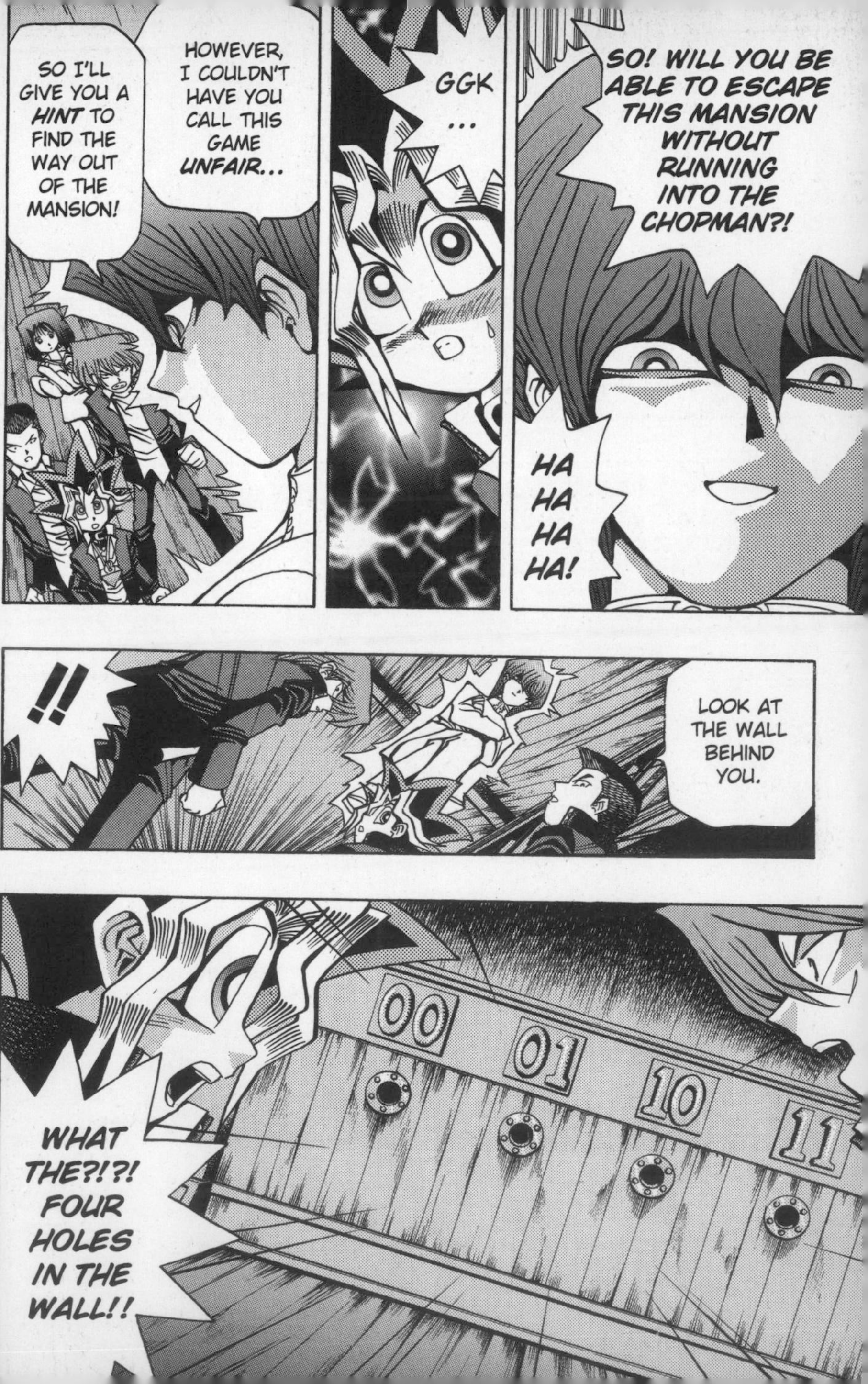
SO! WILL YOU BE ABLE TO ESCAPE THIS MANSION WITHOUT RUNNING INTO THE CHOPMAN?!
HA HA HA HA!
GGK ...
HOWEVER, I COULDN'T HAVE YOU CALL THIS GAME UNFAIR...
SO I'LL GIVE YOU A HINT TO FIND THE WAY OUT OF THE MANSION!
LOOK AT THE WALL BEHIND YOU.
!!
WHAT THE?!?! FOUR HOLES IN THE WALL!!
00
01
10
11

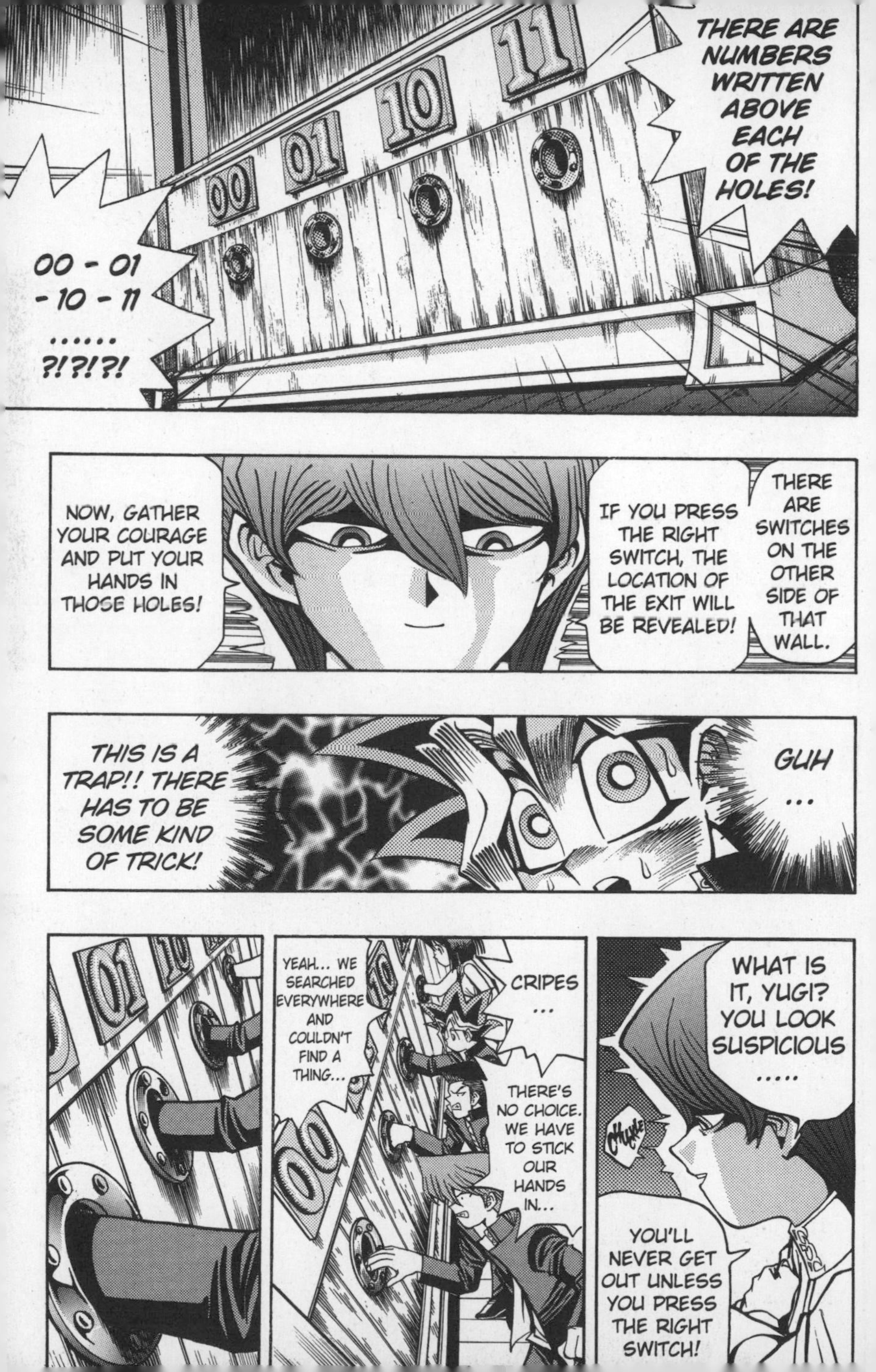
THERE ARE NUMBERS WRITTEN ABOVE EACH OF THE HOLES!
00 - 01 - 10 - 11 ...... ?!?!?!
THERE ARE SWITCHES ON THE OTHER SIDE OF THAT WALL.
IF YOU PRESS THE RIGHT SWITCH, THE LOCATION OF THE EXIT WILL BE REVEALED!
NOW, GATHER YOUR COURAGE AND PUT YOUR HANDS IN THOSE HOLES!
GUH ...
THIS IS A TRAP!! THERE HAS TO BE SOME KIND OF TRICK!
WHAT IS IT, YUGI? YOU LOOK SUSPICIOUS .....
YOU'LL NEVER GET OUT UNLESS YOU PRESS THE RIGHT SWITCH!
CRIPES ...
THERE'S NO CHOICE. WE HAVE TO STICK OUR HANDS IN...
YEAH... WE SEARCHED EVERYWHERE AND COULDN'T FIND A THING...

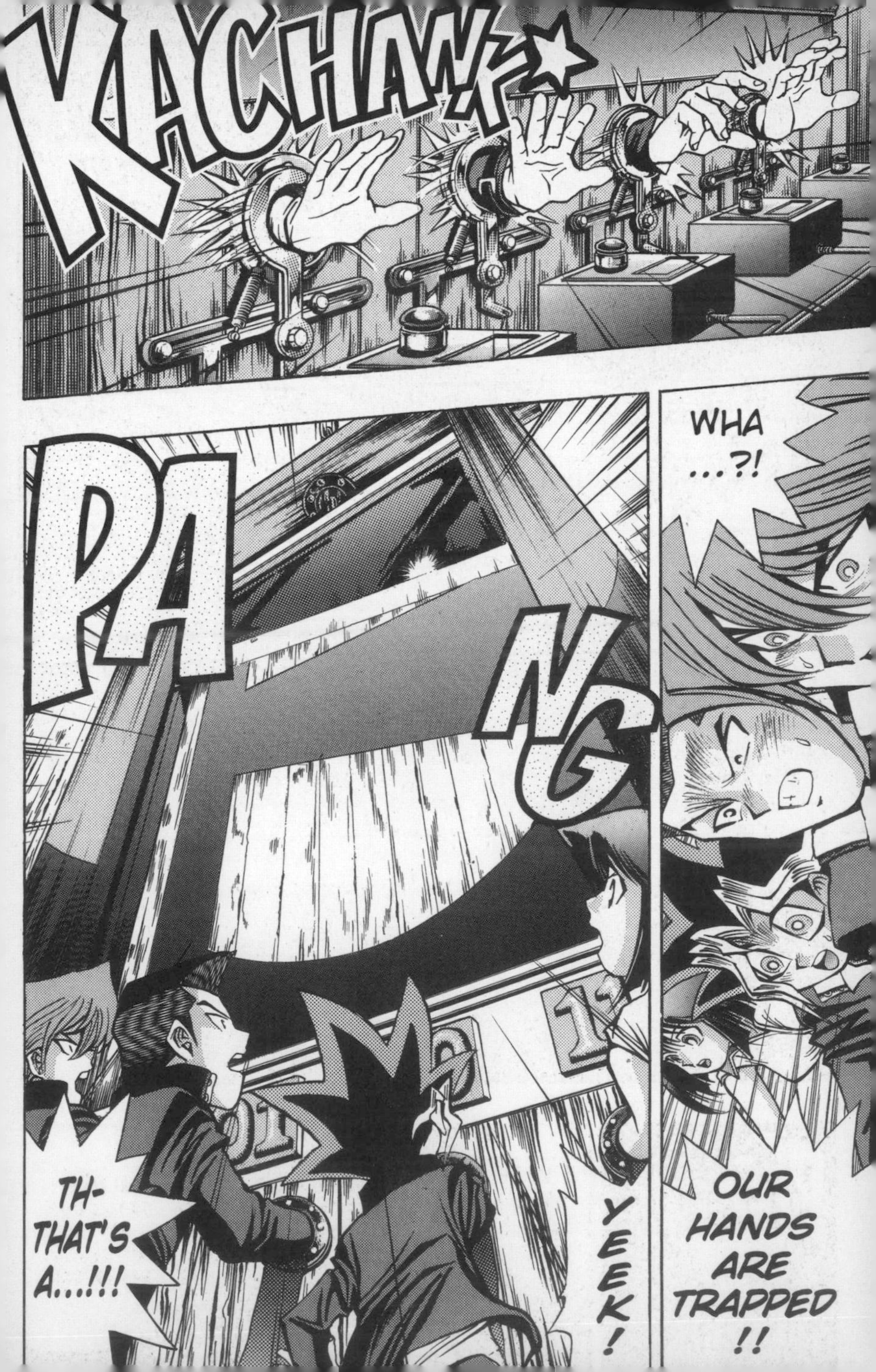
KACHAK!☆
WHA ...?!
OUR HANDS ARE TRAPPED !!
PANG
YEEK!
TH- THAT'S A...!!!

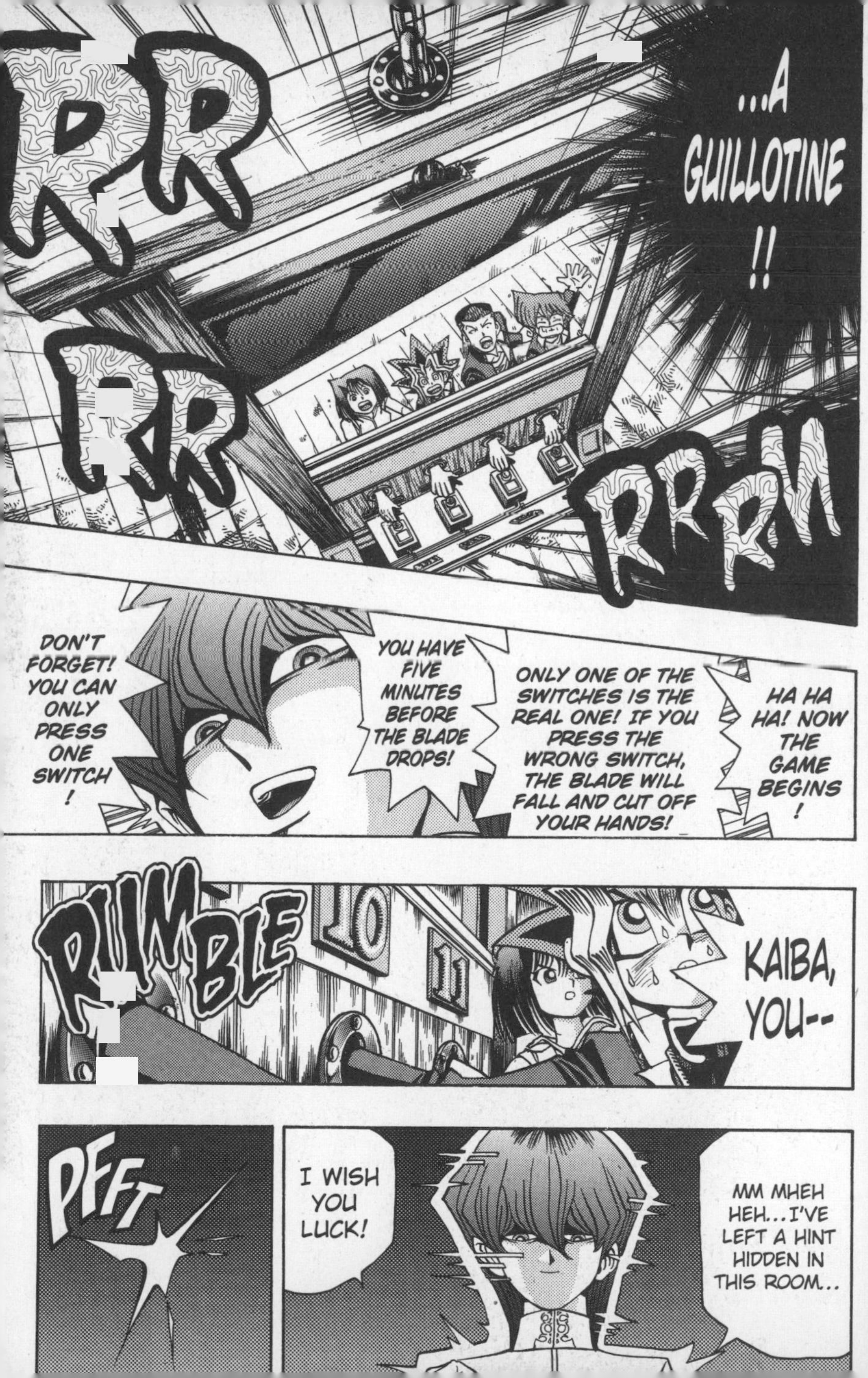
...A GUILLOTINE !!
RRRM
RR
RR
HA HA HA! NOW THE GAME BEGINS!
ONLY ONE OF THE SWITCHES IS THE REAL ONE! IF YOU PRESS THE WRONG SWITCH, THE BLADE WILL FALL AND CUT OFF YOUR HANDS!
YOU HAVE FIVE MINUTES BEFORE THE BLADE DROPS!
DON'T FORGET! YOU CAN ONLY PRESS ONE SWITCH!
KAIBA, YOU--
10
11
RUMBLE
MM MHEH HEH...I'VE LEFT A HINT HIDDEN IN THIS ROOM...
I WISH YOU LUCK!
PFFT

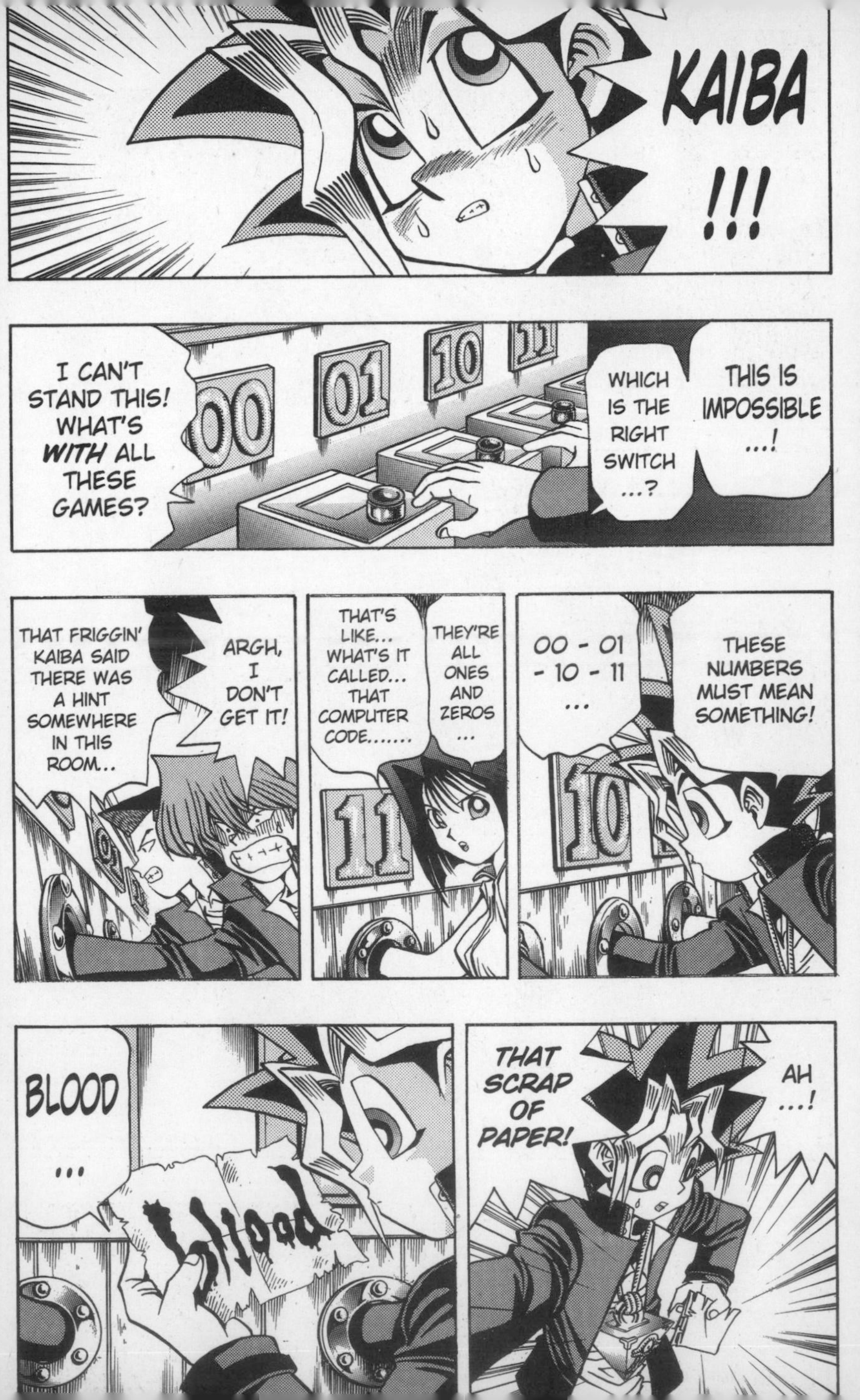
KAIBA !!!
THIS IS IMPOSSIBLE ...!
WHICH IS THE RIGHT SWITCH ...?
I CAN'T STAND THIS! WHAT'S *WITH* ALL THESE GAMES?
THESE NUMBERS MUST MEAN SOMETHING!
00 - 01 - 10 - 11 ...
THEY'RE ALL ONES AND ZEROS ...
THAT'S LIKE... WHAT'S IT CALLED... THAT COMPUTER CODE.......
ARGH, I DON'T GET IT!
THAT FRIGGIN' KAIBA SAID THERE WAS A HINT SOMEWHERE IN THIS ROOM...
AH ...!
THAT SCRAP OF PAPER!
BLOOD ...
blood

READ THIS WAY

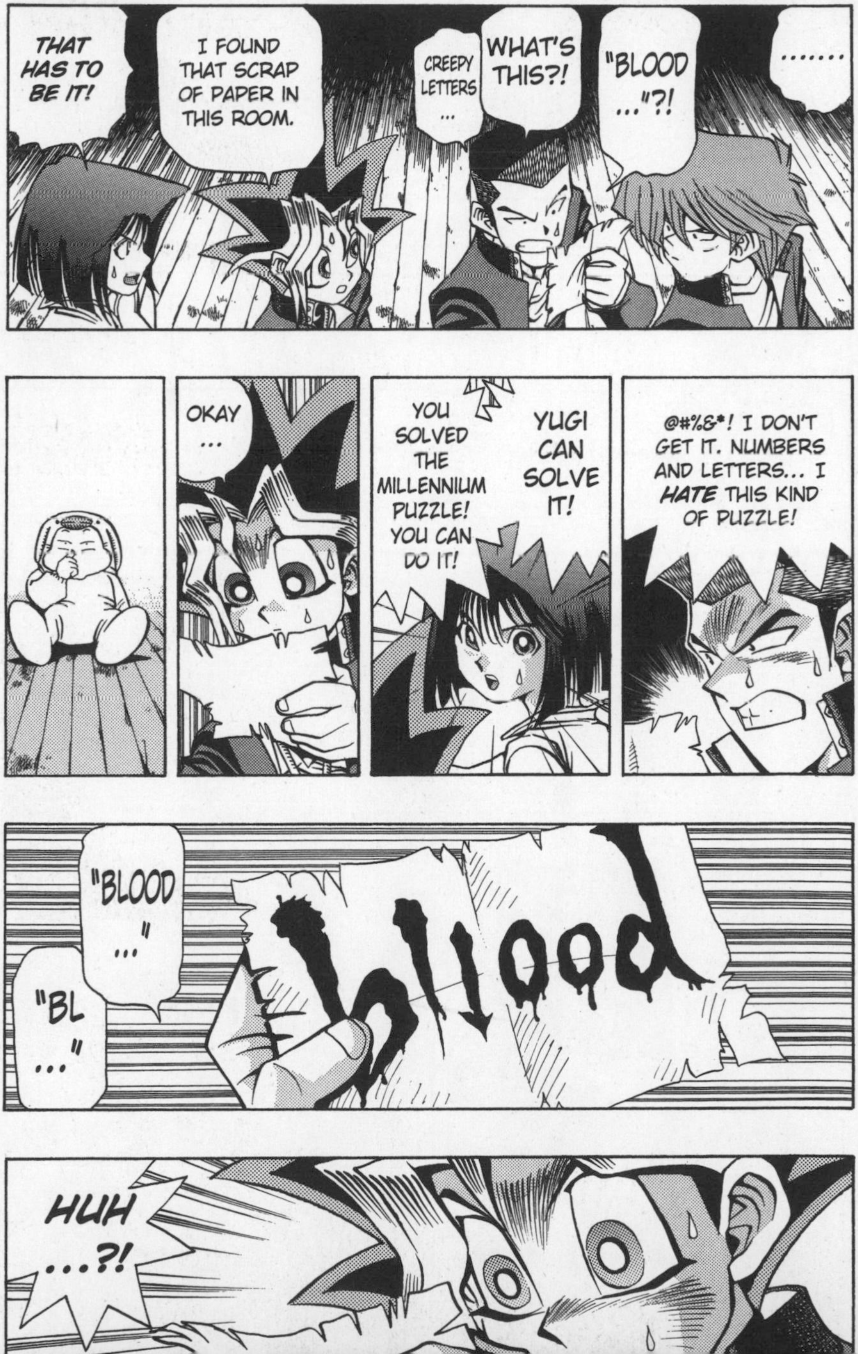

....
"BLOOD ..."?!
WHAT'S THIS?!
CREEPY LETTERS ...
I FOUND THAT SCRAP OF PAPER IN THIS ROOM.
THAT HAS TO BE IT!
@#%&*! I DON'T GET IT. NUMBERS AND LETTERS... I HATE THIS KIND OF PUZZLE!
YUGI CAN SOLVE IT!
YOU SOLVED THE MILLENNIUM PUZZLE! YOU CAN DO IT!
OKAY ...
"BLOOD ..."
"BL ..."
blood
HUH ...?!

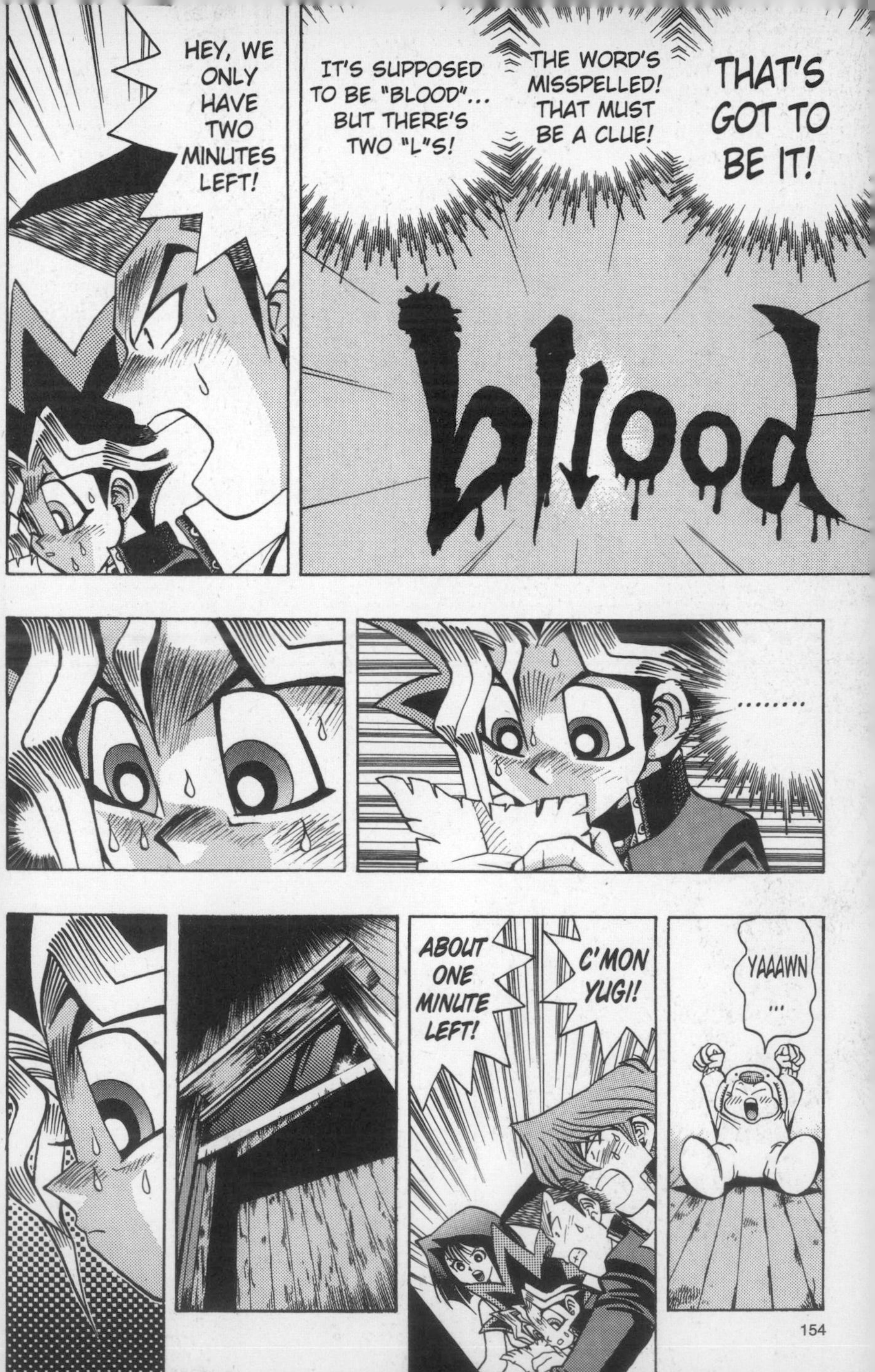
THAT'S GOT TO BE IT!
THE WORD'S MISSPELLED! THAT MUST BE A CLUE!
IT'S SUPPOSED TO BE "BLOOD"... BUT THERE'S TWO "L"S!
blood
HEY, WE ONLY HAVE TWO MINUTES LEFT!
....
YAAAWN ...
C'MON YUGI!
ABOUT ONE MINUTE LEFT!

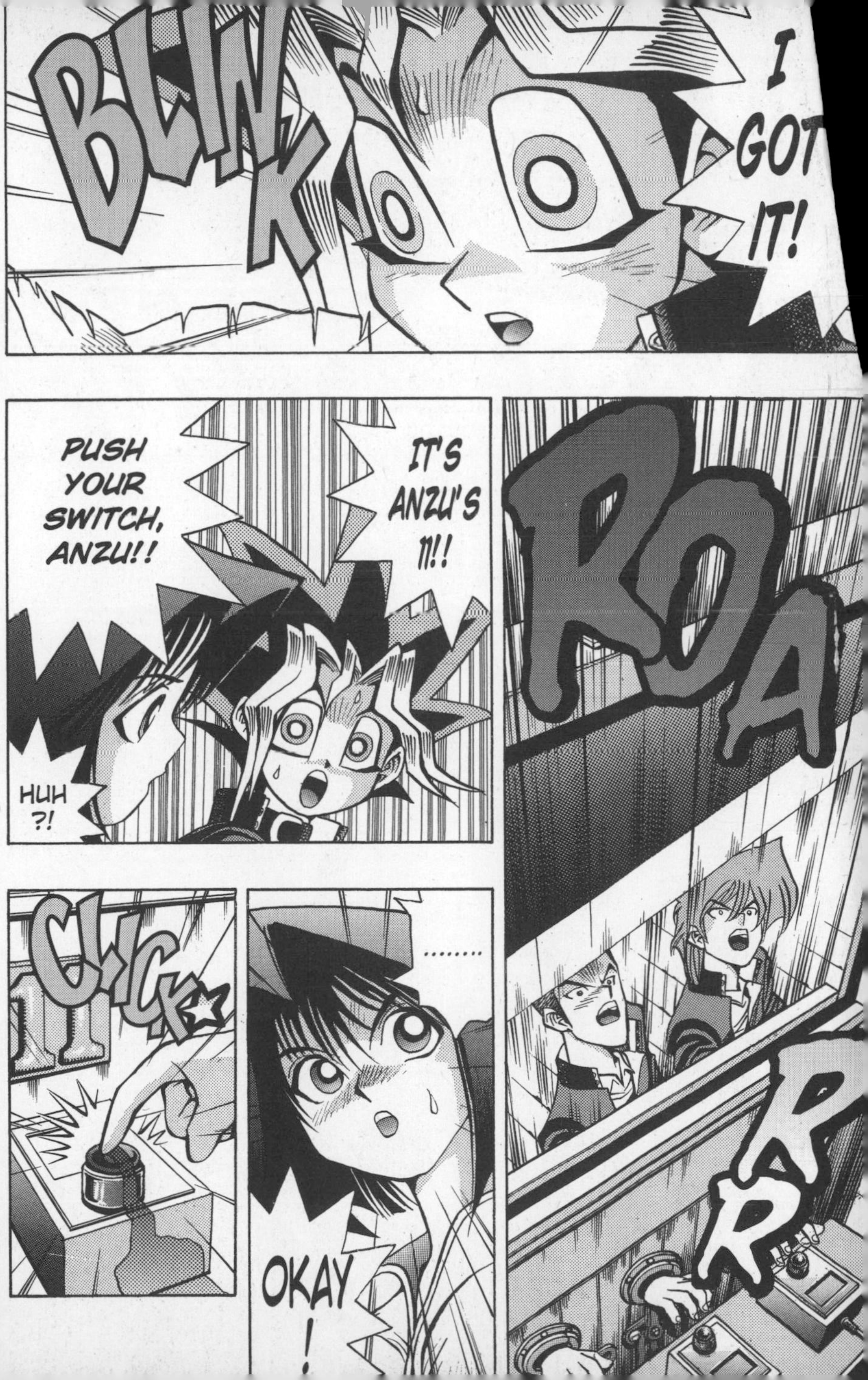
I GOT IT!
BLINK
ROA
R
IT'S ANZU'S 11!!
PUSH YOUR SWITCH, ANZU!!
HUH ?!
OKAY !
....
CLICK

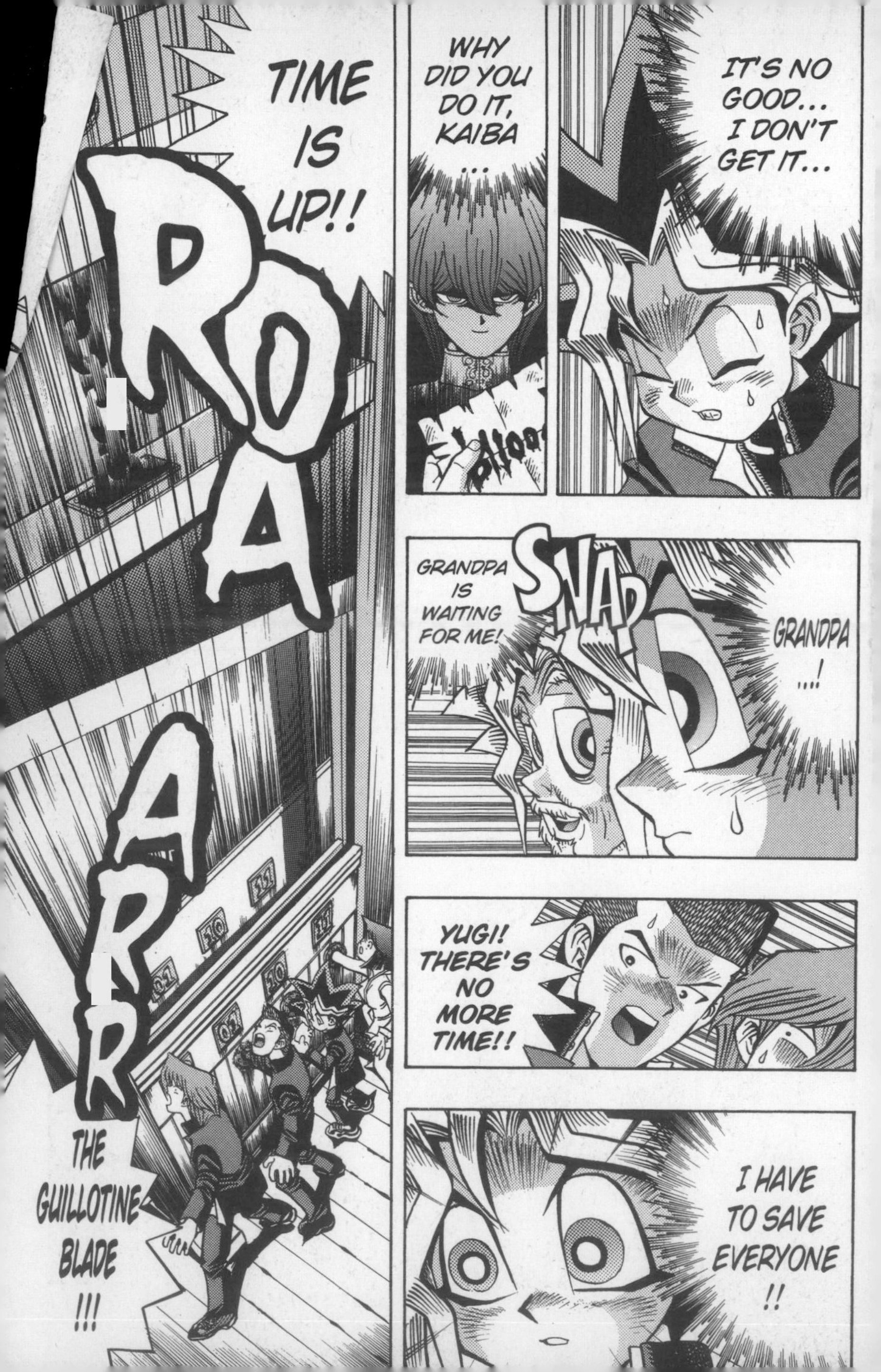
IT'S NO GOOD... I DON'T GET IT...
WHY DID YOU DO IT, KAIBA ...
GRANDPA ...!
SNAP
GRANDPA IS WAITING FOR ME!
YUGI! THERE'S NO MORE TIME!!
I HAVE TO SAVE EVERYONE !!
TIME IS UP!!
ROAAR
THE GUILLOTINE BLADE !!!

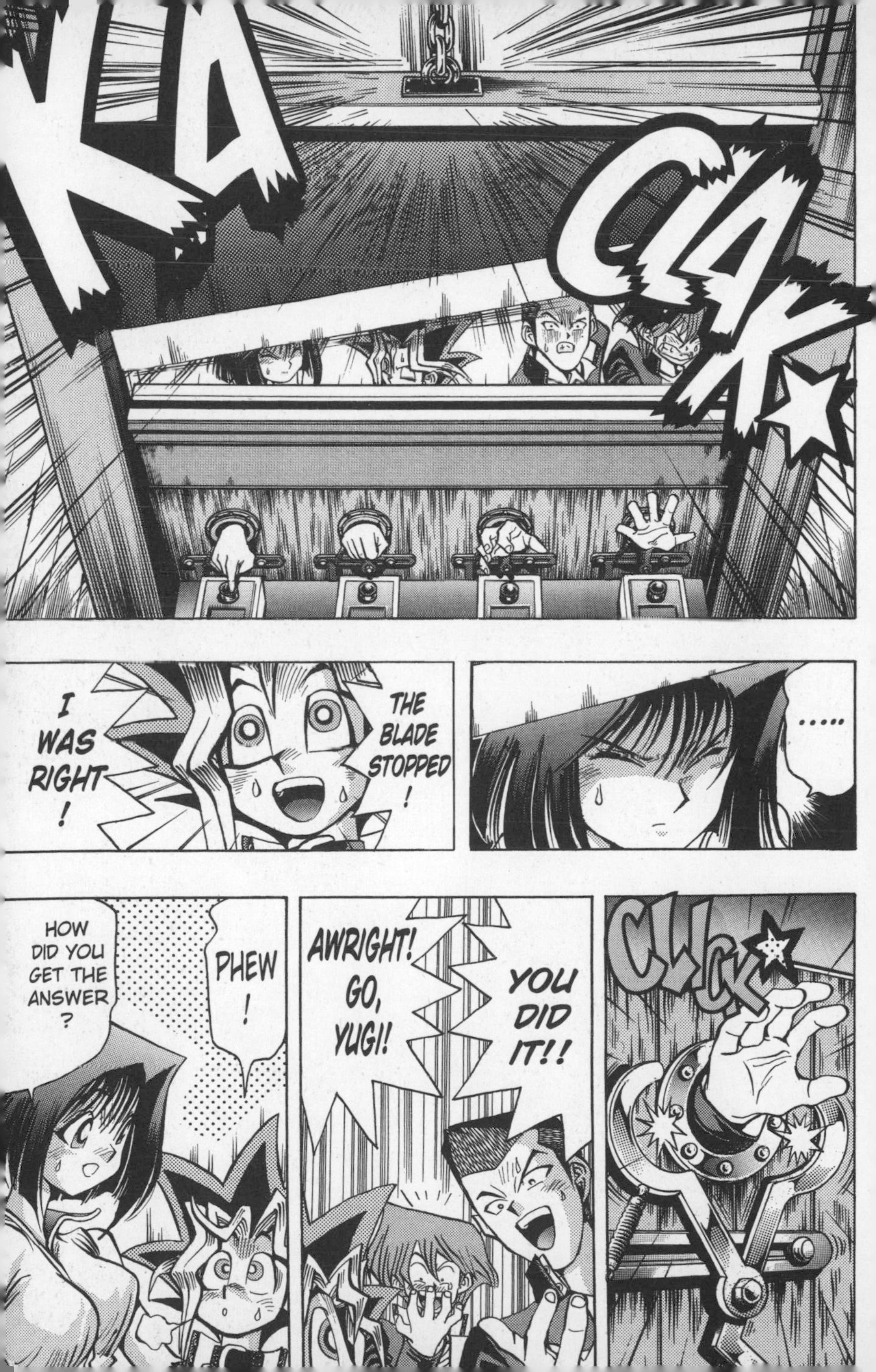
KA
CLACK
.....
THE BLADE STOPPED!
I WAS RIGHT!
CLICK
YOU DID IT!!
AWRIGHT! GO, YUGI!
PHEW!
HOW DID YOU GET THE ANSWER?

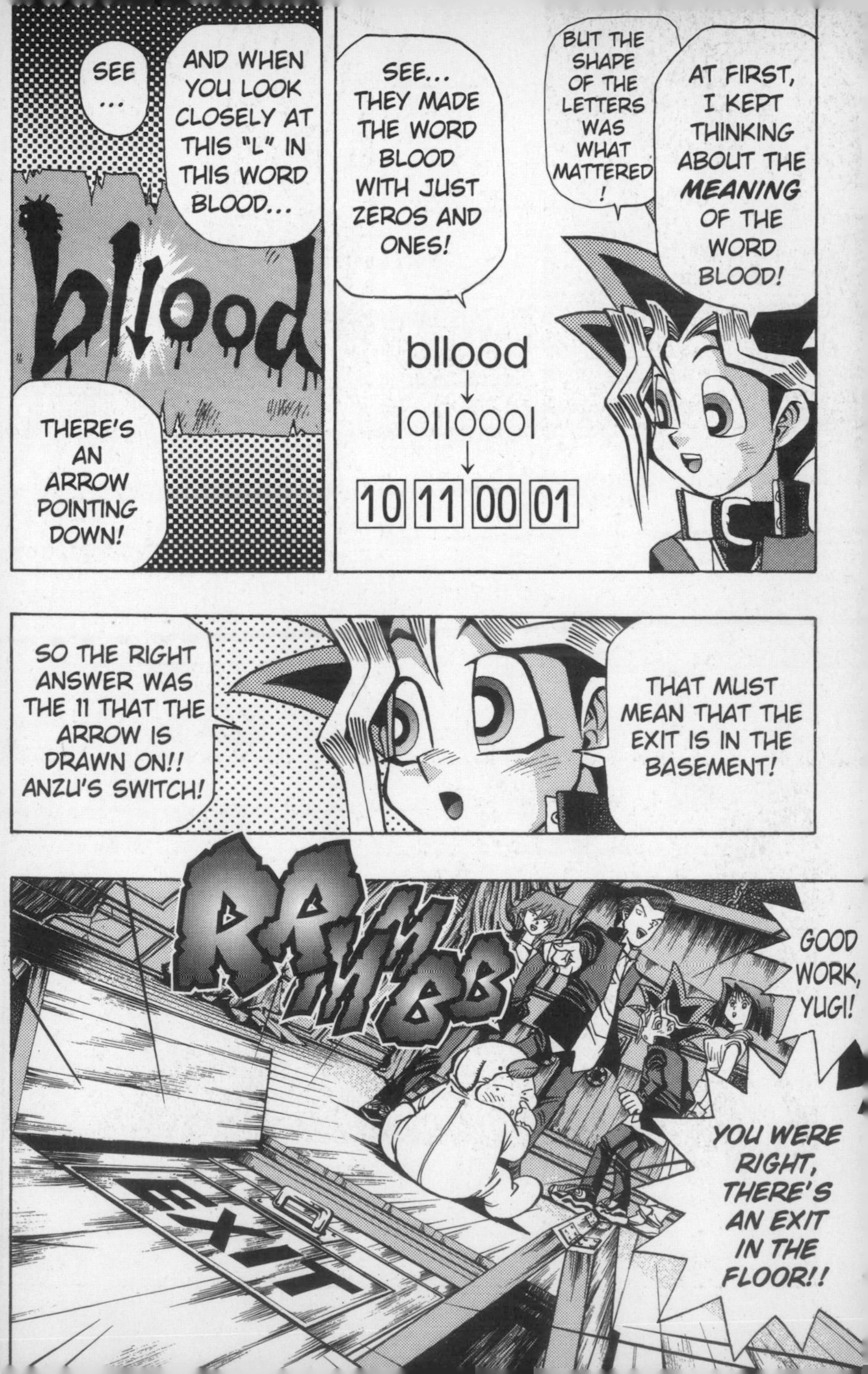
AT FIRST, I KEPT THINKING ABOUT THE ***MEANING*** OF THE WORD BLOOD!
BUT THE SHAPE OF THE LETTERS WAS WHAT MATTERED!
SEE... THEY MADE THE WORD BLOOD WITH JUST ZEROS AND ONES!
bllood
|0||000|
10 11 00 01
AND WHEN YOU LOOK CLOSELY AT THIS "L" IN THIS WORD BLOOD...
SEE...
bllood
THERE'S AN ARROW POINTING DOWN!
THAT MUST MEAN THAT THE EXIT IS IN THE BASEMENT!
SO THE RIGHT ANSWER WAS THE 11 THAT THE ARROW IS DRAWN ON!! ANZU'S SWITCH!
GOOD WORK, YUGI!
YOU WERE RIGHT, THERE'S AN EXIT IN THE FLOOR!!
RAMBB
EXIT

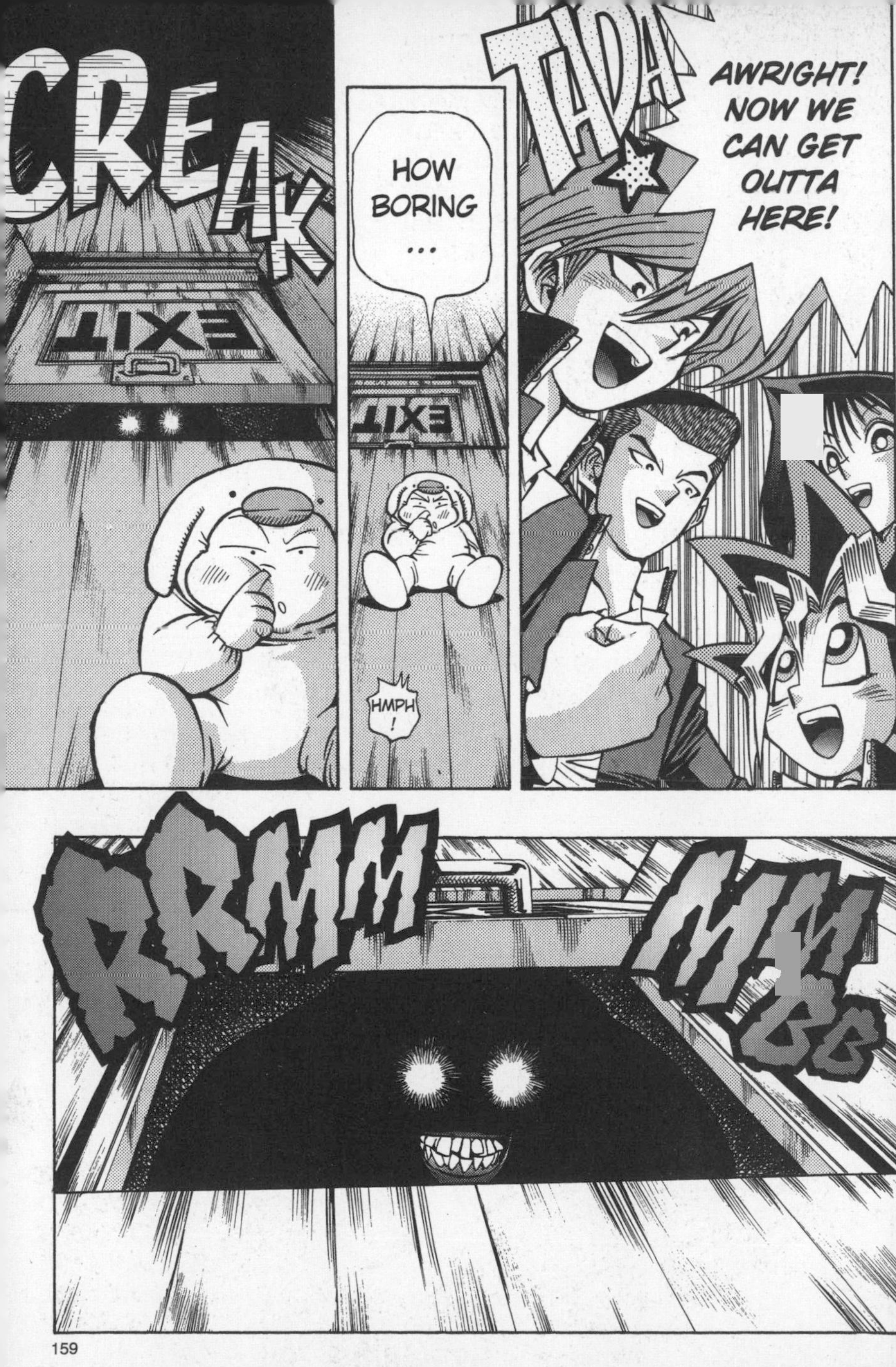

TADA
AWRIGHT! NOW WE CAN GET OUTTA HERE!
HOW BORING ...
HMPH!
CREAK
BRMM
MMBB

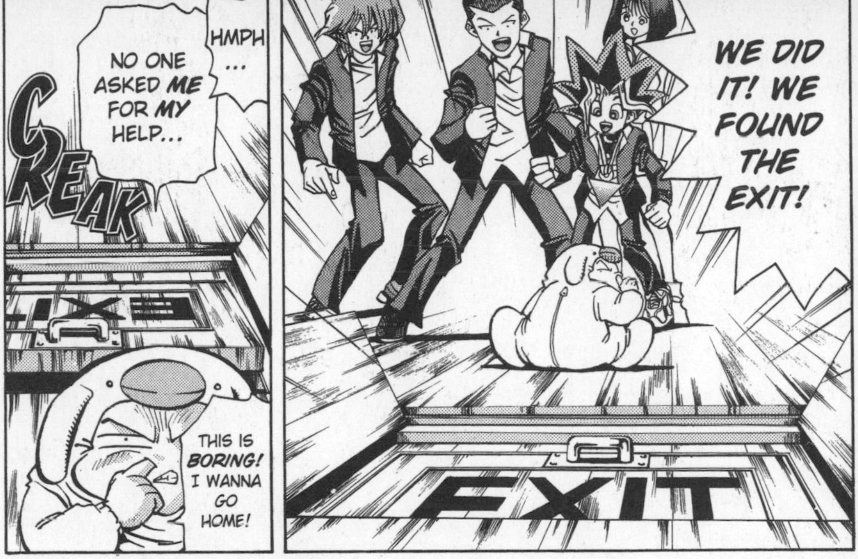
WE DID IT! WE FOUND THE EXIT!
HMPH ...
NO ONE ASKED ME FOR MY HELP...
CREAK
EXIT
THIS IS BORING! I WANNA GO HOME!

Duel 32: Chainsaw Deathmatch!!

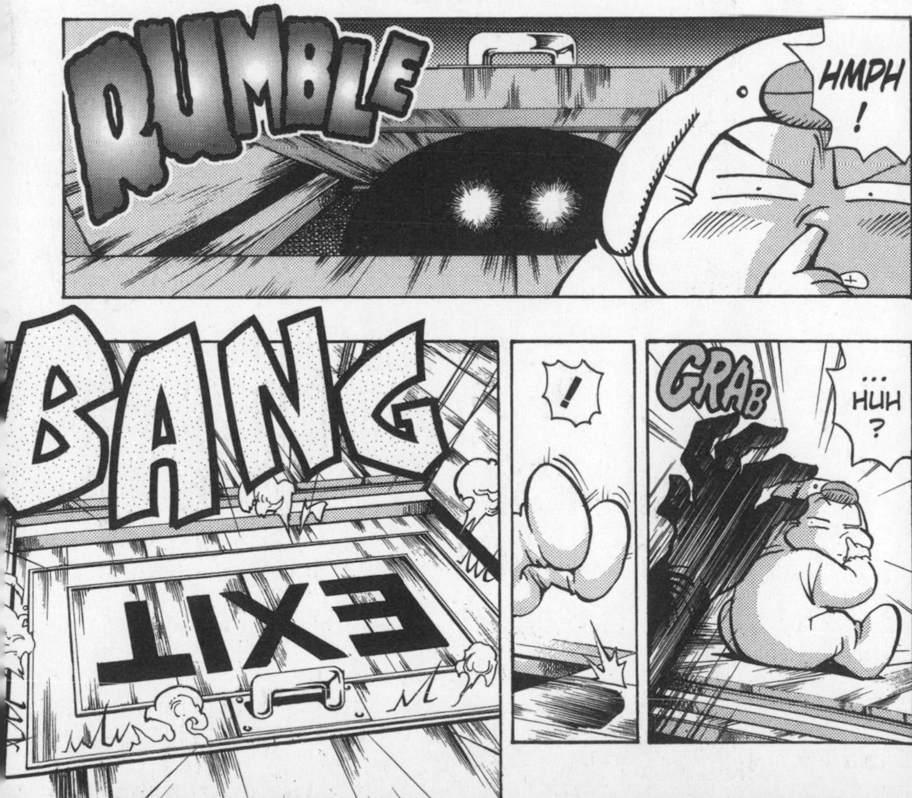
RUMBLE
HMPH!
... HUH?
GRAB
!
BANG
EXIT

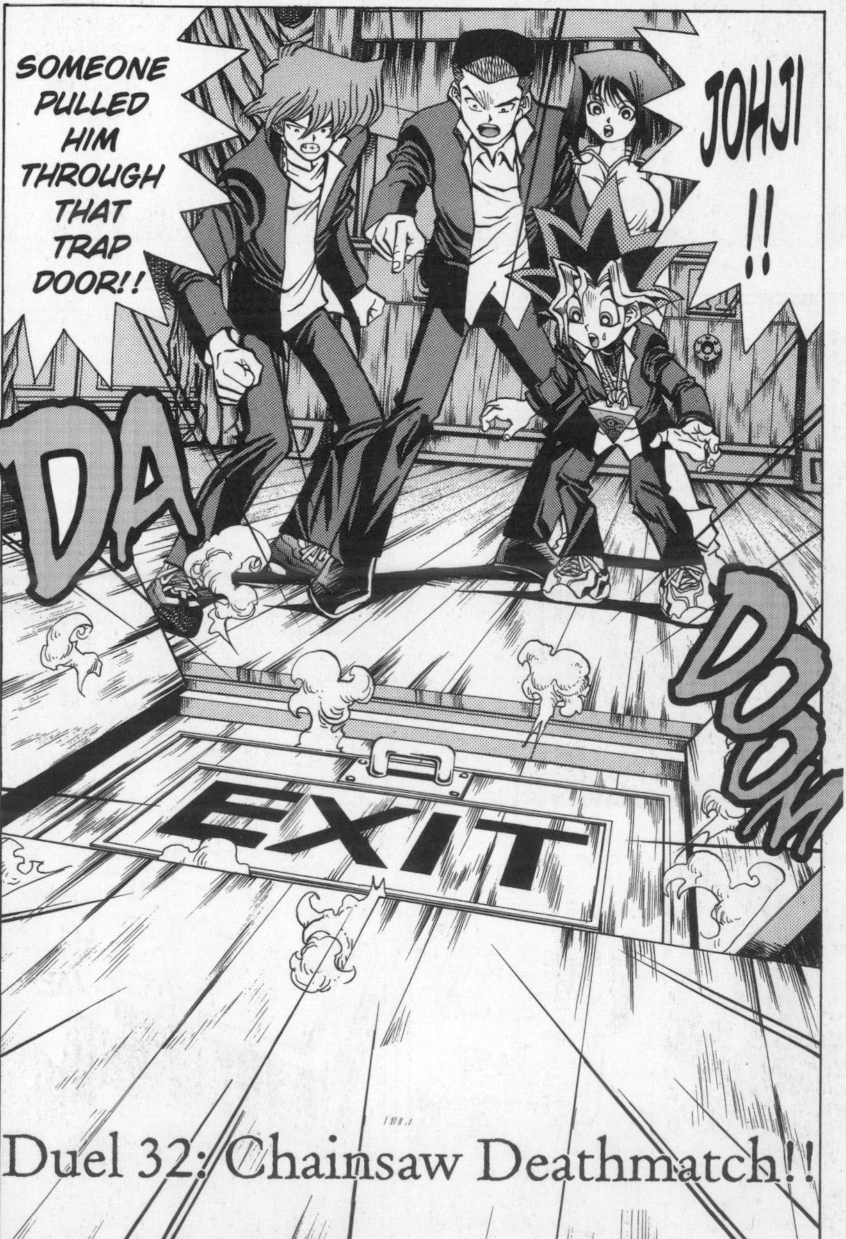
JOHJI!!
SOMEONE PULLED HIM THROUGH THAT TRAP DOOR!!
DA
DOOM
EXIT
Duel 32: Chainsaw Deathmatch!!

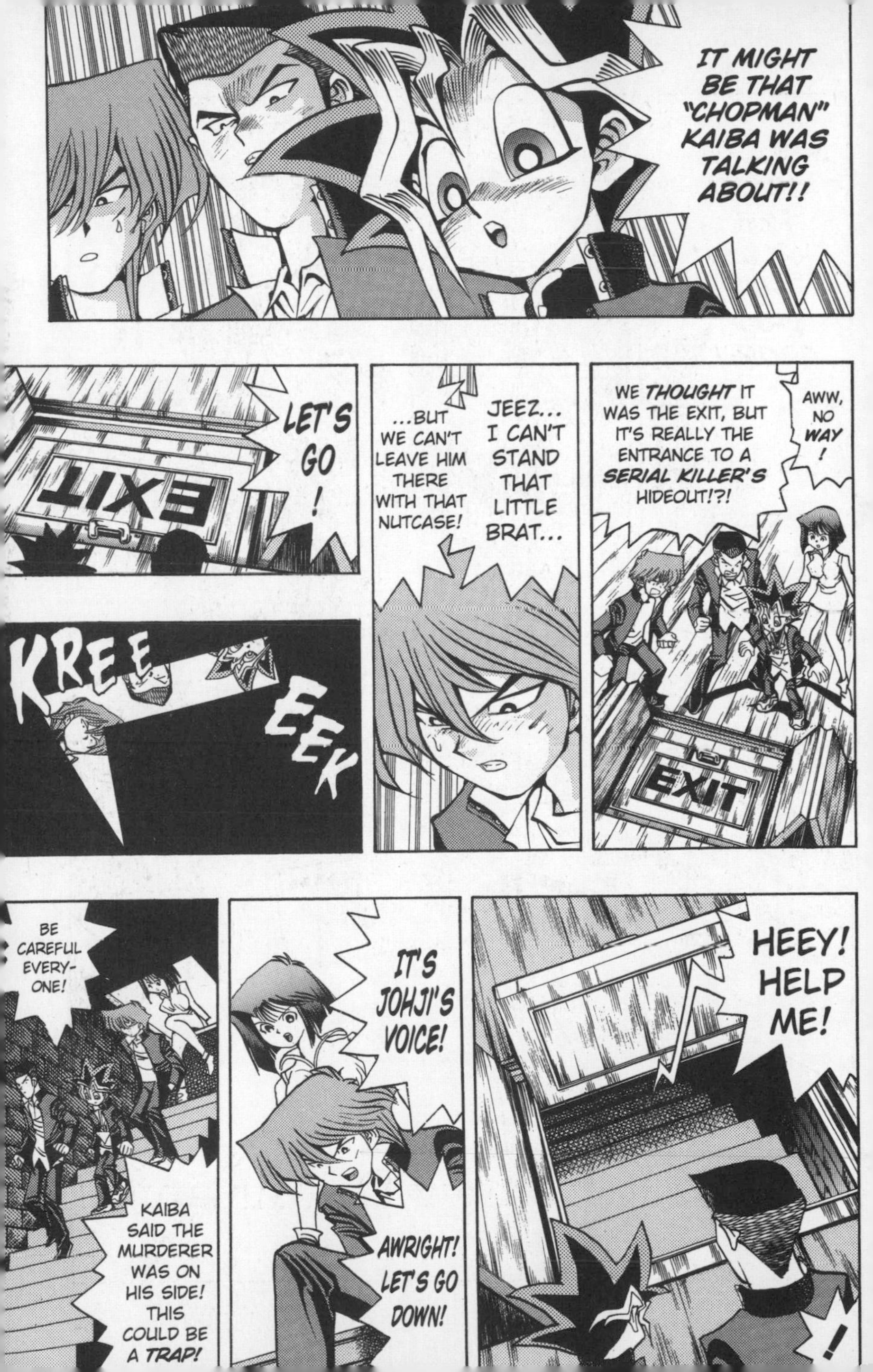
IT MIGHT BE THAT "CHOPMAN" KAIBA WAS TALKING ABOUT!!
AWW, NO WAY!
WE THOUGHT IT WAS THE EXIT, BUT IT'S REALLY THE ENTRANCE TO A SERIAL KILLER'S HIDEOUT!?!
EXIT
JEEZ... I CAN'T STAND THAT LITTLE BRAT...
...BUT WE CAN'T LEAVE HIM THERE WITH THAT NUTCASE!
LET'S GO!
EXIT
KREE
EEK
HEEY! HELP ME!
!
IT'S JOHJI'S VOICE!
AWRIGHT! LET'S GO DOWN!
BE CAREFUL EVERY-ONE!
KAIBA SAID THE MURDERER WAS ON HIS SIDE! THIS COULD BE A TRAP!

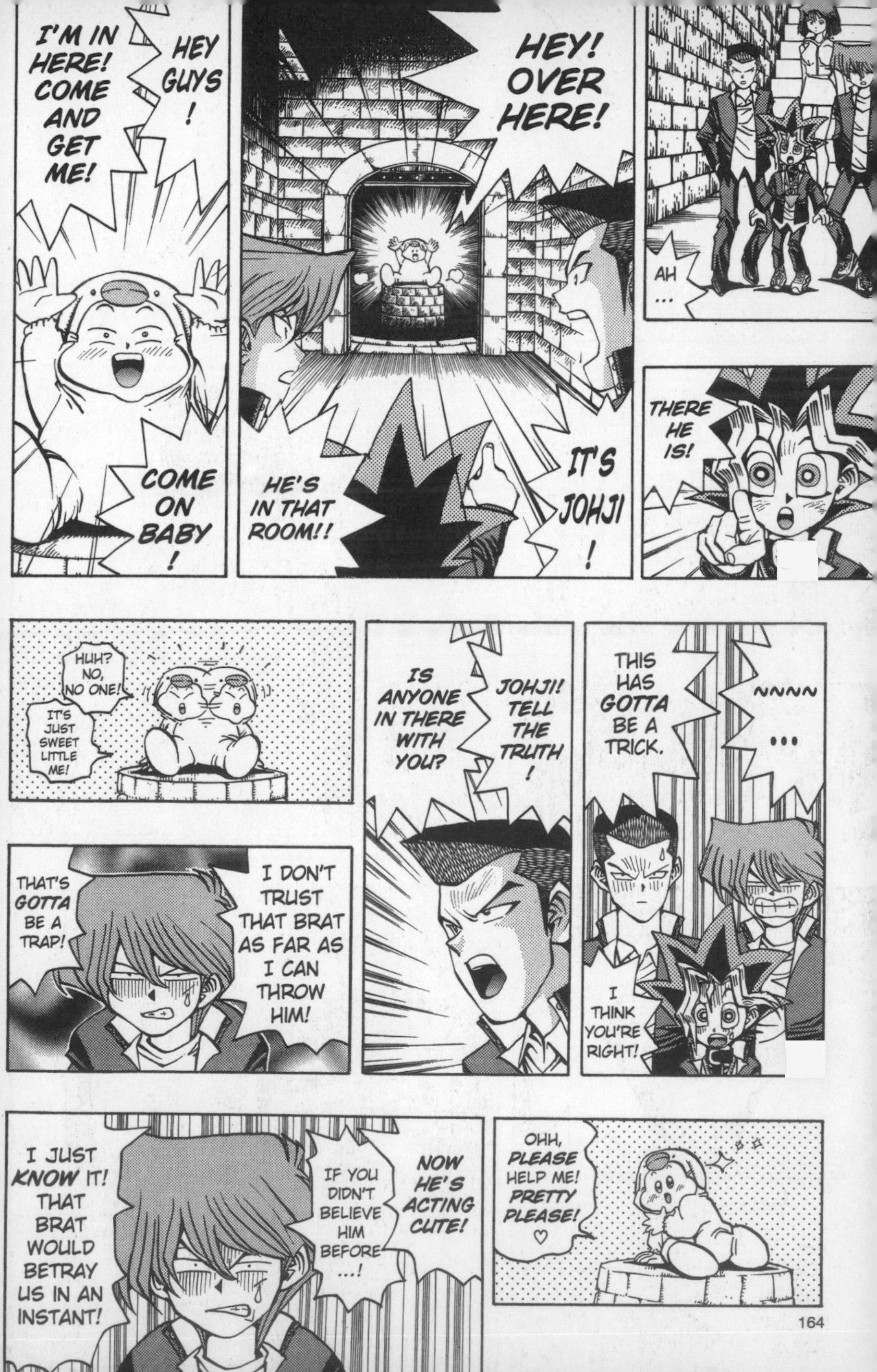
AH ...
THERE HE IS!
HEY! OVER HERE!
IT'S JOHJI!
HE'S IN THAT ROOM!!
I'M IN HERE! COME AND GET ME!
HEY GUYS!
COME ON BABY!
THIS HAS GOTTA BE A TRICK.
NNNN ...
I THINK YOU'RE RIGHT!
JOHJI! TELL THE TRUTH!
IS ANYONE IN THERE WITH YOU?
HUH? NO, NO ONE!
IT'S JUST SWEET LITTLE ME!
I DON'T TRUST THAT BRAT AS FAR AS I CAN THROW HIM!
THAT'S GOTTA BE A TRAP!
OHH, PLEASE HELP ME! PRETTY PLEASE! ♡
NOW HE'S ACTING CUTE!
IF YOU DIDN'T BELIEVE HIM BEFORE ...!
I JUST KNOW IT! THAT BRAT WOULD BETRAY US IN AN INSTANT!

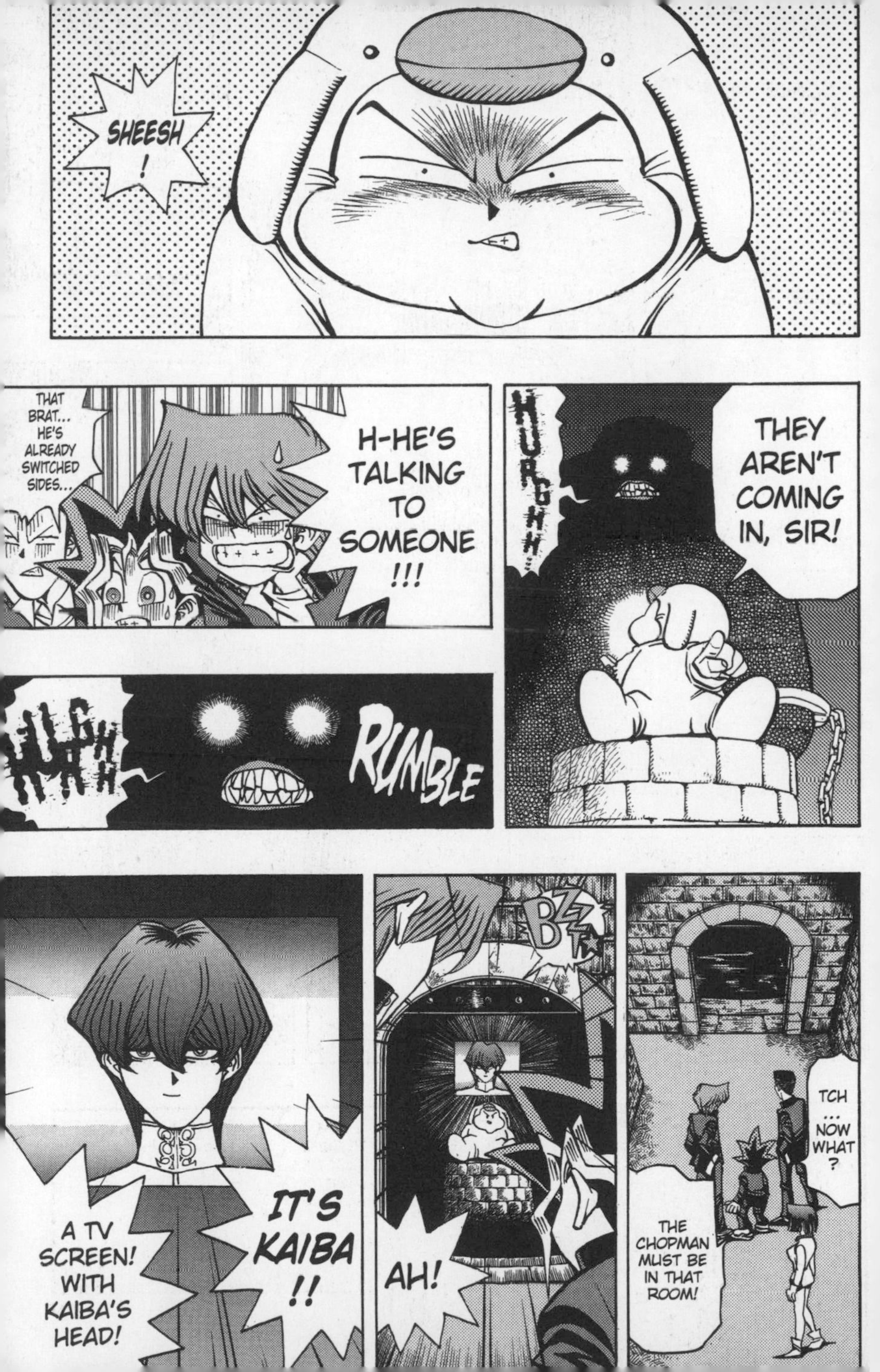
SHEESH !
THEY AREN'T COMING IN, SIR!
HURGHH...
H-HE'S TALKING TO SOMEONE !!!
THAT BRAT... HE'S ALREADY SWITCHED SIDES...
HUGHHH
RUMBLE
TCH ... NOW WHAT ?
THE CHOPMAN MUST BE IN THAT ROOM!
BZZT
AH!
IT'S KAIBA !!
A TV SCREEN! WITH KAIBA'S HEAD!

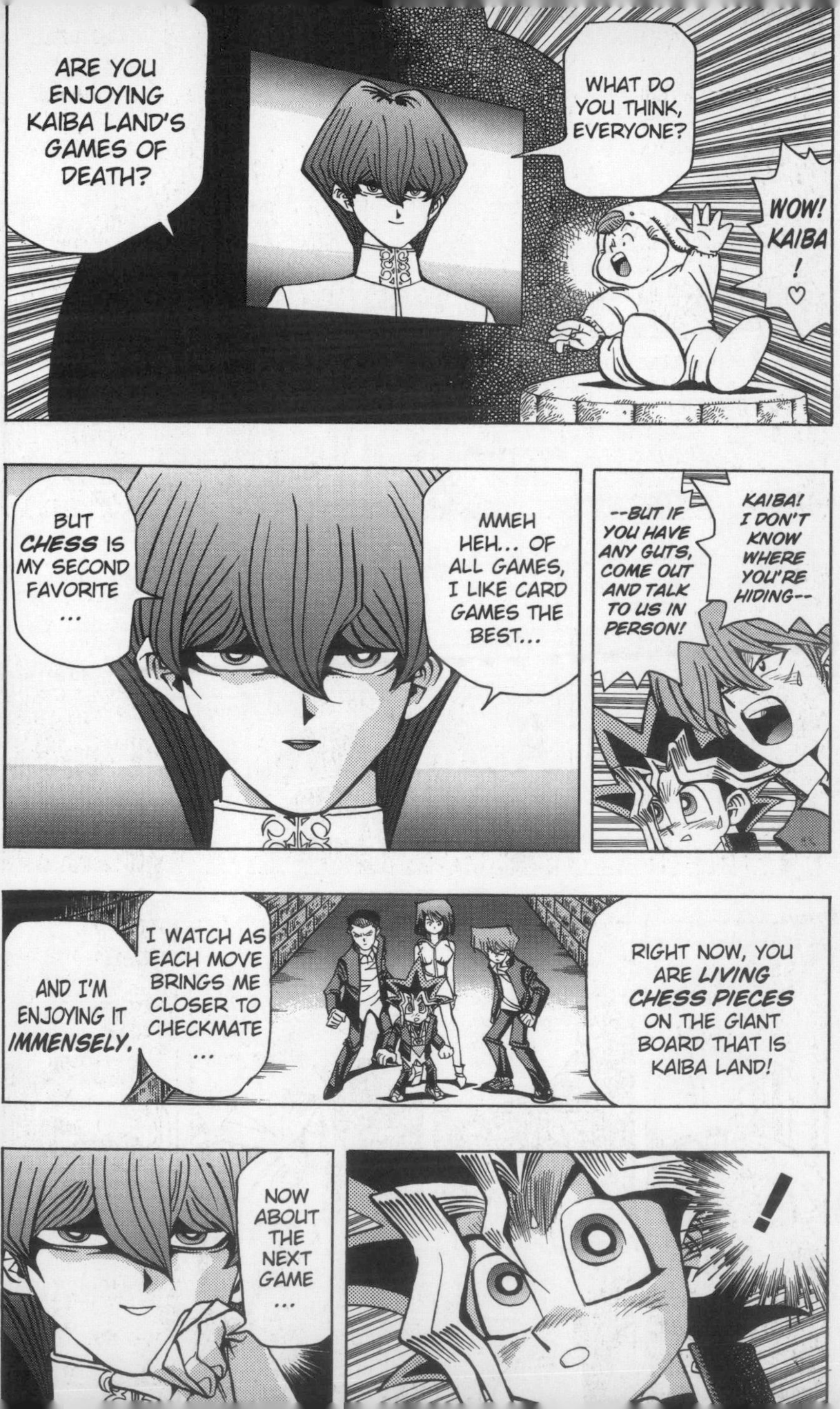
WHAT DO YOU THINK, EVERYONE?
ARE YOU ENJOYING KAIBA LAND'S GAMES OF DEATH?
WOW! KAIBA! ♡
KAIBA! I DON'T KNOW WHERE YOU'RE HIDING--
--BUT IF YOU HAVE ANY GUTS, COME OUT AND TALK TO US IN PERSON!
MMEH HEH... OF ALL GAMES, I LIKE CARD GAMES THE BEST...
BUT CHESS IS MY SECOND FAVORITE ...
RIGHT NOW, YOU ARE LIVING CHESS PIECES ON THE GIANT BOARD THAT IS KAIBA LAND!
I WATCH AS EACH MOVE BRINGS ME CLOSER TO CHECKMATE ...
AND I'M ENJOYING IT IMMENSELY.
!
NOW ABOUT THE NEXT GAME ...

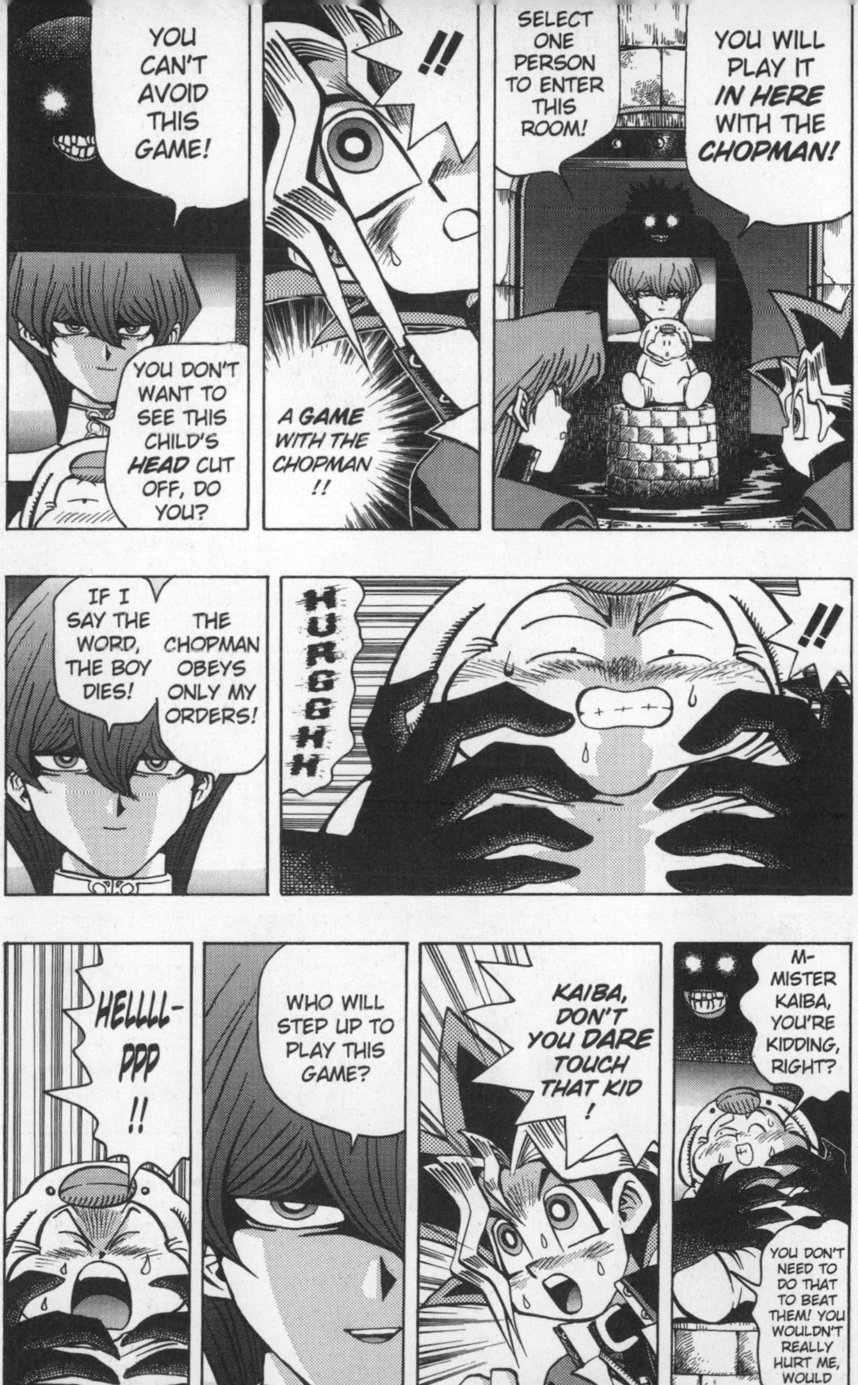
YOU WILL PLAY IT *IN HERE* WITH THE *CHOPMAN!*
SELECT ONE PERSON TO ENTER THIS ROOM!
!!
A *GAME* WITH THE CHOPMAN !!
YOU CAN'T AVOID THIS GAME!
YOU DON'T WANT TO SEE THIS CHILD'S *HEAD* CUT OFF, DO YOU?
!!
HURGGHH
IF I SAY THE WORD, THE BOY DIES!
THE CHOPMAN OBEYS ONLY MY ORDERS!
M-MISTER KAIBA, YOU'RE KIDDING, RIGHT?
YOU DON'T NEED TO DO THAT TO BEAT THEM! YOU WOULDN'T REALLY HURT ME, WOULD YOU?
KAIBA, DON'T YOU DARE TOUCH THAT KID!
WHO WILL STEP UP TO PLAY THIS GAME?
HELLLL-PPP !!

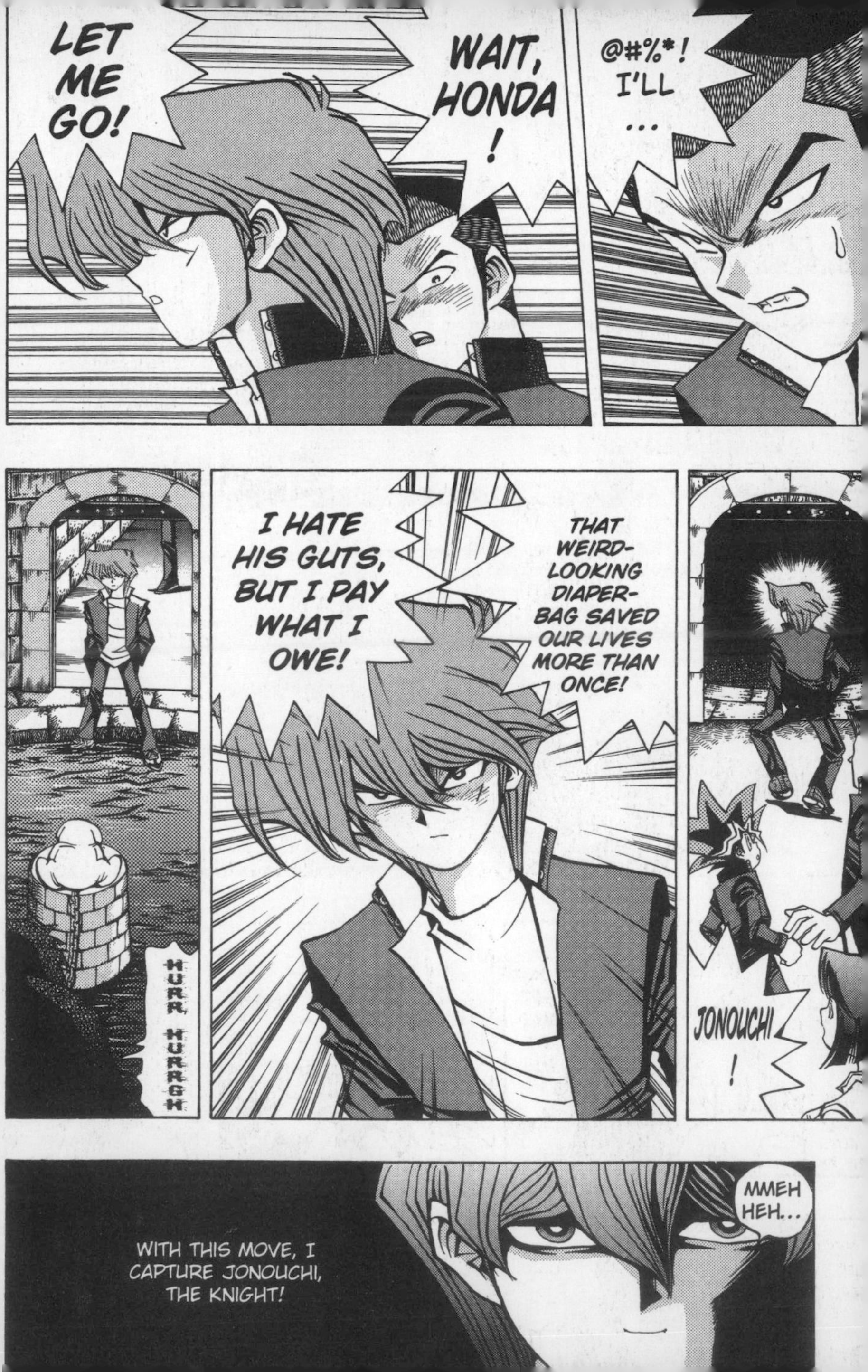
@#%*! I'LL ...
WAIT, HONDA!
LET ME GO!
JONOUCHI!
THAT WEIRD-LOOKING DIAPER-BAG SAVED OUR LIVES MORE THAN ONCE!
I HATE HIS GUTS, BUT I PAY WHAT I OWE!
HURR, HURRGH
MMEH HEH...
WITH THIS MOVE, I CAPTURE JONOUCHI, THE KNIGHT!

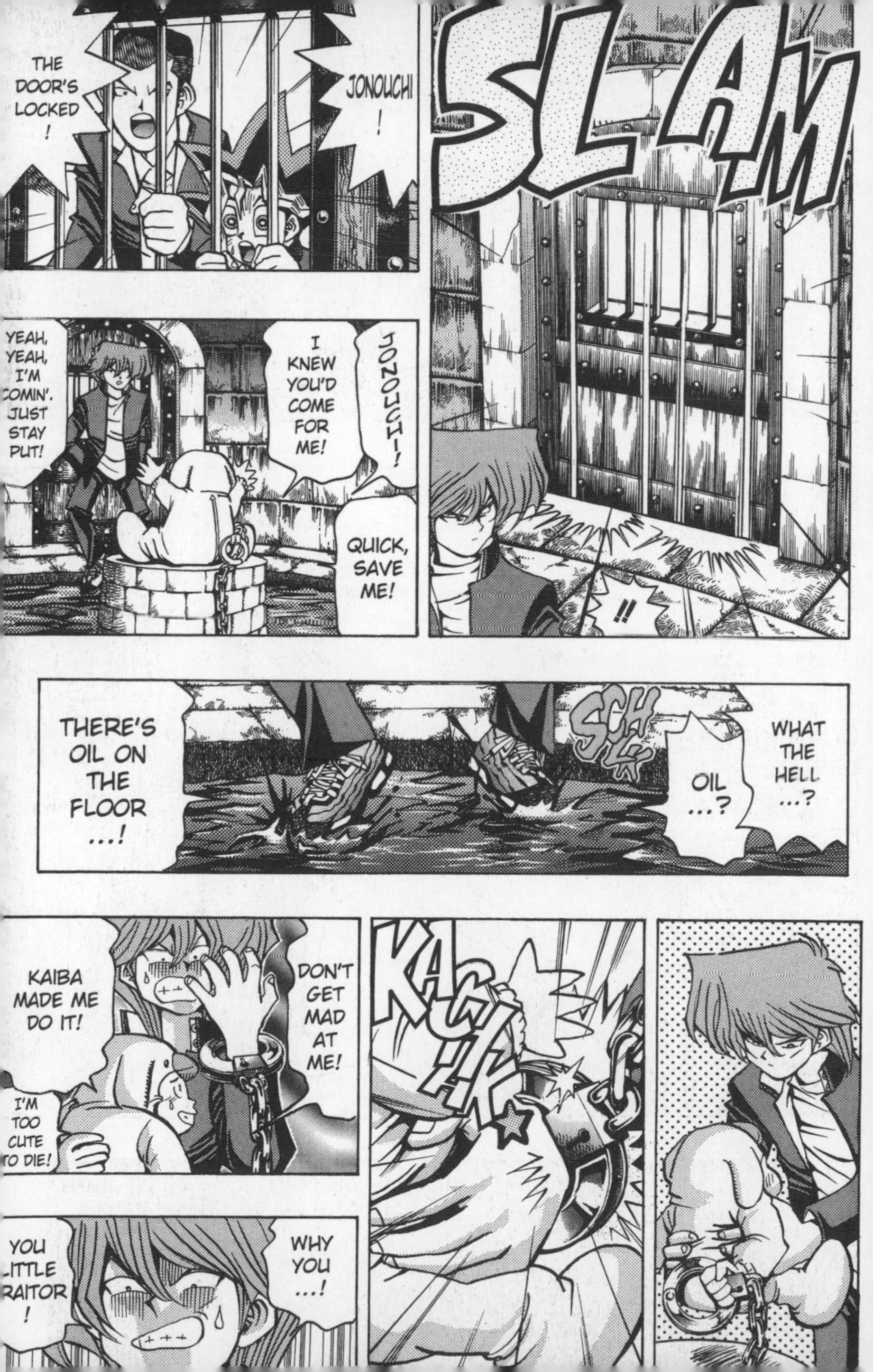
SLAM
!!
JONOUCHI!
THE DOOR'S LOCKED!
JONOUCHI-!
I KNEW YOU'D COME FOR ME!
QUICK, SAVE ME!
YEAH, YEAH, I'M COMIN'. JUST STAY PUT!
WHAT THE HELL...?
SCH
OIL...?
THERE'S OIL ON THE FLOOR...!
DON'T GET MAD AT ME!
KAIBA MADE ME DO IT!
I'M TOO CUTE TO DIE!
WHY YOU...!
YOU LITTLE RAITOR!

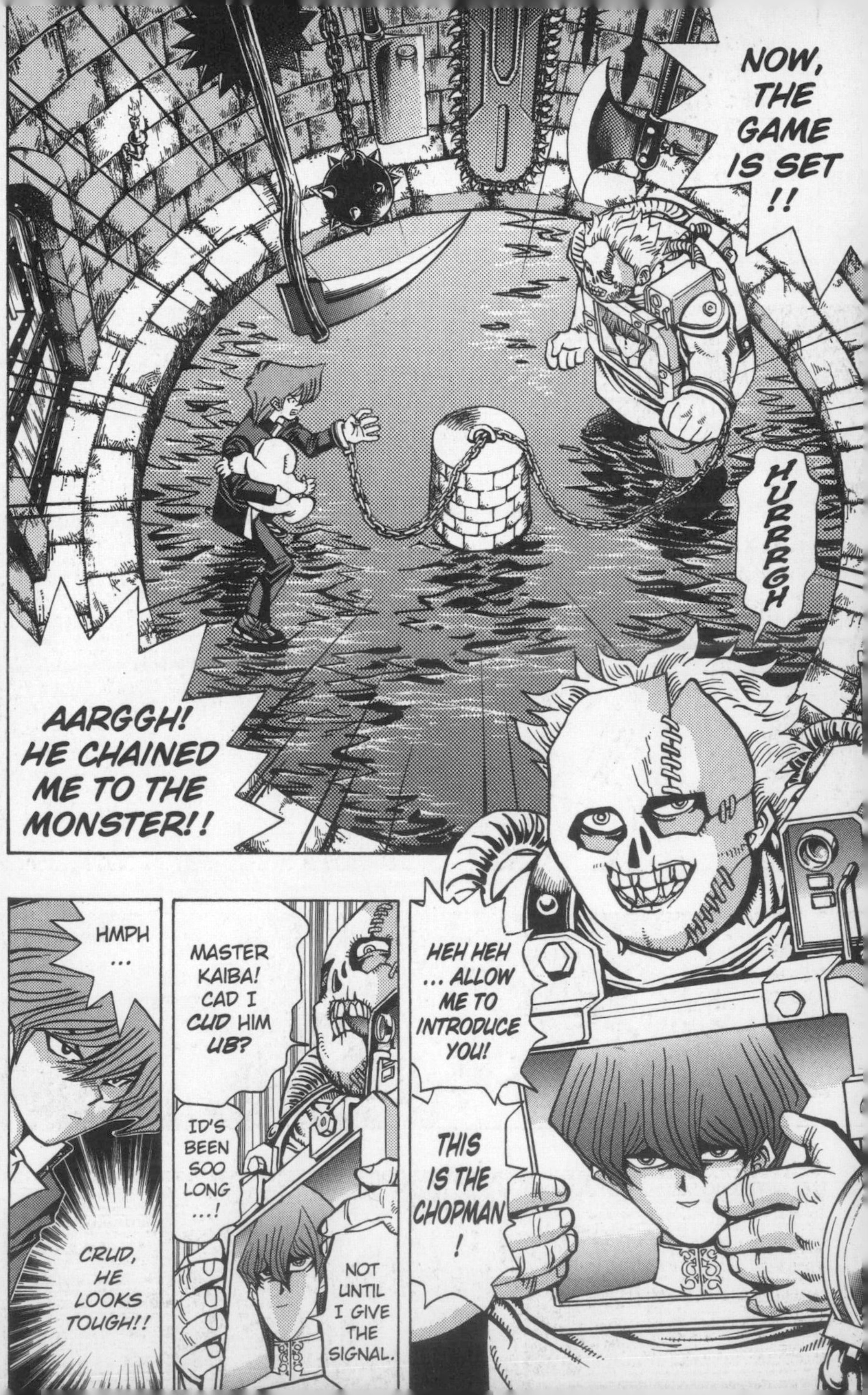
NOW, THE GAME IS SET !!
HURRRGH
AARGGH! HE CHAINED ME TO THE MONSTER!!
HEH HEH ... ALLOW ME TO INTRODUCE YOU!
THIS IS THE CHOPMAN !
MASTER KAIBA! CAD I CUD HIM UB?
ID'S BEEN SOO LONG ...!
NOT UNTIL I GIVE THE SIGNAL.
HMPH ...
CRUD, HE LOOKS TOUGH!!

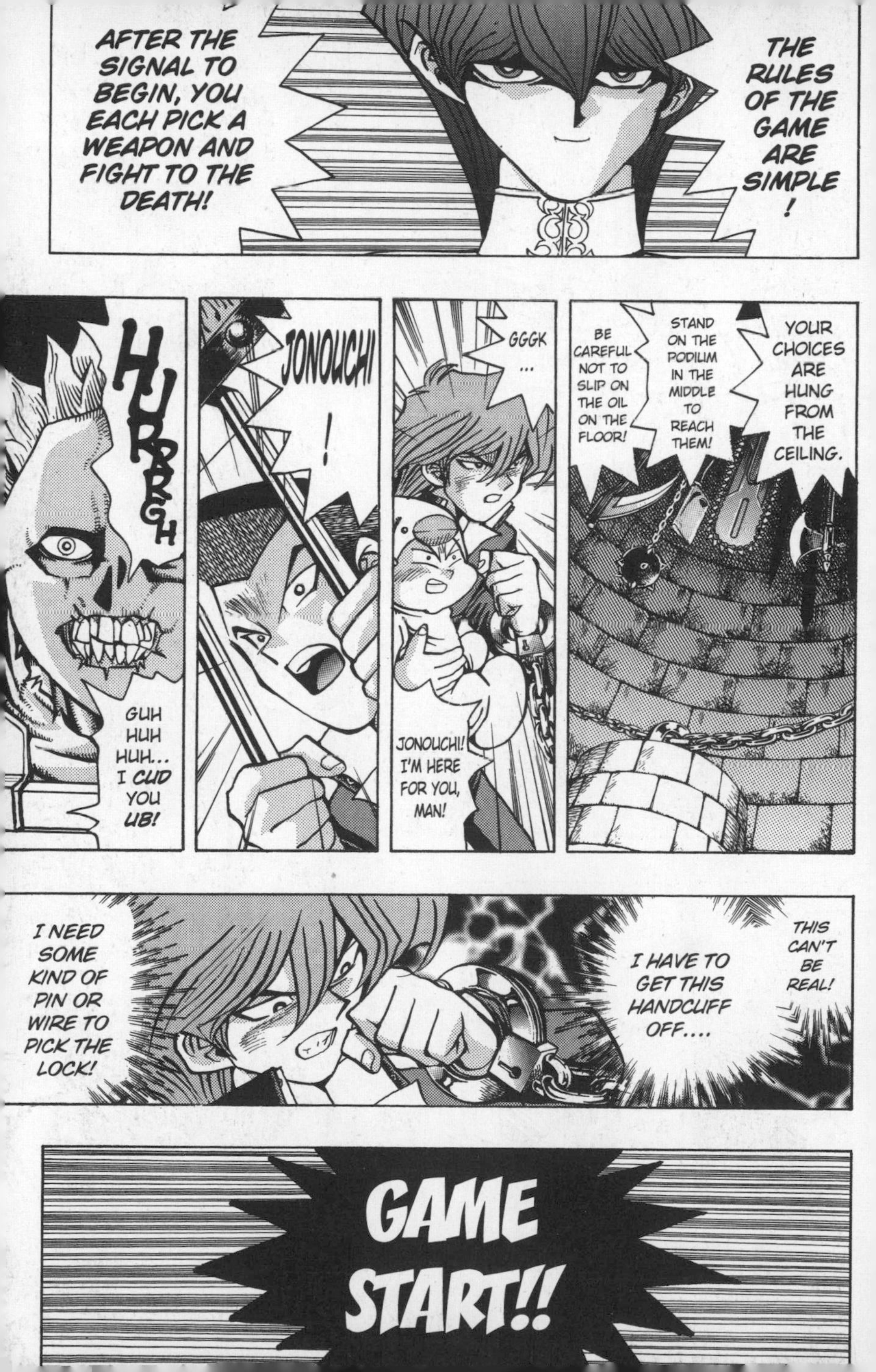
THE RULES OF THE GAME ARE SIMPLE!
AFTER THE SIGNAL TO BEGIN, YOU EACH PICK A WEAPON AND FIGHT TO THE DEATH!
YOUR CHOICES ARE HUNG FROM THE CEILING.
STAND ON THE PODIUM IN THE MIDDLE TO REACH THEM!
BE CAREFUL NOT TO SLIP ON THE OIL ON THE FLOOR!
GGGK ...
JONOUCHI! I'M HERE FOR YOU, MAN!
JONOUCHI!
HURRRGH
GUH HUH HUH... I CUD YOU UB!
THIS CAN'T BE REAL!
I HAVE TO GET THIS HANDCUFF OFF....
I NEED SOME KIND OF PIN OR WIRE TO PICK THE LOCK!
GAME START!!

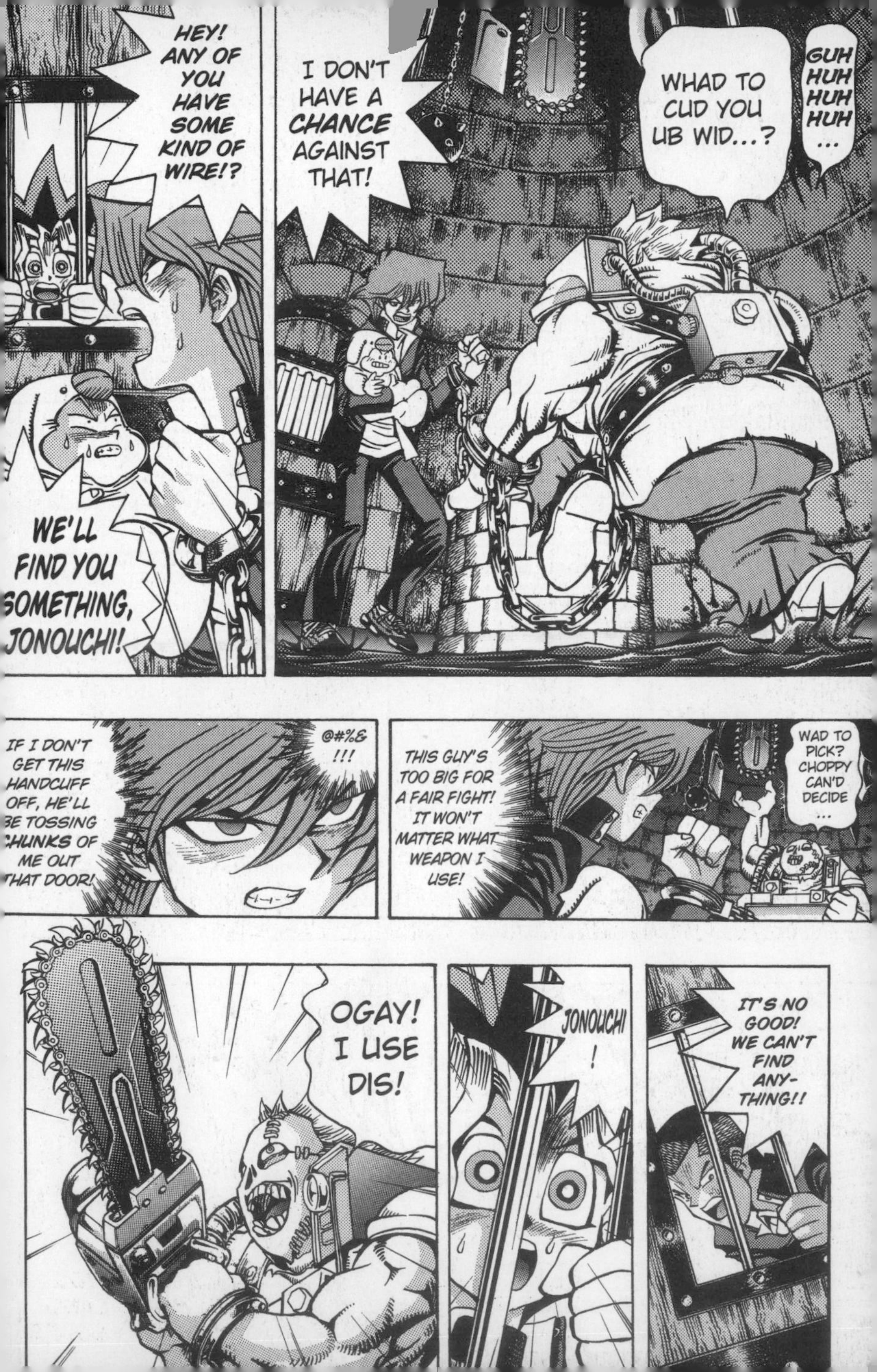
GUH HUH HUH HUH ...
WHAD TO CUD YOU UB WID...?
I DON'T HAVE A CHANCE AGAINST THAT!
HEY! ANY OF YOU HAVE SOME KIND OF WIRE!?
WE'LL FIND YOU SOMETHING, JONOUCHI!
WAD TO PICK? CHOPPY CAN'D DECIDE ...
THIS GUY'S TOO BIG FOR A FAIR FIGHT! IT WON'T MATTER WHAT WEAPON I USE!
@#%& !!!
IF I DON'T GET THIS HANDCUFF OFF, HE'LL BE TOSSING CHUNKS OF ME OUT THAT DOOR!
IT'S NO GOOD! WE CAN'T FIND ANY-THING!!
JONOUCHI !
OGAY! I USE DIS!

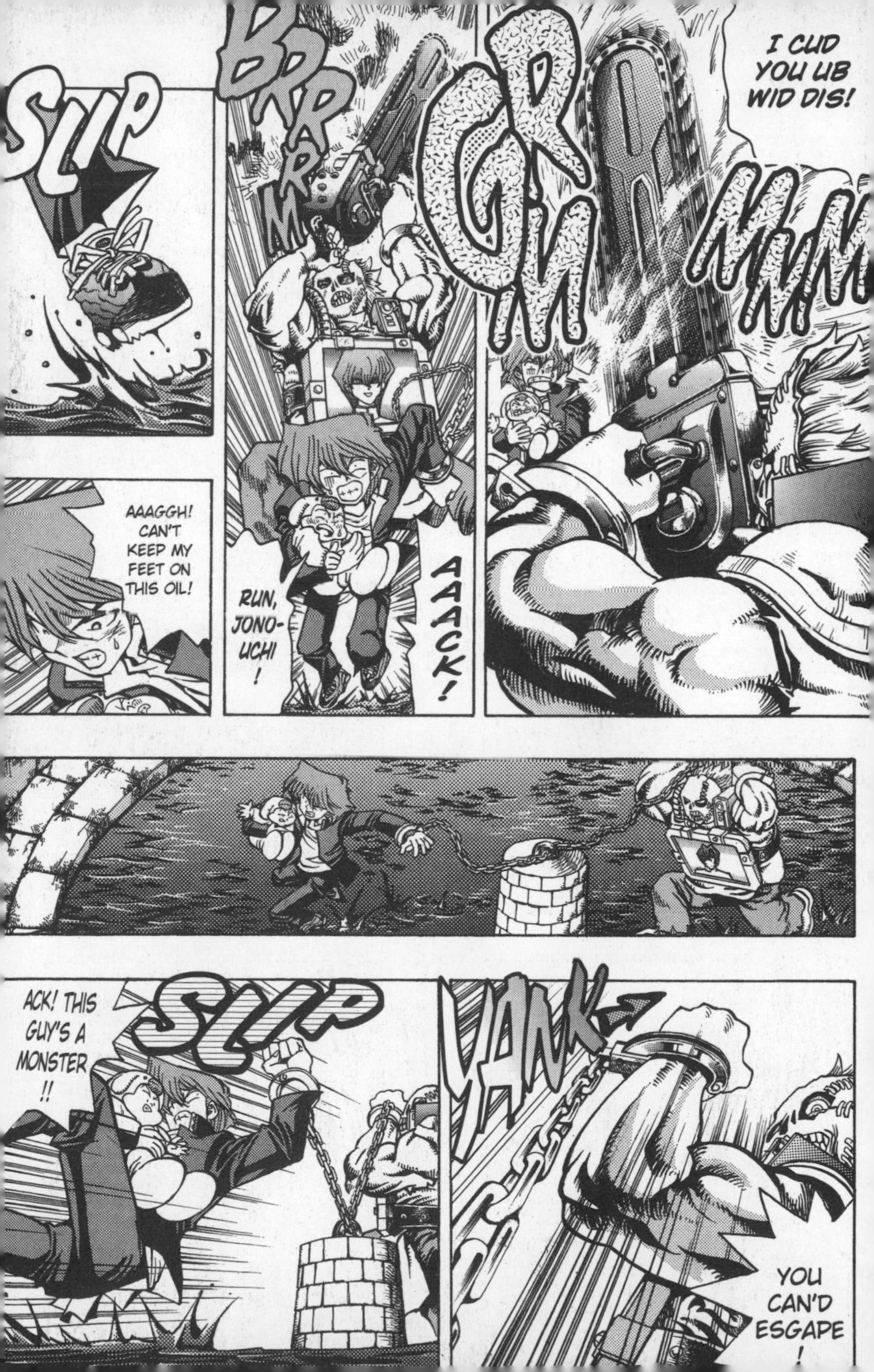
I CUD YOU UB WID DIS!
RUN, JONO-UCHI!
AAAACK!
SLIP
AAAGGH! CAN'T KEEP MY FEET ON THIS OIL!
YANK
YOU CAN'D ESGAPE!
ACK! THIS GUY'S A MONSTER!!
SLIP

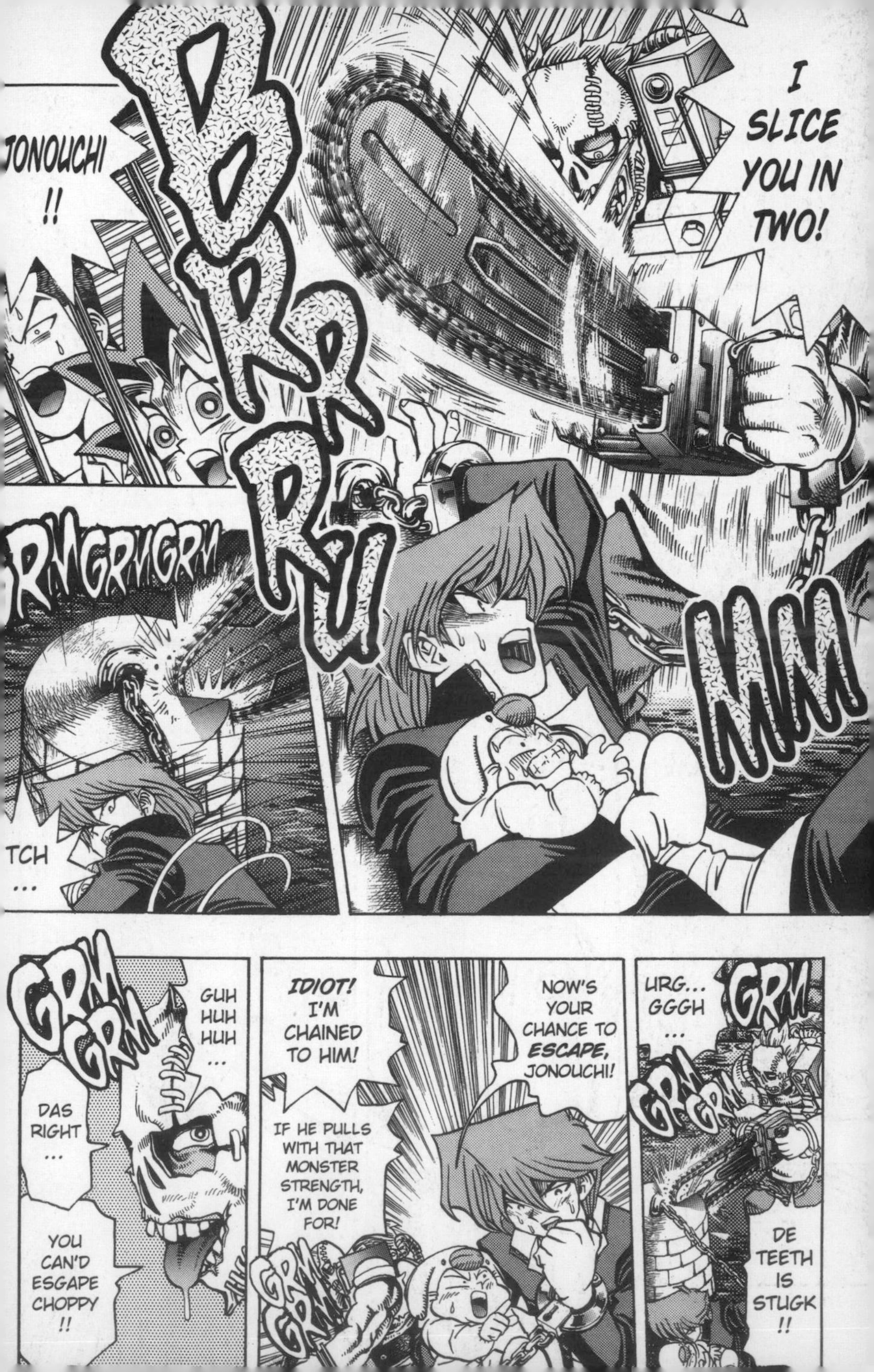
I SLICE YOU IN TWO!
BRRRRU
JONOUCHI !!
MMM
RMGRMGRM
TCH ...
URG... GGGH ...
GRM
GRM GRM
DE TEETH IS STUGK !!
NOW'S YOUR CHANCE TO ESCAPE, JONOUCHI!
IDIOT! I'M CHAINED TO HIM!
IF HE PULLS WITH THAT MONSTER STRENGTH, I'M DONE FOR!
GRM GRM
GRM GRM
GUH HUH HUH ...
DAS RIGHT ...
YOU CAN'D ESGAPE CHOPPY !!

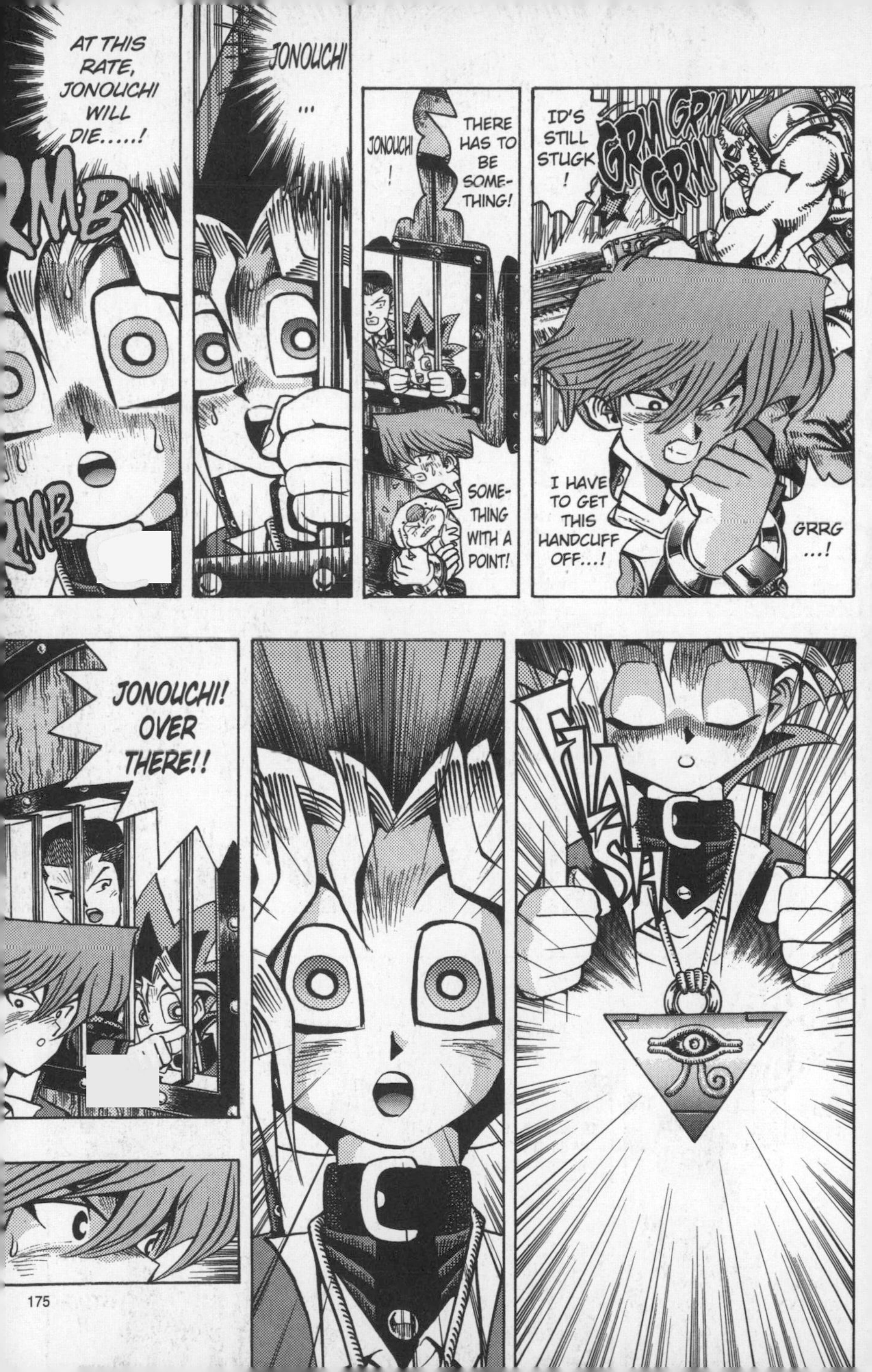
ID'S STILL STUGK !
GRM GRM GRM
I HAVE TO GET THIS HANDCUFF OFF...!
GRRG ...!
THERE HAS TO BE SOME-THING!
JONOUCHI !
SOME-THING WITH A POINT!
JONOUCHI ...
AT THIS RATE, JONOUCHI WILL DIE.....!
RMB
RMB
JONOUCHI! OVER THERE!!

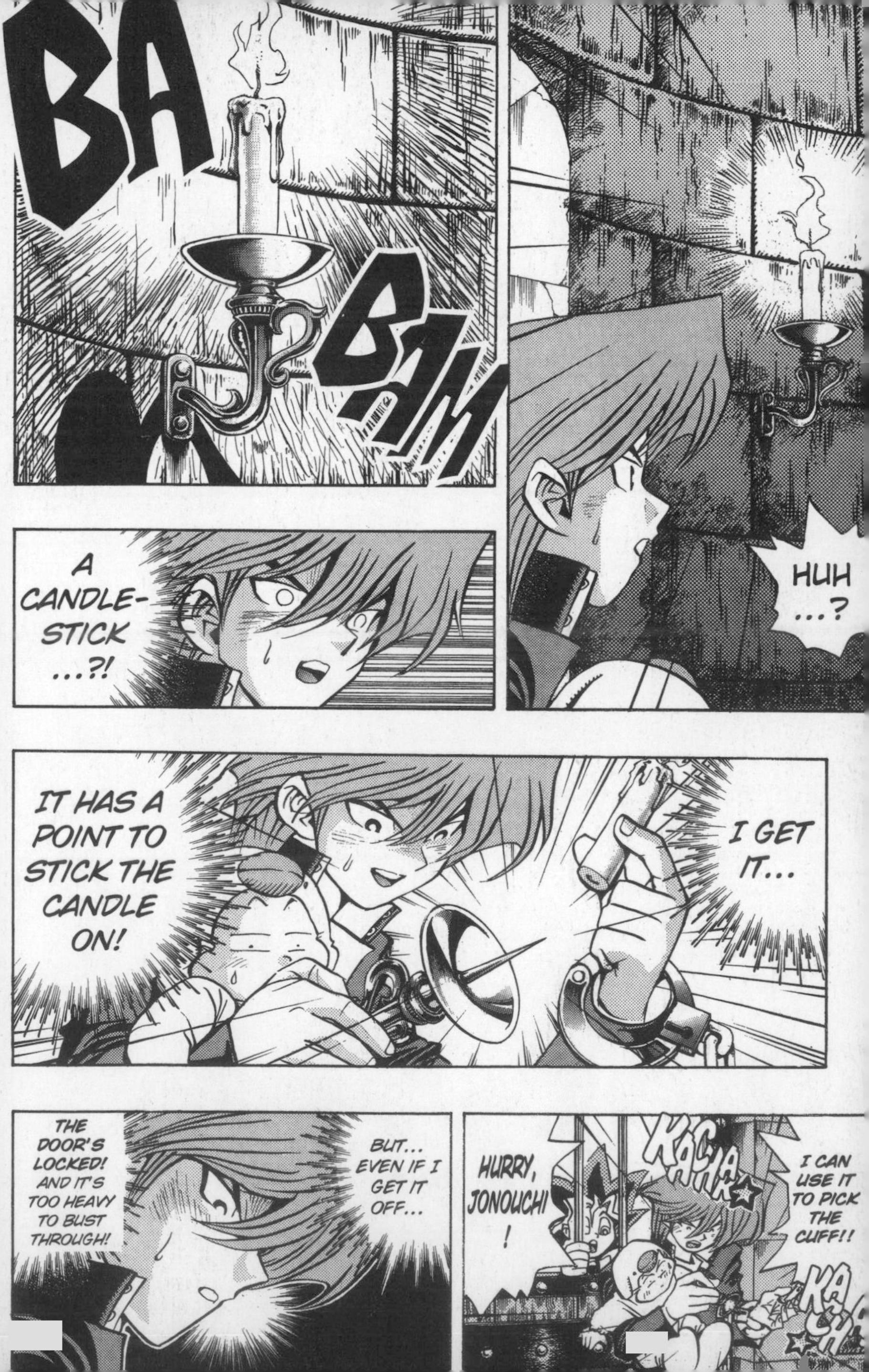
HUH ...?
BA
BAM
A CANDLE-STICK ...?!
I GET IT...
IT HAS A POINT TO STICK THE CANDLE ON!
I CAN USE IT TO PICK THE CUFF!!
KACHA
HURRY, JONOUCHI!
KACHA
BUT... EVEN IF I GET IT OFF...
THE DOOR'S LOCKED! AND IT'S TOO HEAVY TO BUST THROUGH!

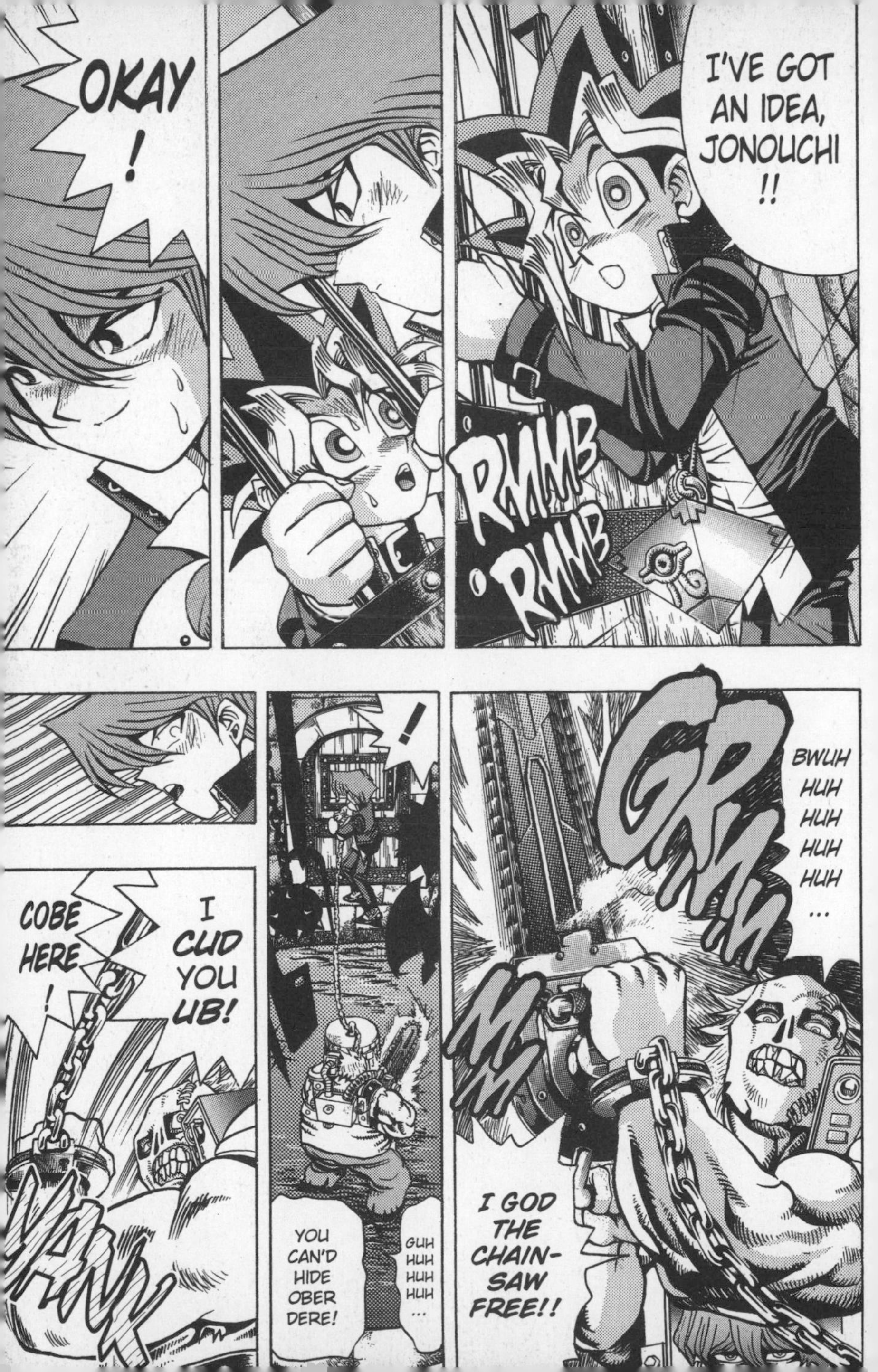
I'VE GOT AN IDEA, JONOUCHI!!
RMMB RMMB
OKAY!
GRMM
BWUH HUH HUH HUH HUH...
I GOD THE CHAIN-SAW FREE!!
!
GUH HUH HUH HUH...
YOU CAN'D HIDE OBER DERE!
I CUD YOU UB!
COBE HERE!

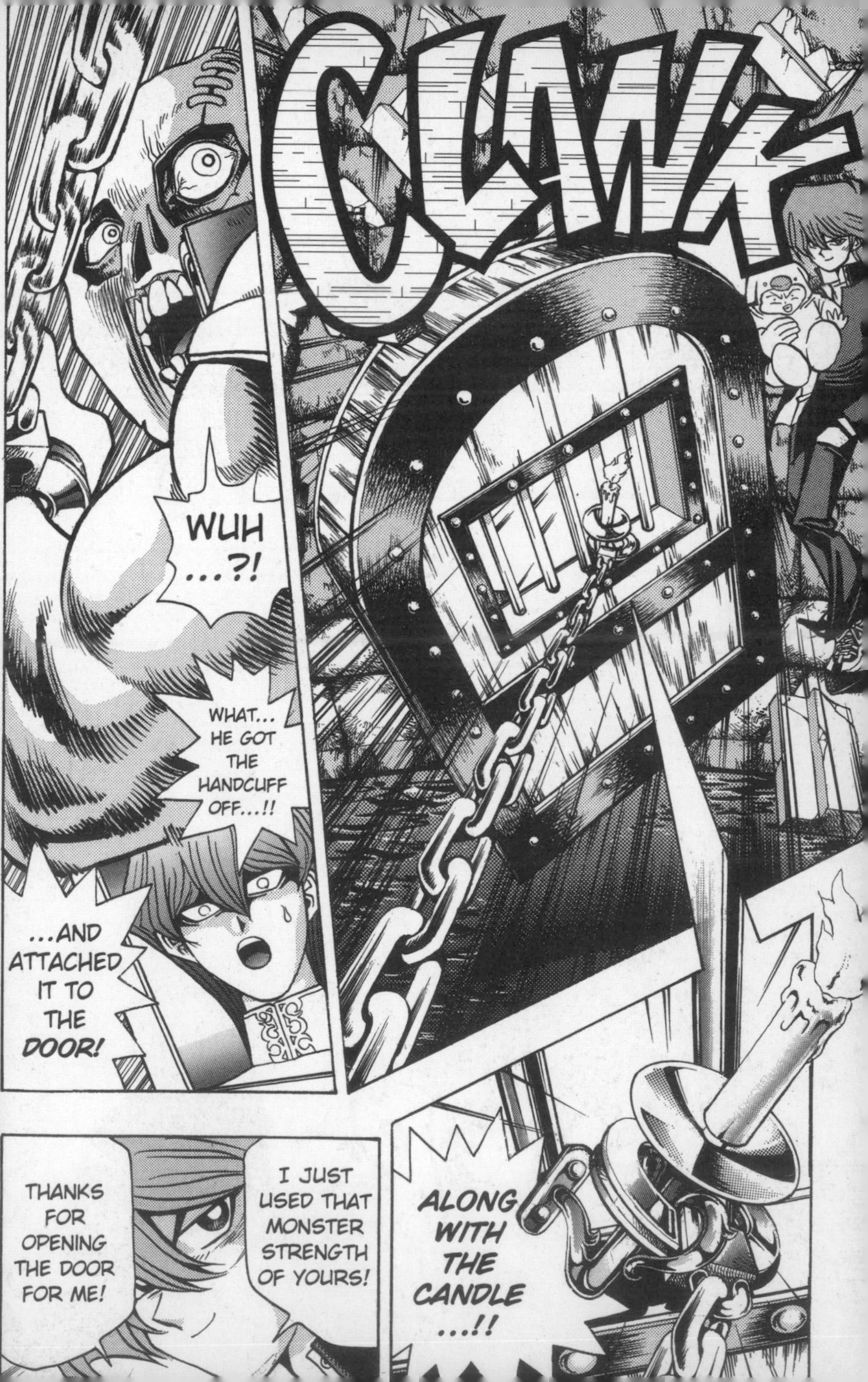
CLANK
WUH ...?!
WHAT... HE GOT THE HANDCUFF OFF...!!
...AND ATTACHED IT TO THE DOOR!
ALONG WITH THE CANDLE ...!!
I JUST USED THAT MONSTER STRENGTH OF YOURS!
THANKS FOR OPENING THE DOOR FOR ME!

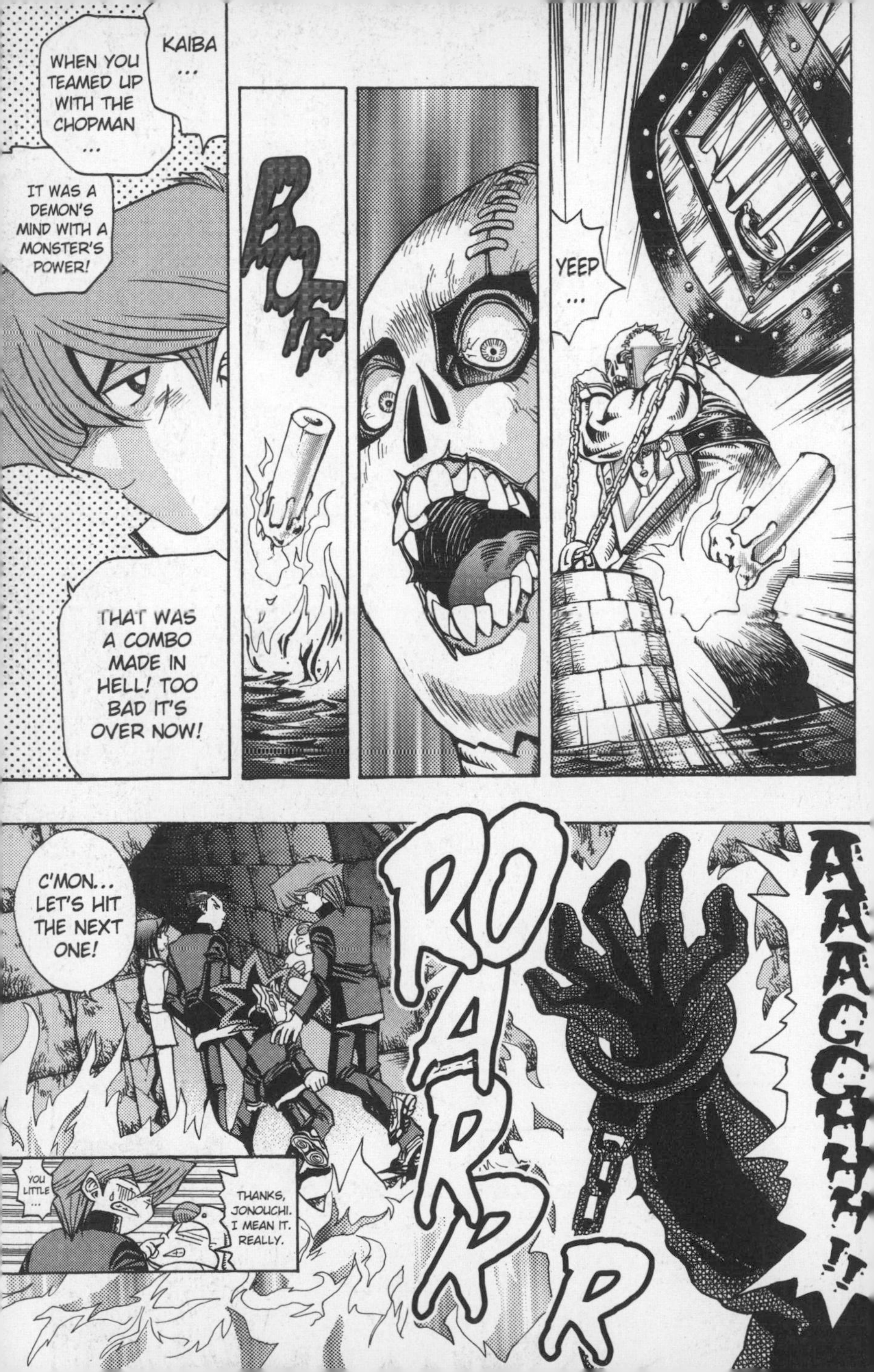
YEEP ...
BOFF
KAIBA ...
WHEN YOU TEAMED UP WITH THE CHOPMAN ...
IT WAS A DEMON'S MIND WITH A MONSTER'S POWER!
THAT WAS A COMBO MADE IN HELL! TOO BAD IT'S OVER NOW!
AAAGHH!!
ROARR
C'MON... LET'S HIT THE NEXT ONE!
THANKS, JONOUCHI. I MEAN IT. REALLY.
YOU LITTLE ...

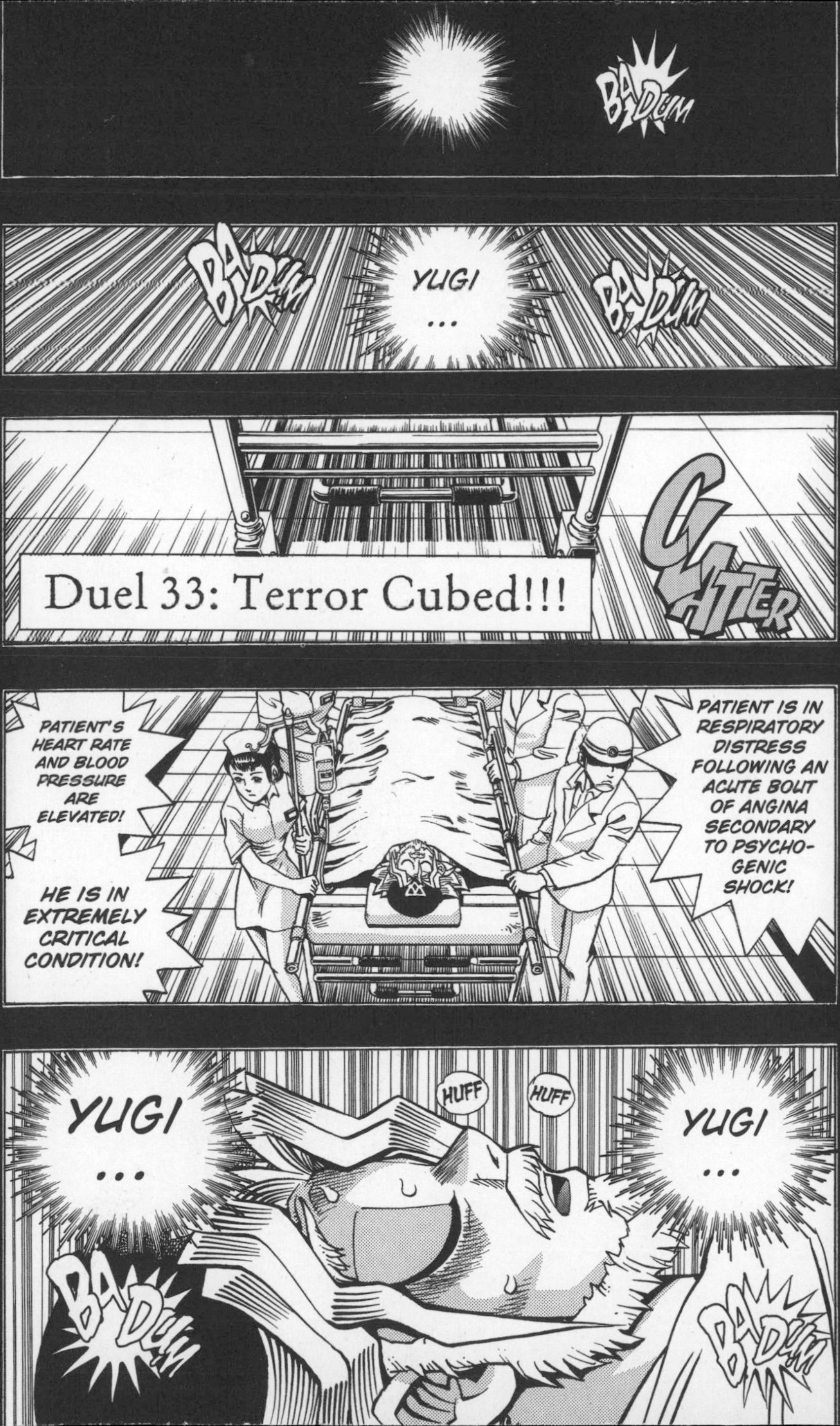
BA-DUM
BA-DUM
YUGI ...
BA-DUM
CLATTER
Duel 33: Terror Cubed!!!
PATIENT IS IN RESPIRATORY DISTRESS FOLLOWING AN ACUTE BOUT OF ANGINA SECONDARY TO PSYCHO-GENIC SHOCK!
PATIENT'S HEART RATE AND BLOOD PRESSURE ARE ELEVATED!
HE IS IN EXTREMELY CRITICAL CONDITION!
YUGI ...
HUFF
HUFF
YUGI ...
BA-DUM
BA-DUM

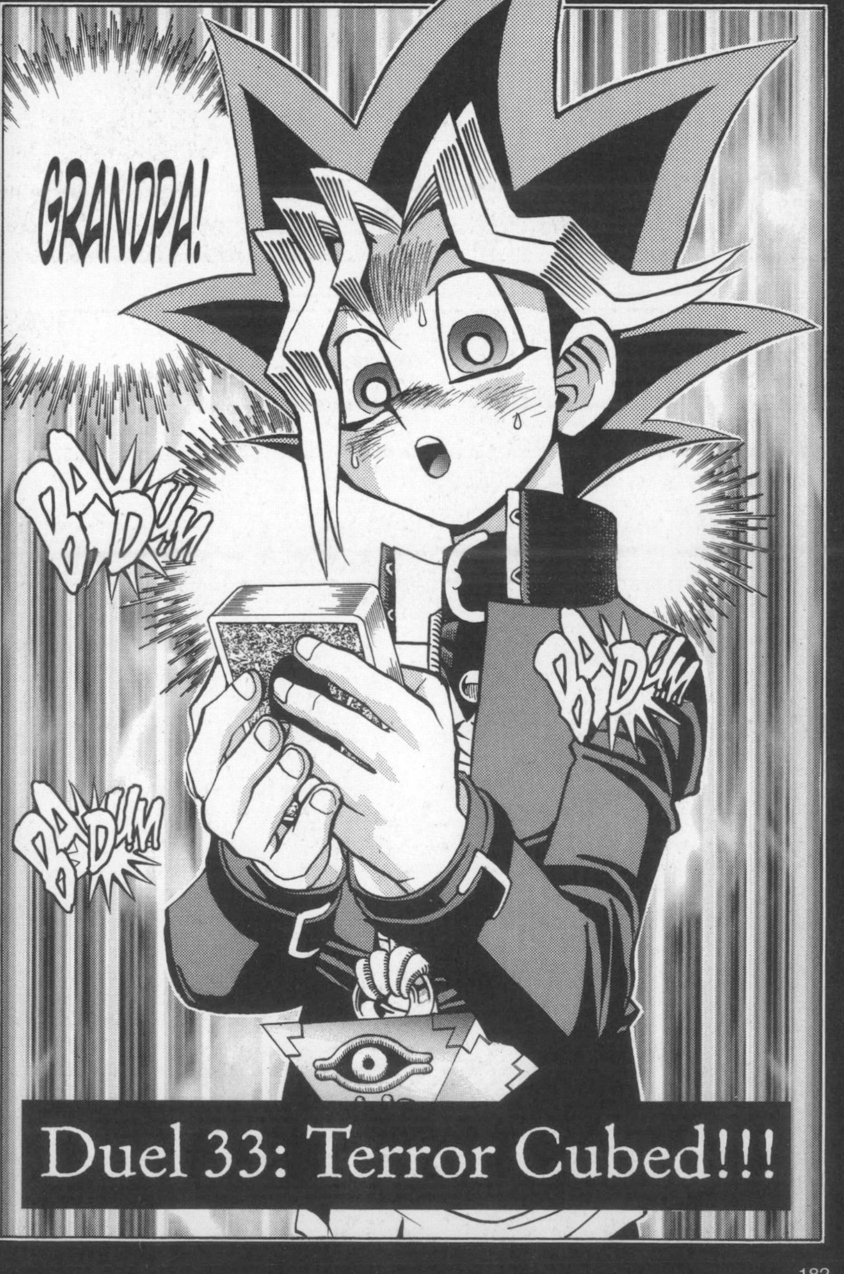
GRANDPA!
BA-DUM
BA-DUM
BA-DUM

Duel 33: Terror Cubed!!!

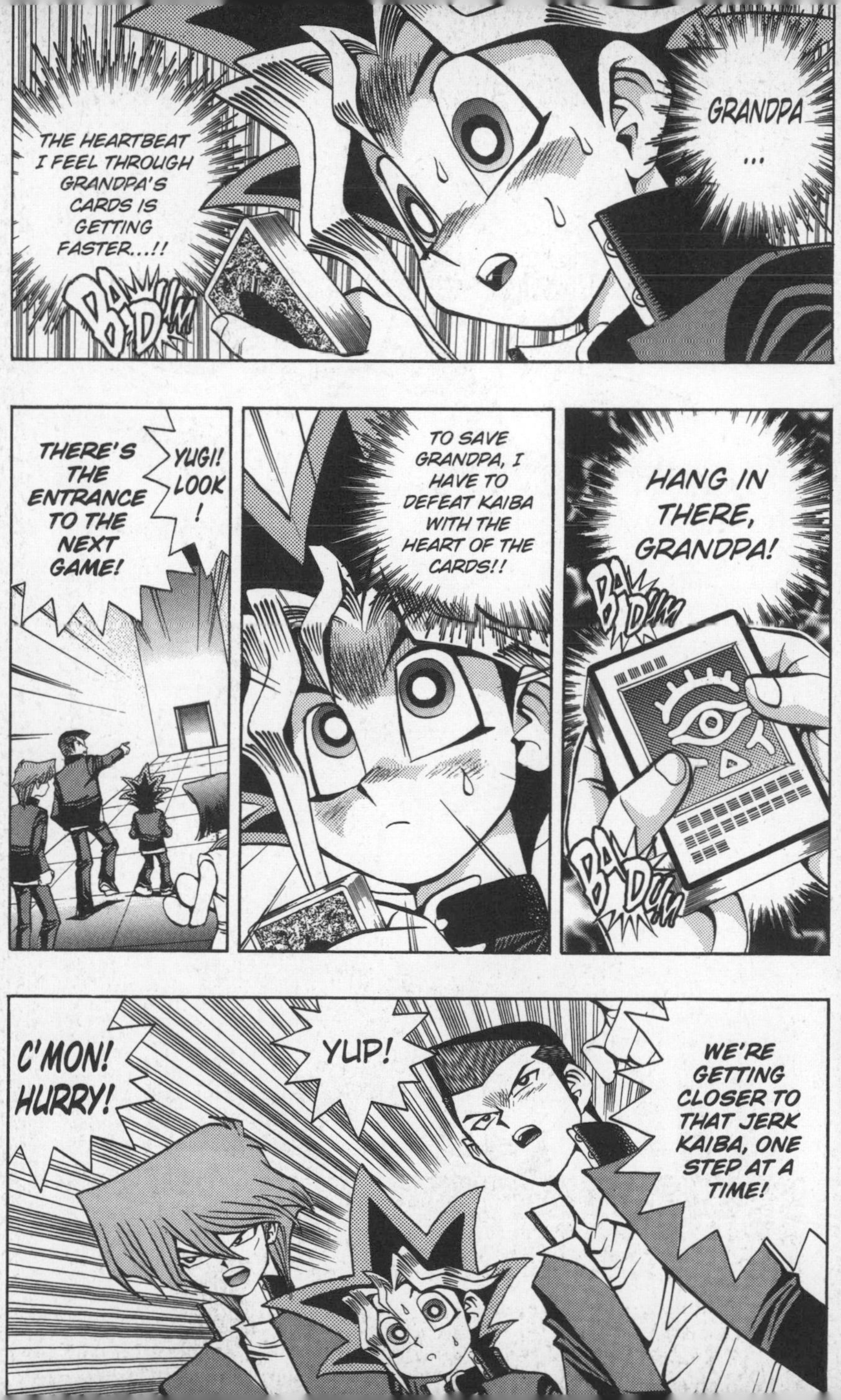
GRANDPA ...
THE HEARTBEAT I FEEL THROUGH GRANDPA'S CARDS IS GETTING FASTER...!!
BA-DUM
HANG IN THERE, GRANDPA!
BA-DUM
BA-DUM
TO SAVE GRANDPA, I HAVE TO DEFEAT KAIBA WITH THE HEART OF THE CARDS!!
YUGI! LOOK!
THERE'S THE ENTRANCE TO THE NEXT GAME!
WE'RE GETTING CLOSER TO THAT JERK KAIBA, ONE STEP AT A TIME!
YUP!
C'MON! HURRY!

READ THIS WAY

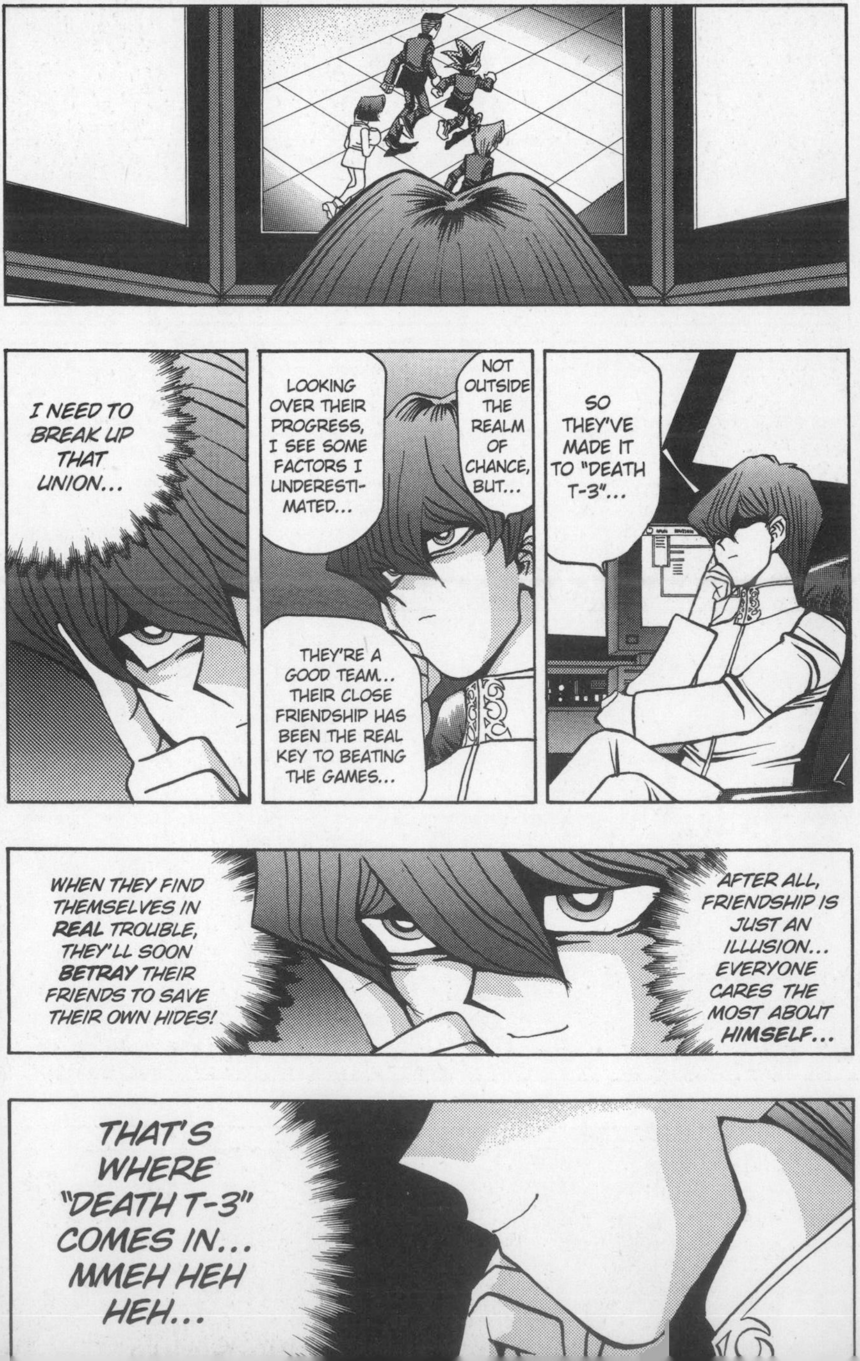

SO THEY'VE MADE IT TO "DEATH T-3"...
NOT OUTSIDE THE REALM OF CHANCE, BUT...
LOOKING OVER THEIR PROGRESS, I SEE SOME FACTORS I UNDERESTIMATED...
THEY'RE A GOOD TEAM... THEIR CLOSE FRIENDSHIP HAS BEEN THE REAL KEY TO BEATING THE GAMES...
I NEED TO BREAK UP THAT UNION...
AFTER ALL, FRIENDSHIP IS JUST AN ILLUSION... EVERYONE CARES THE MOST ABOUT HIMSELF...
WHEN THEY FIND THEMSELVES IN REAL TROUBLE, THEY'LL SOON BETRAY THEIR FRIENDS TO SAVE THEIR OWN HIDES!
THAT'S WHERE "DEATH T-3" COMES IN... MMEH HEH HEH...

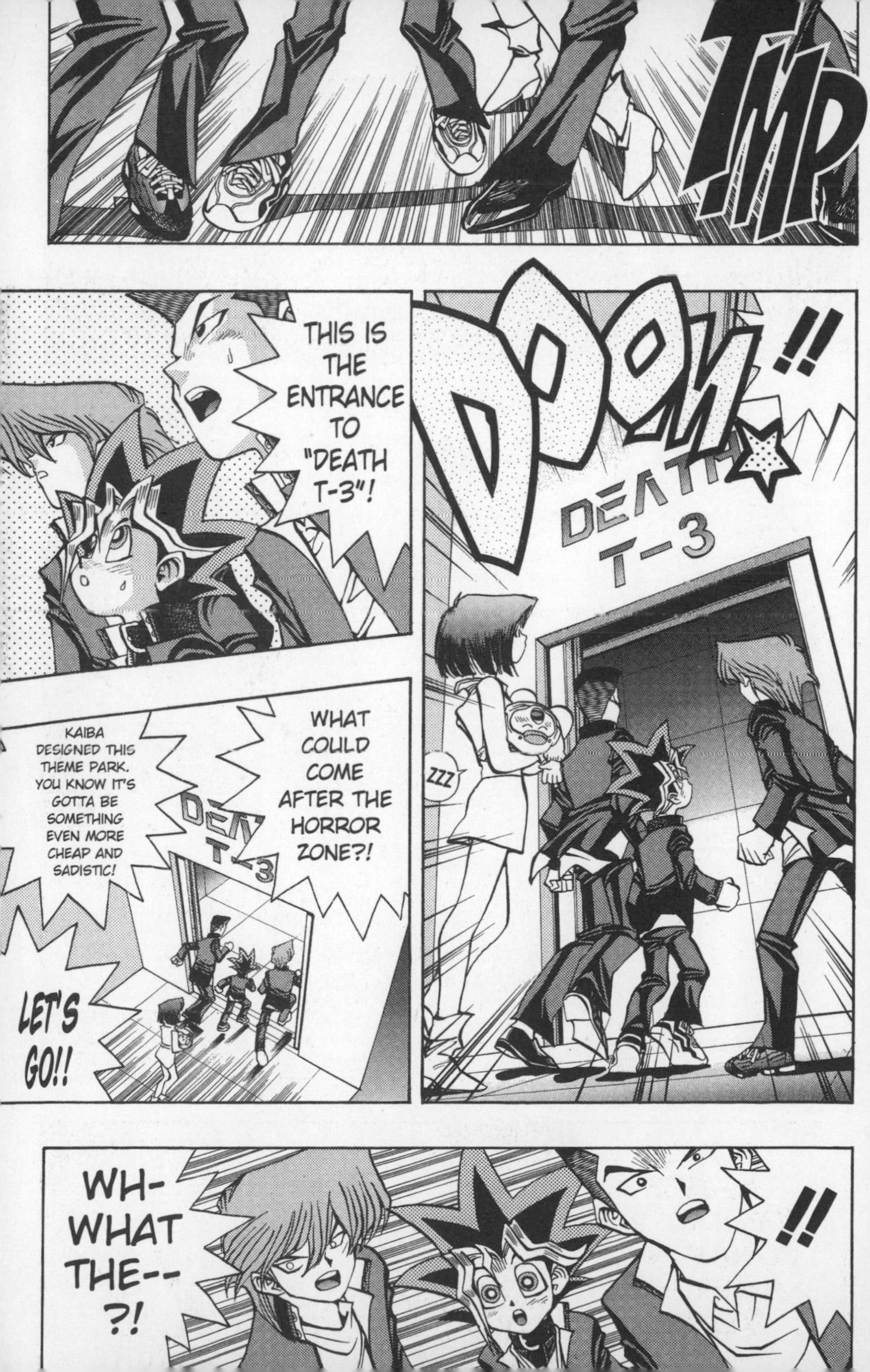
TMP
DOOM!!
DEATH T-3
ZZZ
THIS IS THE ENTRANCE TO "DEATH T-3"!
WHAT COULD COME AFTER THE HORROR ZONE?!
KAIBA DESIGNED THIS THEME PARK. YOU KNOW IT'S GOTTA BE SOMETHING EVEN MORE CHEAP AND SADISTIC!
LET'S GO!!
!!
WH- WHAT THE-- ?!

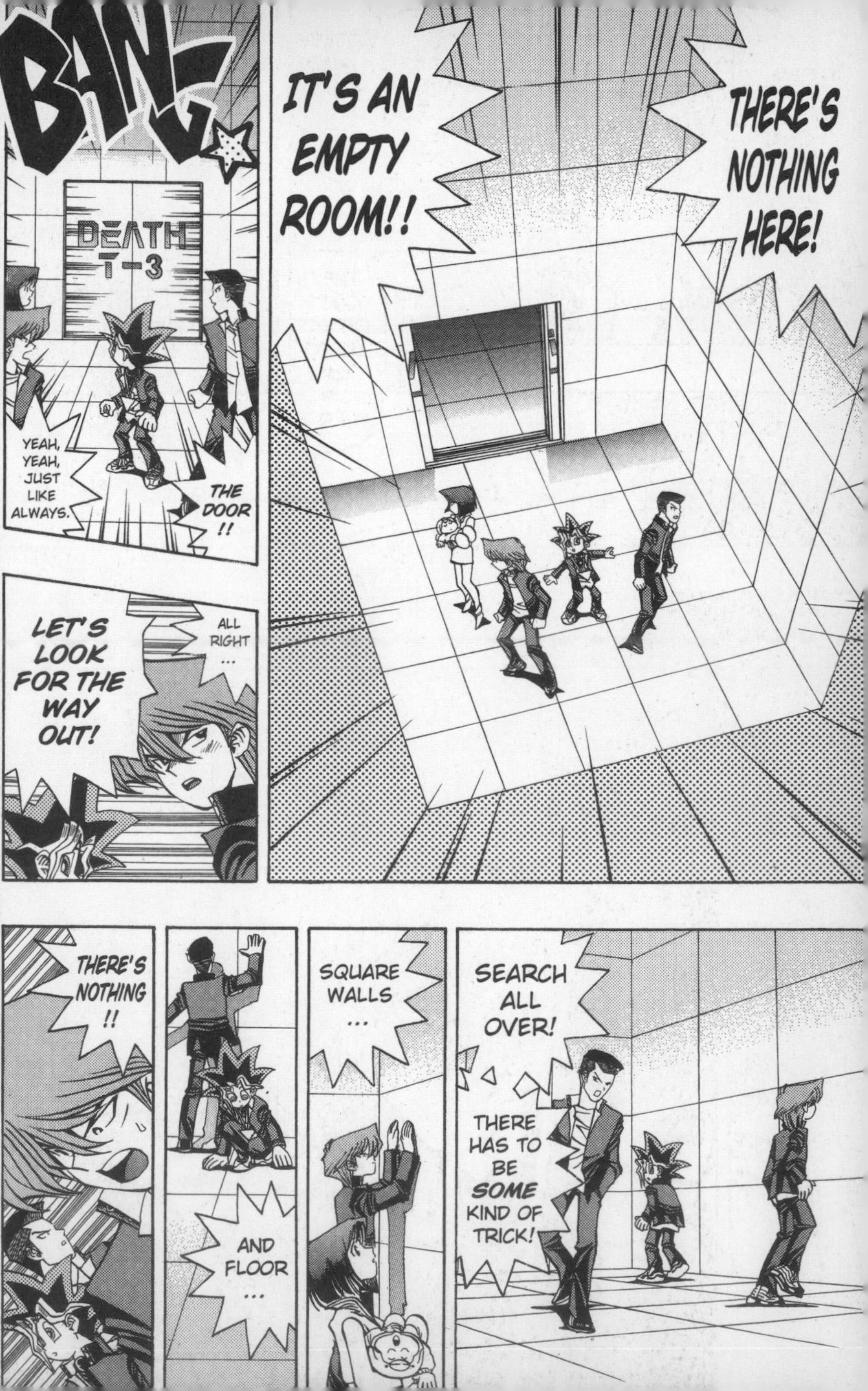
THERE'S NOTHING HERE!
IT'S AN EMPTY ROOM!!
BAN
DEATH T-3
THE DOOR!!
YEAH, YEAH, JUST LIKE ALWAYS.
ALL RIGHT...
LET'S LOOK FOR THE WAY OUT!
SEARCH ALL OVER!
THERE HAS TO BE SOME KIND OF TRICK!
SQUARE WALLS...
AND FLOOR...
THERE'S NOTHING!!

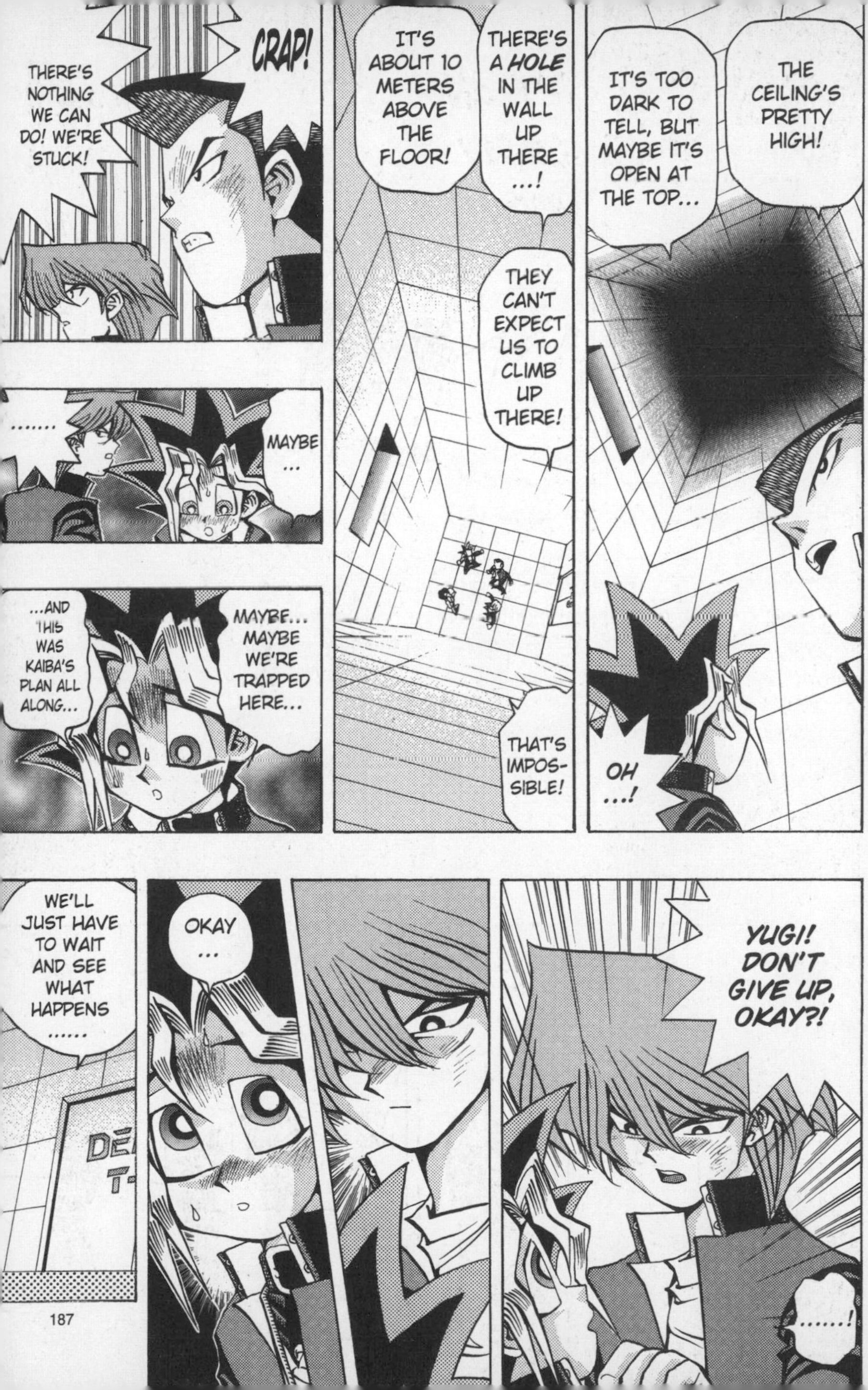
THE CEILING'S PRETTY HIGH!
IT'S TOO DARK TO TELL, BUT MAYBE IT'S OPEN AT THE TOP...
OH ...!
THERE'S A *HOLE* IN THE WALL UP THERE ...!
IT'S ABOUT 10 METERS ABOVE THE FLOOR!
THEY CAN'T EXPECT US TO CLIMB UP THERE!
THAT'S IMPOSSIBLE!
CRAP!
THERE'S NOTHING WE CAN DO! WE'RE STUCK!
MAYBE ...
....
MAYBE... MAYBE WE'RE TRAPPED HERE...
...AND THIS WAS KAIBA'S PLAN ALL ALONG...
YUGI! DON'T GIVE UP, OKAY?!
.......!
OKAY ...
WE'LL JUST HAVE TO WAIT AND SEE WHAT HAPPENS ......

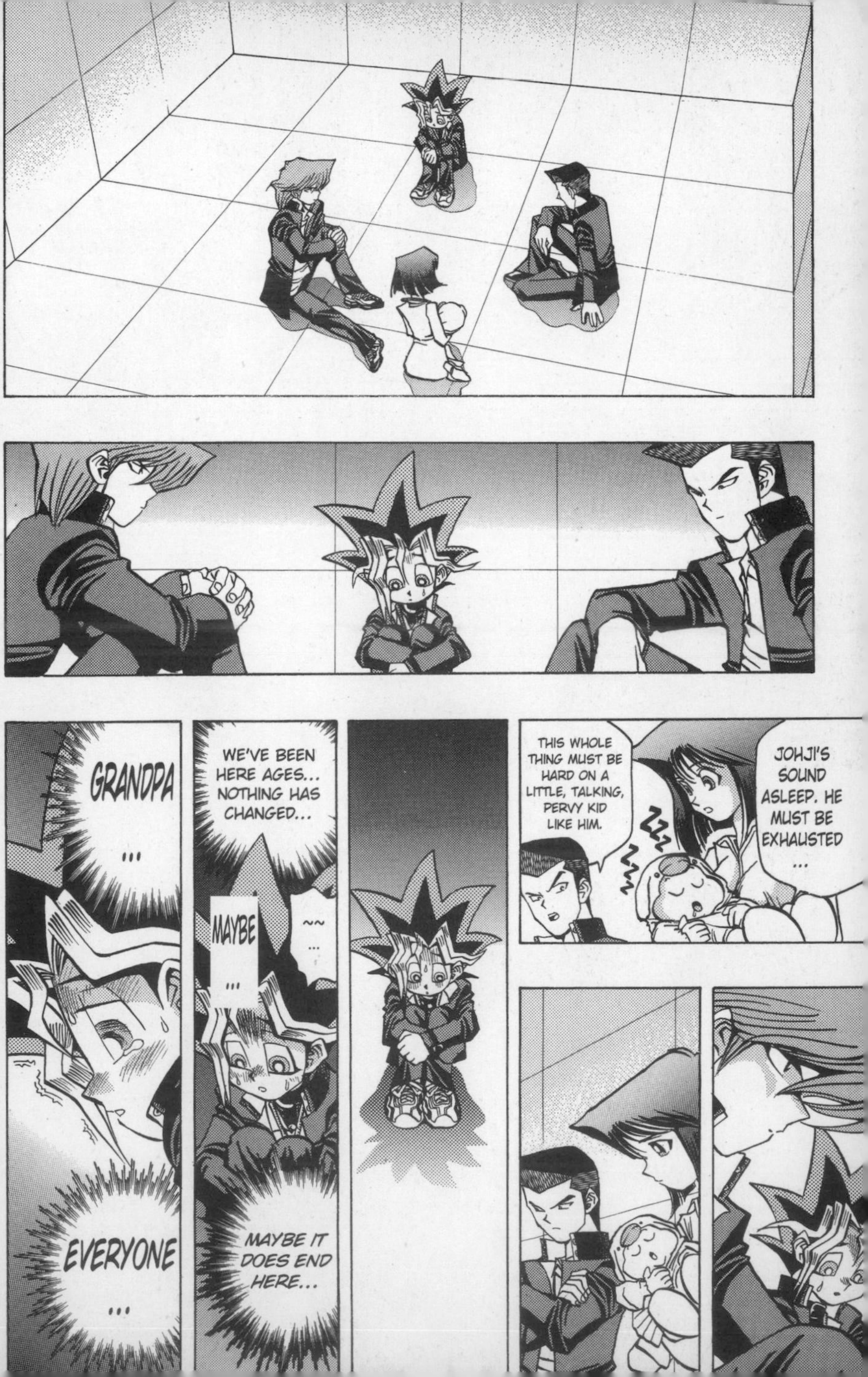
JOHJI'S SOUND ASLEEP. HE MUST BE EXHAUSTED ...
THIS WHOLE THING MUST BE HARD ON A LITTLE, TALKING, PERVY KID LIKE HIM.
ZZZ
WE'VE BEEN HERE AGES... NOTHING HAS CHANGED...
~~ ...
MAYBE ...
MAYBE IT DOES END HERE...
GRANDPA ...
EVERYONE ...

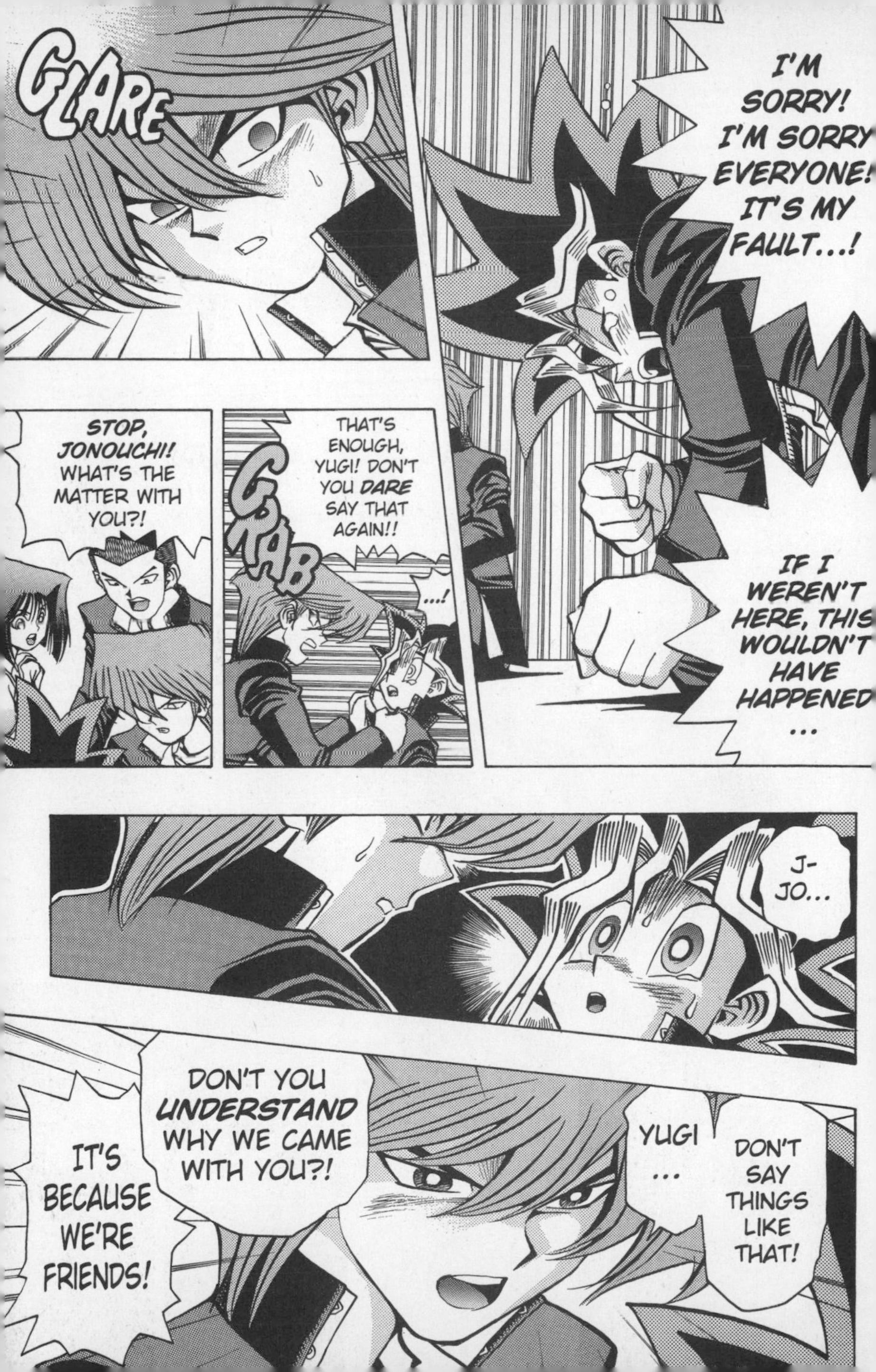
I'M SORRY! I'M SORRY EVERYONE! IT'S MY FAULT...!
IF I WEREN'T HERE, THIS WOULDN'T HAVE HAPPENED...
GLARE
THAT'S ENOUGH, YUGI! DON'T YOU DARE SAY THAT AGAIN!!
GRAB
...!
STOP, JONOUCHI!! WHAT'S THE MATTER WITH YOU?!
J-JO...
YUGI...
DON'T SAY THINGS LIKE THAT!
DON'T YOU UNDERSTAND WHY WE CAME WITH YOU?!
IT'S BECAUSE WE'RE FRIENDS!

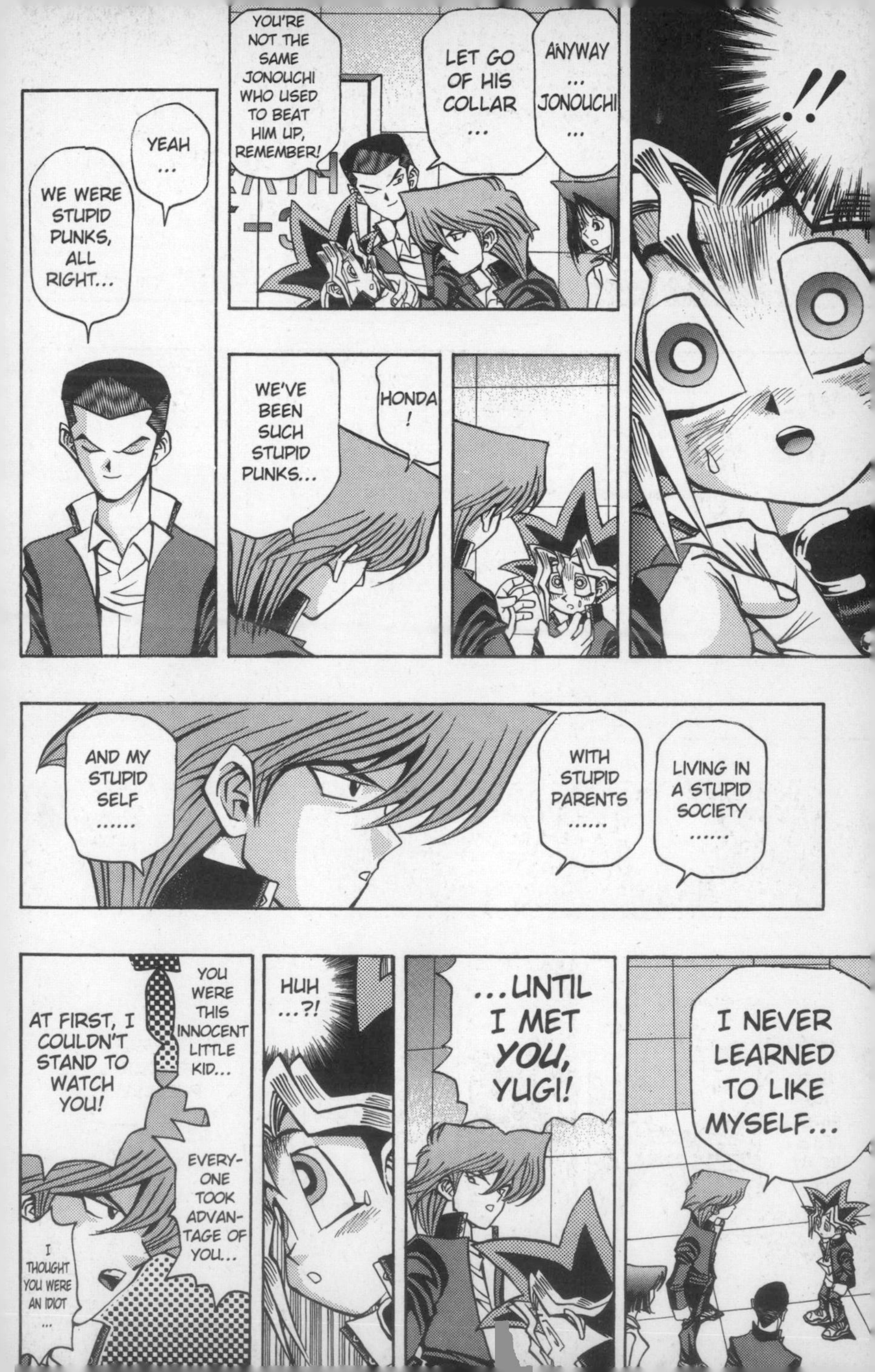
!!
ANYWAY ... JONOUCHI ...
LET GO OF HIS COLLAR ...
YOU'RE NOT THE SAME JONOUCHI WHO USED TO BEAT HIM UP, REMEMBER!
HONDA!
WE'VE BEEN SUCH STUPID PUNKS...
YEAH ...
WE WERE STUPID PUNKS, ALL RIGHT...
LIVING IN A STUPID SOCIETY ......
WITH STUPID PARENTS ......
AND MY STUPID SELF ......
I NEVER LEARNED TO LIKE MYSELF...
...UNTIL I MET *YOU*, YUGI!
HUH ...?!
YOU WERE THIS INNOCENT LITTLE KID...
AT FIRST, I COULDN'T STAND TO WATCH YOU!
EVERY-ONE TOOK ADVAN-TAGE OF YOU...
I THOUGHT YOU WERE AN IDIOT ...

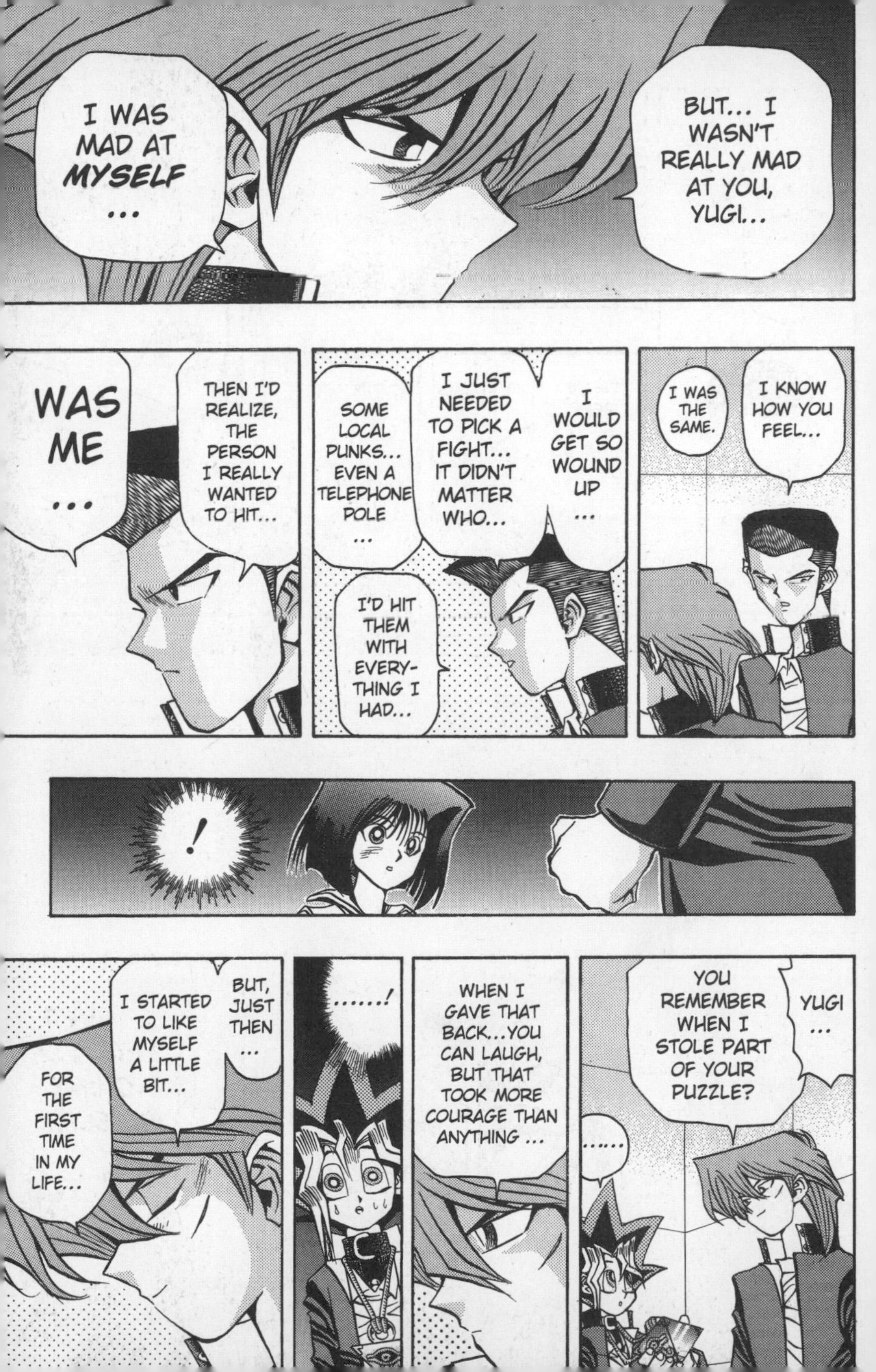
BUT... I WASN'T REALLY MAD AT YOU, YUGI...
I WAS MAD AT *MYSELF* ...
I KNOW HOW YOU FEEL...
I WAS THE SAME.
I WOULD GET SO WOUND UP ...
I JUST NEEDED TO PICK A FIGHT... IT DIDN'T MATTER WHO...
SOME LOCAL PUNKS... EVEN A TELEPHONE POLE ...
I'D HIT THEM WITH EVERYTHING I HAD...
THEN I'D REALIZE, THE PERSON I REALLY WANTED TO HIT...
WAS ME ...
!
YUGI ...
YOU REMEMBER WHEN I STOLE PART OF YOUR PUZZLE?
......
WHEN I GAVE THAT BACK...YOU CAN LAUGH, BUT THAT TOOK MORE COURAGE THAN ANYTHING ...
......!
BUT, JUST THEN ...
I STARTED TO LIKE MYSELF A LITTLE BIT...
FOR THE FIRST TIME IN MY LIFE...

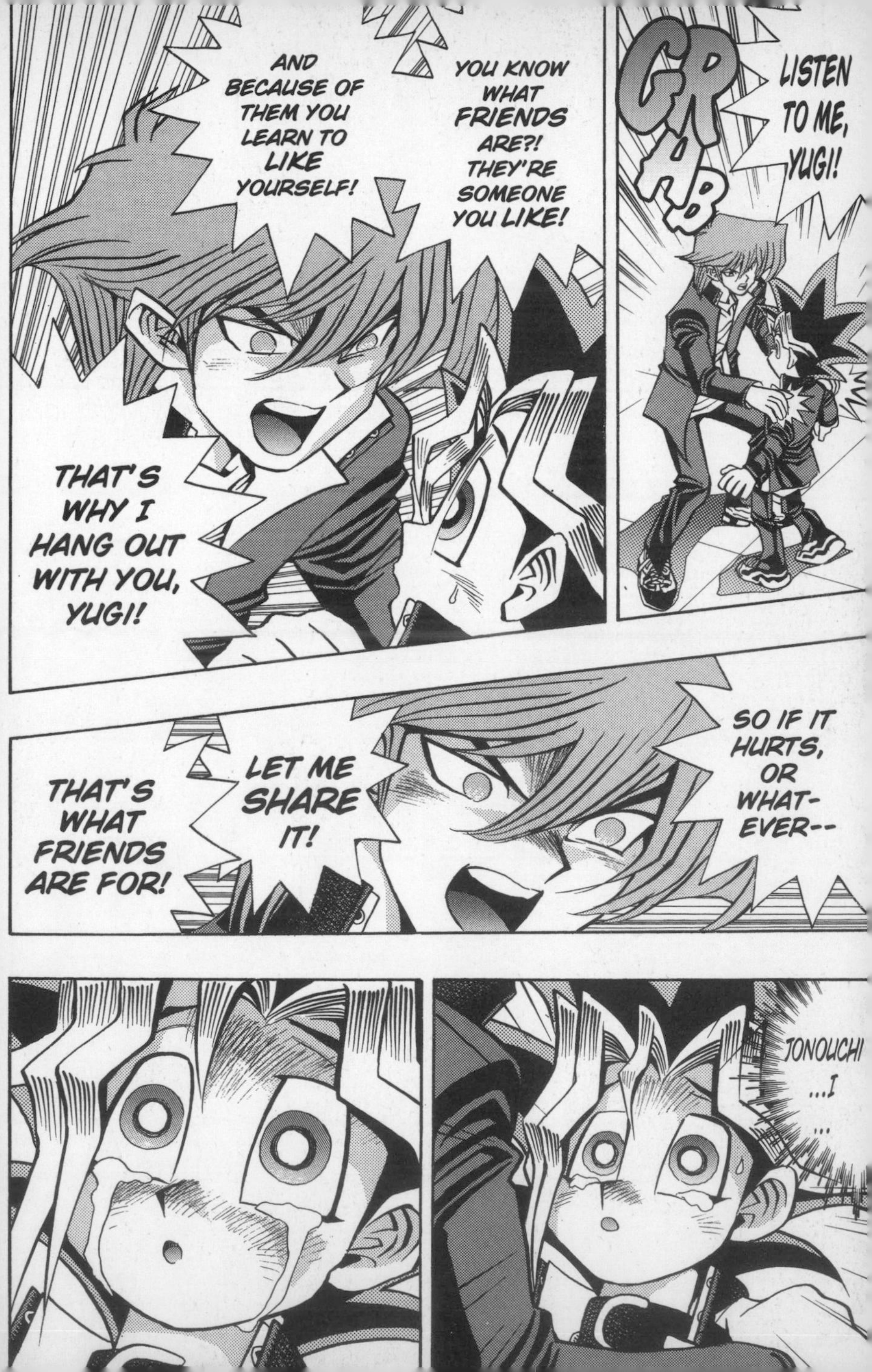
LISTEN TO ME, YUGI!
GRAB
YOU KNOW WHAT FRIENDS ARE?! THEY'RE SOMEONE YOU LIKE!
AND BECAUSE OF THEM YOU LEARN TO LIKE YOURSELF!
THAT'S WHY I HANG OUT WITH YOU, YUGI!
SO IF IT HURTS, OR WHAT-EVER--
LET ME SHARE IT!
THAT'S WHAT FRIENDS ARE FOR!
JONOUCHI ...I ...

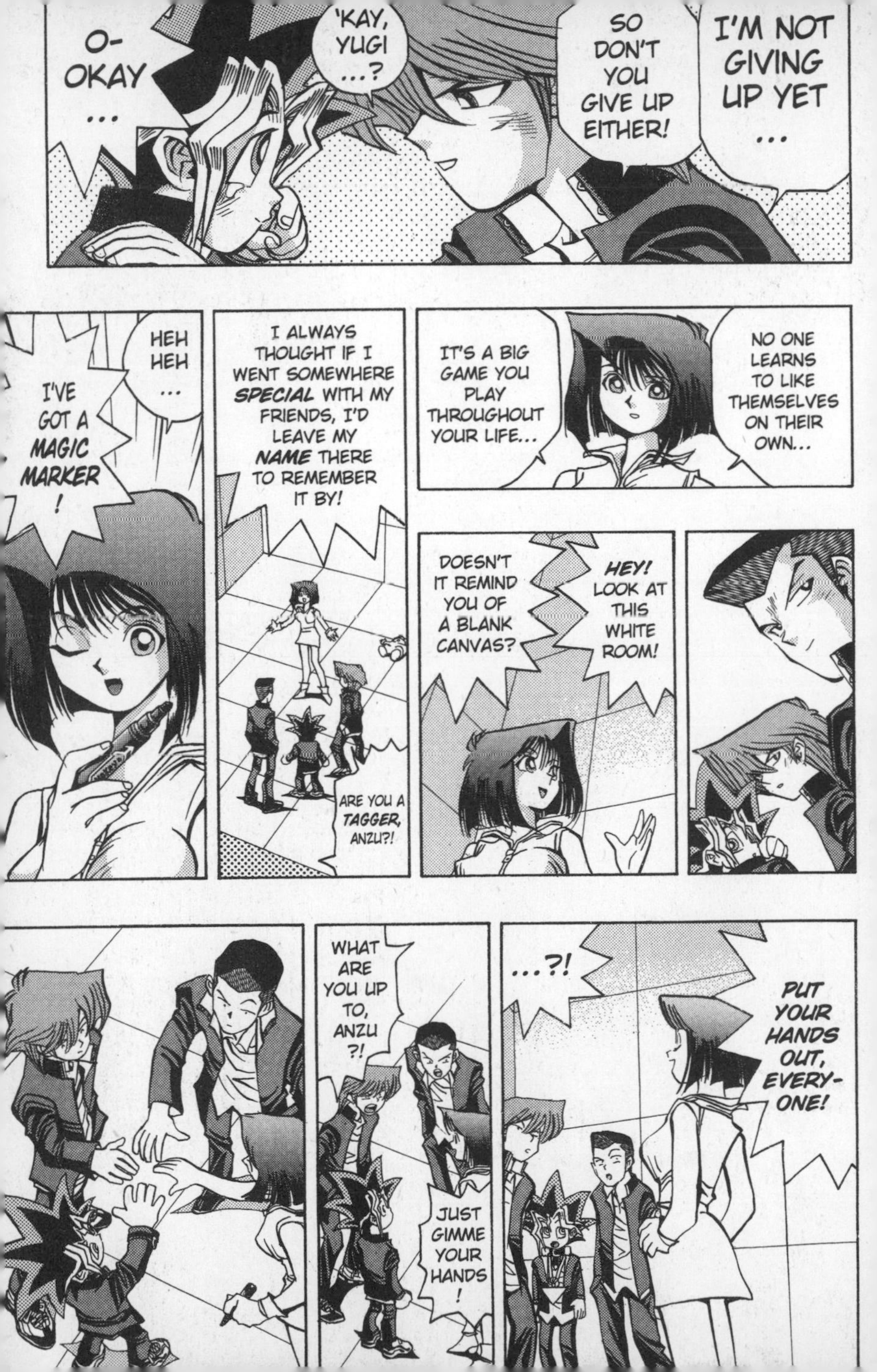
I'M NOT GIVING UP YET ...
SO DON'T YOU GIVE UP EITHER!
'KAY, YUGI ...?
O-OKAY ...
NO ONE LEARNS TO LIKE THEMSELVES ON THEIR OWN...
IT'S A BIG GAME YOU PLAY THROUGHOUT YOUR LIFE...
HEY! LOOK AT THIS WHITE ROOM!
DOESN'T IT REMIND YOU OF A BLANK CANVAS?
I ALWAYS THOUGHT IF I WENT SOMEWHERE SPECIAL WITH MY FRIENDS, I'D LEAVE MY NAME THERE TO REMEMBER IT BY!
ARE YOU A TAGGER, ANZU?!
HEH HEH ...
I'VE GOT A MAGIC MARKER !
PUT YOUR HANDS OUT, EVERY-ONE!
...?!
WHAT ARE YOU UP TO, ANZU ?!
JUST GIMME YOUR HANDS !

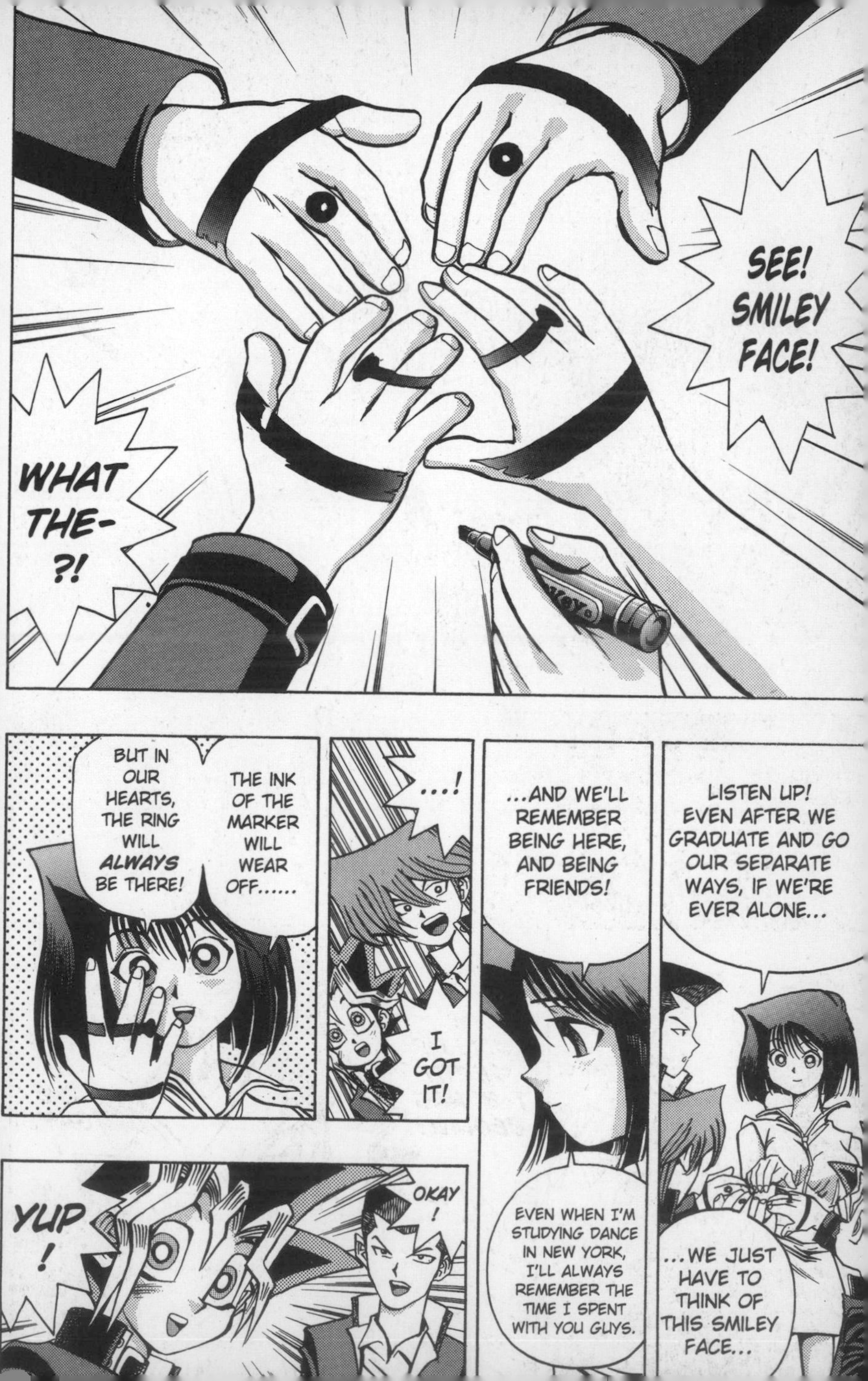
SEE! SMILEY FACE!
WHAT THE- ?!
LISTEN UP! EVEN AFTER WE GRADUATE AND GO OUR SEPARATE WAYS, IF WE'RE EVER ALONE...
...WE JUST HAVE TO THINK OF THIS SMILEY FACE...
...AND WE'LL REMEMBER BEING HERE, AND BEING FRIENDS!
EVEN WHEN I'M STUDYING DANCE IN NEW YORK, I'LL ALWAYS REMEMBER THE TIME I SPENT WITH YOU GUYS.
...!
I GOT IT!
OKAY!
YUP!
BUT IN OUR HEARTS, THE RING WILL *ALWAYS* BE THERE!
THE INK OF THE MARKER WILL WEAR OFF......

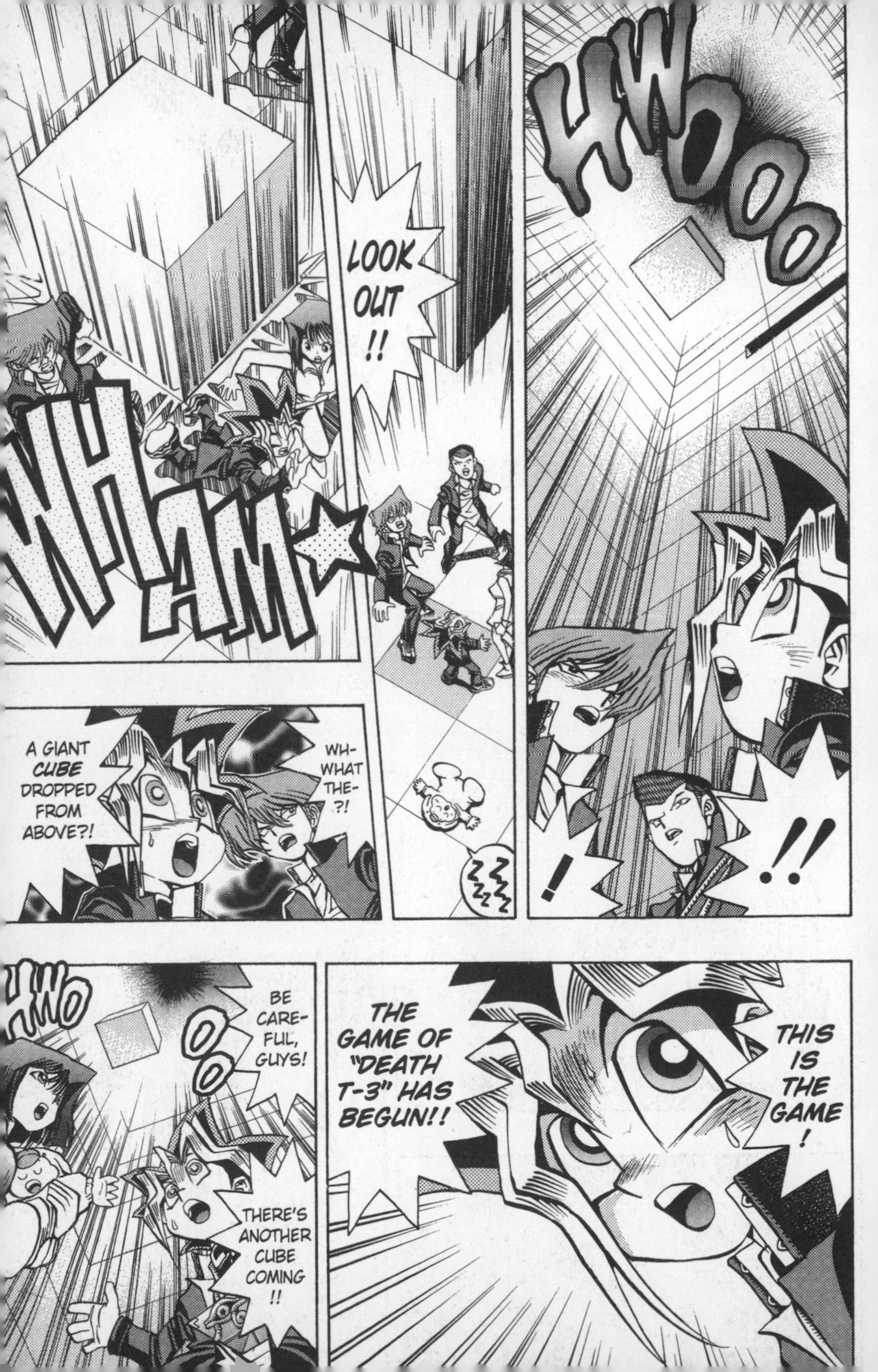
HWOOO
!!
!
LOOK OUT !!
ZZZZZ
WHAM
A GIANT CUBE DROPPED FROM ABOVE?!
WH-WHAT THE-?!
THIS IS THE GAME!
THE GAME OF "DEATH T-3" HAS BEGUN!!
BE CAREFUL, GUYS!
HWOOO
THERE'S ANOTHER CUBE COMING!!

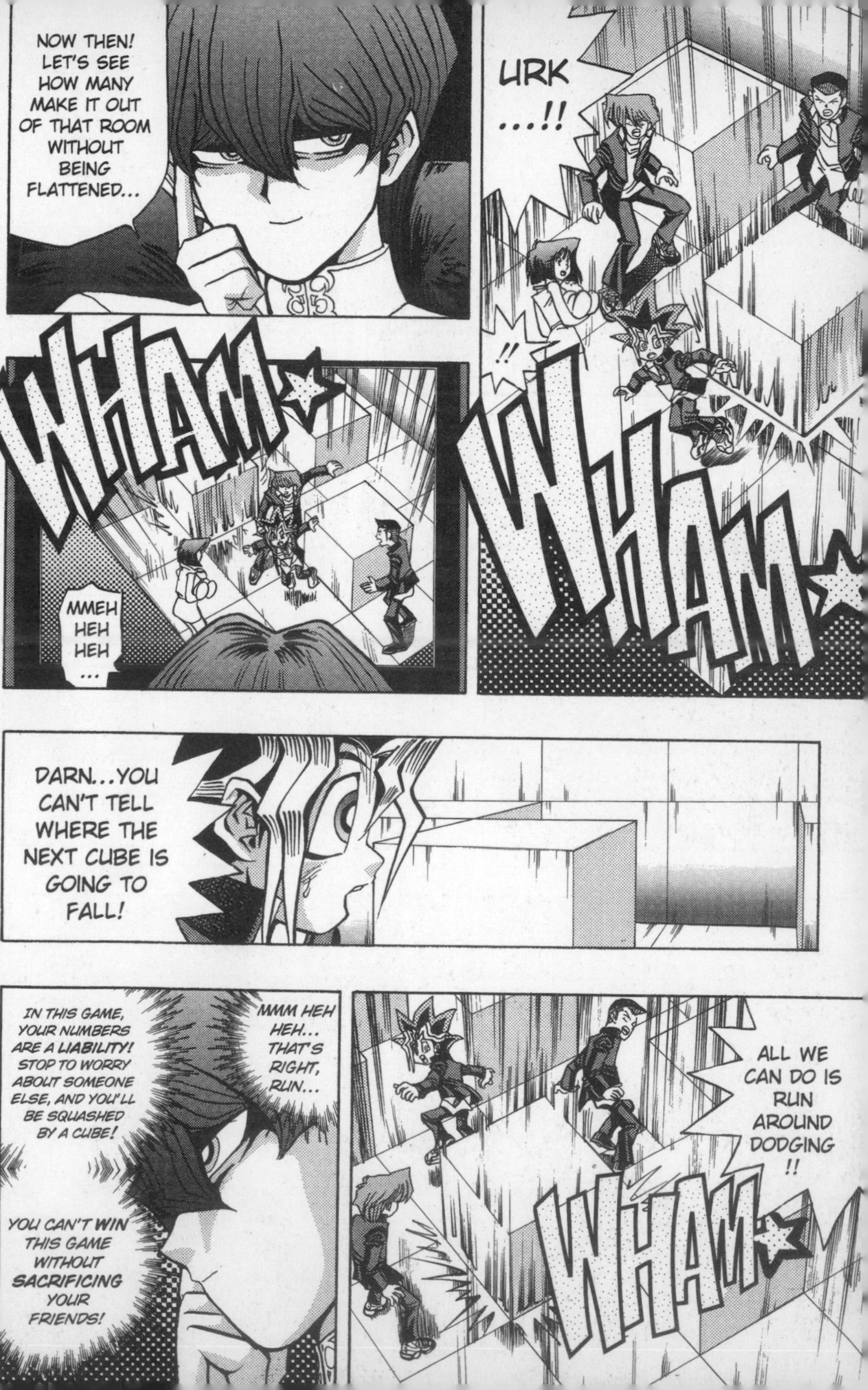
URK
...!!
!!
WHAM☆
NOW THEN! LET'S SEE HOW MANY MAKE IT OUT OF THAT ROOM WITHOUT BEING FLATTENED...
WHAM☆
MMEH HEH HEH ...
DARN...YOU CAN'T TELL WHERE THE NEXT CUBE IS GOING TO FALL!
ALL WE CAN DO IS RUN AROUND DODGING !!
WHAM☆
MMM HEH HEH... THAT'S RIGHT, RUN...
IN THIS GAME, YOUR NUMBERS ARE A LIABILITY! STOP TO WORRY ABOUT SOMEONE ELSE, AND YOU'LL BE SQUASHED BY A CUBE!
YOU CAN'T WIN THIS GAME WITHOUT SACRIFICING YOUR FRIENDS!

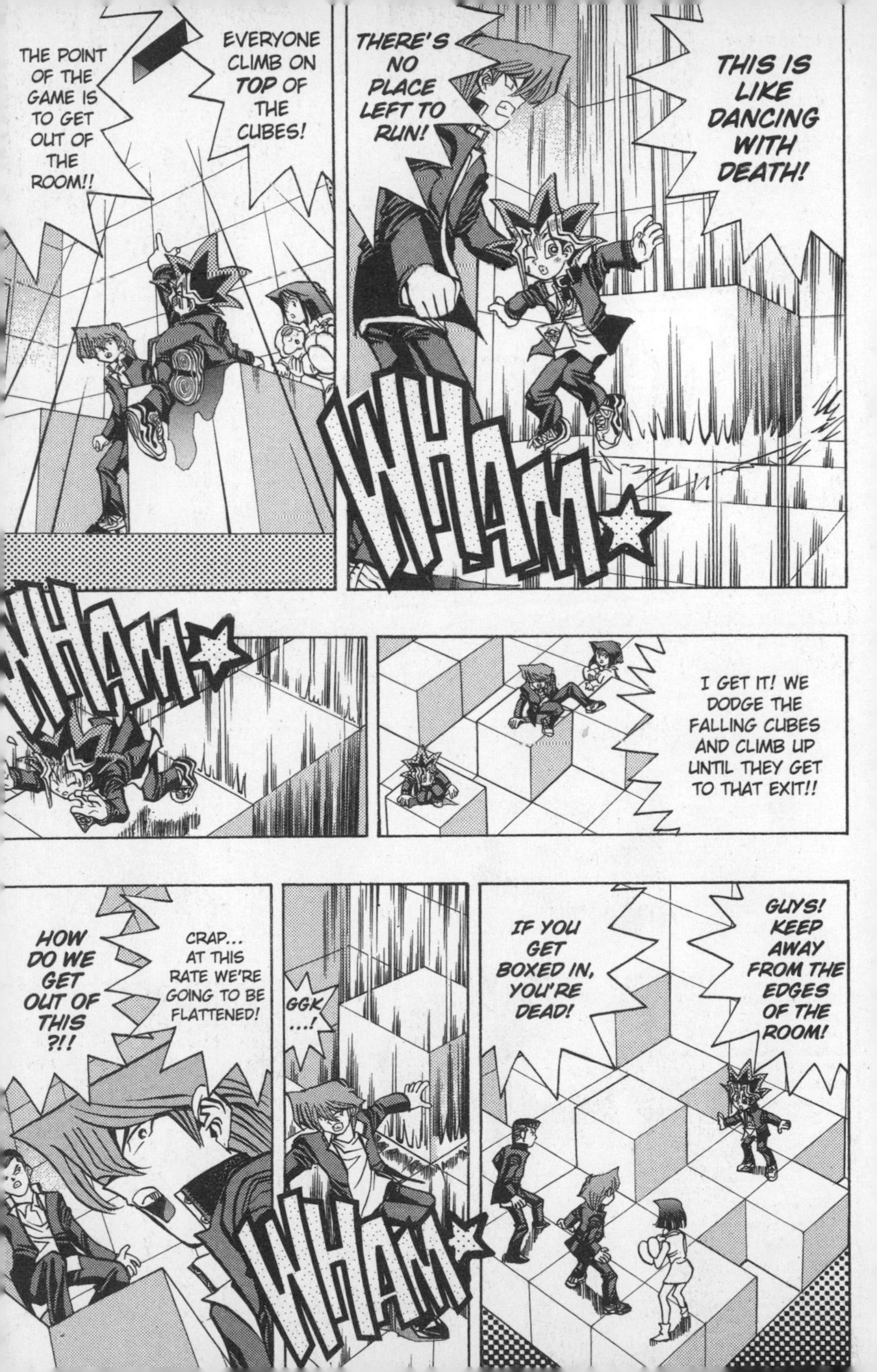
THIS IS LIKE DANCING WITH DEATH!
THERE'S NO PLACE LEFT TO RUN!
WHAM
EVERYONE CLIMB ON TOP OF THE CUBES!
THE POINT OF THE GAME IS TO GET OUT OF THE ROOM!!
I GET IT! WE DODGE THE FALLING CUBES AND CLIMB UP UNTIL THEY GET TO THAT EXIT!!
WHAM
GUYS! KEEP AWAY FROM THE EDGES OF THE ROOM!
IF YOU GET BOXED IN, YOU'RE DEAD!
GGK ...!
CRAP... AT THIS RATE WE'RE GOING TO BE FLATTENED!
HOW DO WE GET OUT OF THIS ?!!
WHAM

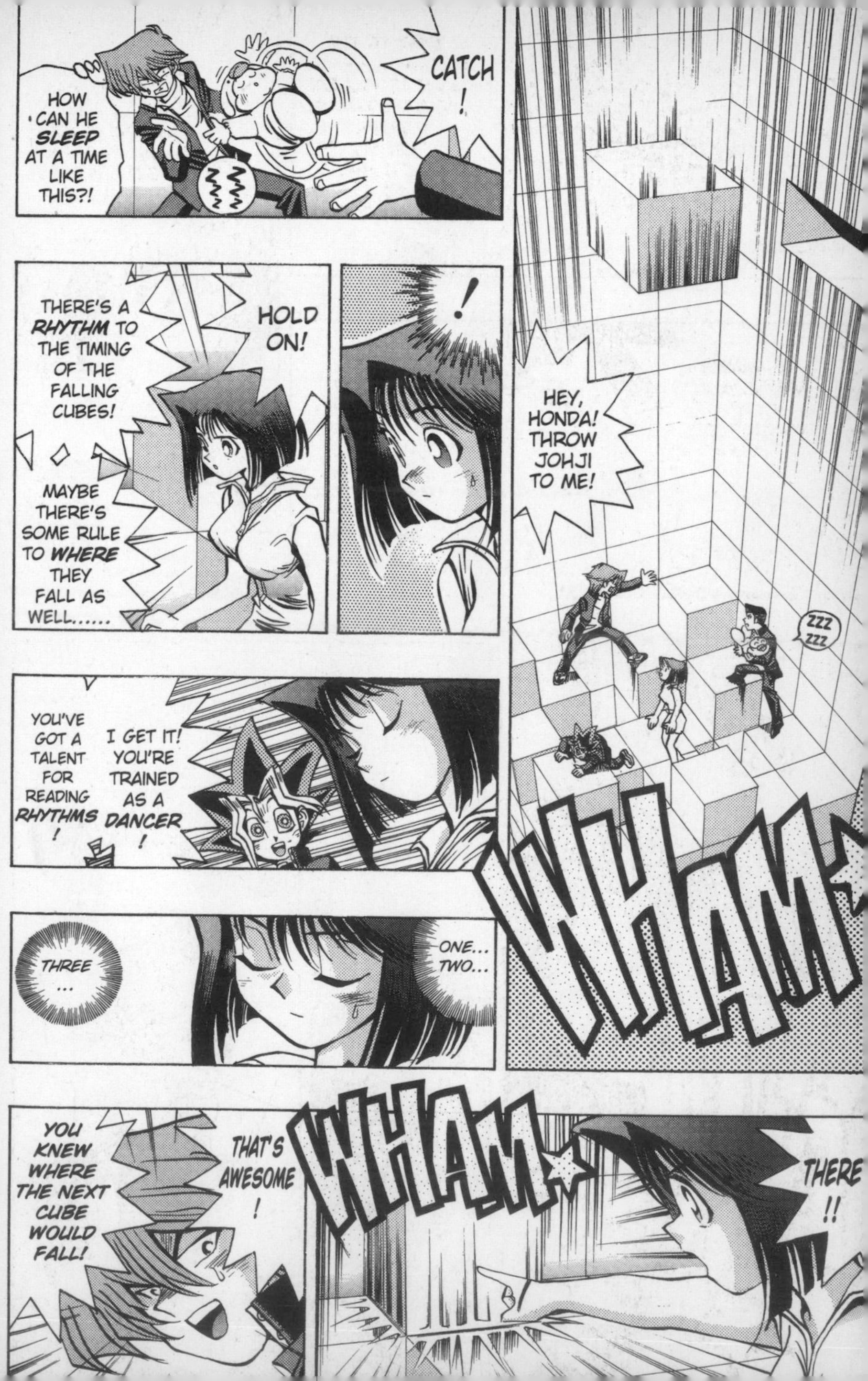
HEY, HONDA! THROW JOHJI TO ME!
ZZZ ZZZ
WHAM
CATCH!
HOW CAN HE SLEEP AT A TIME LIKE THIS?!
ZZZZ
!
HOLD ON!
THERE'S A RHYTHM TO THE TIMING OF THE FALLING CUBES!
MAYBE THERE'S SOME RULE TO WHERE THEY FALL AS WELL......
I GET IT! YOU'RE TRAINED AS A DANCER!
YOU'VE GOT A TALENT FOR READING RHYTHMS!
ONE... TWO...
THREE...
THERE!!
WHAM
THAT'S AWESOME!
YOU KNEW WHERE THE NEXT CUBE WOULD FALL!

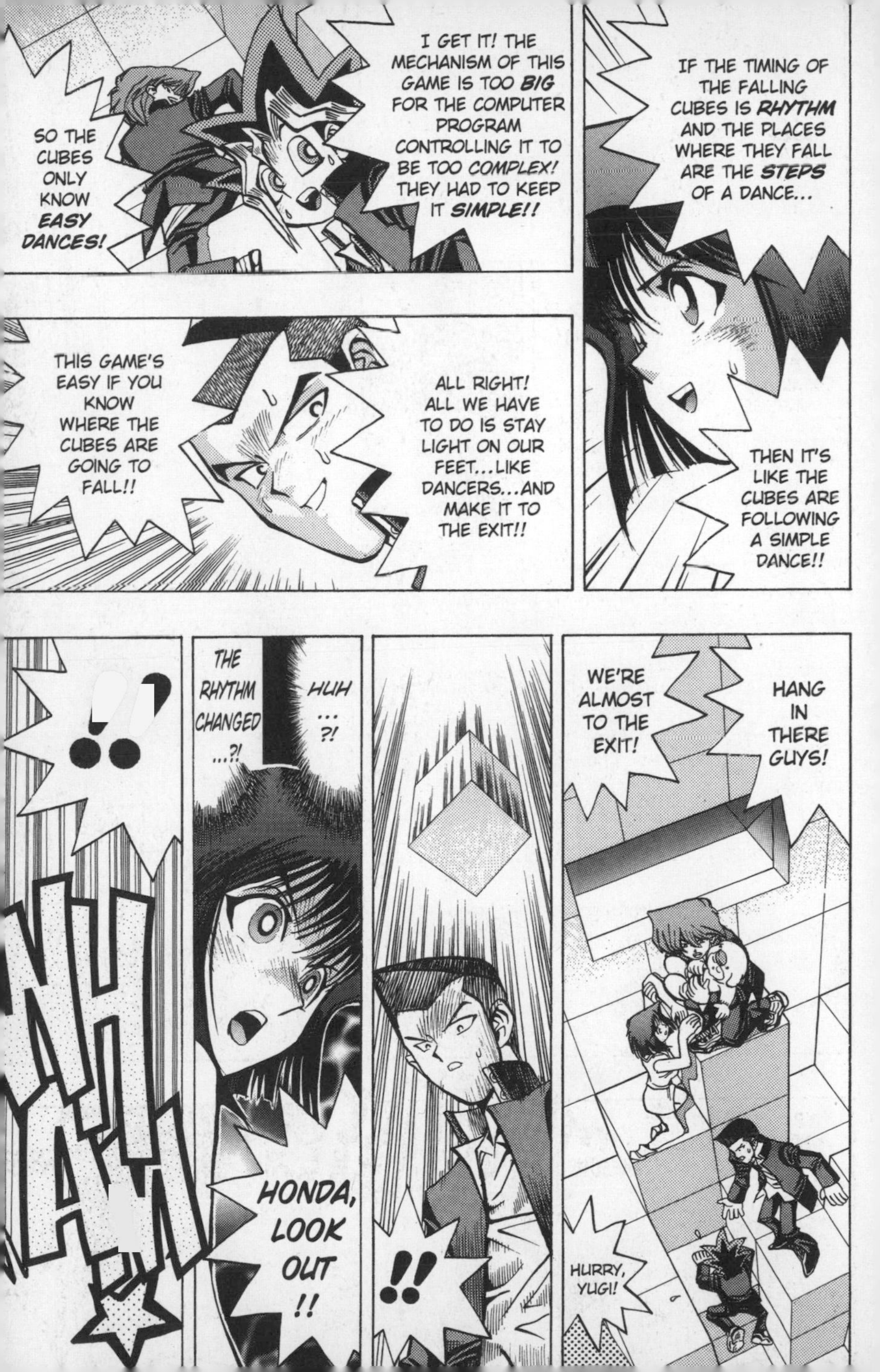
IF THE TIMING OF THE FALLING CUBES IS RHYTHM AND THE PLACES WHERE THEY FALL ARE THE STEPS OF A DANCE...
I GET IT! THE MECHANISM OF THIS GAME IS TOO BIG FOR THE COMPUTER PROGRAM CONTROLLING IT TO BE TOO COMPLEX! THEY HAD TO KEEP IT SIMPLE!!
SO THE CUBES ONLY KNOW EASY DANCES!
THEN IT'S LIKE THE CUBES ARE FOLLOWING A SIMPLE DANCE!!
ALL RIGHT! ALL WE HAVE TO DO IS STAY LIGHT ON OUR FEET...LIKE DANCERS...AND MAKE IT TO THE EXIT!!
THIS GAME'S EASY IF YOU KNOW WHERE THE CUBES ARE GOING TO FALL!!
HANG IN THERE GUYS!
WE'RE ALMOST TO THE EXIT!
HURRY, YUGI!
!!
HUH ...?!
THE RHYTHM CHANGED ...?!
HONDA, LOOK OUT !!
!!
AH

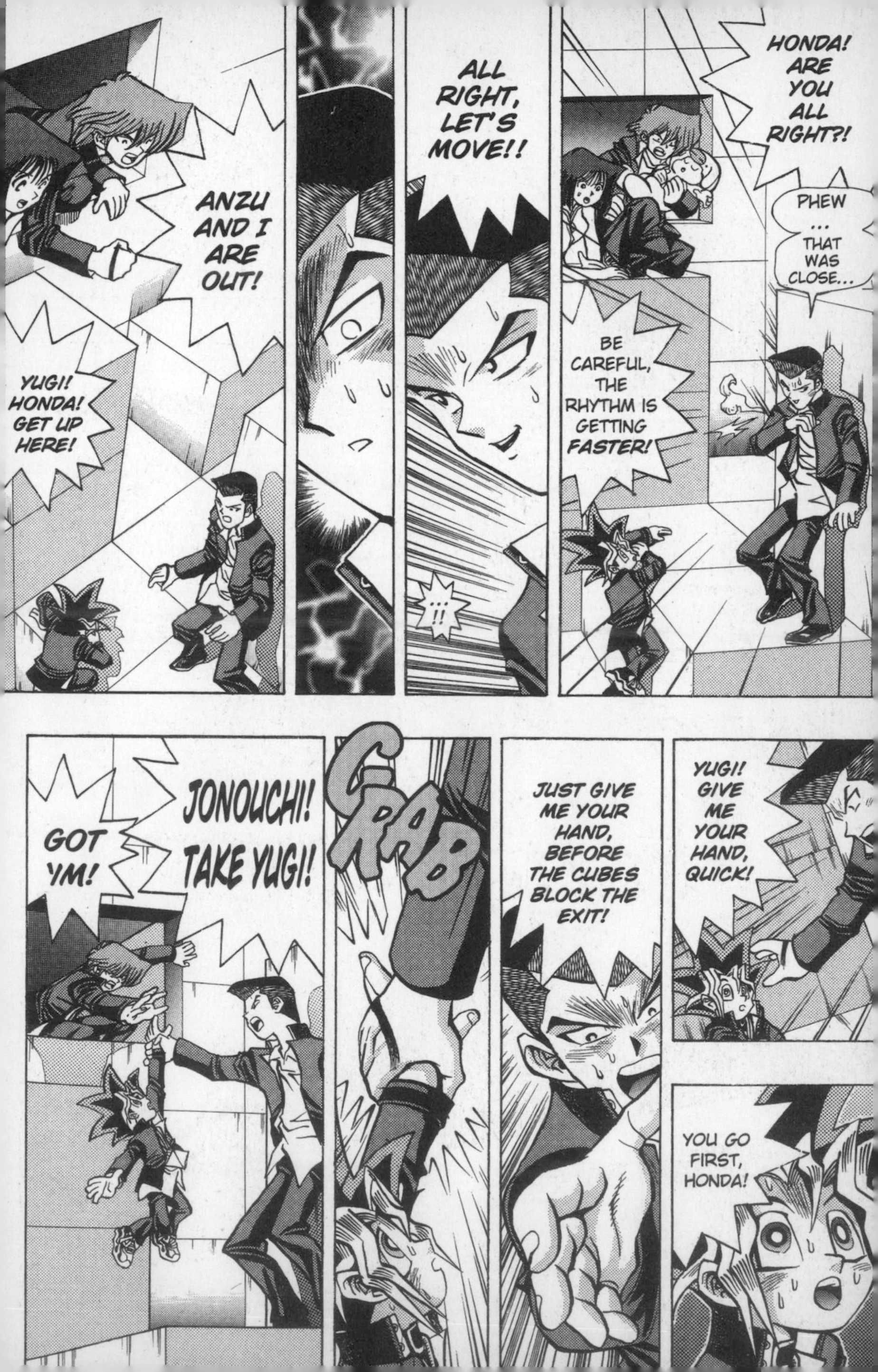
HONDA! ARE YOU ALL RIGHT?!
PHEW ... THAT WAS CLOSE...
BE CAREFUL, THE RHYTHM IS GETTING FASTER!
ALL RIGHT, LET'S MOVE!!
!!
ANZU AND I ARE OUT!
YUGI! HONDA! GET UP HERE!
YUGI! GIVE ME YOUR HAND, QUICK!
YOU GO FIRST, HONDA!
JUST GIVE ME YOUR HAND, BEFORE THE CUBES BLOCK THE EXIT!
GRAB
JONOUCHI! TAKE YUGI!
GOT 'YM!

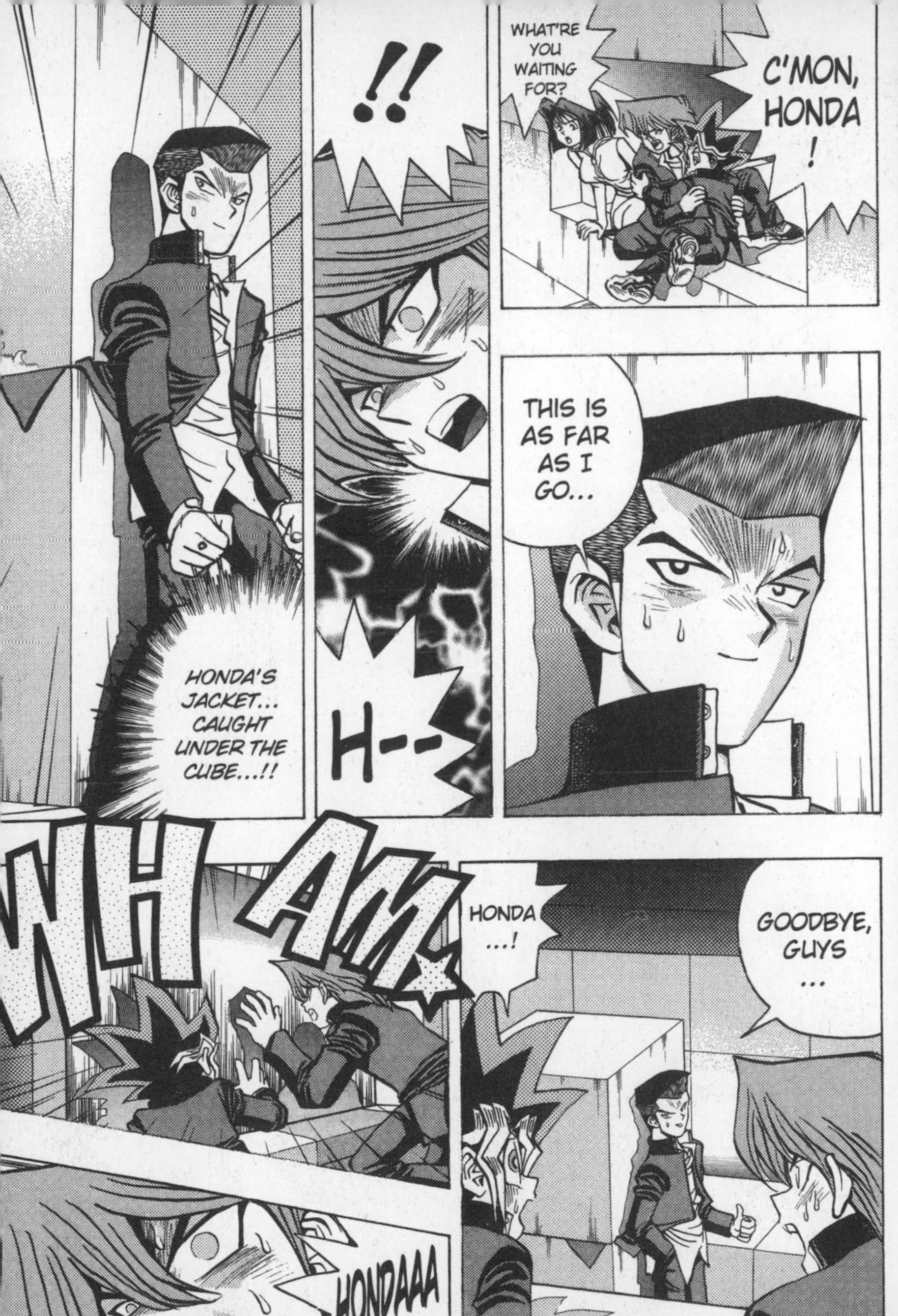
WHAT'RE YOU WAITING FOR?
C'MON, HONDA!
THIS IS AS FAR AS I GO...
!!
H--
HONDA'S JACKET... CAUGHT UNDER THE CUBE...!!
GOODBYE, GUYS...
HONDA...!
WHAM
HONDAAA!!

TO BE CONTINUED IN YU-GI-OH VOL. 5!

SPECIAL BONUS!

THRILLING BOARD GAME!

Number of Players: 1-5

What You Need:
- A 6-sided die
- Something to use as game pieces (coins, pebbles, etc.)

How to Play:
- Place your game pieces on the "Start" space on page 203!
- Roll the die to see who goes first. The players take turns rolling the die and moving according to the rules below!

☆ ⚀ • When you roll a 1, you can move one or two spaces (your choice) *in a straight line* in any direction you want. (But not diagonally!)

☆ ⚁ ⚂ ⚃ ⚄
• When you roll a 2, 3, 4 or 5, you must move one space according to the chart below!

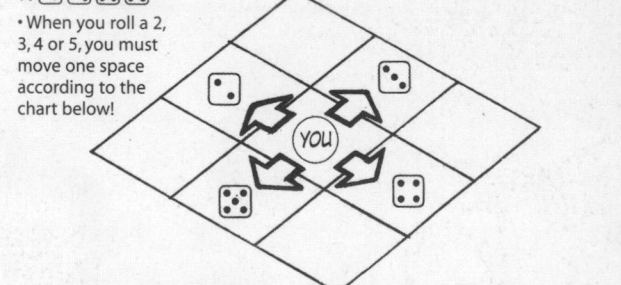

☆ ⚅ • When you roll a 6, you can move one or two spaces (your choice) in any direction you want. You can even change direction, like going up and then right. (You still can't move diagonally, though.)

- If the dice says to go into a rock wall (like the top of page 203), just stop at the edge. You cannot go into a rock wall.
- If the dice says to go over the edge (like the bottom of page 203), *you fall off and you have to return to "Start" on page 203!* If you're playing alone, the game is over.
- You can also push other players off the edge! (See figure 1.)

FIGURE 1

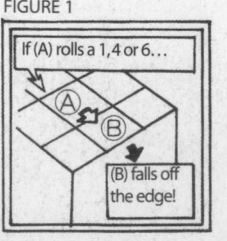

If (A) rolls a 1, 4 or 6…

(B) falls off the edge!

THE FIRST ONE TO MAKE IT TO THE GOAL (ON PAGE 207) WINS!

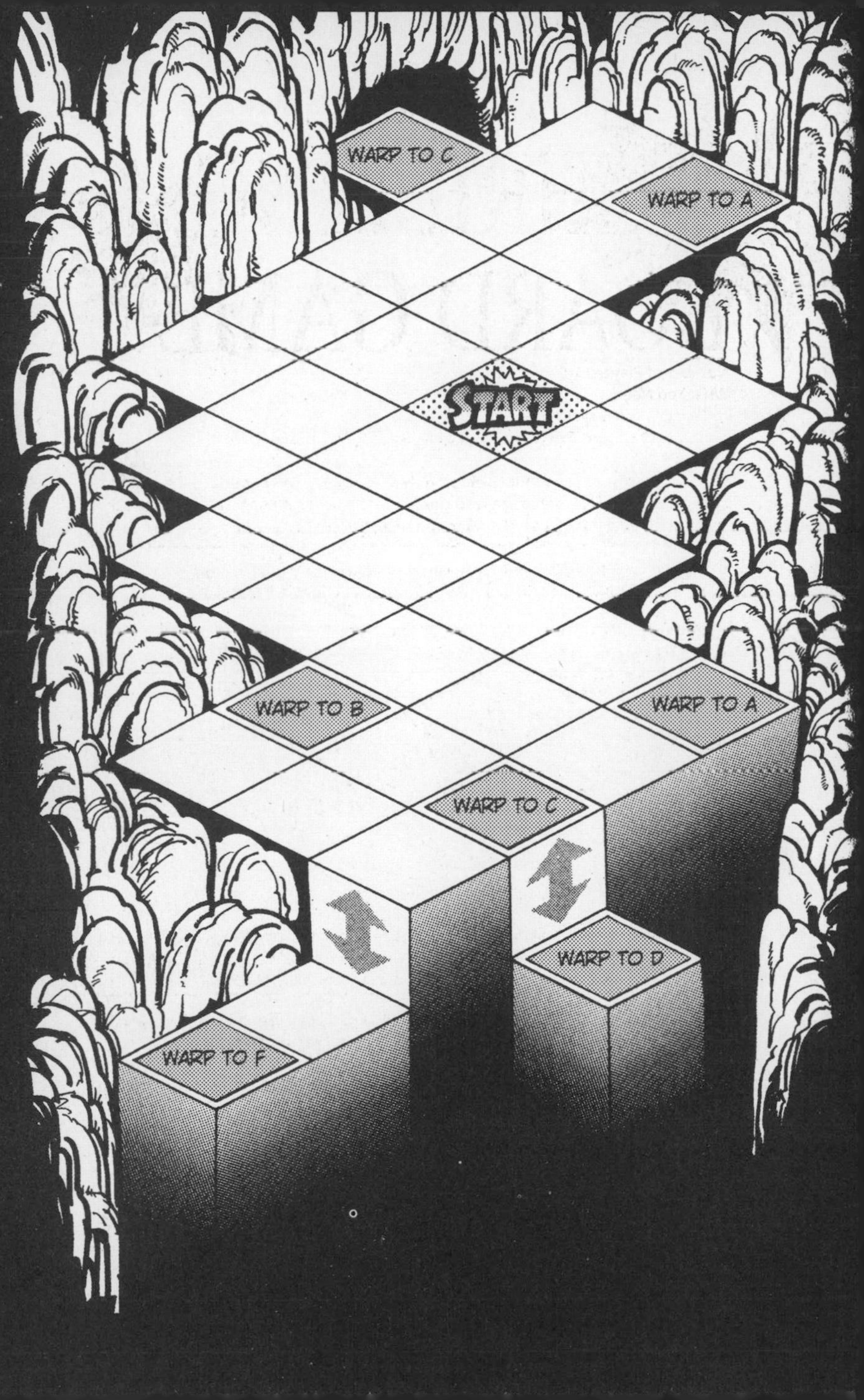
WARP TO C
WARP TO A
START
WARP TO B
WARP TO A
WARP TO C
WARP TO D
WARP TO F

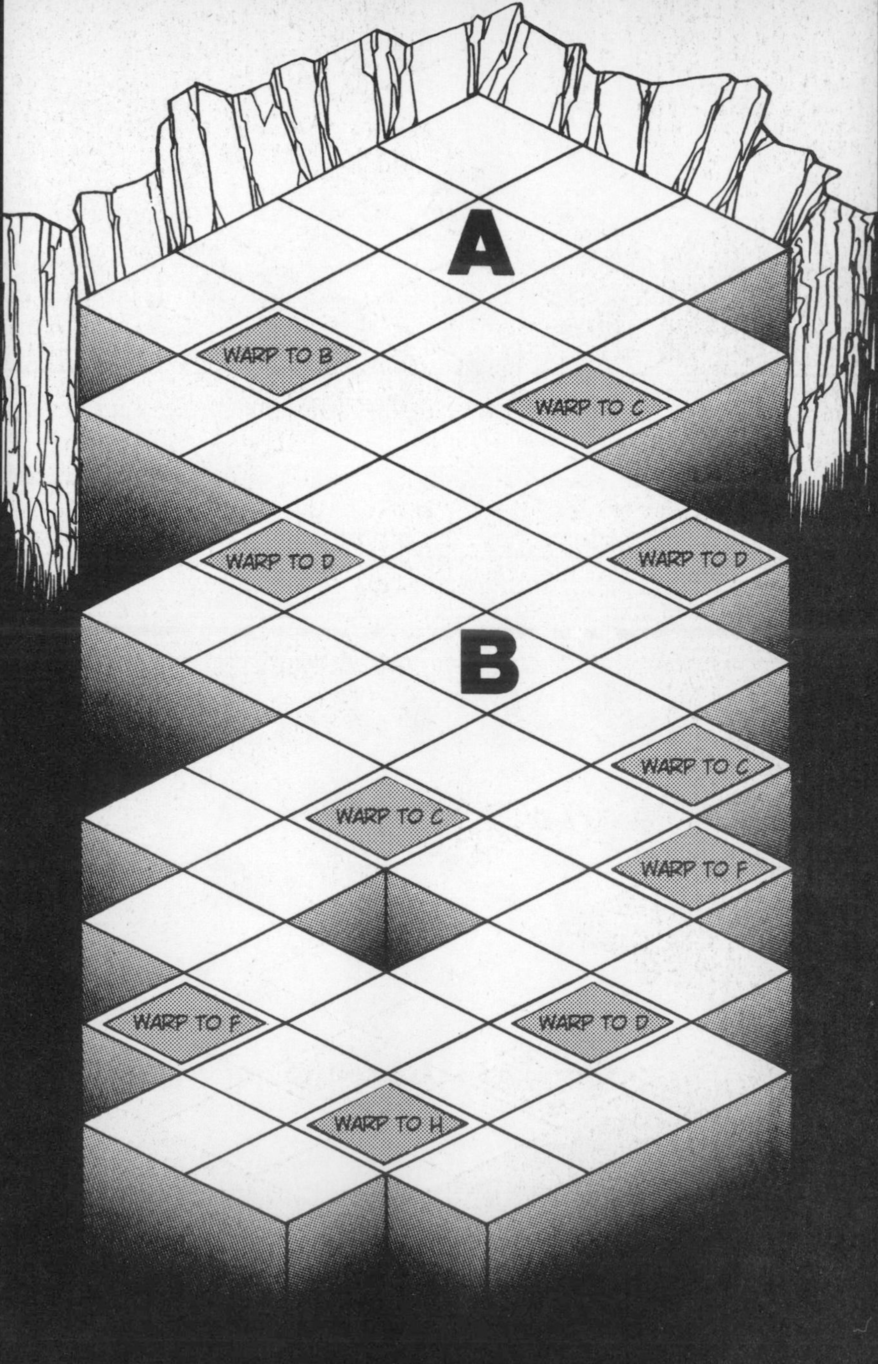
A
WARP TO B
WARP TO C
WARP TO D
WARP TO D
B
WARP TO C
WARP TO C
WARP TO F
WARP TO F
WARP TO D
WARP TO H

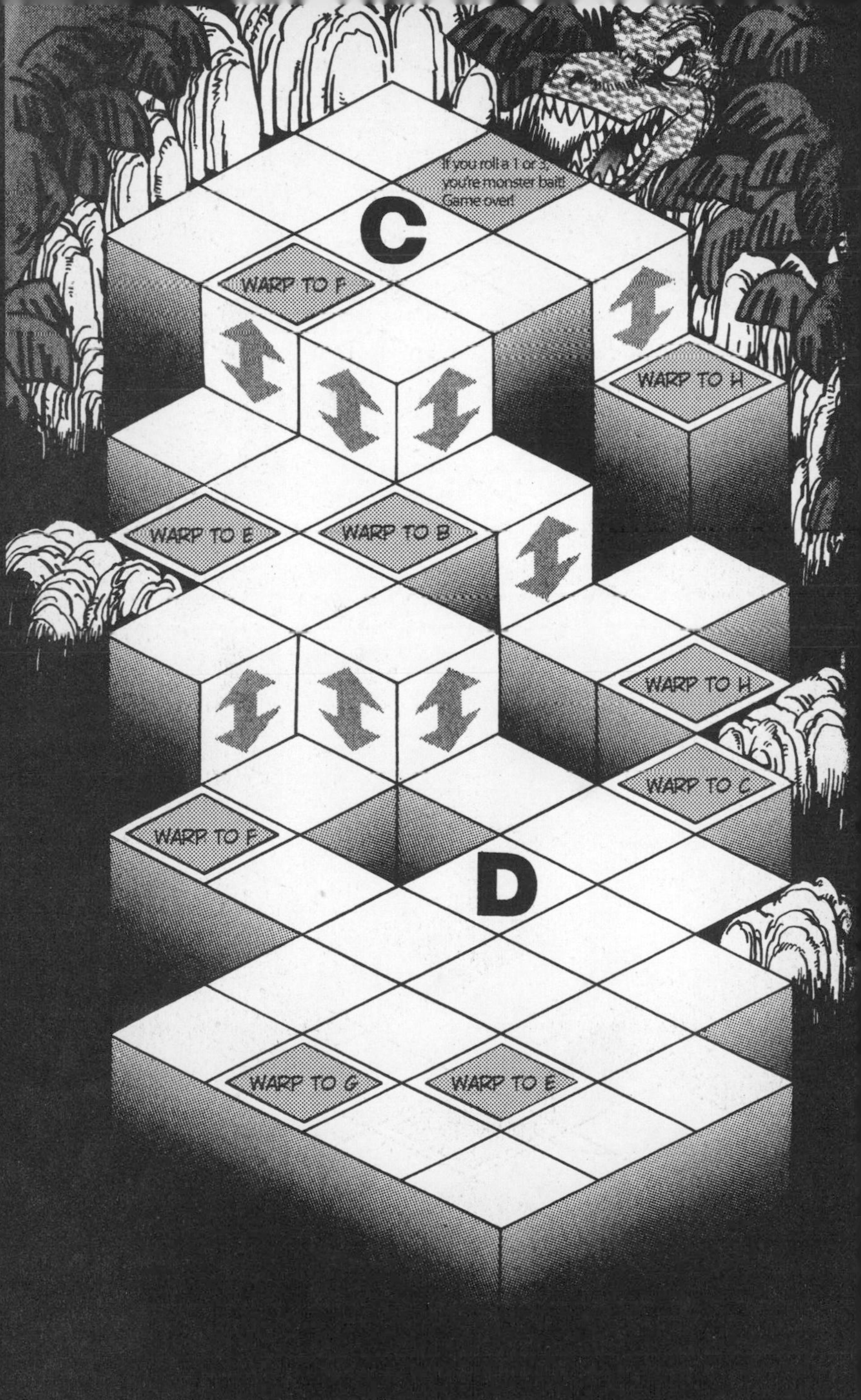
If you roll a 1 or 3, you're monster bait! Game over!
C
WARP TO F
WARP TO H
WARP TO E
WARP TO B
WARP TO H
WARP TO C
WARP TO F
D
WARP TO G
WARP TO E

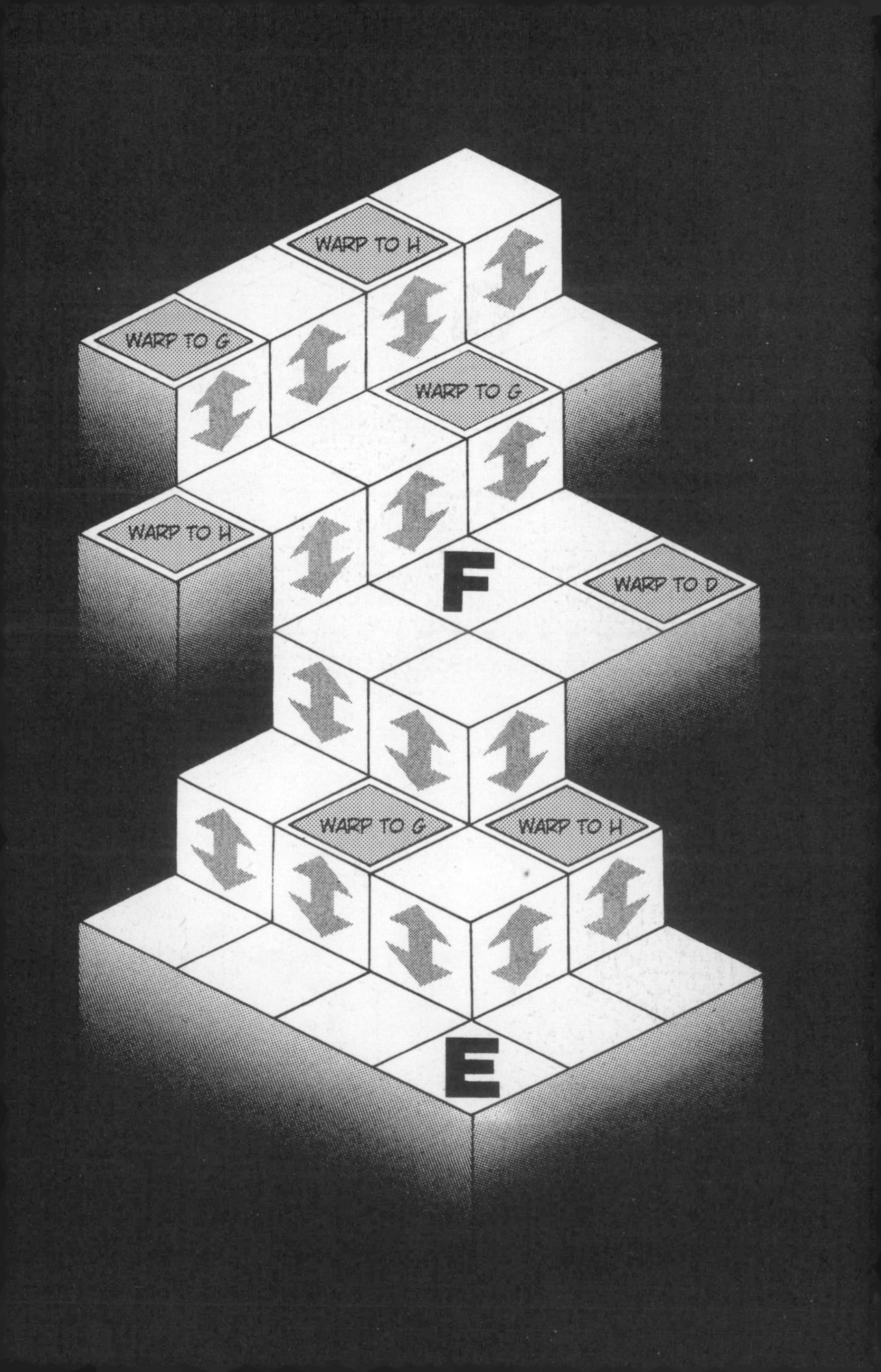
WARP TO H
WARP TO G
WARP TO G
WARP TO H
F
WARP TO D
WARP TO G
WARP TO H
E

LOSE A TURN
G
WARP TO C
GOAL
WARP TO D
WARP TO F
LOSE A TURN
H
WARP TO B
WARP TO A
WARP TO G
WARP TO G

MASTER OF THE CARDS

Collectible card games first appeared in **Yu-Gi-Oh!** in Duels 9 and 10, "The Cards with Teeth" (see **Yu-Gi-Oh!** volume 2). As **Yu-Gi-Oh!** fans know, the manga and anime version of the "Duel Monsters" card game has simpler rules than the real-world version. Also, many of the card names are different between the English and Japanese versions. Here's a rundown of the cards in this graphic novel.

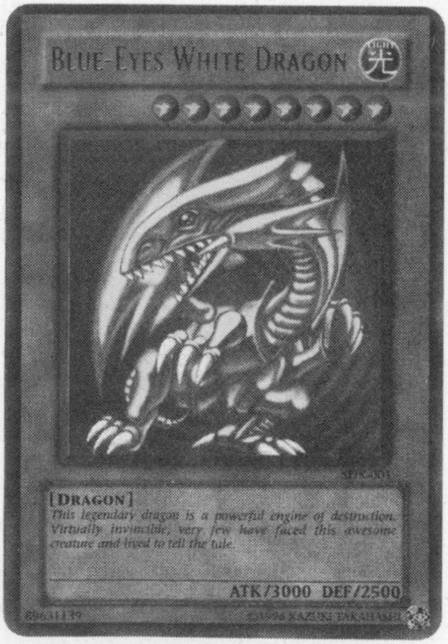
BLUE-EYES WHITE DRAGON
[DRAGON]
This legendary dragon is a powerful engine of destruction. Virtually invincible, very few have faced this awesome creature and lived to tell the tale.
ATK/3000 DEF/2500

1. Blue-Eyes White Dragon
In the manga, this card is extremely rare—only a few are supposed to exist.

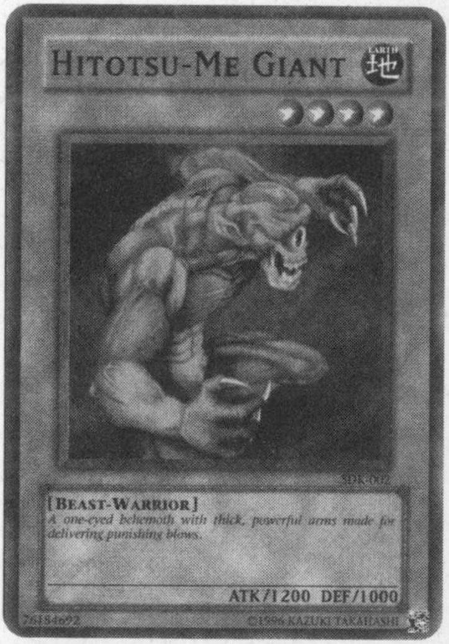
HITOTSU-ME GIANT
[BEAST-WARRIOR]
A one-eyed behemoth with thick, powerful arms made for delivering punishing blows.
ATK/1200 DEF/1000
©1996 KAZUKI TAKAHASHI

2. Hitotsu-me Giant
Known as "Cyclops" in the original Japanese. "Hitotsu-me" is Japanese for "one-eyed."

IN THE NEXT VOLUME...

Yugi, Jonouchi and Anzu have made it to the end of the "Death-T"—the *Theme Park of Death*! Now, Yugi must survive the last two steps of Kaiba's revenge alone. The first, a rematch at "Capsule Monster Chess" with Kaiba's little brother Mokuba. The second, a rematch at "Duel Monsters" with Kaiba himself! But can Yugi's faith, and his grandfather's deck-building, beat Kaiba's three "Blue-Lyes White Dragon" cards?

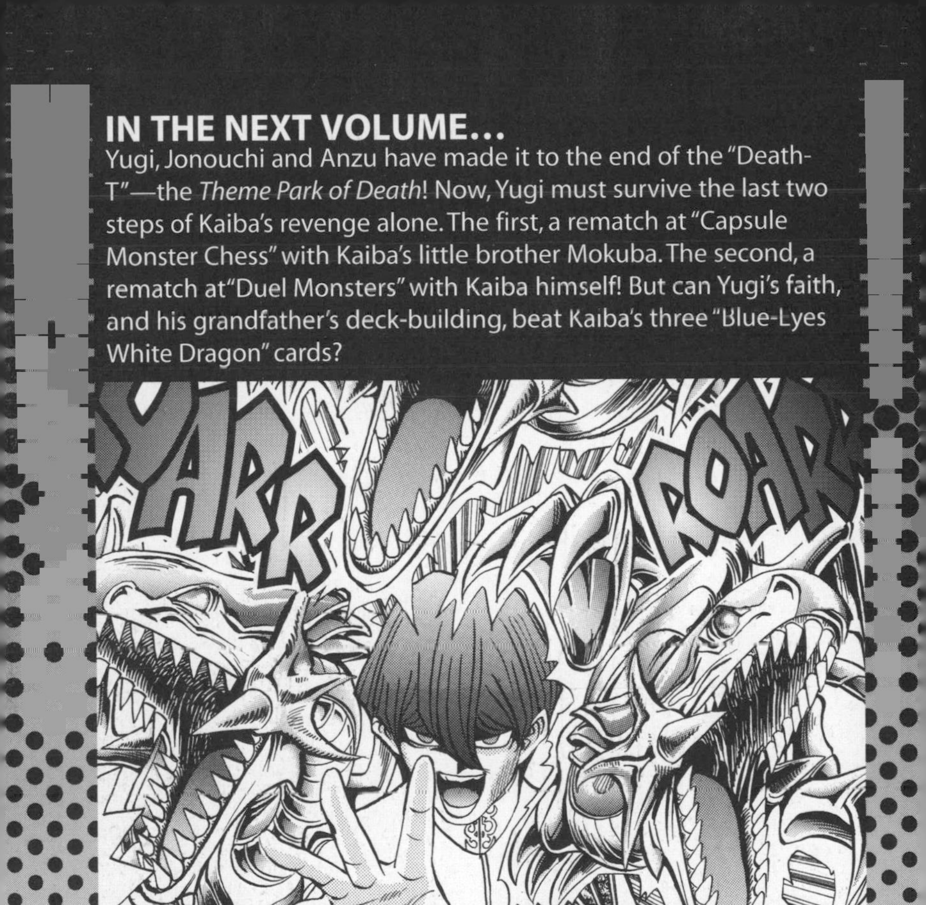
ROAR
YARR

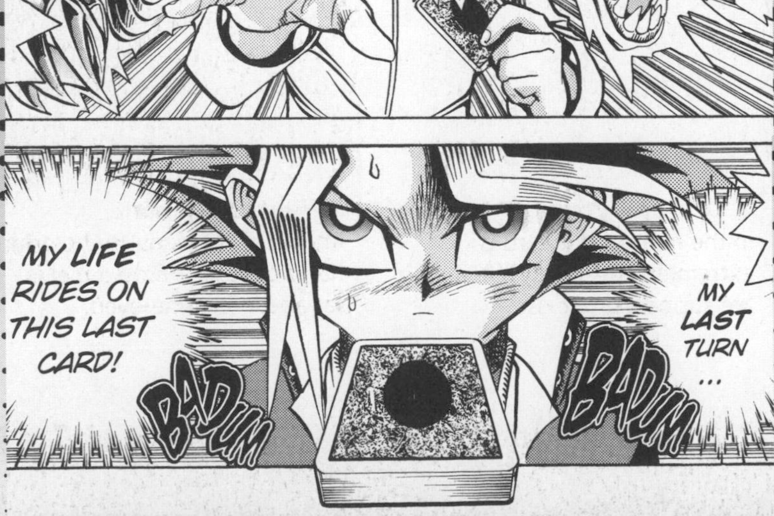
MY LAST TURN ...
BADUM
MY LIFE RIDES ON THIS LAST CARD!
BADUM

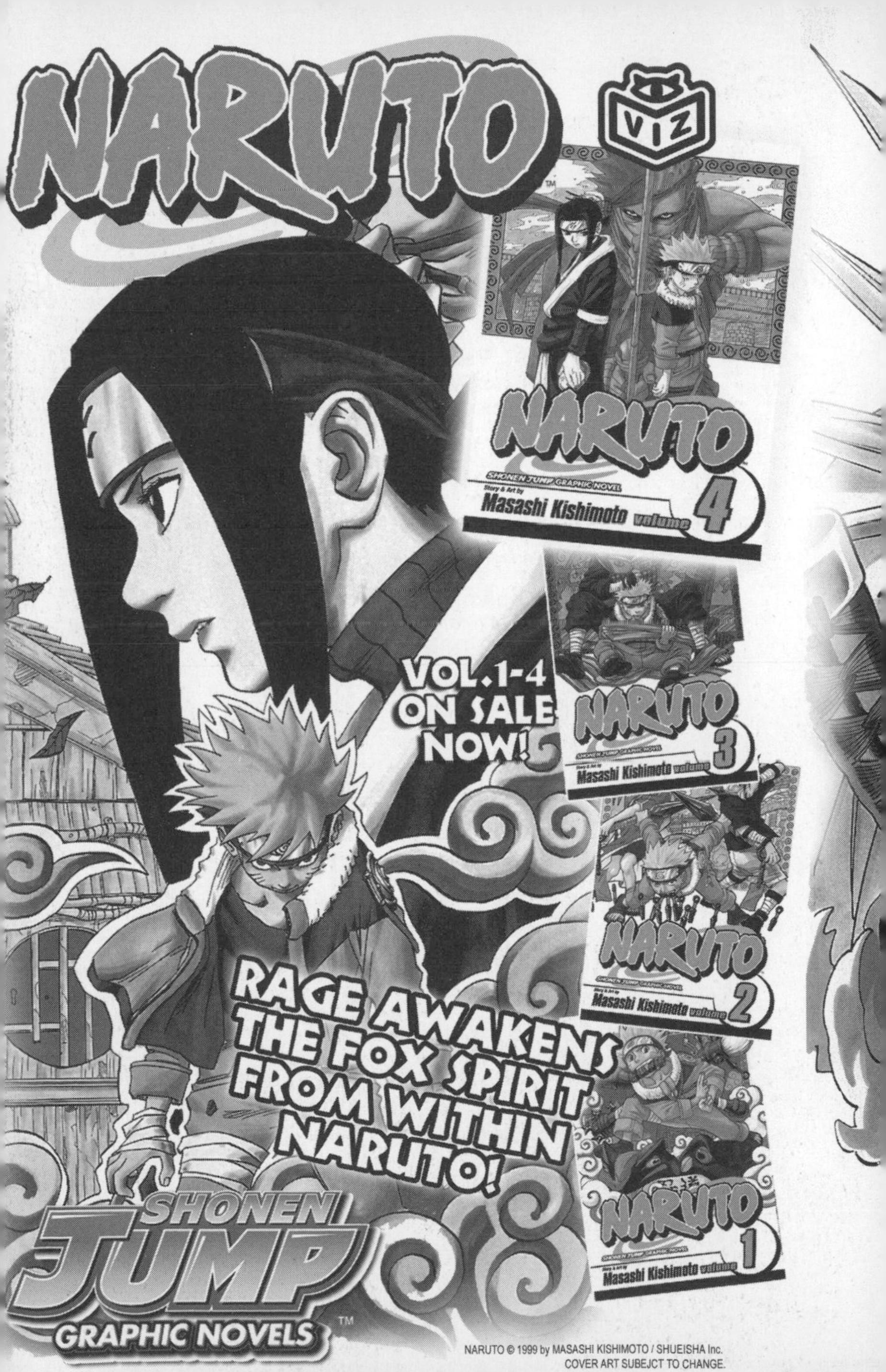
NARUTO
VIZ
NARUTO
SHONEN JUMP GRAPHIC NOVEL
Story & Art by
Masashi Kishimoto volume 4
VOL.1-4
ON SALE
NOW!
NARUTO
SHONEN JUMP GRAPHIC NOVEL
Masashi Kishimoto volume 3
NARUTO
Masashi Kishimoto volume 2
RAGE AWAKENS
THE FOX SPIRIT
FROM WITHIN
NARUTO!
NARUTO
Masashi Kishimoto volume 1
SHONEN
JUMP
GRAPHIC NOVELS

LUFFY AND HIS CREW
CATCH BLACK CAT FEVER!
ONE PIECE
For Whom the Bell Tolls
Only $7.95 Each!
Volumes 1-5 on Sale Now!
ONE PIECE
Now Airing on the FoxBox!
SHONEN JUMP GRAPHIC NOVELS
On Sale At:
www.shonenjump.com
Also available at your local bookstore, comic store and Suncoast Motion Picture Company.
COMIC SHOP LOCATOR SERVICE
888-COMIC-BOOK
888-266-4226

SHONEN JUMP™
THE WORLD'S MOST POPULAR MANGA

COMPLETE OUR SURVEY AND LET US KNOW WHAT YOU THINK!

☐ Please do NOT send me information about VIZ and SHONEN JUMP products, news and events, special offers, or other information.

☐ Please do NOT send me information from VIZ's trusted business partners.

Name: ______________________

Address: ______________________

City: ____________ **State:** ______ **Zip:** ____________

E-mail: ______________________

☐ **Male** ☐ **Female** **Date of Birth** (mm/dd/yyyy): ___/___/_____ (Under 13? Parental consent required)

What race/ethnicity do you consider yourself? (please check one)

☐ Asian/Pacific Islander ☐ Black/African American ☐ Hispanic/Latino
☐ Native American/Alaskan Native ☐ White/Caucasian ☐ Other: __________

What SHONEN JUMP Graphic Novel did you purchase? (indicate title purchased)

____

What other SHONEN JUMP Graphic Novels, if any, do you own? (indicate title(s) owned)

____

____

Reason for purchase: (check all that apply)

☐ Special offer ☐ Favorite title ☐ Gift
☐ Recommendation ☐ Read in SHONEN JUMP Magazine
☐ Read excerpt in the SHONEN JUMP Compilation Edition
☐ Other ______________________

Where did you make your purchase? (please check one)

☐ Comic store ☐ Bookstore ☐ Mass/Grocery Store
☐ Newsstand ☐ Video/Video Game Store ☐ Other: __________
☐ Online (site: ______________________)

Do you read SHONEN JUMP Magazine?

- [ ] Yes
- [ ] No **(if no, skip the next two questions)**

Do you subscribe?

- [ ] Yes
- [ ] No

If you do not subscribe, how often do you [illegible] ONEN JUMP Magazi[illegible]?

- [ ] 1-3 issues a year
- [ ] 4-6 issues a year
- [ ] more than 7 issues a year

What genre of manga would you like to read as a SHONEN JUMP Graphic Novel?
(please check two)

- [ ] Adventure
- [ ] Comic Strip
- [ ] Science Fiction
- [ ] Fighting
- [ ] Horror
- [ ] Romance
- [ ] Fantasy
- [ ] Sports

Which do you prefer? (please check one)

- [ ] Reading right-to-left
- [ ] Reading left-to-right

Which do you prefer? (please check one)

- [ ] Sound effects in English
- [ ] Sound effects in Japanese with English captions
- [ ] Sound effects in Japanese only with a glossary at the back

THANK YOU! Please send the completed form to:

VIZ Survey
42 Catharine St.
Poughkeepsie, NY 12601

All information provided will be used for internal purposes only. We promise not to sell or otherwise divulge your information.